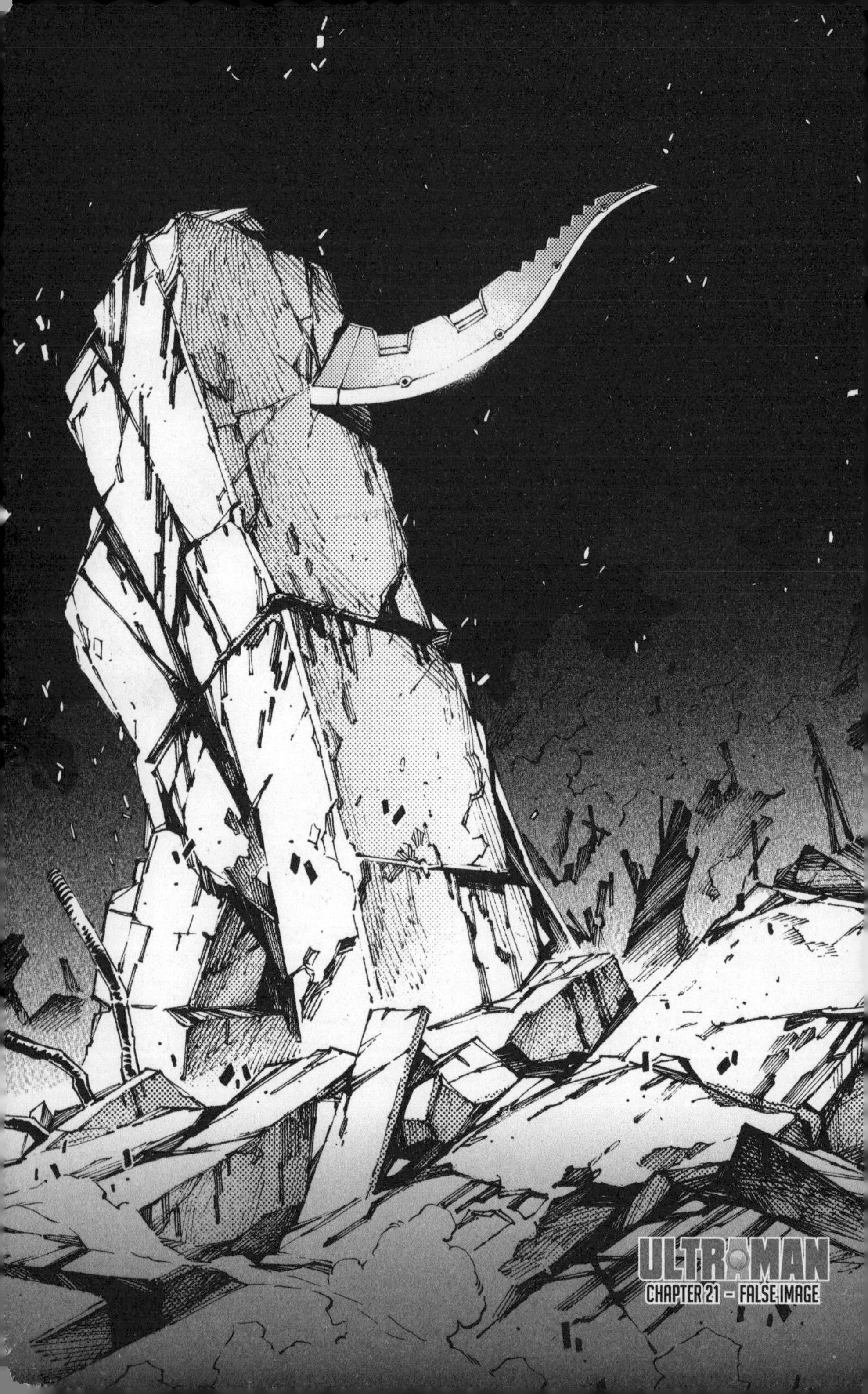
ULTRAMAN
CHAPTER 21 - FALSE IMAGE

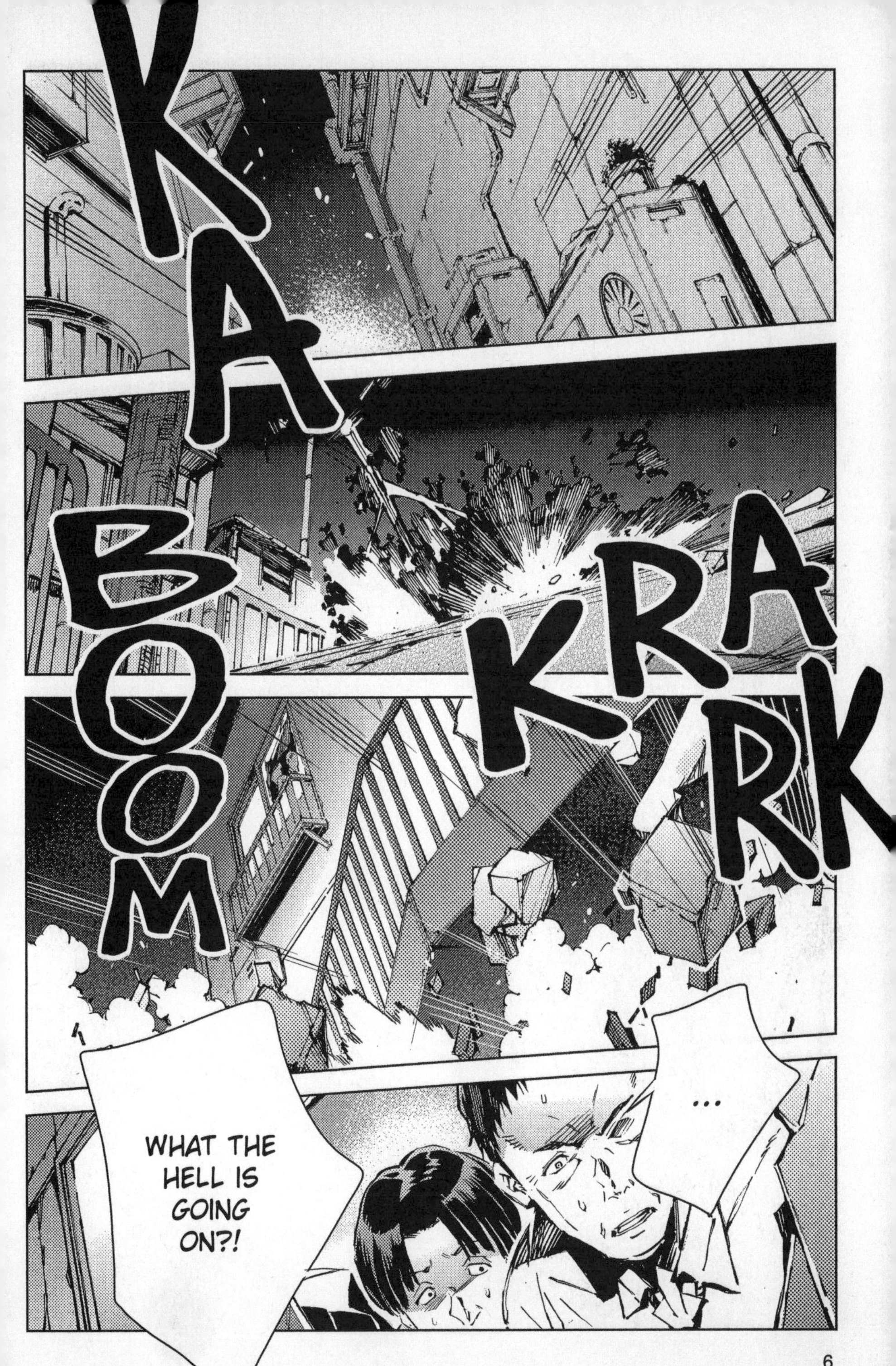
KA
BOOM
KRAKRK
RA
RK
...
WHAT THE HELL IS GOING ON?!

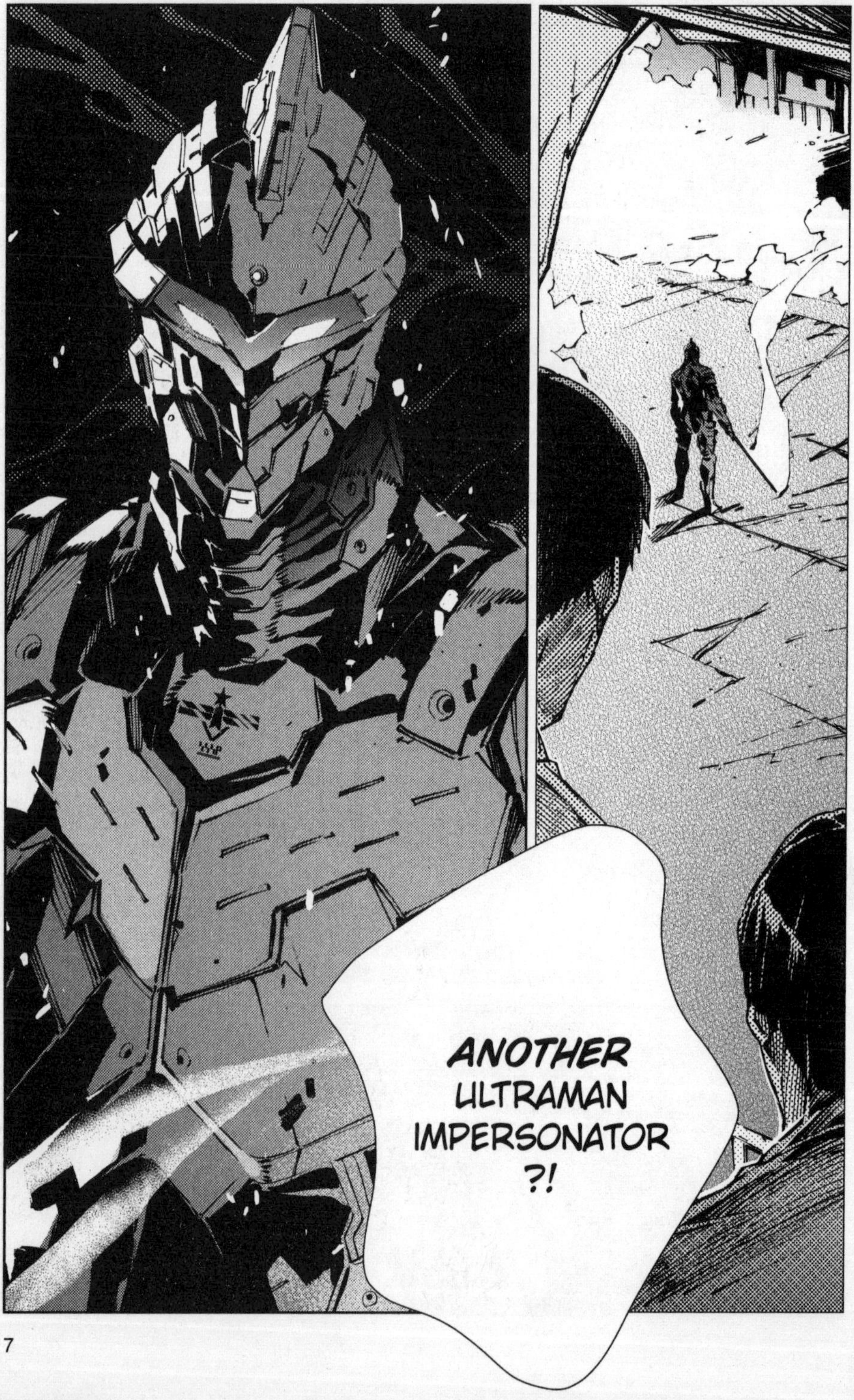
ANOTHER ULTRAMAN IMPERSONATOR ?!

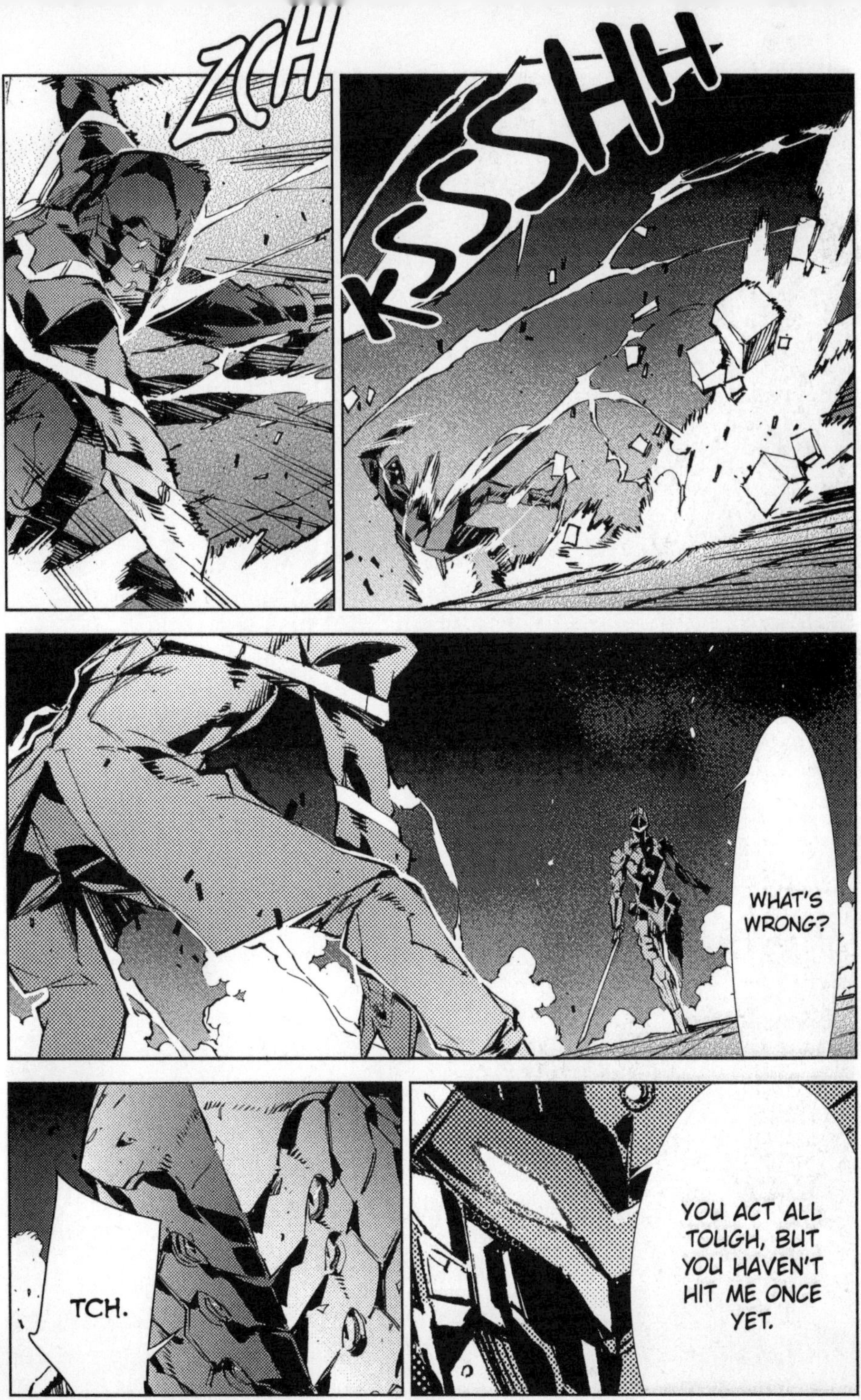
KSSHH
ZCH
WHAT'S WRONG?
YOU ACT ALL TOUGH, BUT YOU HAVEN'T HIT ME ONCE YET.
TCH.

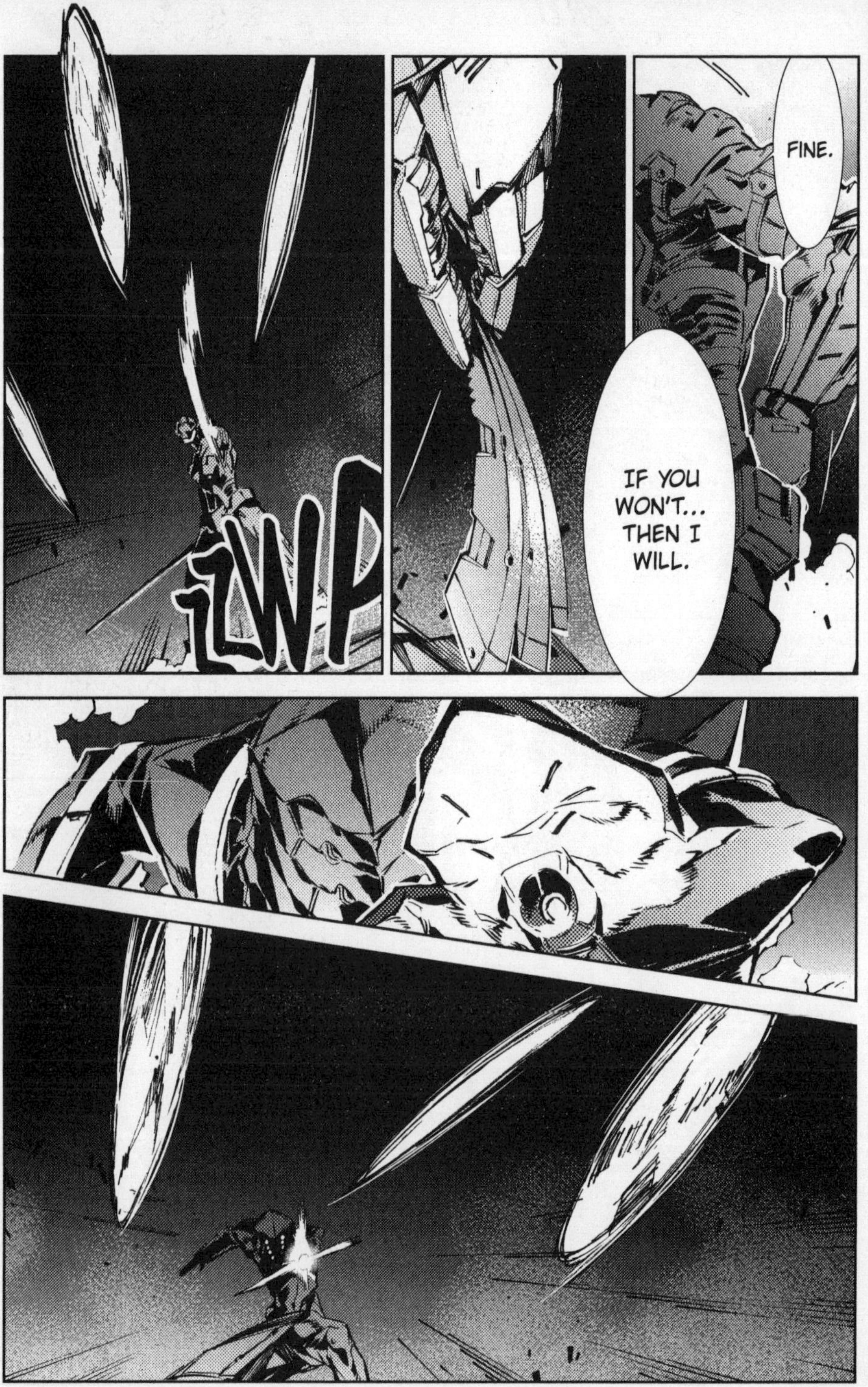
FINE.
IF YOU WON'T... THEN I WILL.
ZWP

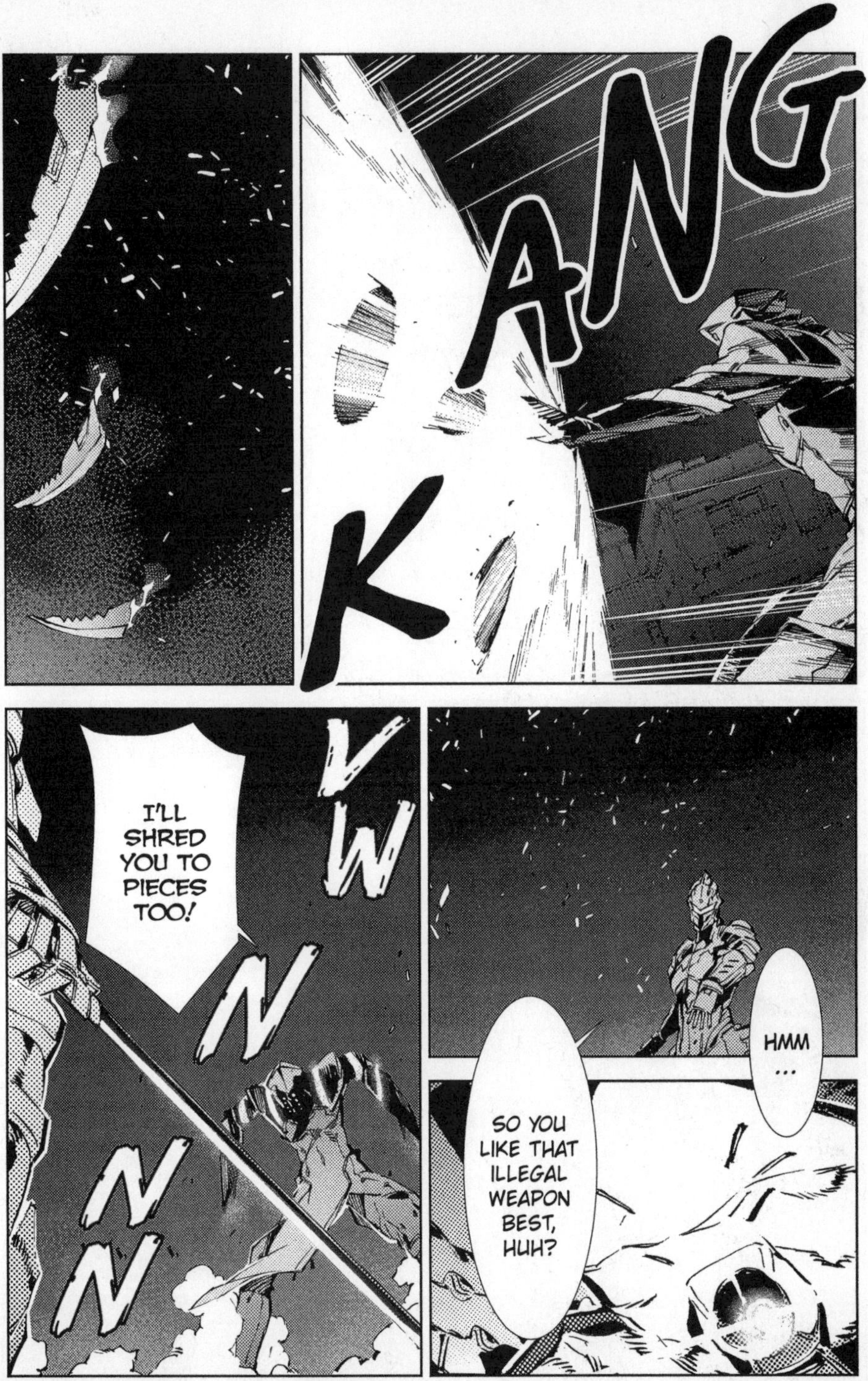
KANG
HMM...
SO YOU LIKE THAT ILLEGAL WEAPON BEST, HUH?
I'LL SHRED YOU TO PIECES TOO!
VWNNNN

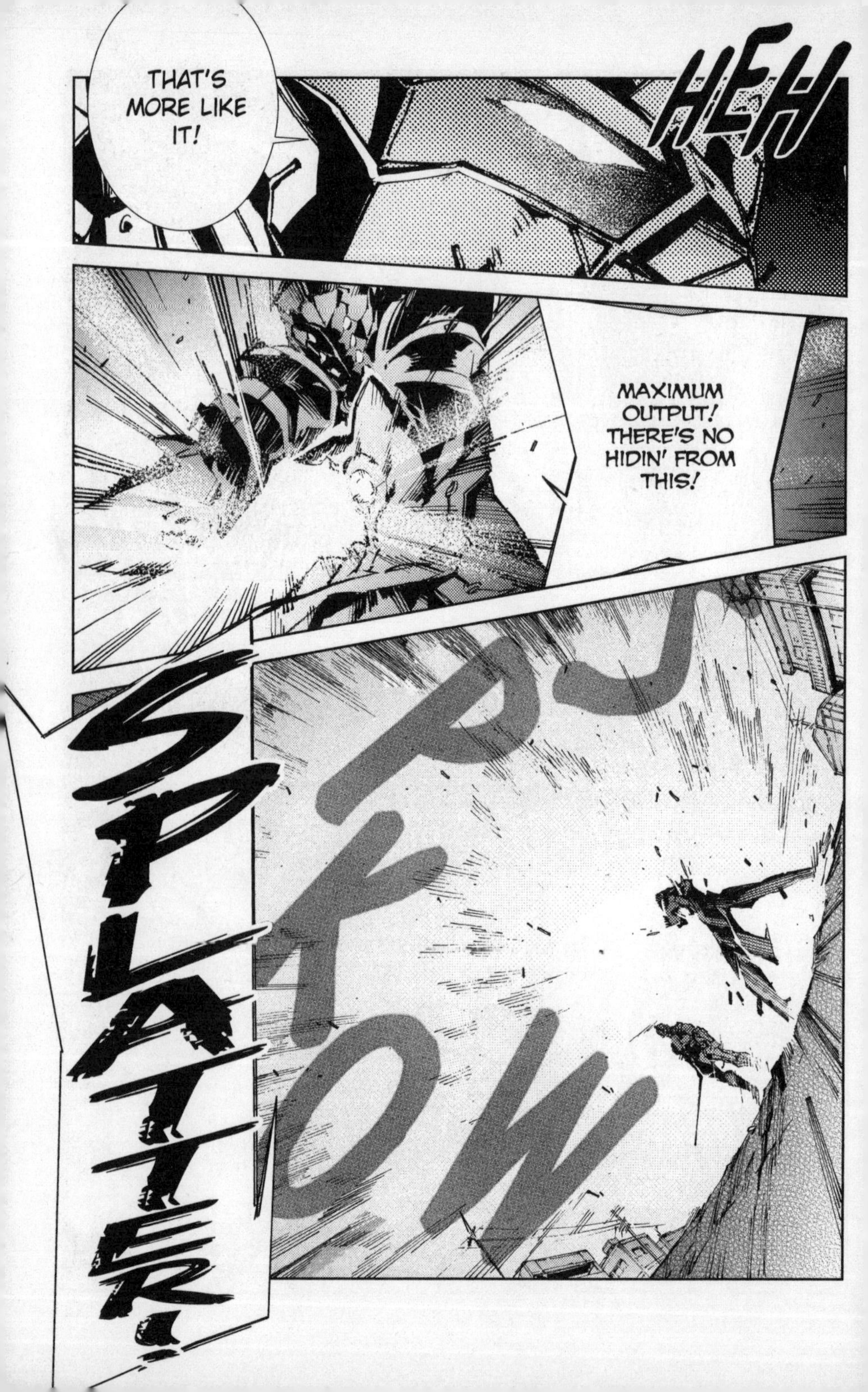
HEH
THAT'S MORE LIKE IT!
MAXIMUM OUTPUT! THERE'S NO HIDIN' FROM THIS!
SPLATTER
PKOW

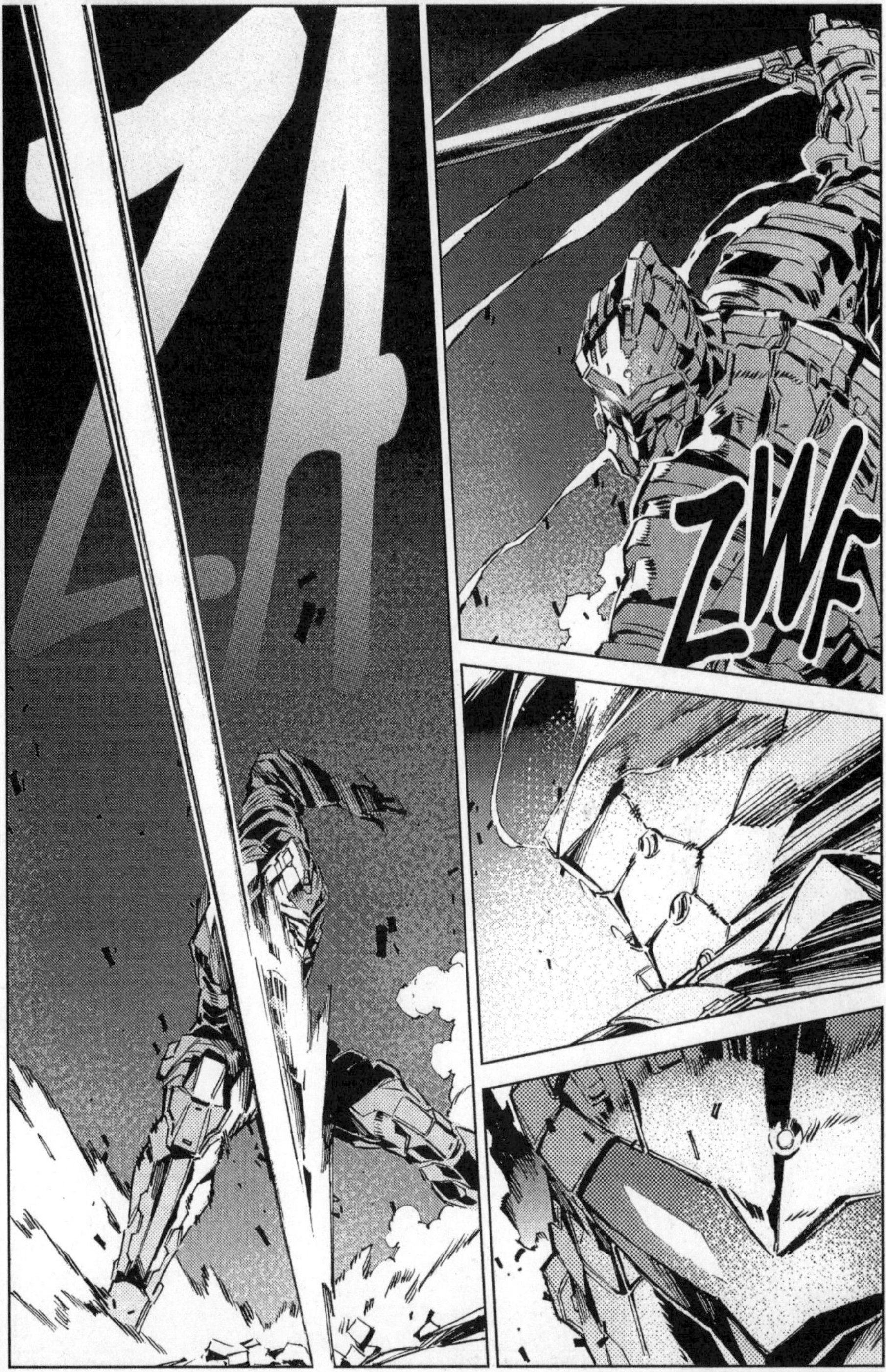
ZWF
ZA

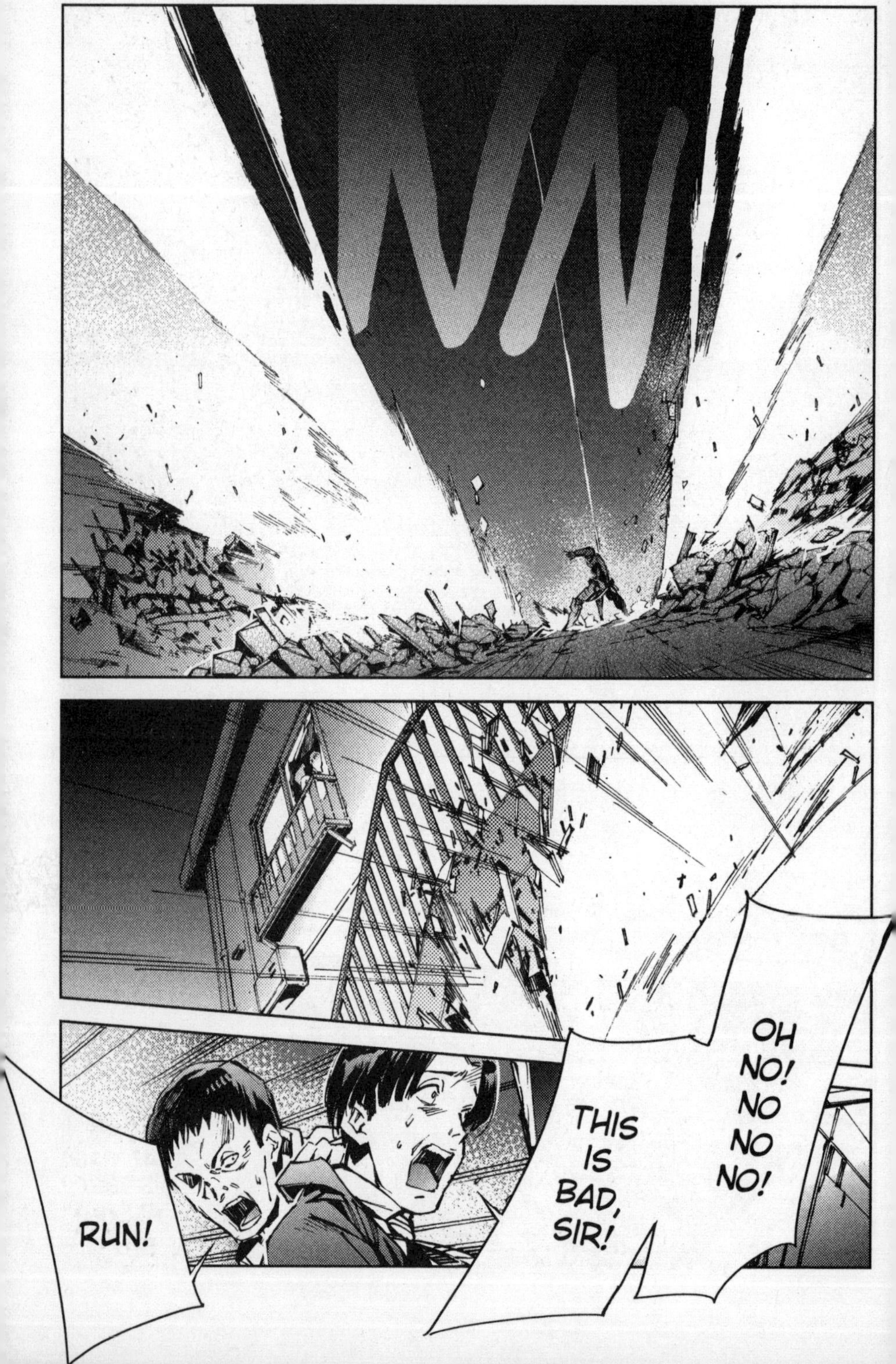
OH NO! NO NO NO!
THIS IS BAD, SIR!
RUN!

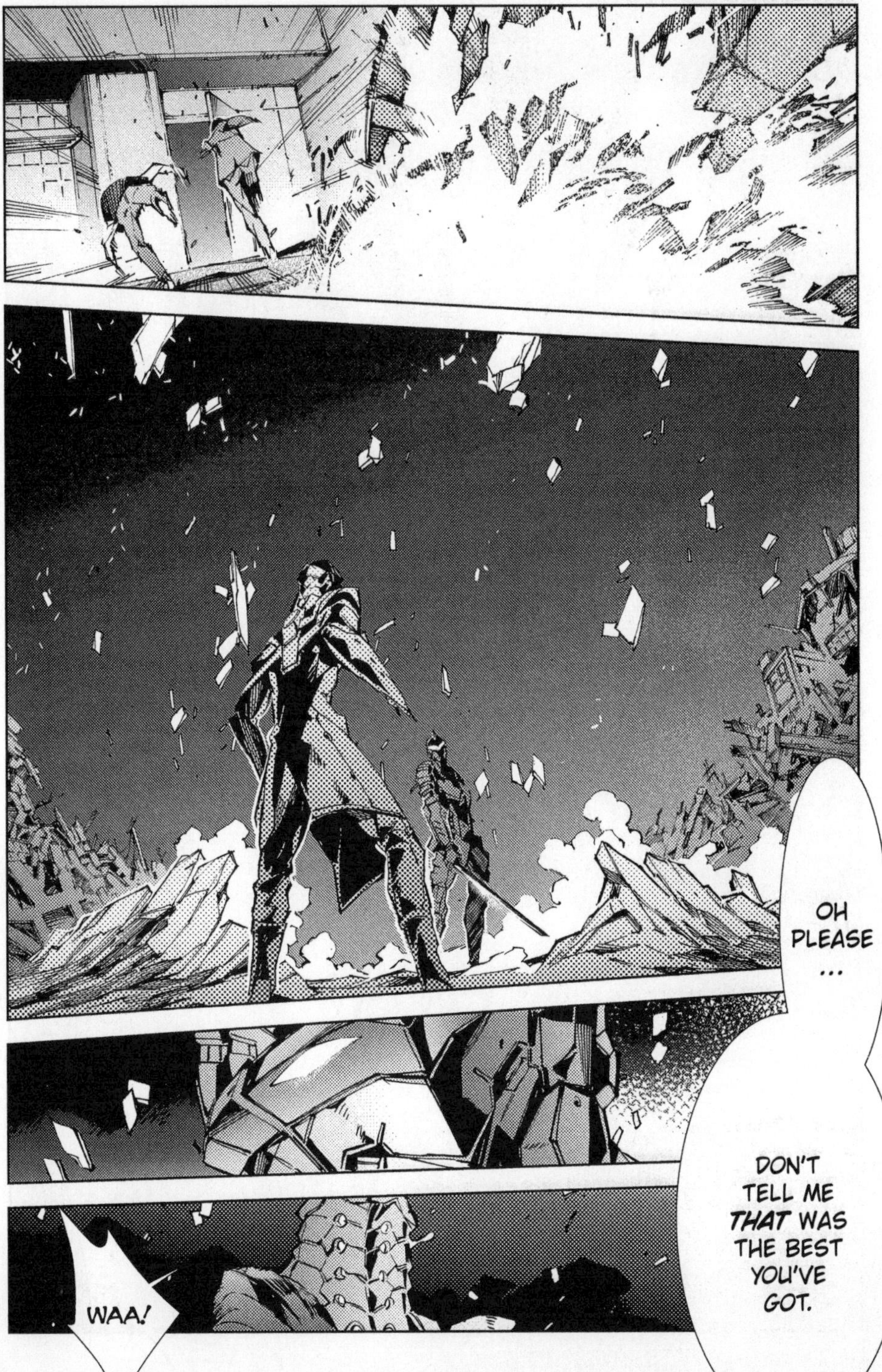
OH PLEASE ...
DON'T TELL ME *THAT* WAS THE BEST YOU'VE GOT.
WAA!

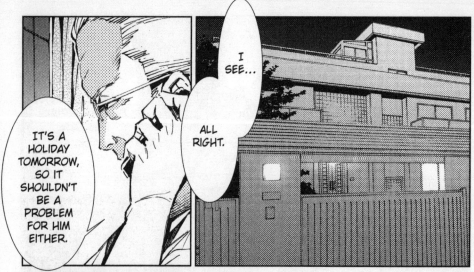

I SEE...

ALL RIGHT.

IT'S A HOLIDAY TOMORROW, SO IT SHOULDN'T BE A PROBLEM FOR HIM EITHER.

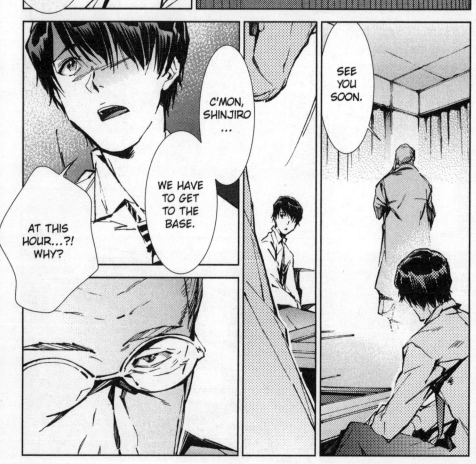

C'MON, SHINJIRO...

WE HAVE TO GET TO THE BASE.

AT THIS HOUR...?! WHY?

SEE YOU SOON.

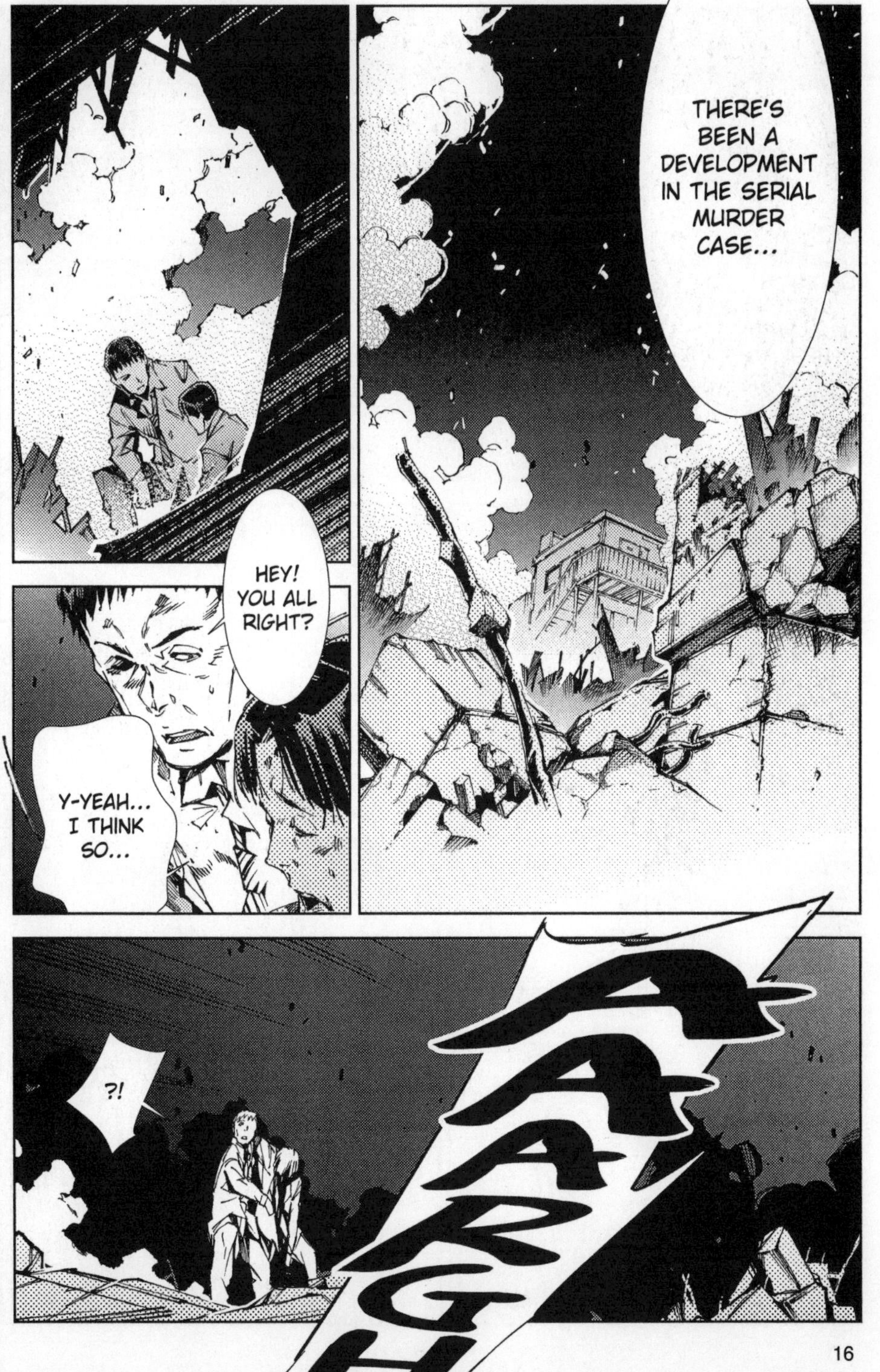
THERE'S BEEN A DEVELOPMENT IN THE SERIAL MURDER CASE...
HEY! YOU ALL RIGHT?
Y-YEAH... I THINK SO...
AAARGH
?!

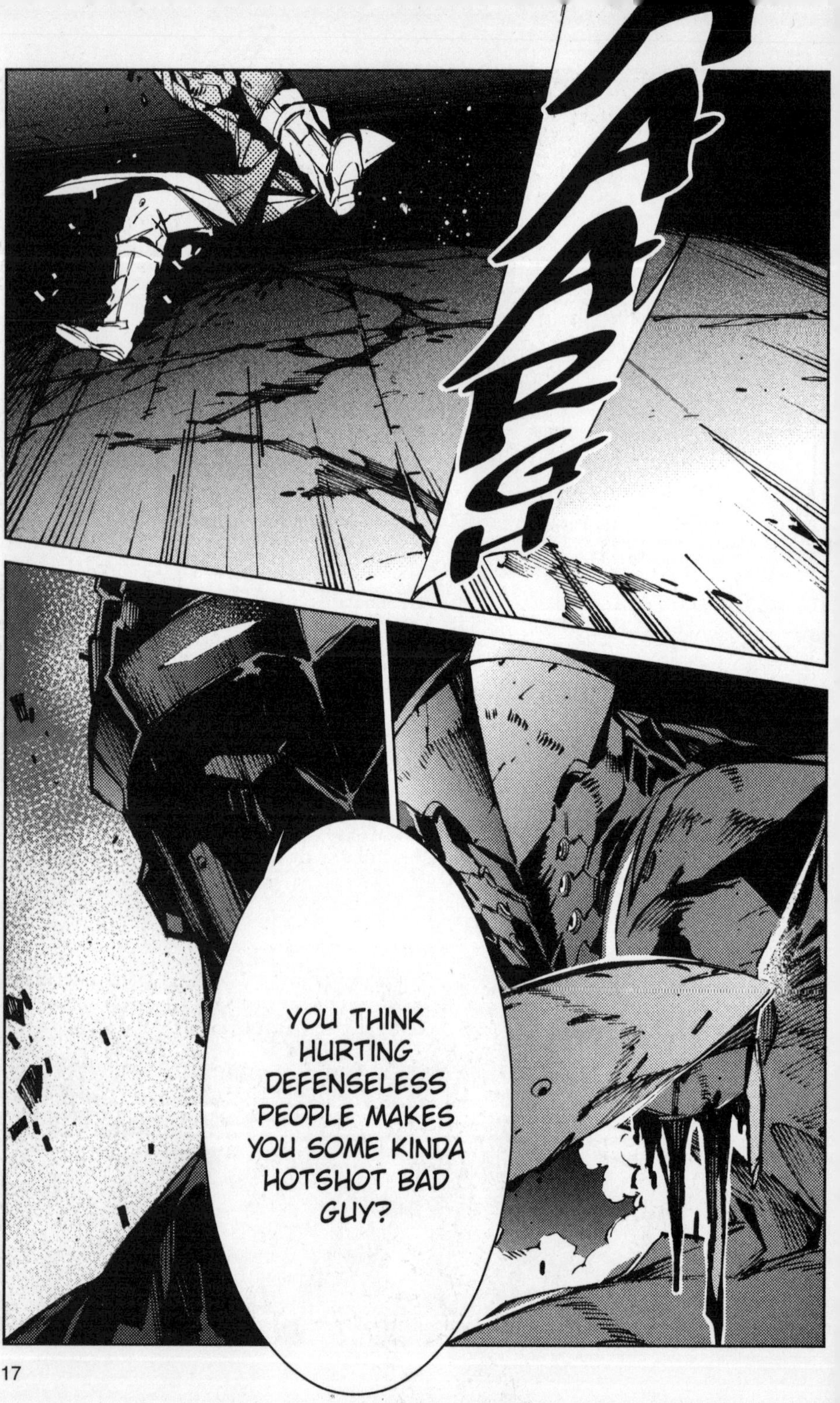
AAARGH!
YOU THINK HURTING DEFENSELESS PEOPLE MAKES YOU SOME KINDA HOTSHOT BAD GUY?

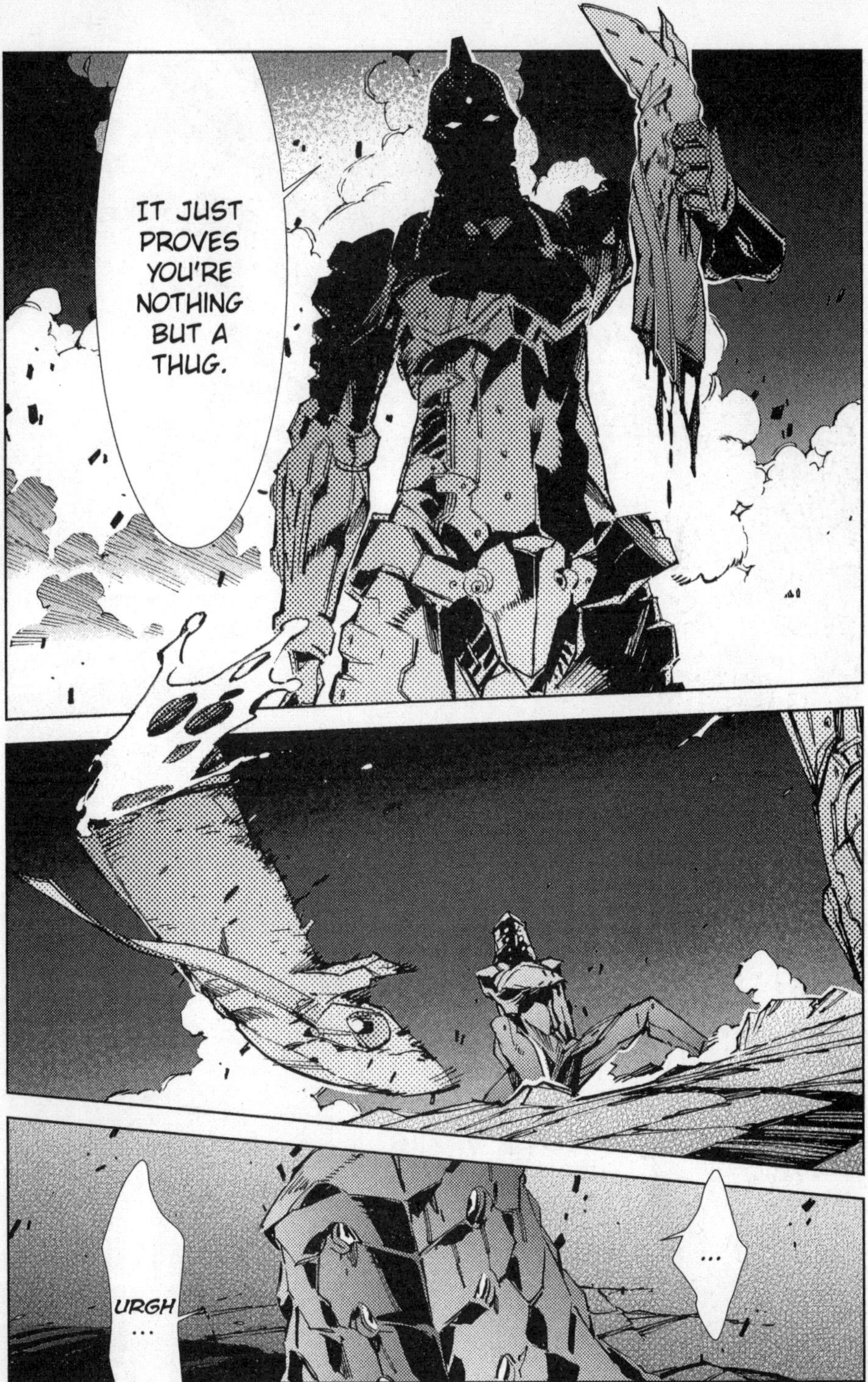
IT JUST PROVES YOU'RE NOTHING BUT A THUG.
...
URGH ...

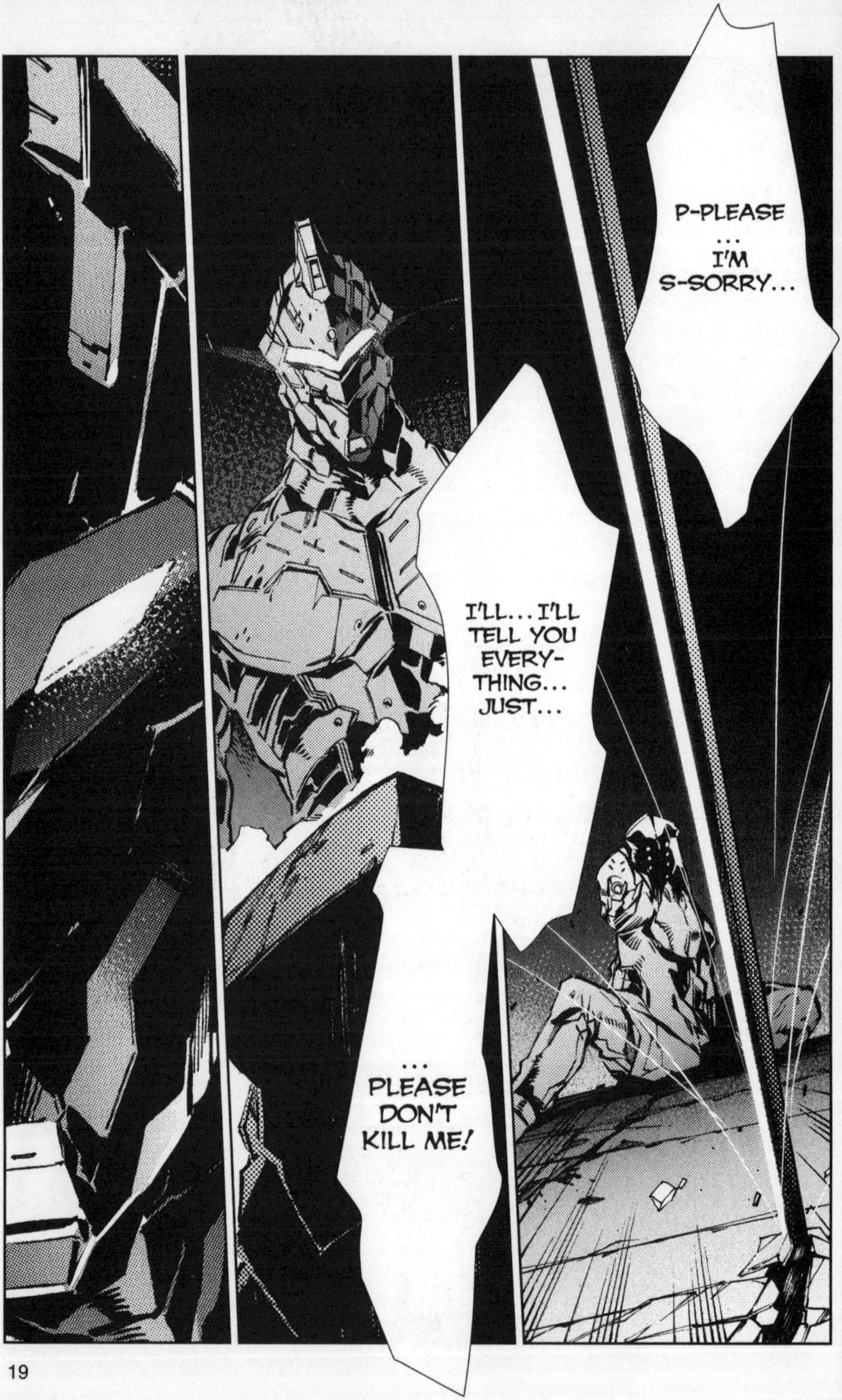
P-PLEASE ... I'M S-SORRY...
I'LL... I'LL TELL YOU EVERY-THING... JUST...
... PLEASE DON'T KILL ME!

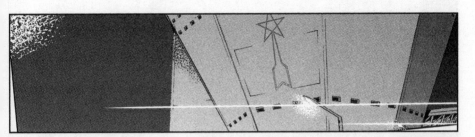

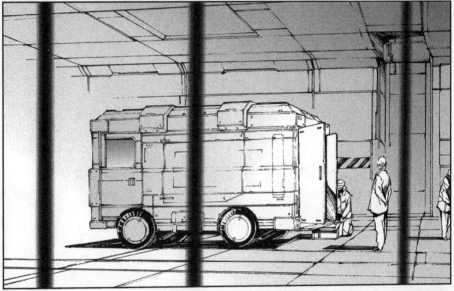

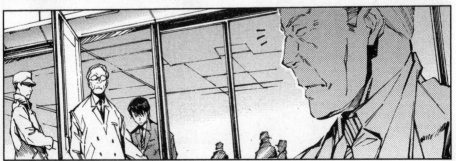

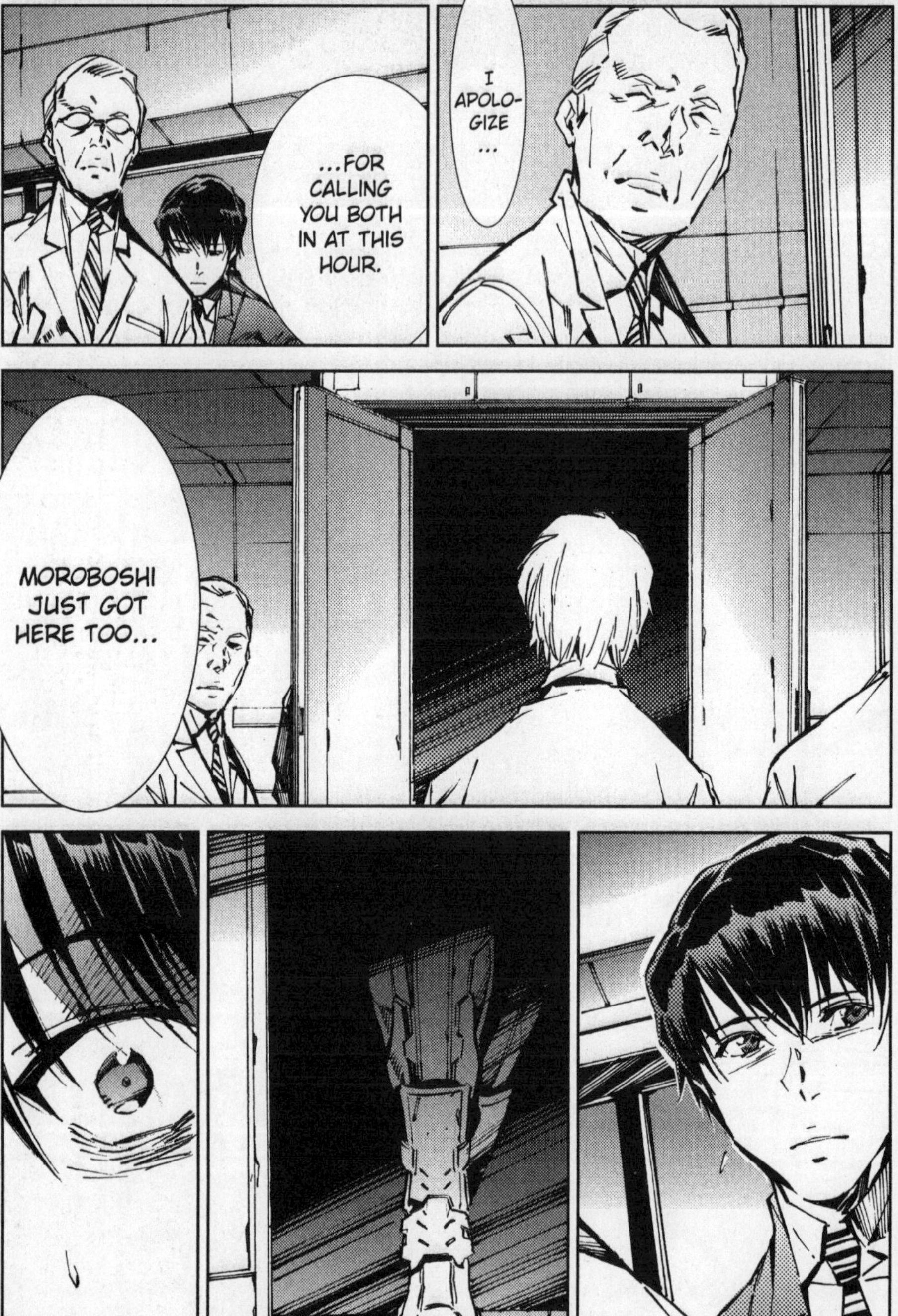
I APOLOGIZE...
...FOR CALLING YOU BOTH IN AT THIS HOUR.
MOROBOSHI JUST GOT HERE TOO...

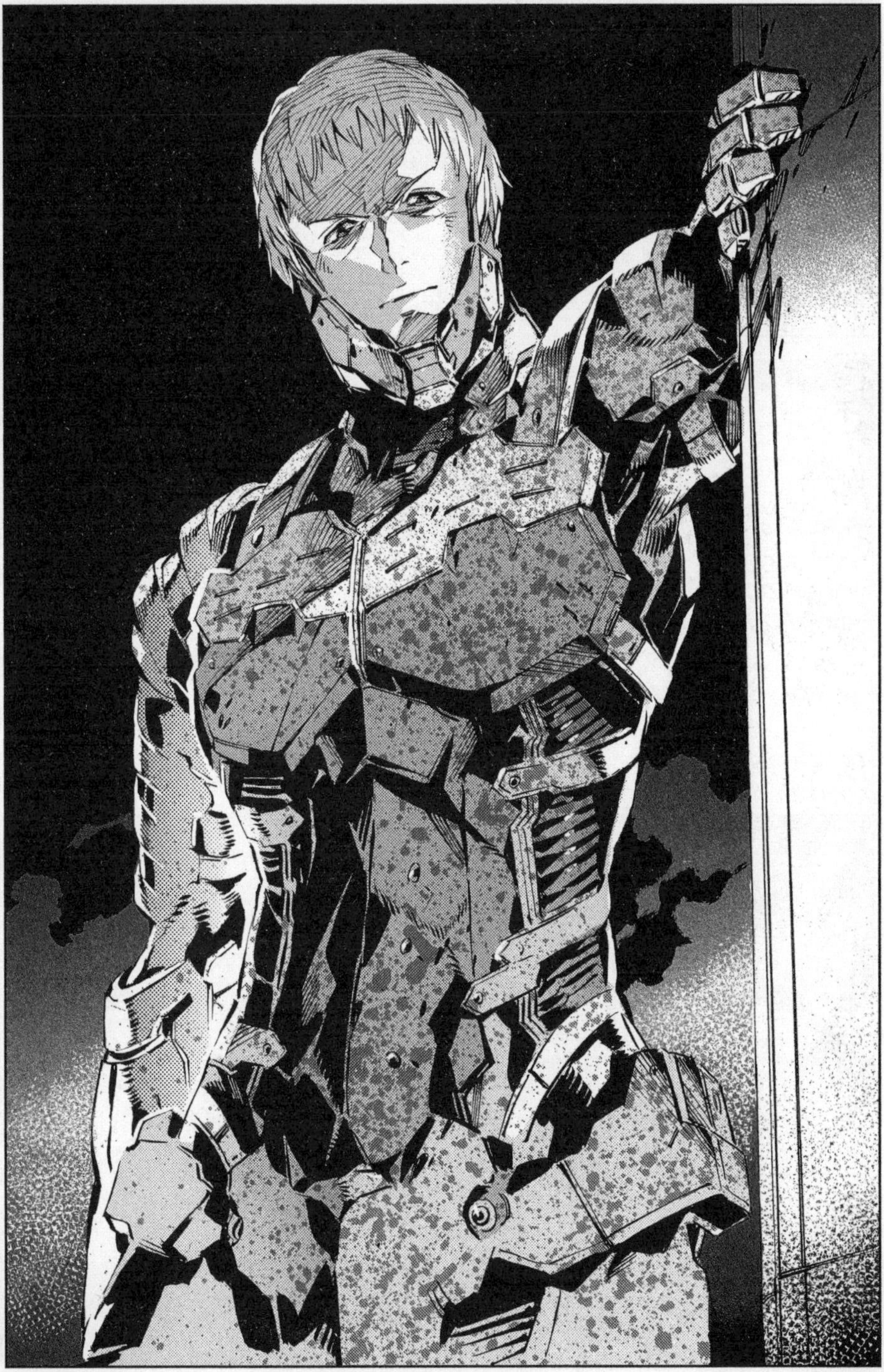

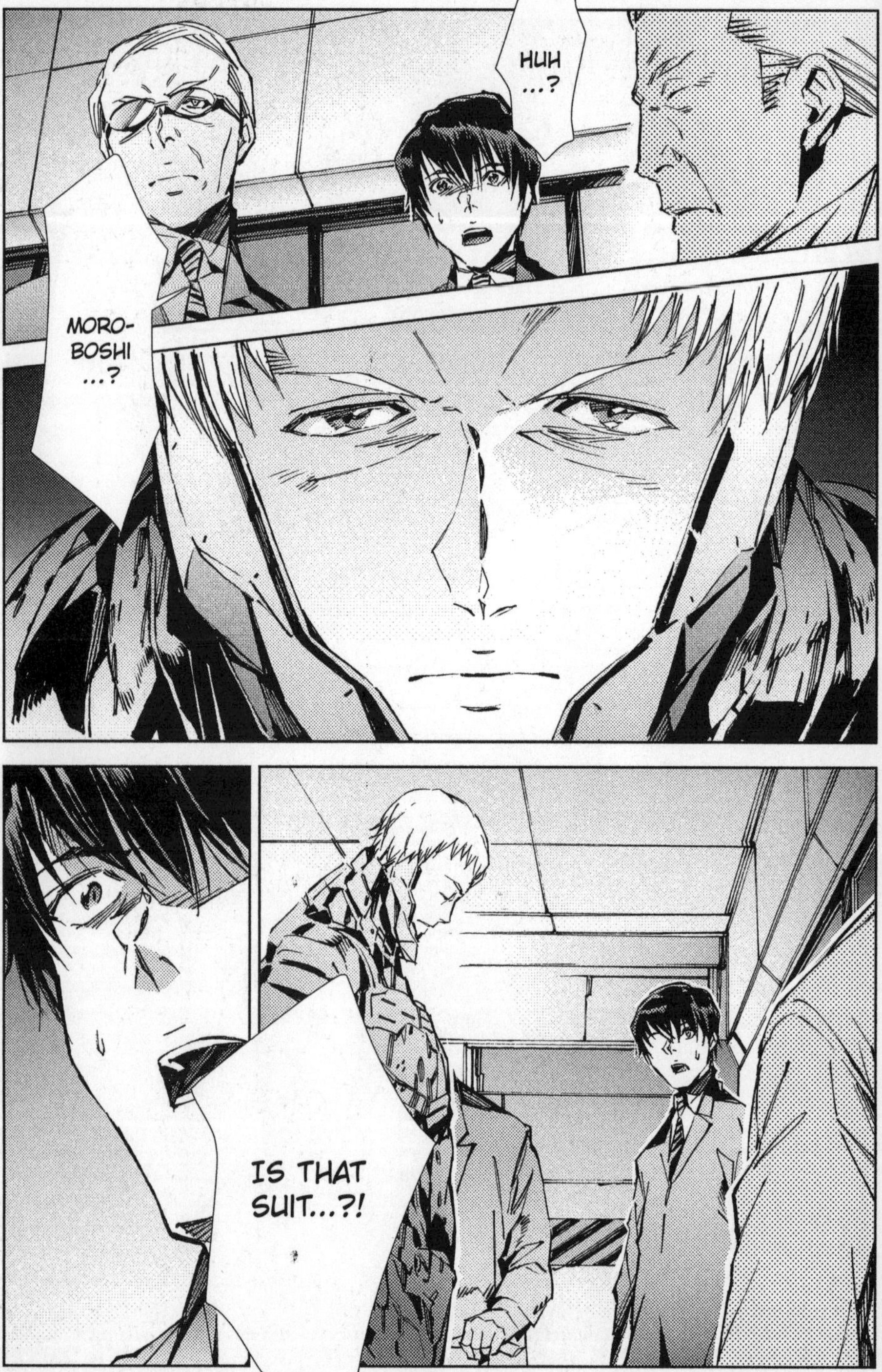
HUH ...?
MORO-BOSHI ...?
IS THAT SUIT...?!

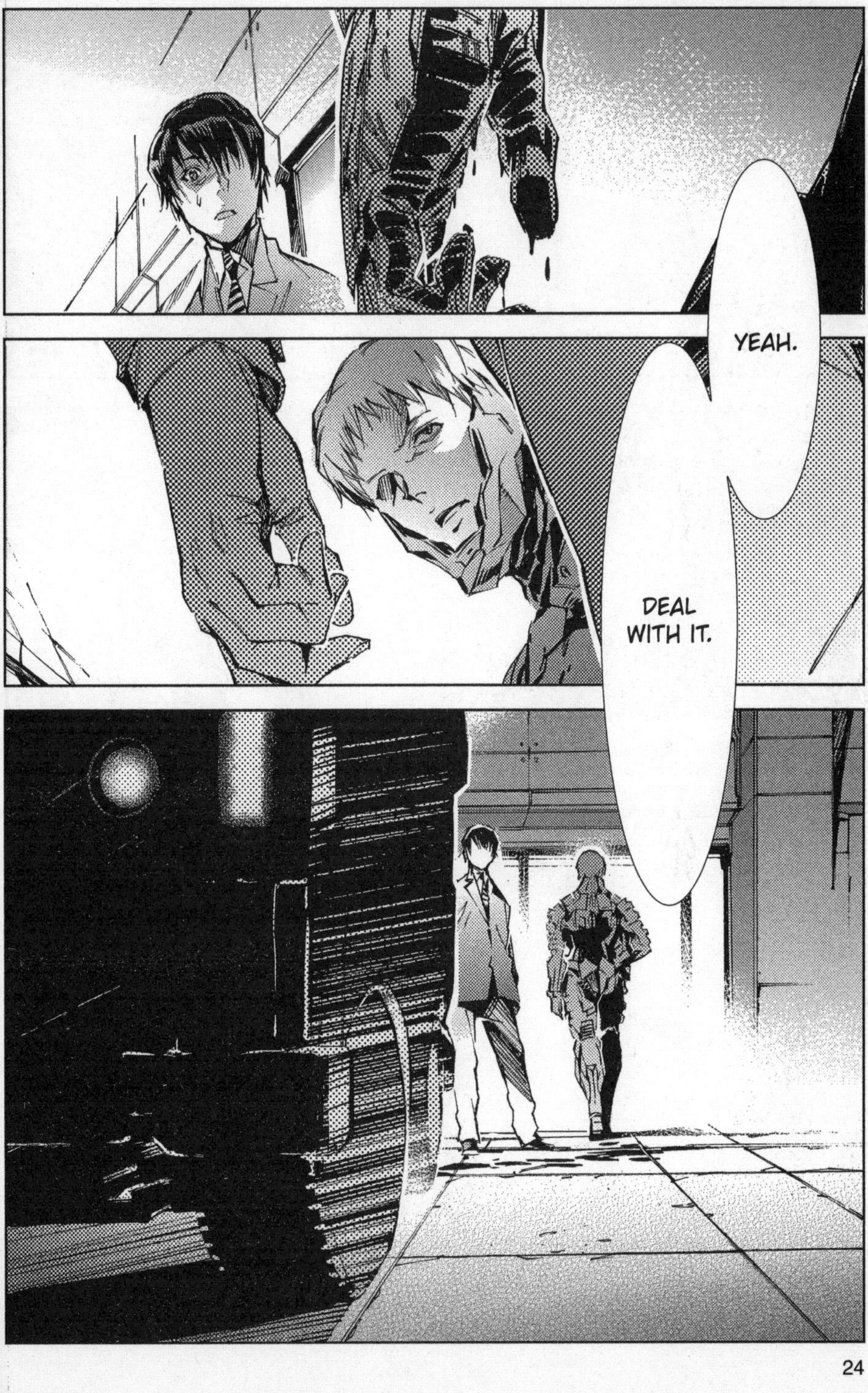
YEAH.
DEAL WITH IT.

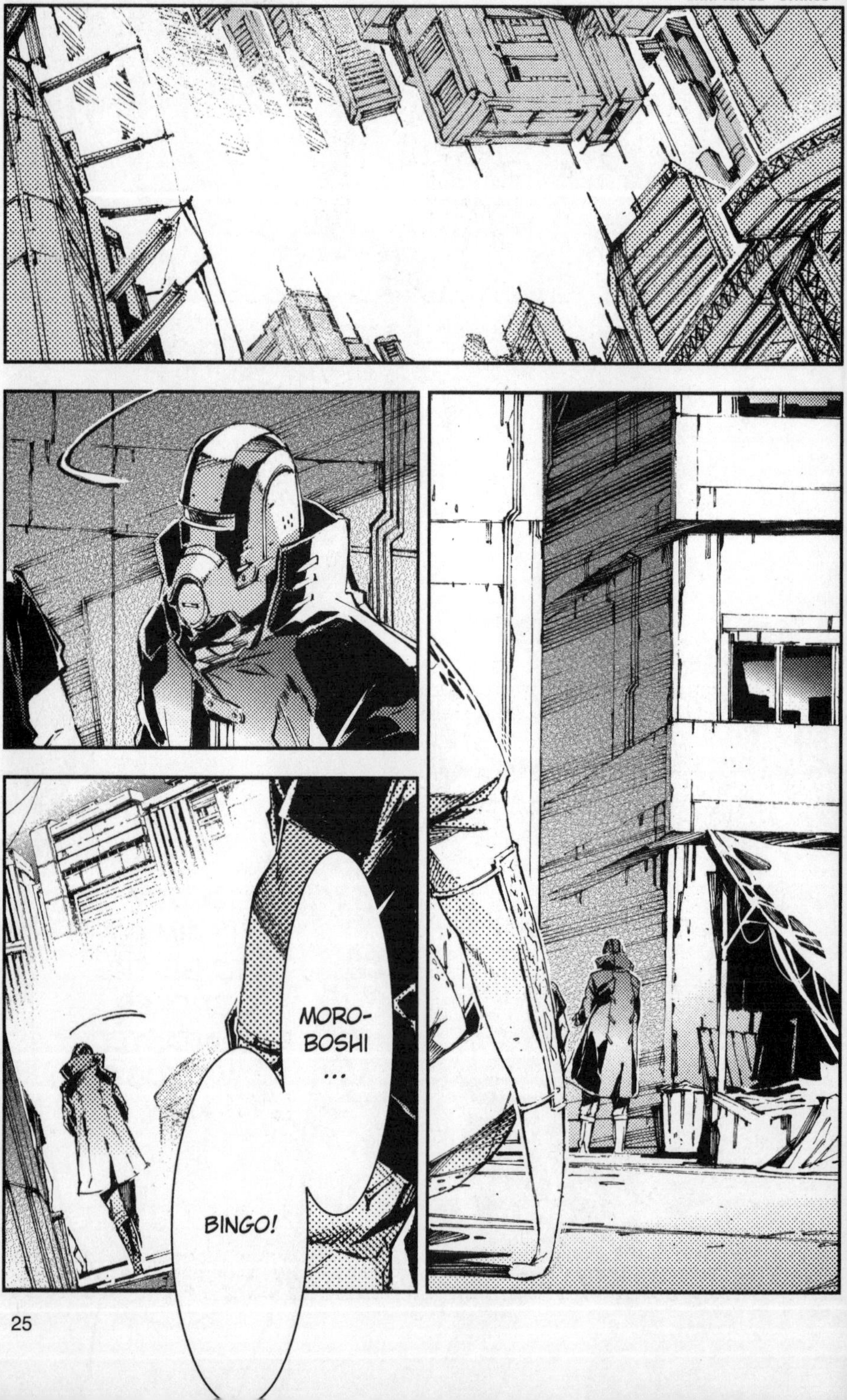
MORO-
BOSHI
...
BINGO!

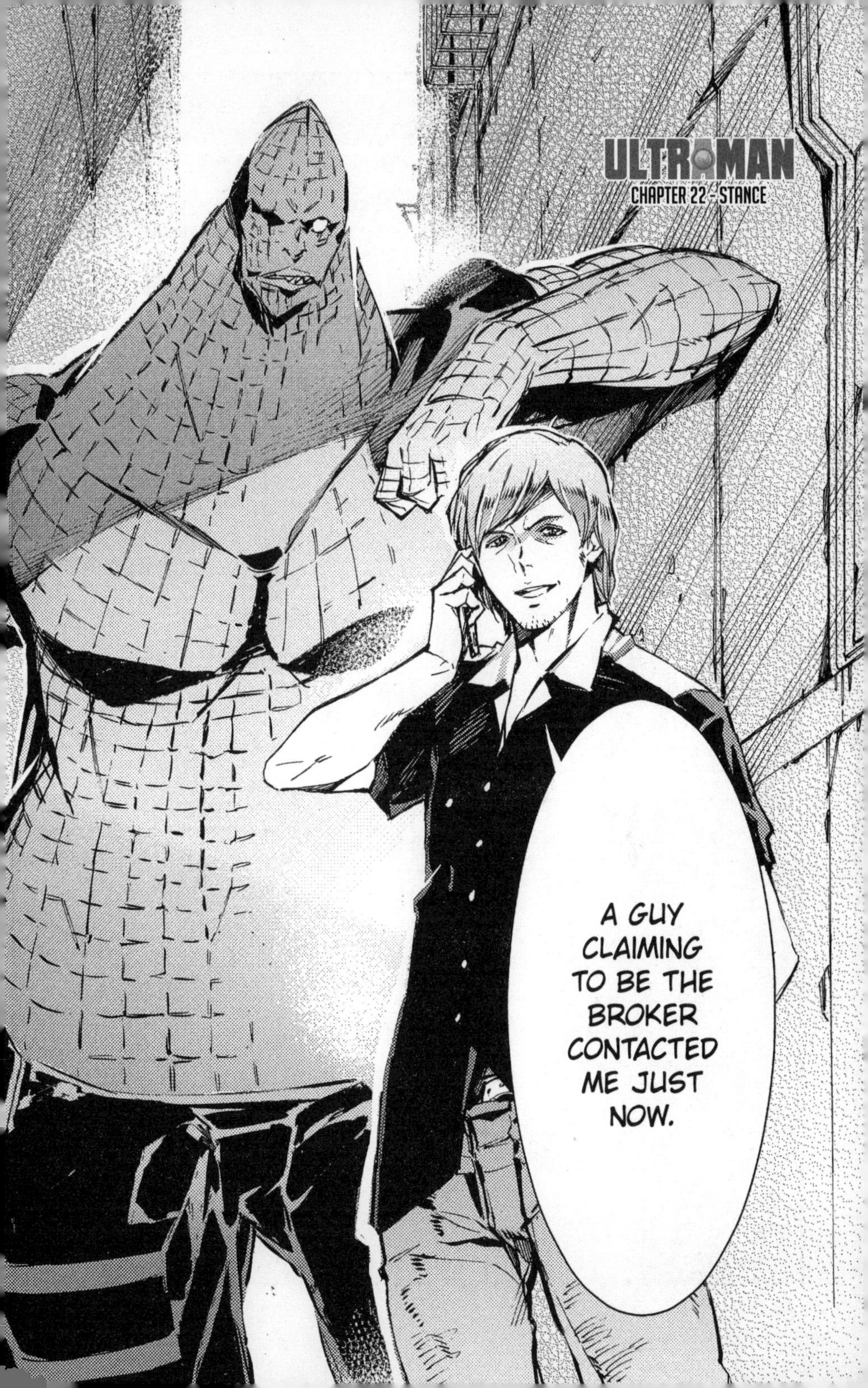
ULTRAMAN
CHAPTER 22 - STANCE
A GUY CLAIMING TO BE THE BROKER CONTACTED ME JUST NOW.

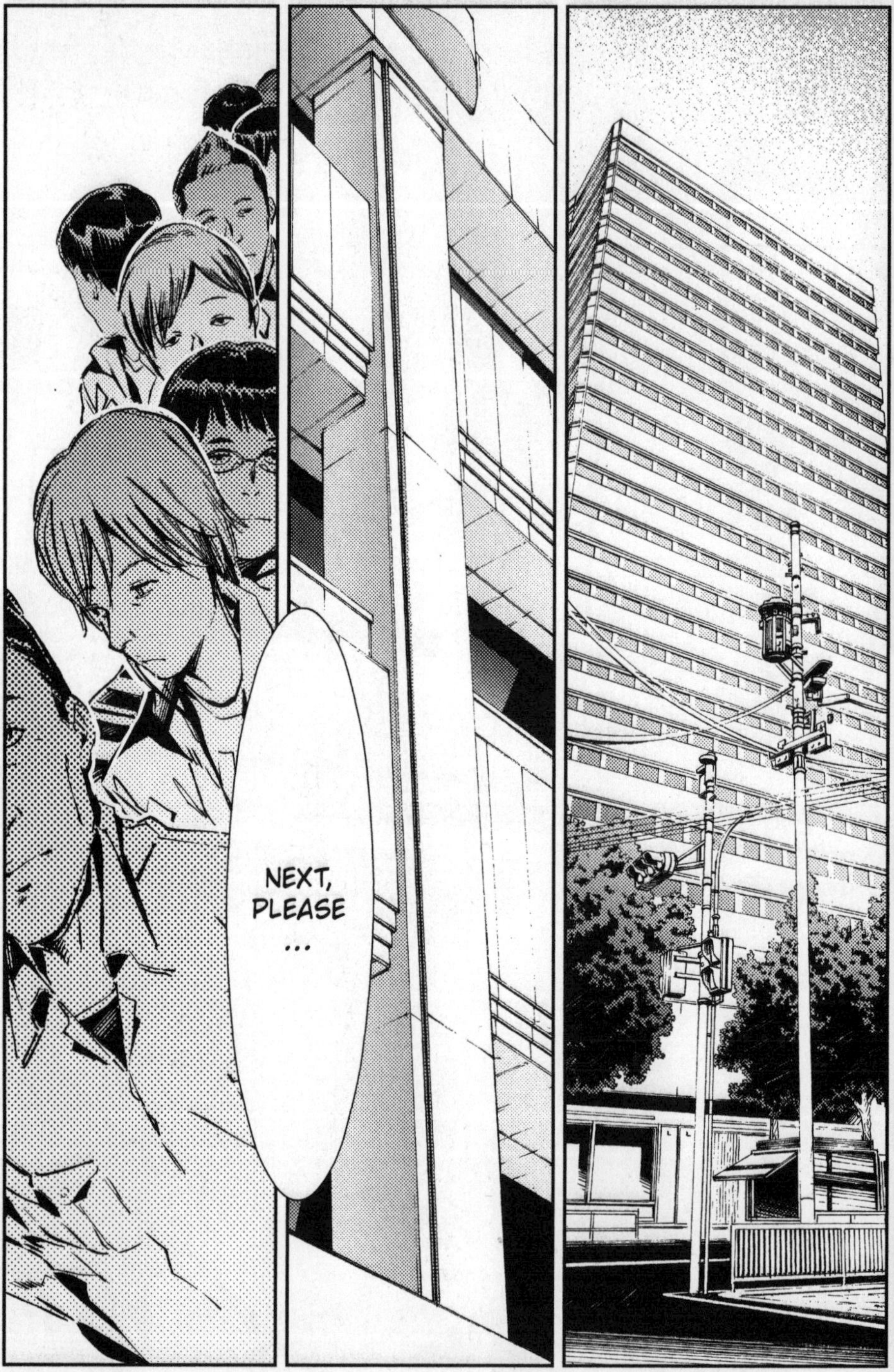
NEXT, PLEASE ...

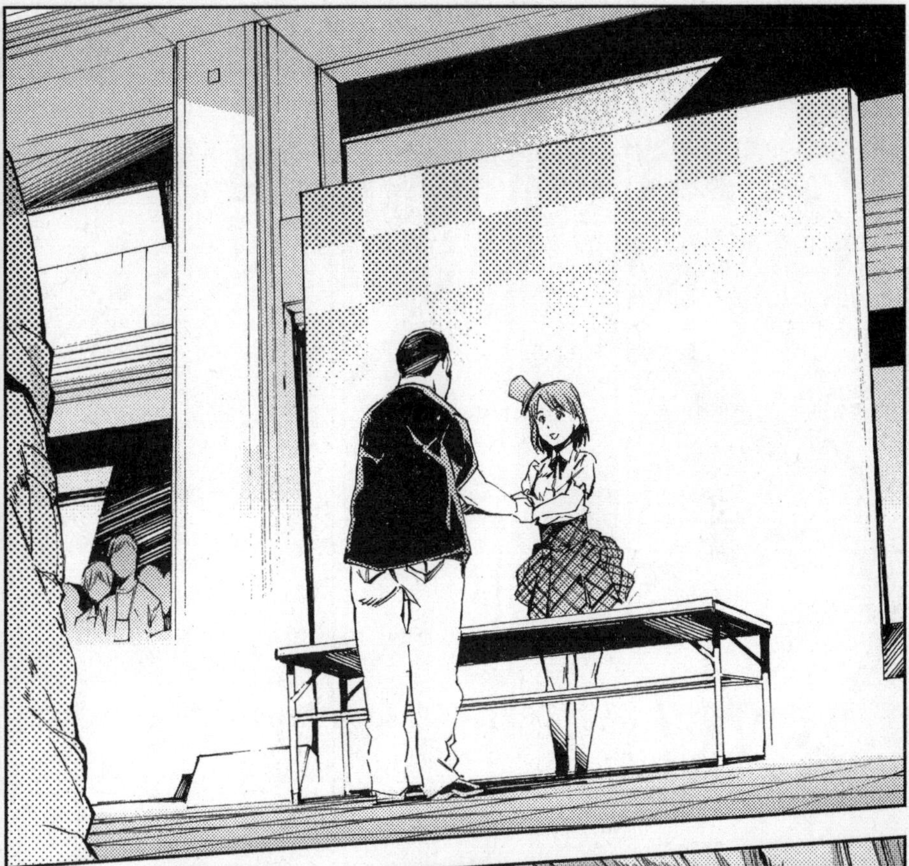
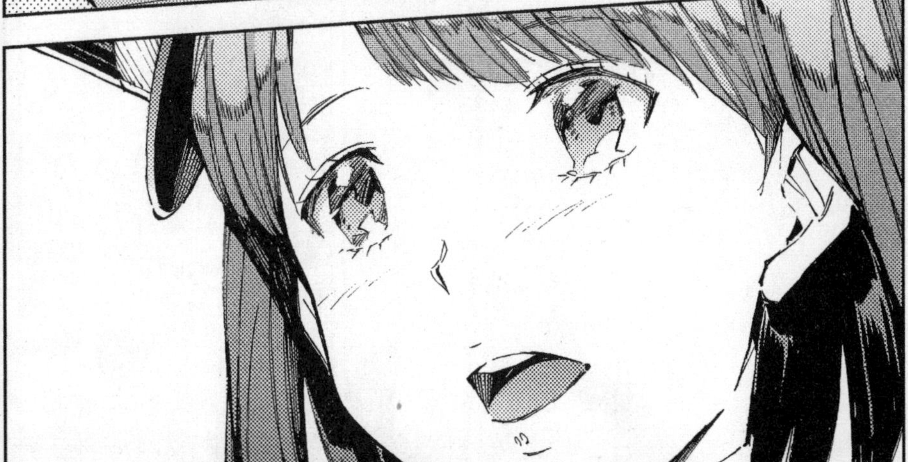

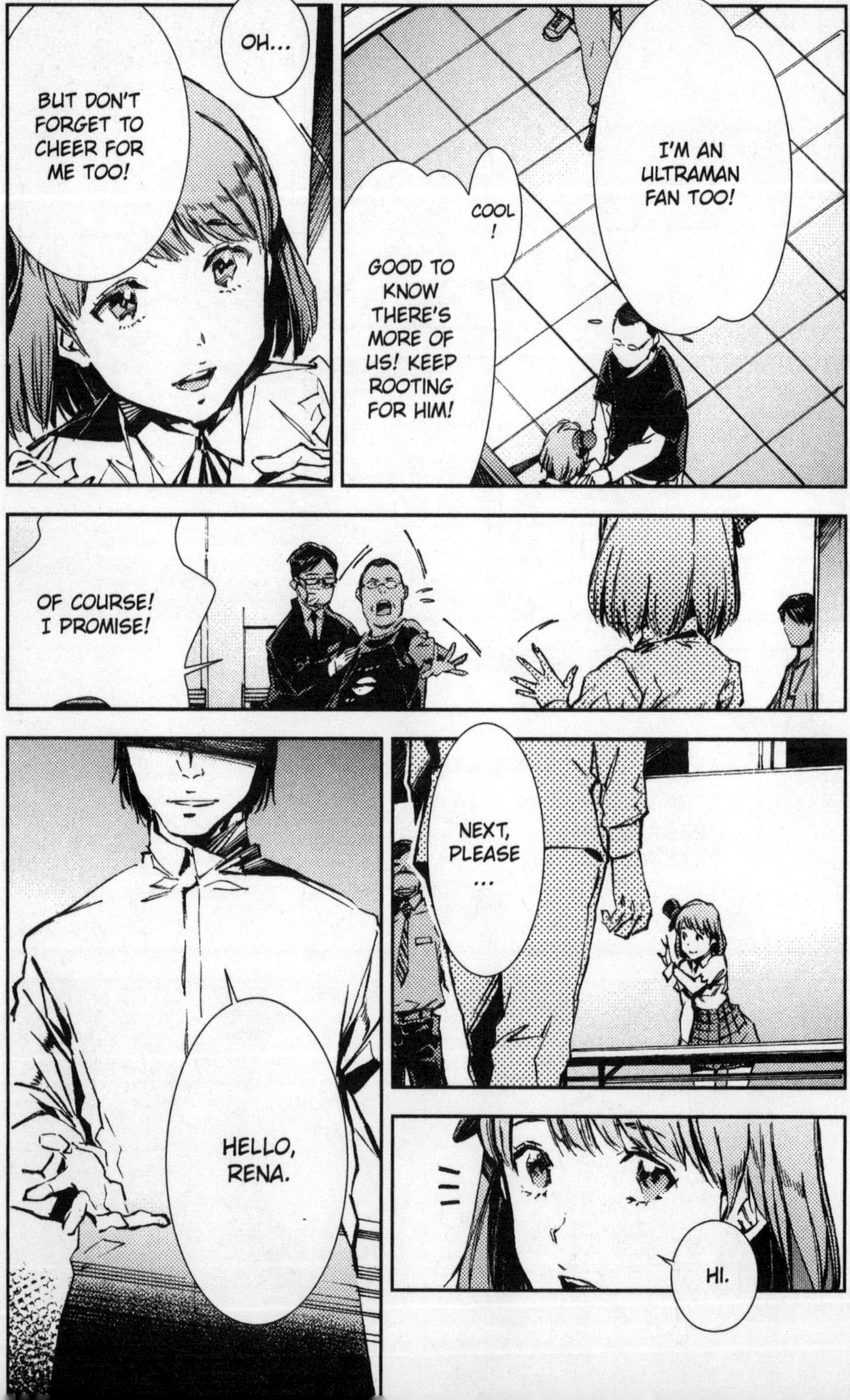
I'M AN ULTRAMAN FAN TOO!
COOL!
GOOD TO KNOW THERE'S MORE OF US! KEEP ROOTING FOR HIM!
OH...
BUT DON'T FORGET TO CHEER FOR ME TOO!
OF COURSE! I PROMISE!
NEXT, PLEASE ...
HELLO, RENA.
HI.

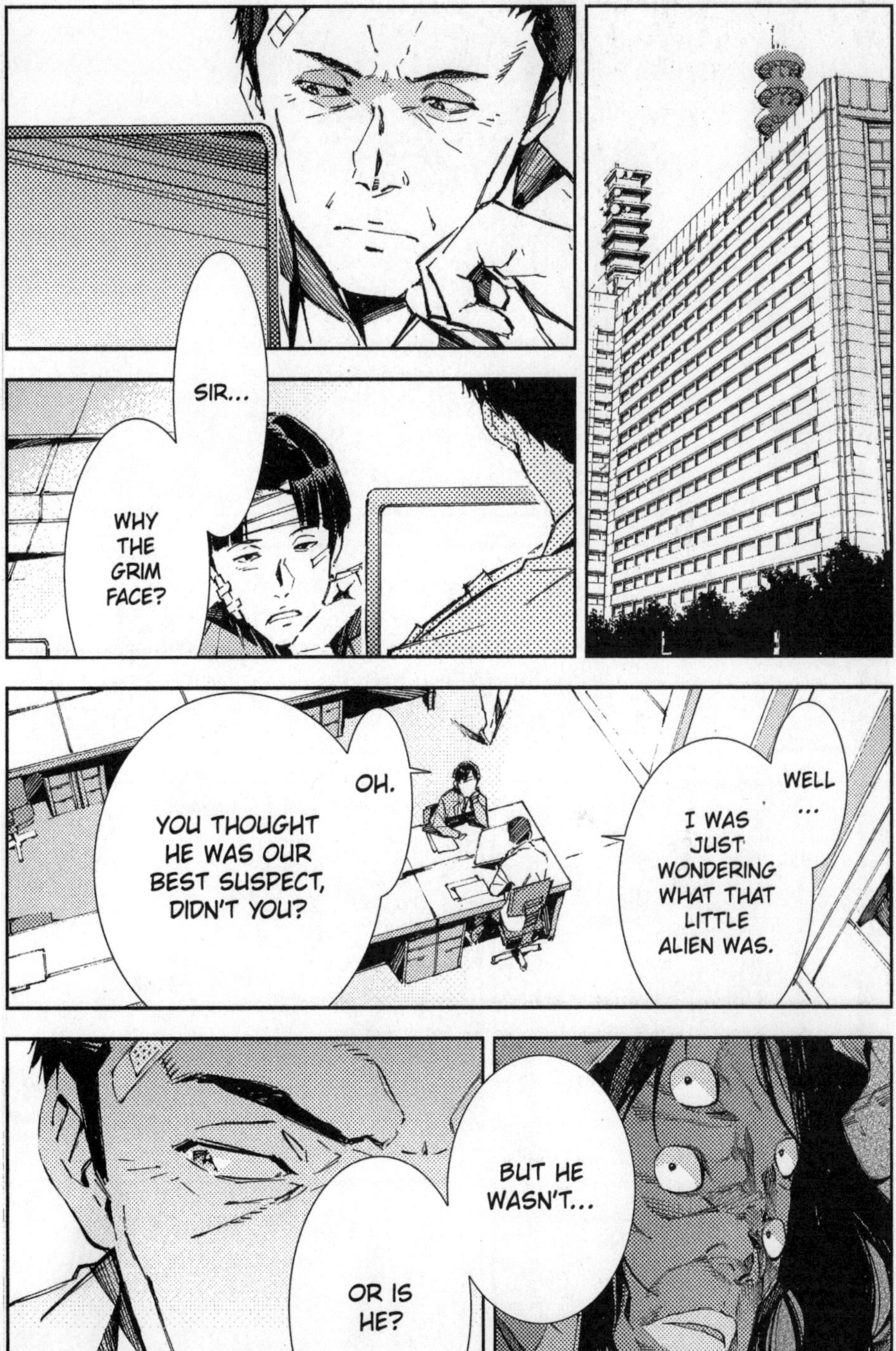
SIR...
WHY THE GRIM FACE?
WELL... I WAS JUST WONDERING WHAT THAT LITTLE ALIEN WAS.
OH.
YOU THOUGHT HE WAS OUR BEST SUSPECT, DIDN'T YOU?
BUT HE WASN'T...
OR IS HE?

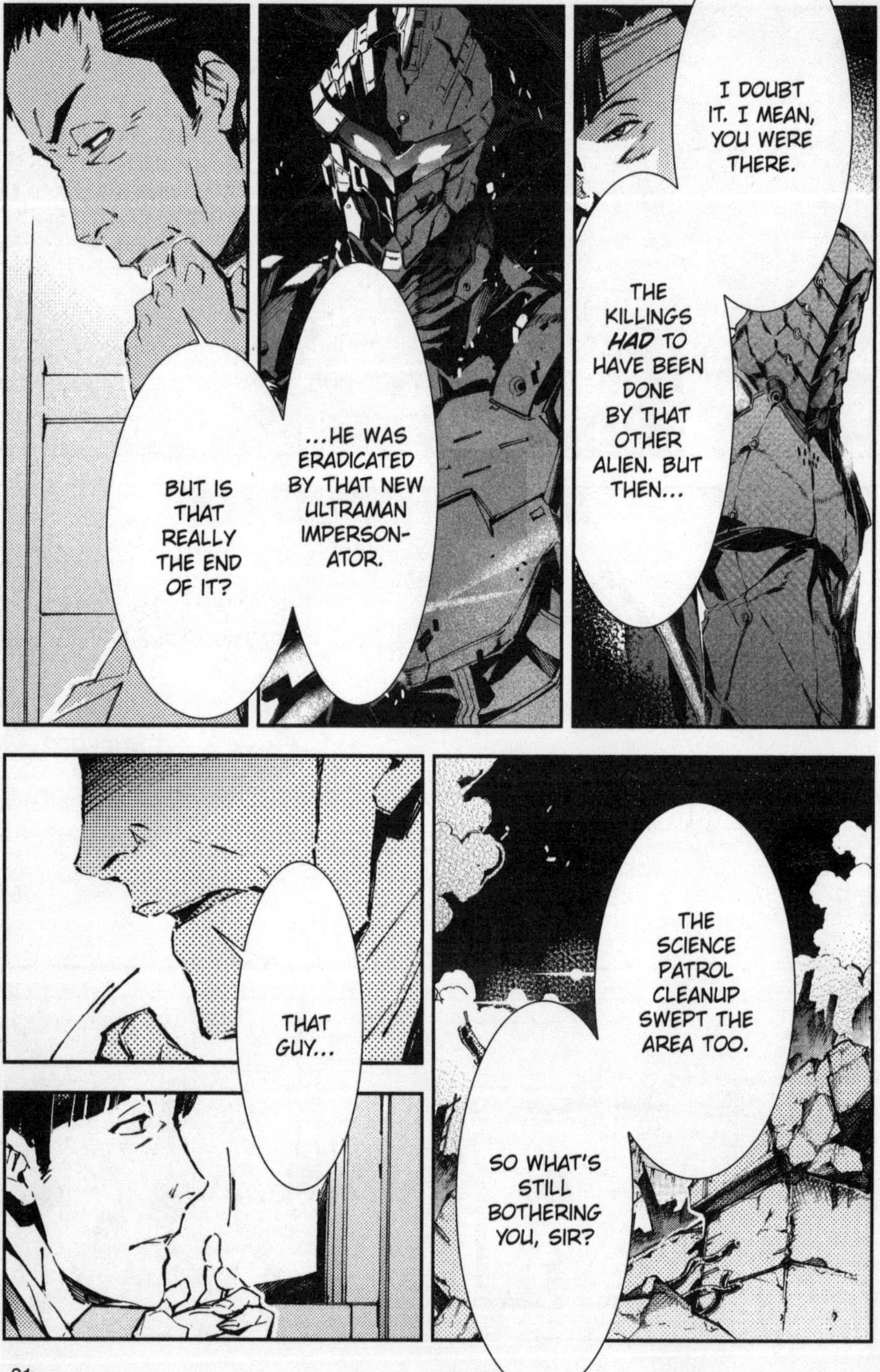
I DOUBT IT. I MEAN, YOU WERE THERE.
THE KILLINGS *HAD* TO HAVE BEEN DONE BY THAT OTHER ALIEN. BUT THEN...
...HE WAS ERADICATED BY THAT NEW ULTRAMAN IMPERSON-ATOR.
BUT IS THAT REALLY THE END OF IT?
THE SCIENCE PATROL CLEANUP SWEPT THE AREA TOO.
SO WHAT'S STILL BOTHERING YOU, SIR?
THAT GUY...

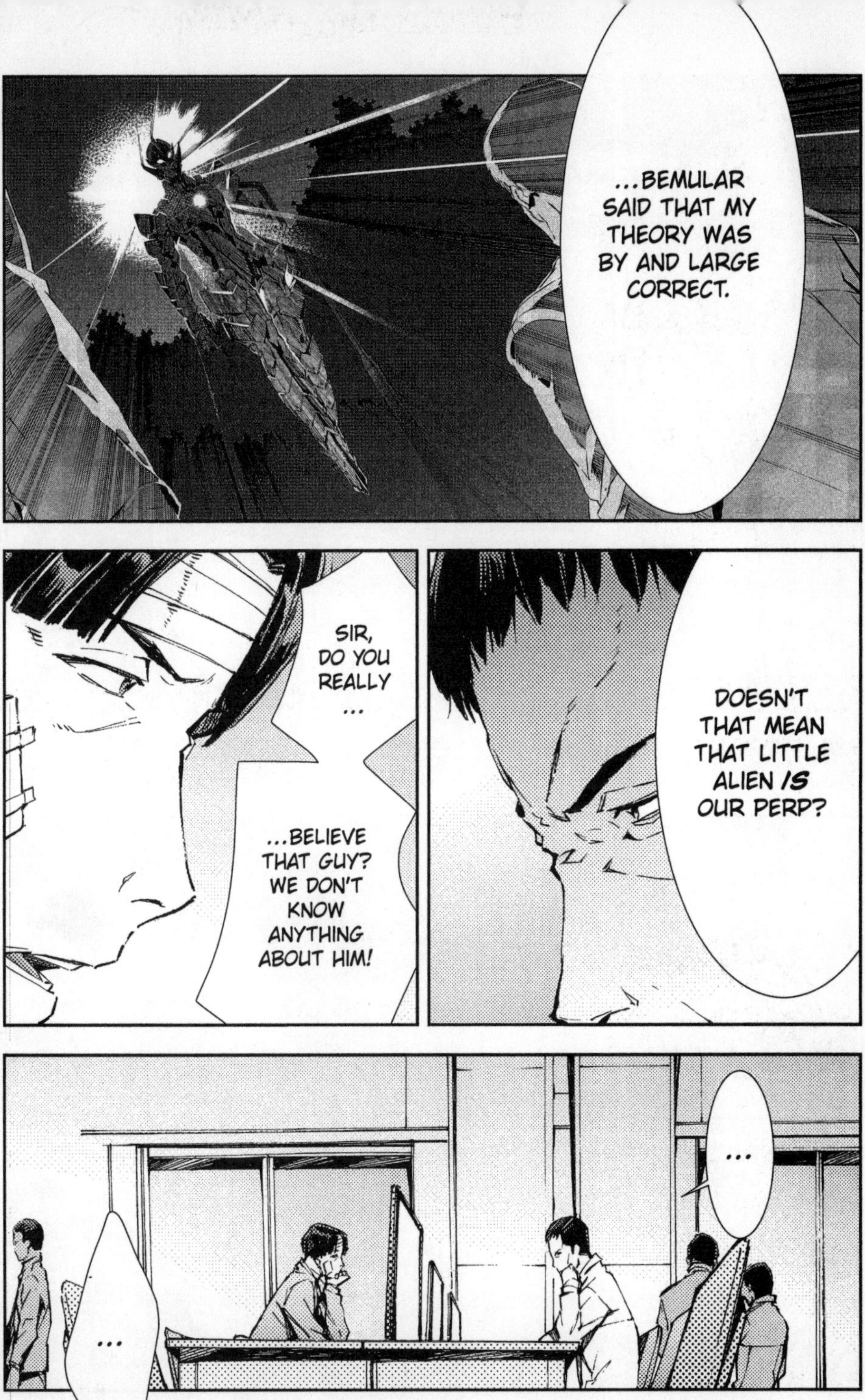
...BEMULAR SAID THAT MY THEORY WAS BY AND LARGE CORRECT.
DOESN'T THAT MEAN THAT LITTLE ALIEN *IS* OUR PERP?
SIR, DO YOU REALLY ...
...BELIEVE THAT GUY? WE DON'T KNOW ANYTHING ABOUT HIM!
...
...

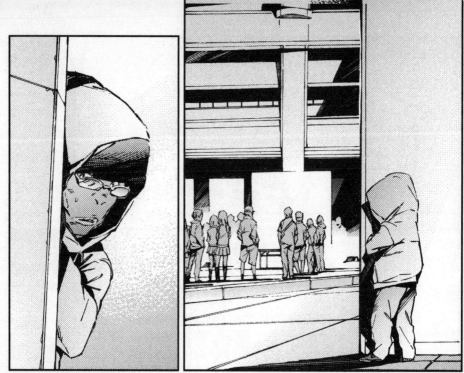

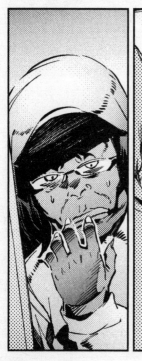

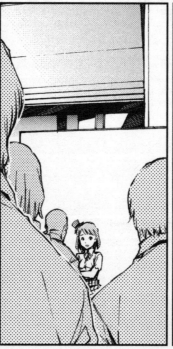

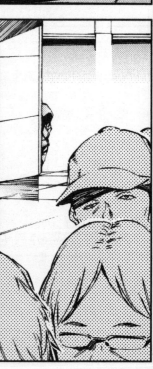

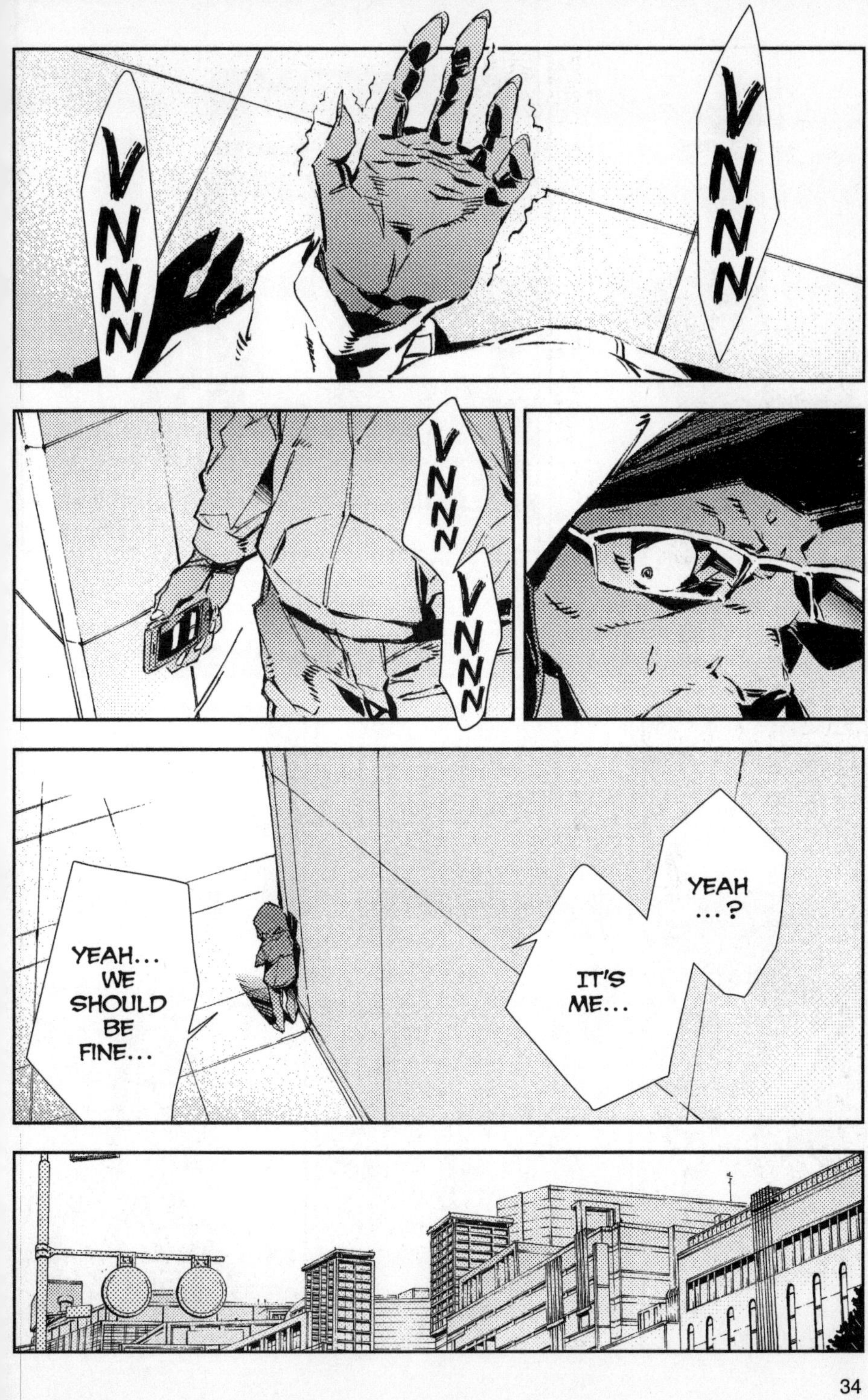
VNNN
VNNN
VNNN
VNNN
YEAH...?
IT'S ME...
YEAH... WE SHOULD BE FINE...

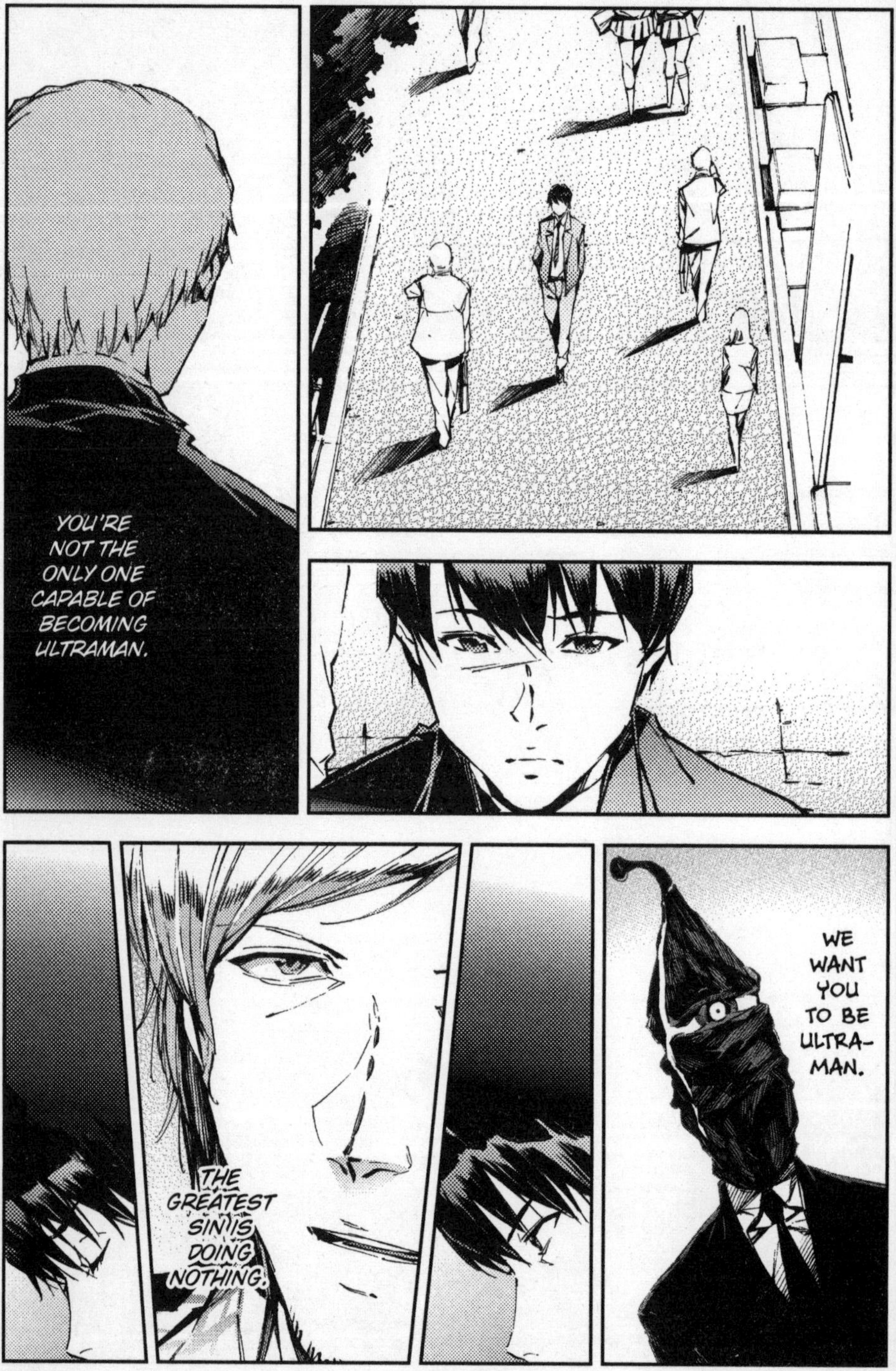
YOU'RE NOT THE ONLY ONE CAPABLE OF BECOMING ULTRAMAN.
WE WANT YOU TO BE ULTRA-MAN.
THE GREATEST SIN IS DOING NOTHING.

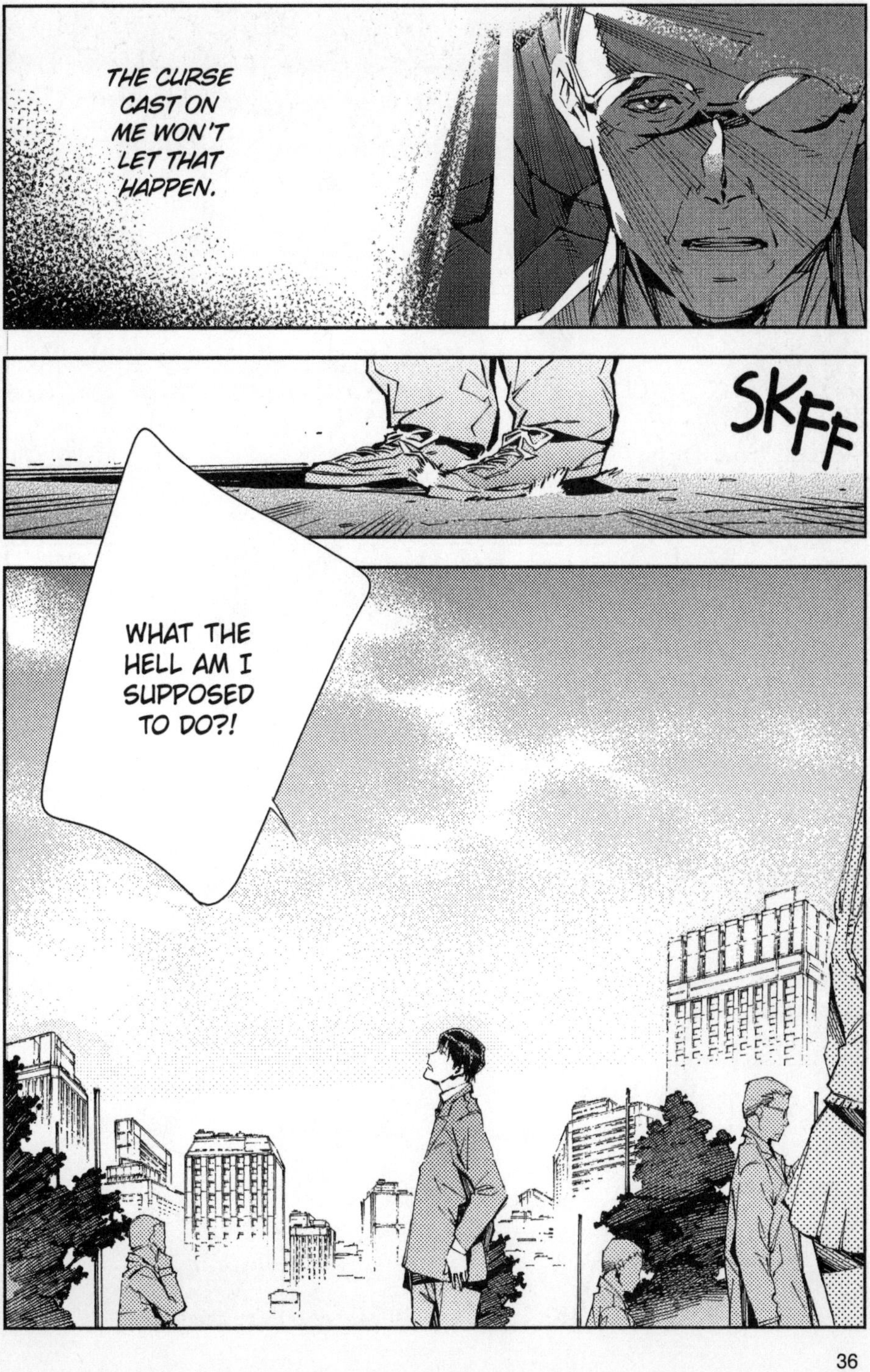
THE CURSE CAST ON ME WON'T LET THAT HAPPEN.
SKFF
WHAT THE HELL AM I SUPPOSED TO DO?!

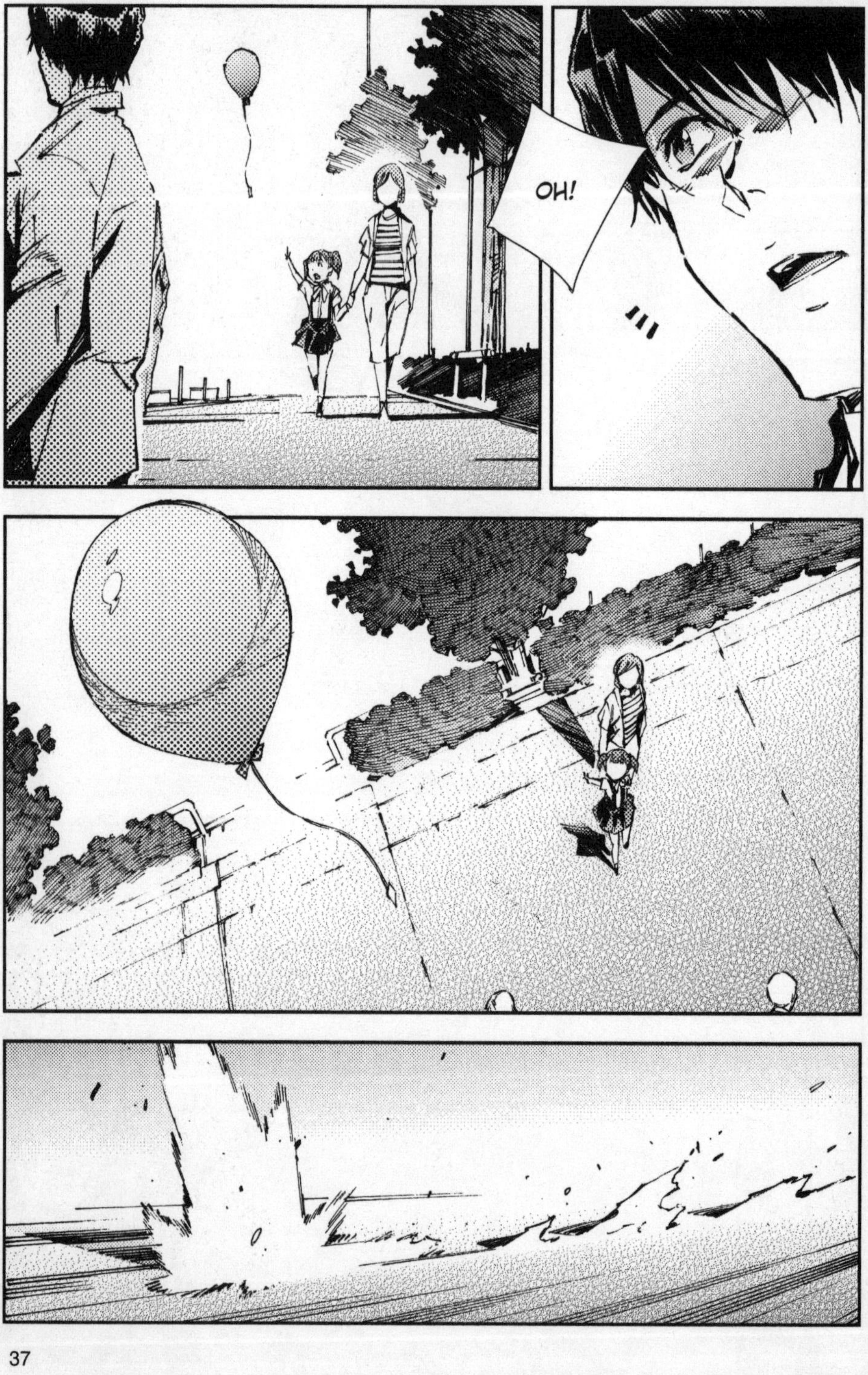
OH!

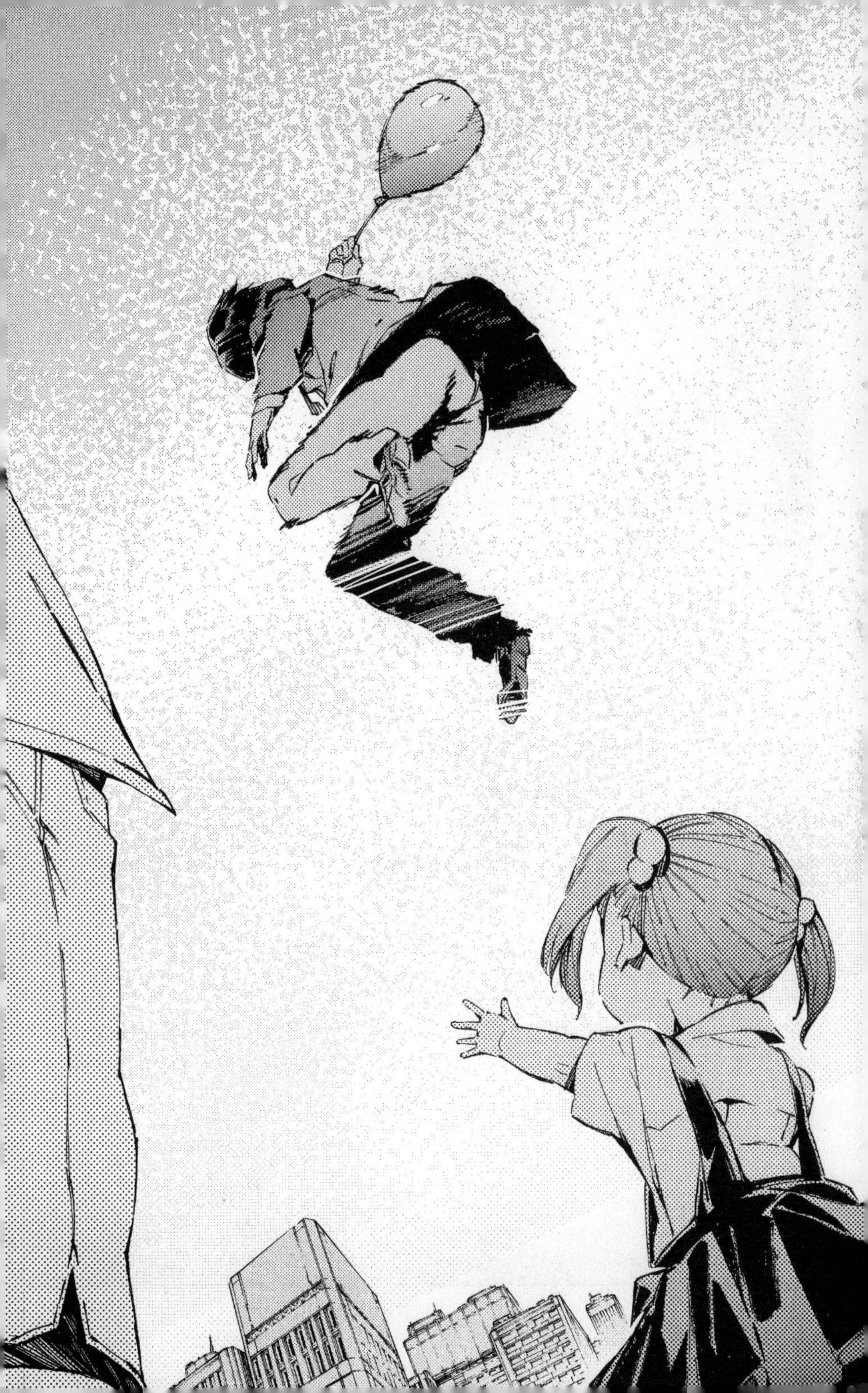

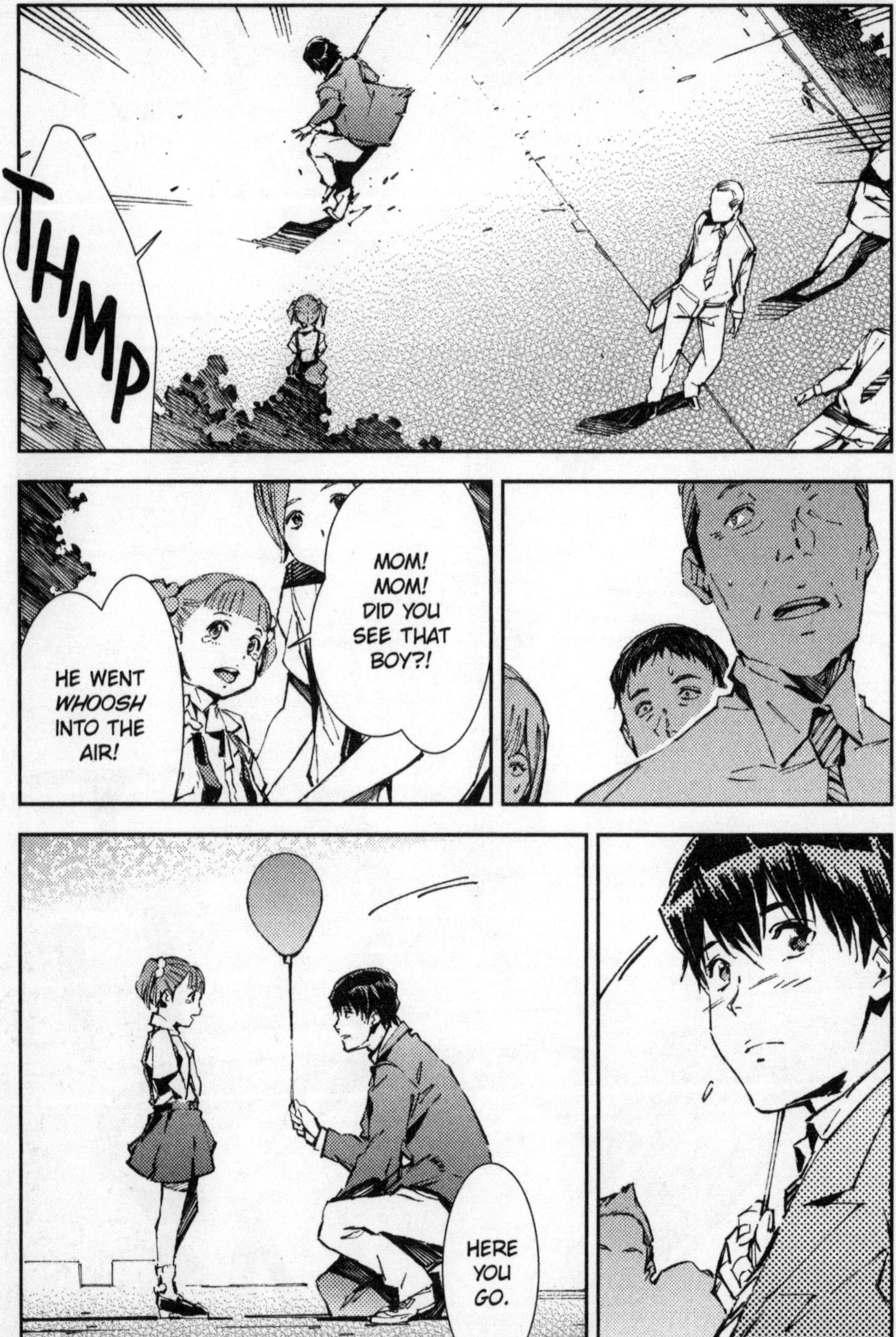
THMP
MOM! MOM! DID YOU SEE THAT BOY?!
HE WENT *WHOOSH* INTO THE AIR!
HERE YOU GO.

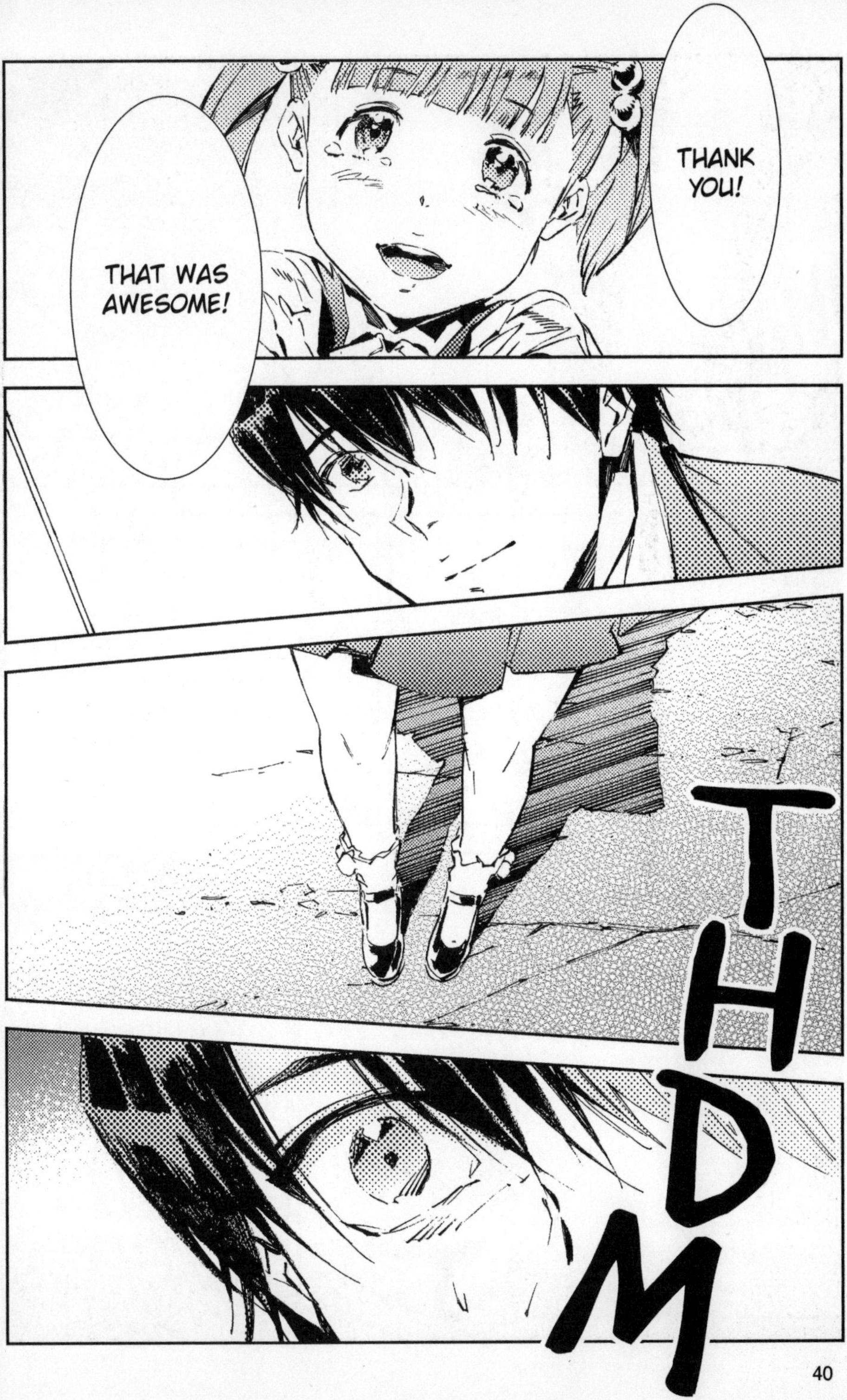
THANK YOU!
THAT WAS AWESOME!
THDM

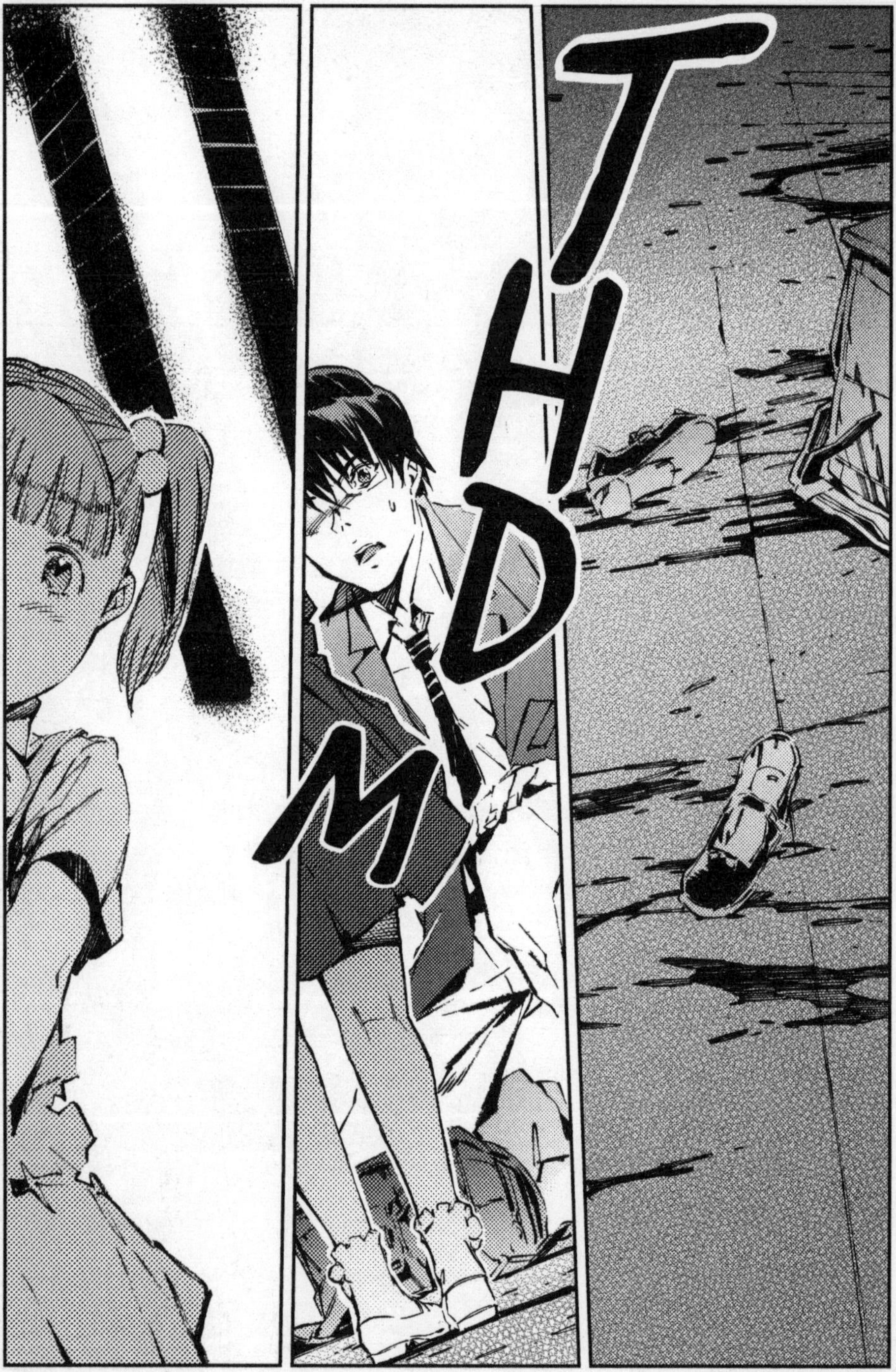

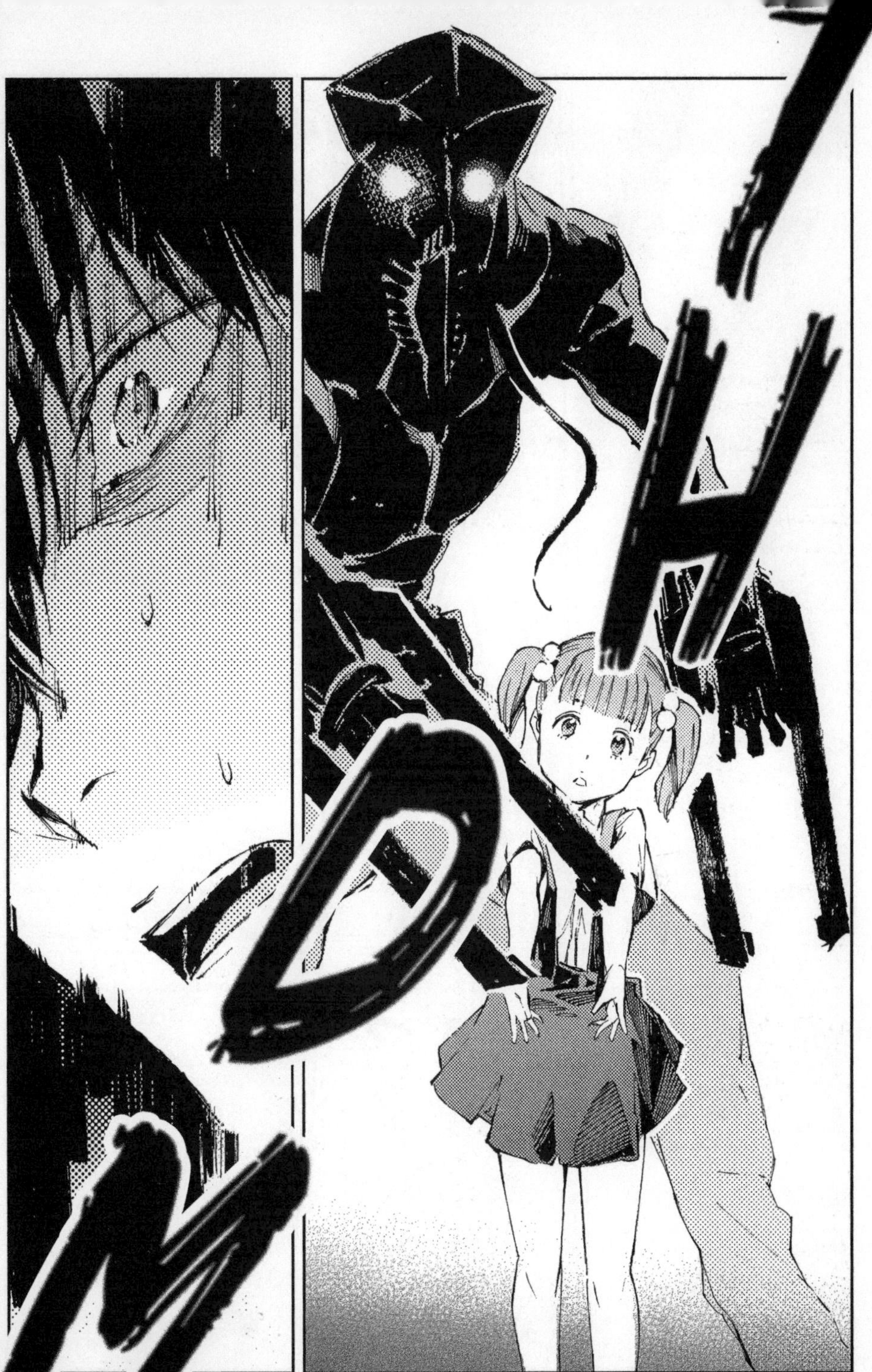

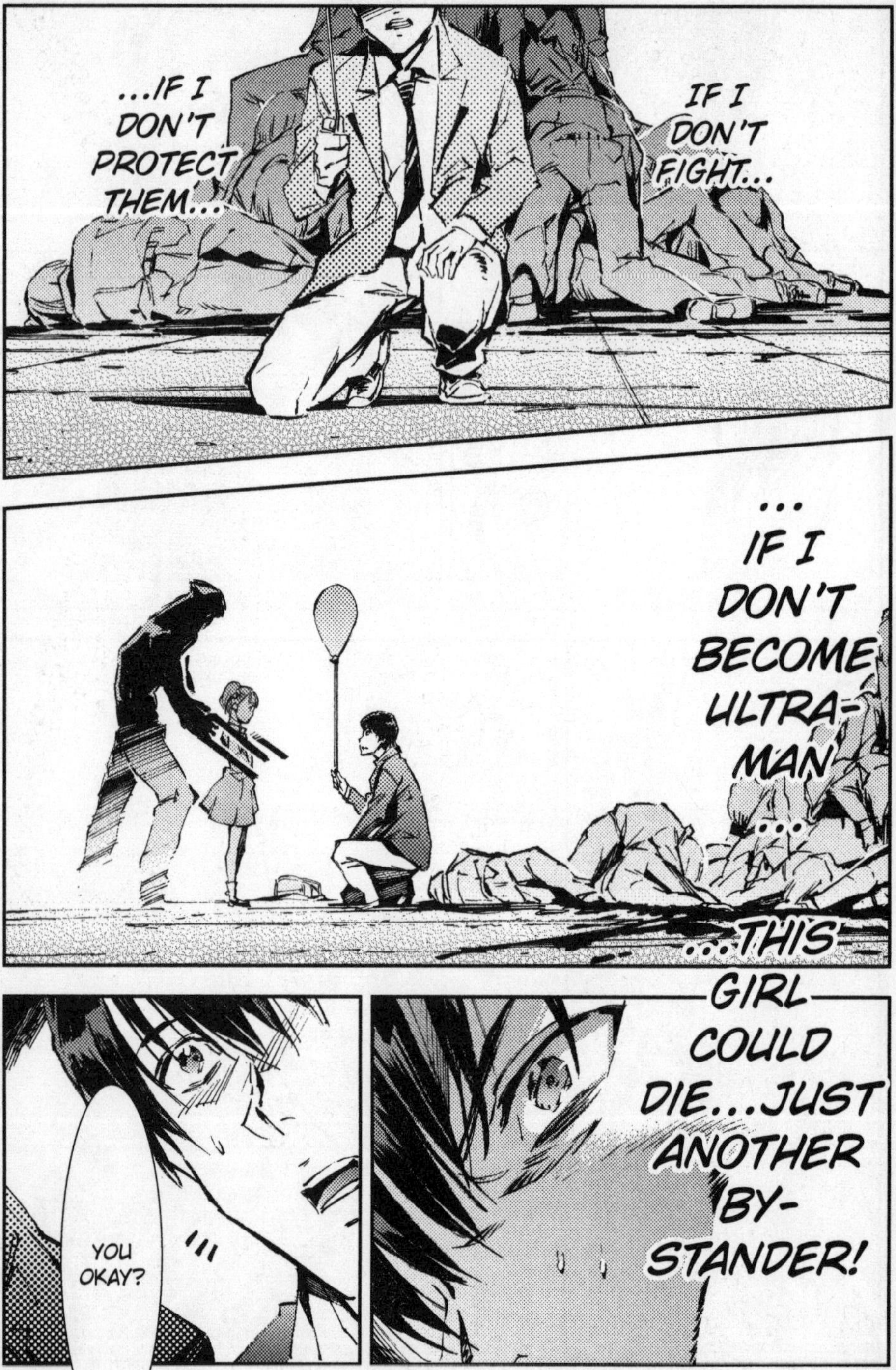
IF I DON'T FIGHT...
...IF I DON'T PROTECT THEM...
... IF I DON'T BECOME ULTRA-MAN ...
...THIS GIRL COULD DIE...JUST ANOTHER BY-STANDER!
YOU OKAY?

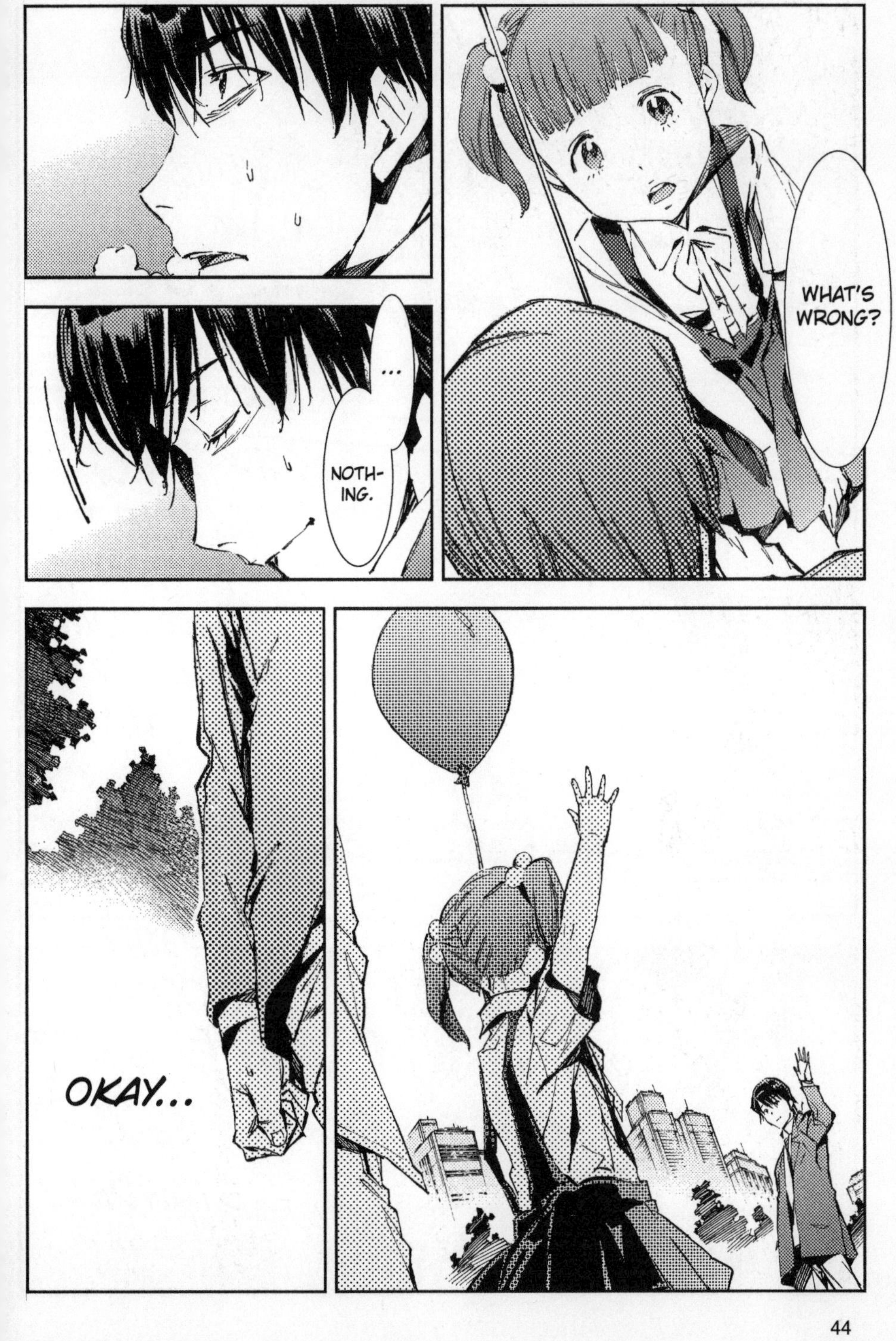
WHAT'S WRONG?
...
NOTH-ING.
OKAY...

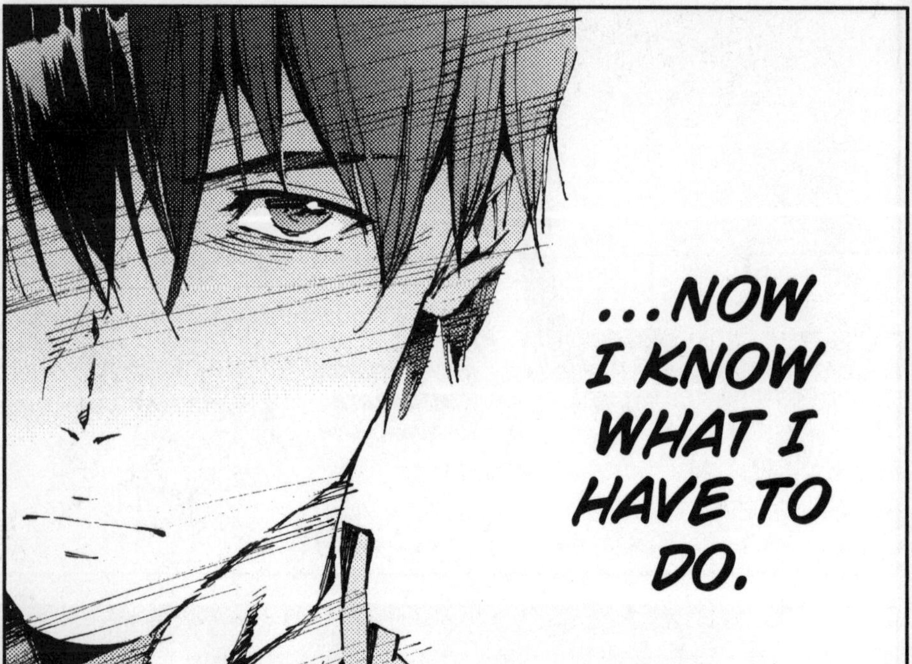
...NOW I KNOW WHAT I HAVE TO DO.

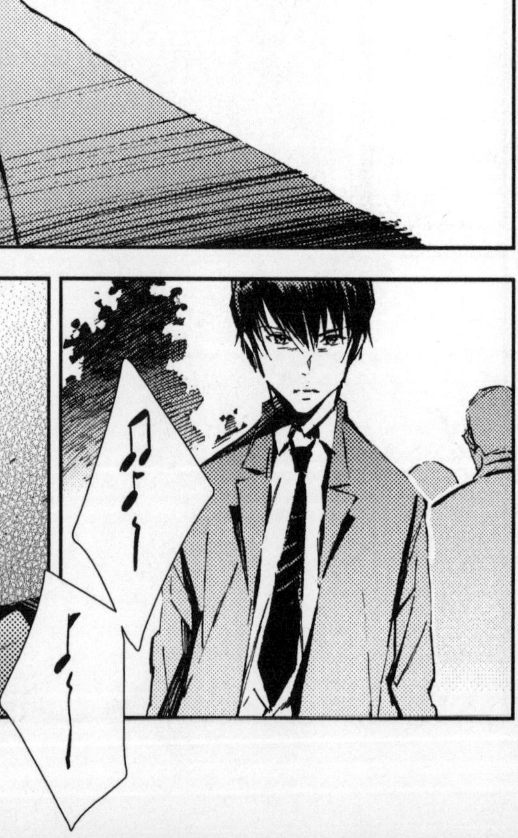

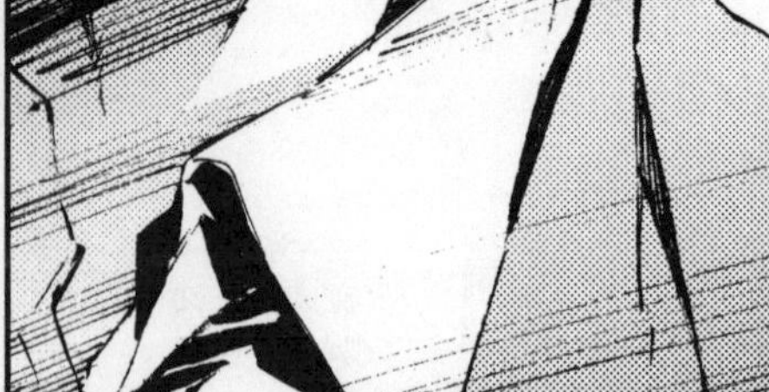
Mr. Ide

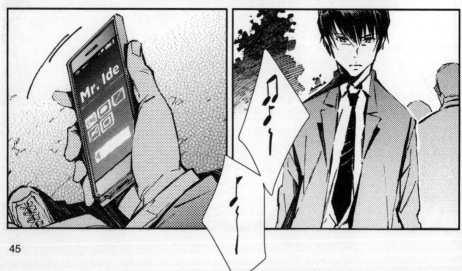

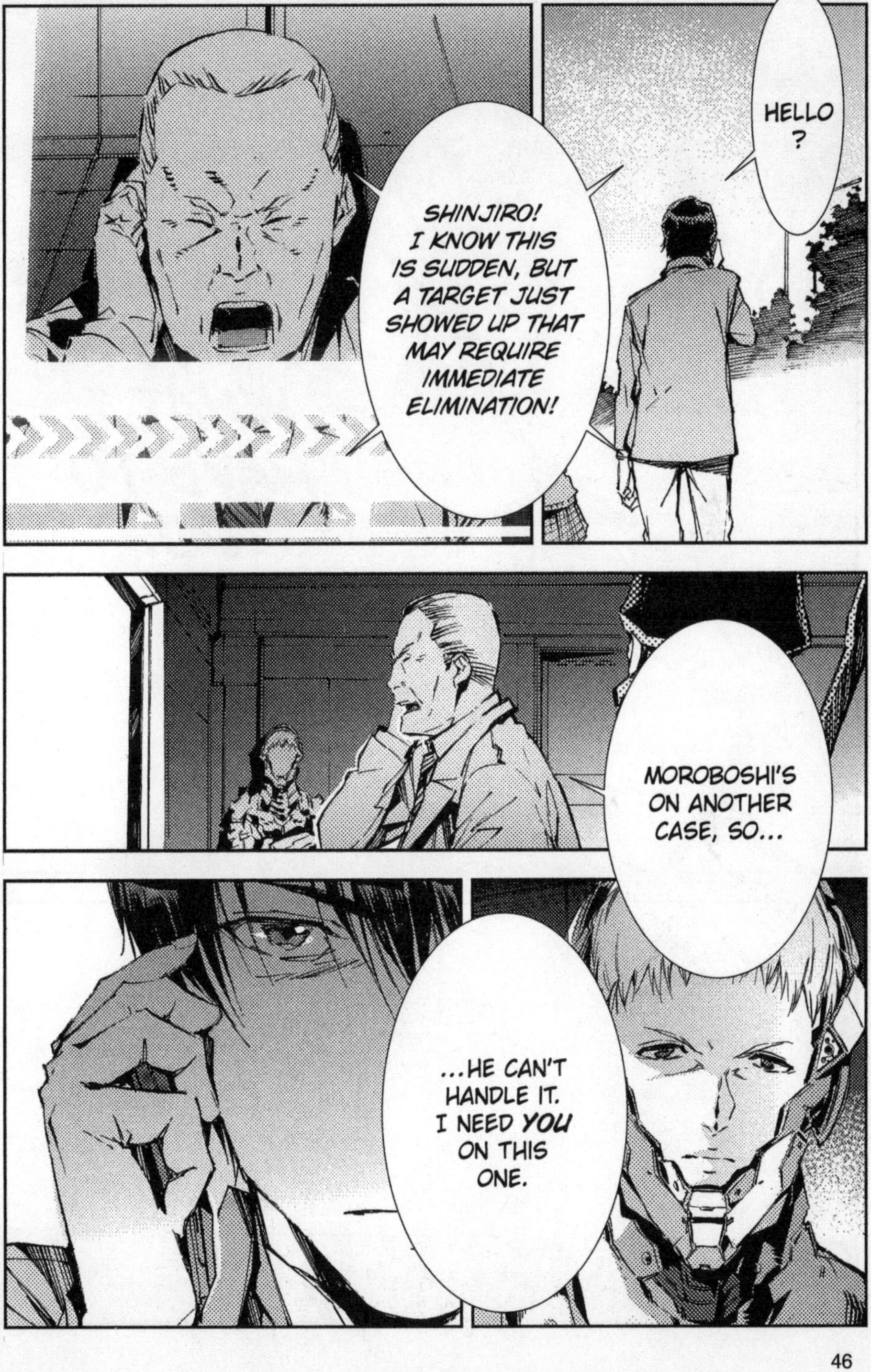
HELLO ?
SHINJIRO! I KNOW THIS IS SUDDEN, BUT A TARGET JUST SHOWED UP THAT MAY REQUIRE IMMEDIATE ELIMINATION!
MOROBOSHI'S ON ANOTHER CASE, SO...
...HE CAN'T HANDLE IT. I NEED *YOU* ON THIS ONE.

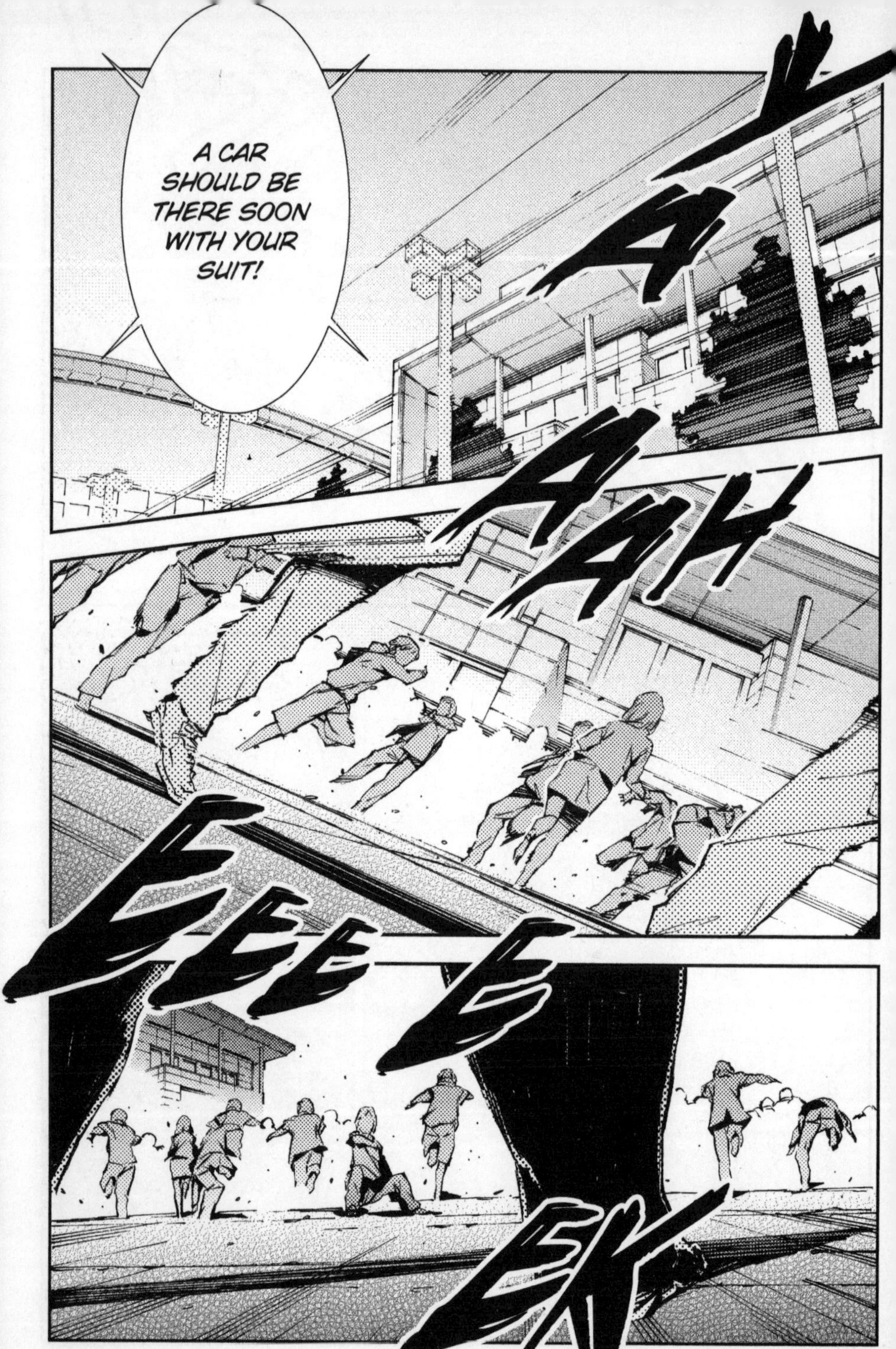
A CAR SHOULD BE THERE SOON WITH YOUR SUIT!
YAAAH
EEEEEK

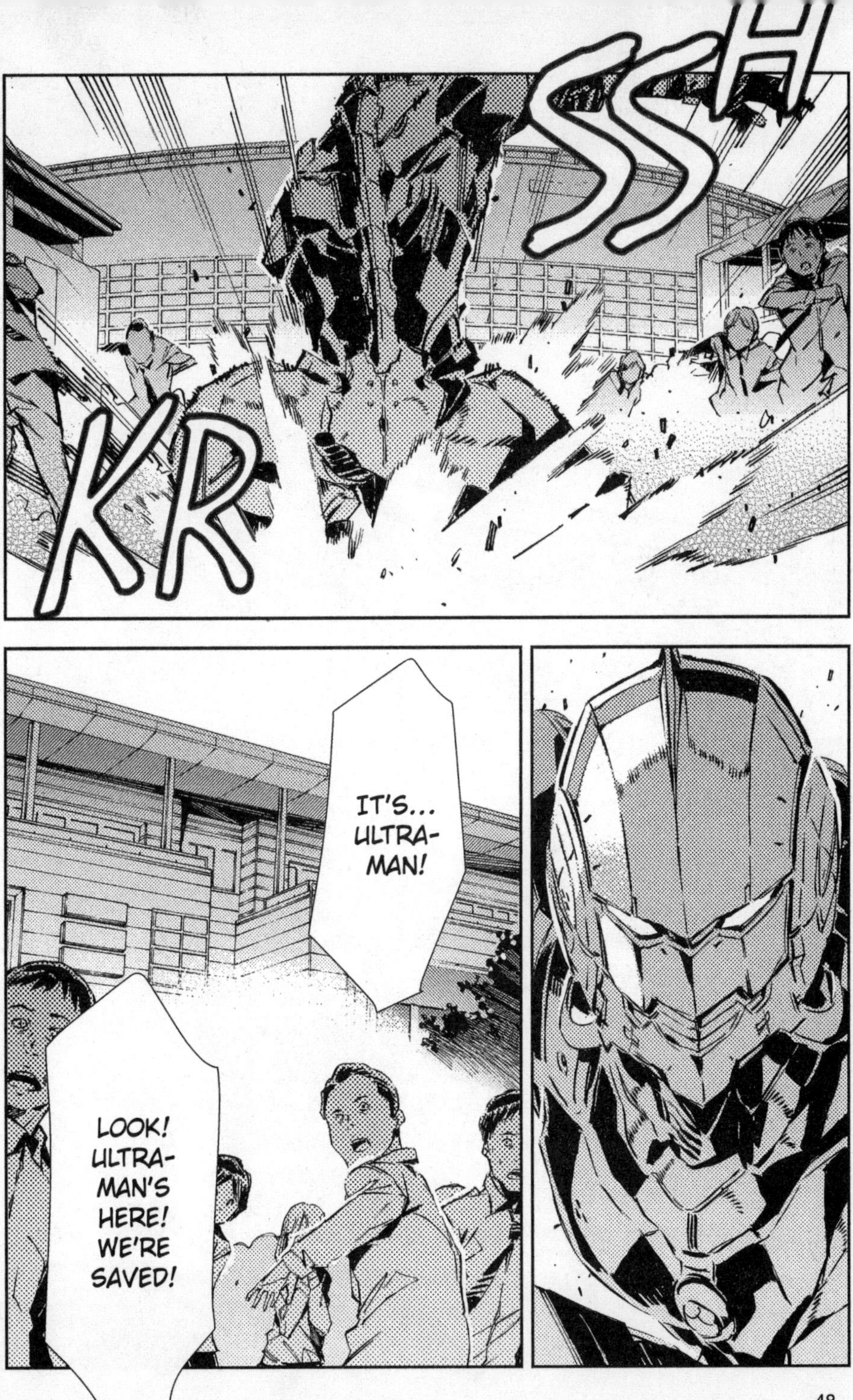
KR
SSH
IT'S... ULTRA-MAN!
LOOK! ULTRA-MAN'S HERE! WE'RE SAVED!

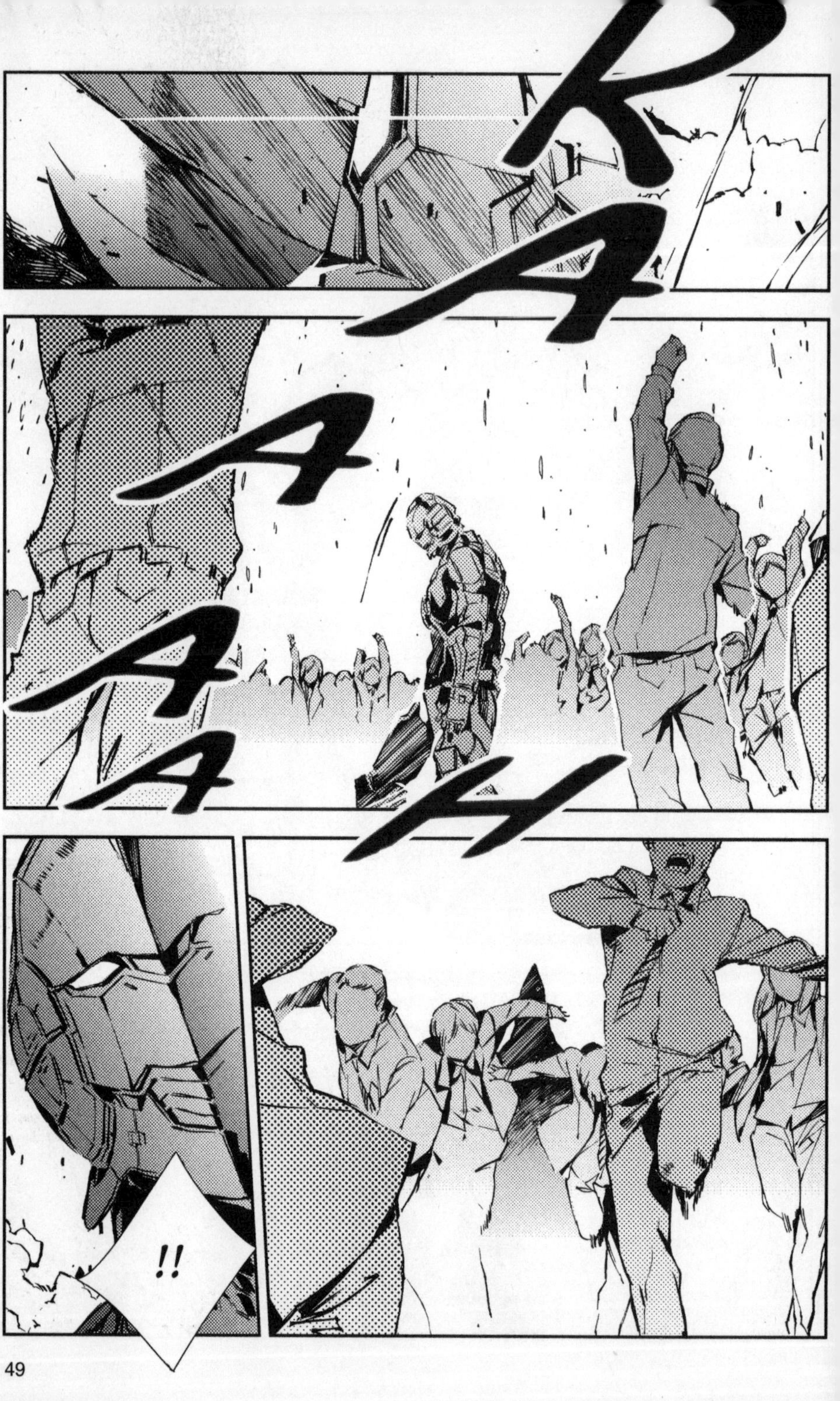
RAAAAAH
!!

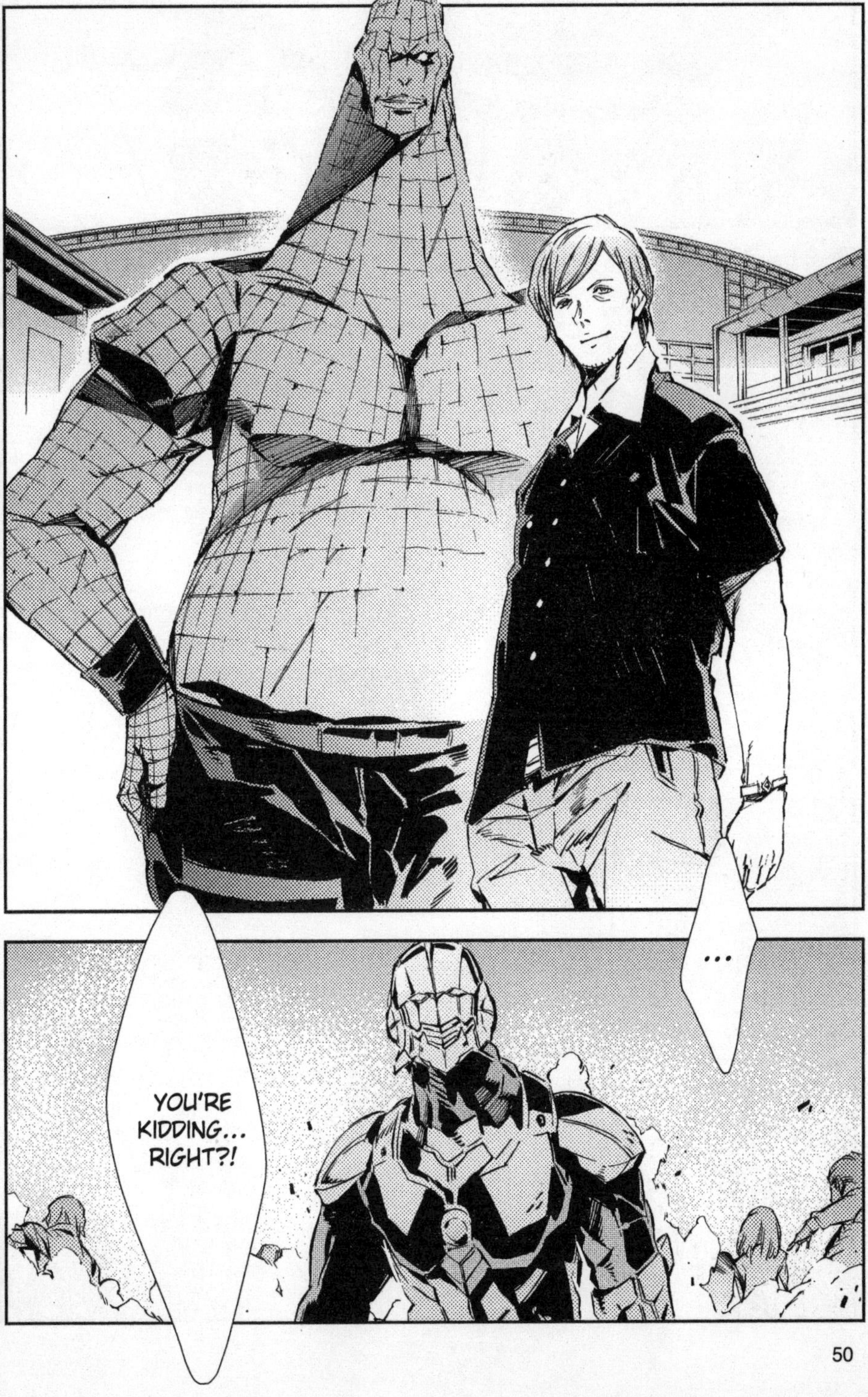
...
YOU'RE KIDDING... RIGHT?!

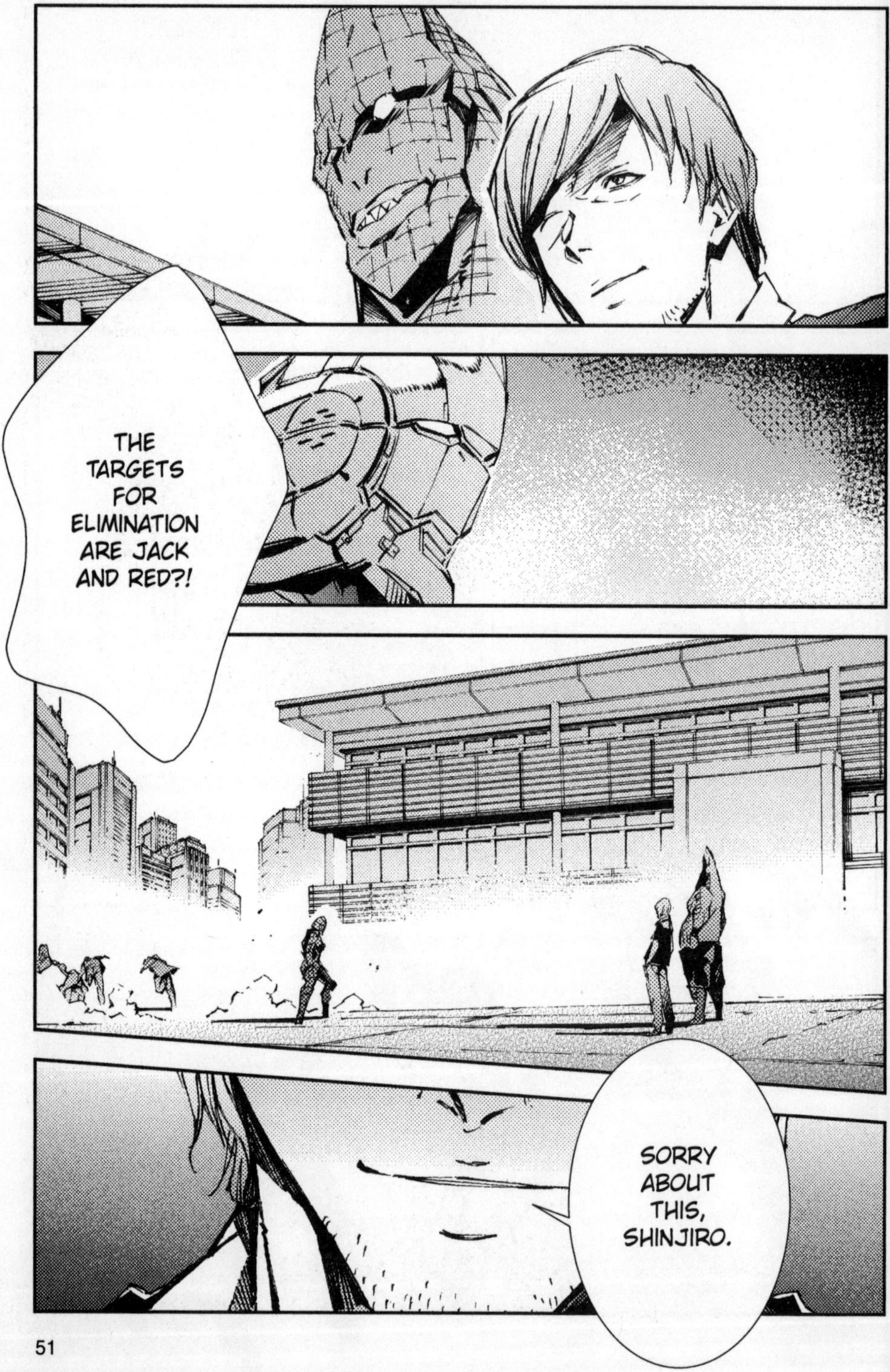
THE TARGETS FOR ELIMINATION ARE JACK AND RED?!
SORRY ABOUT THIS, SHINJIRO.

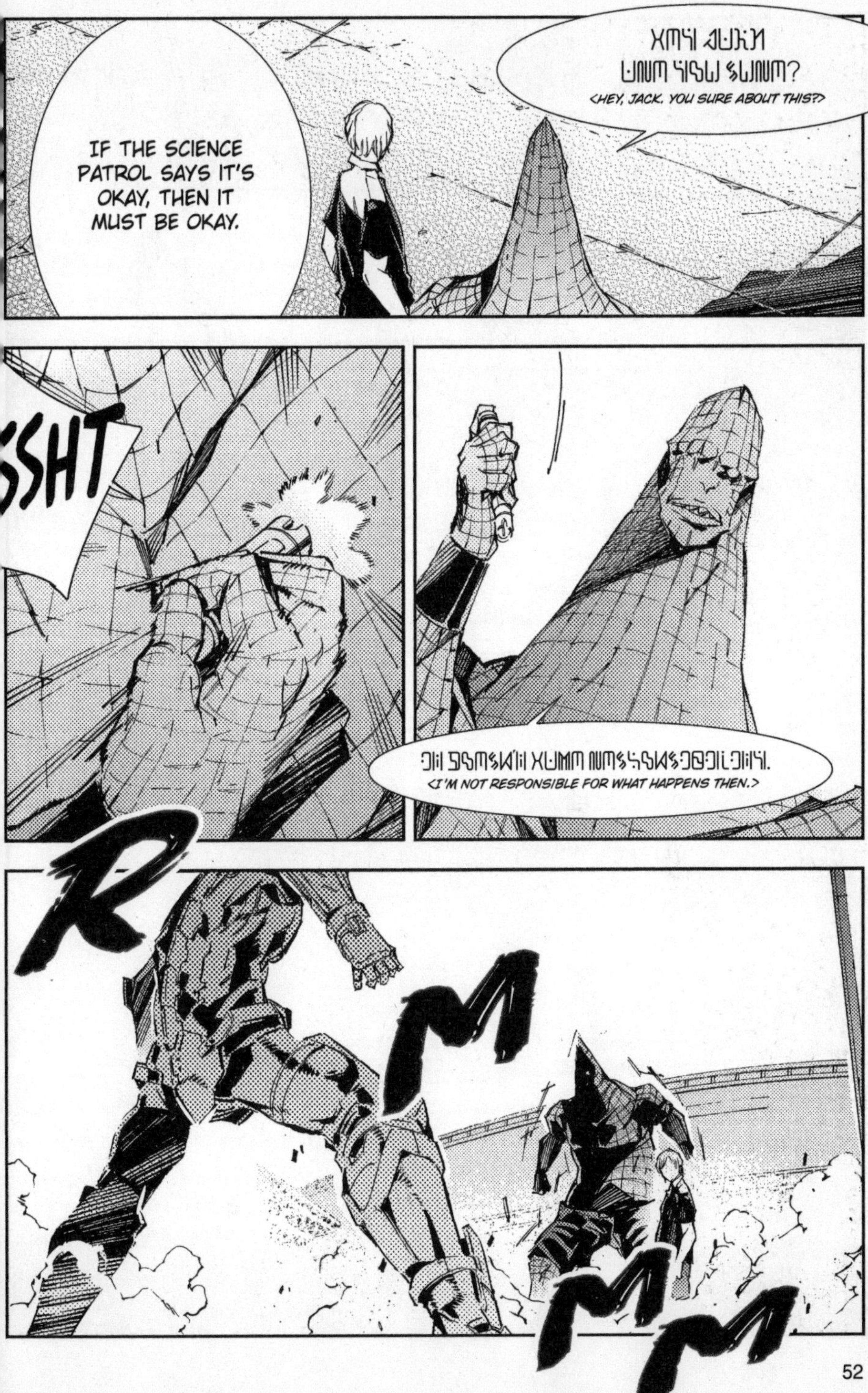
<HEY, JACK. YOU SURE ABOUT THIS?>
IF THE SCIENCE PATROL SAYS IT'S OKAY, THEN IT MUST BE OKAY.
<I'M NOT RESPONSIBLE FOR WHAT HAPPENS THEN.>
SSHT
RMMM

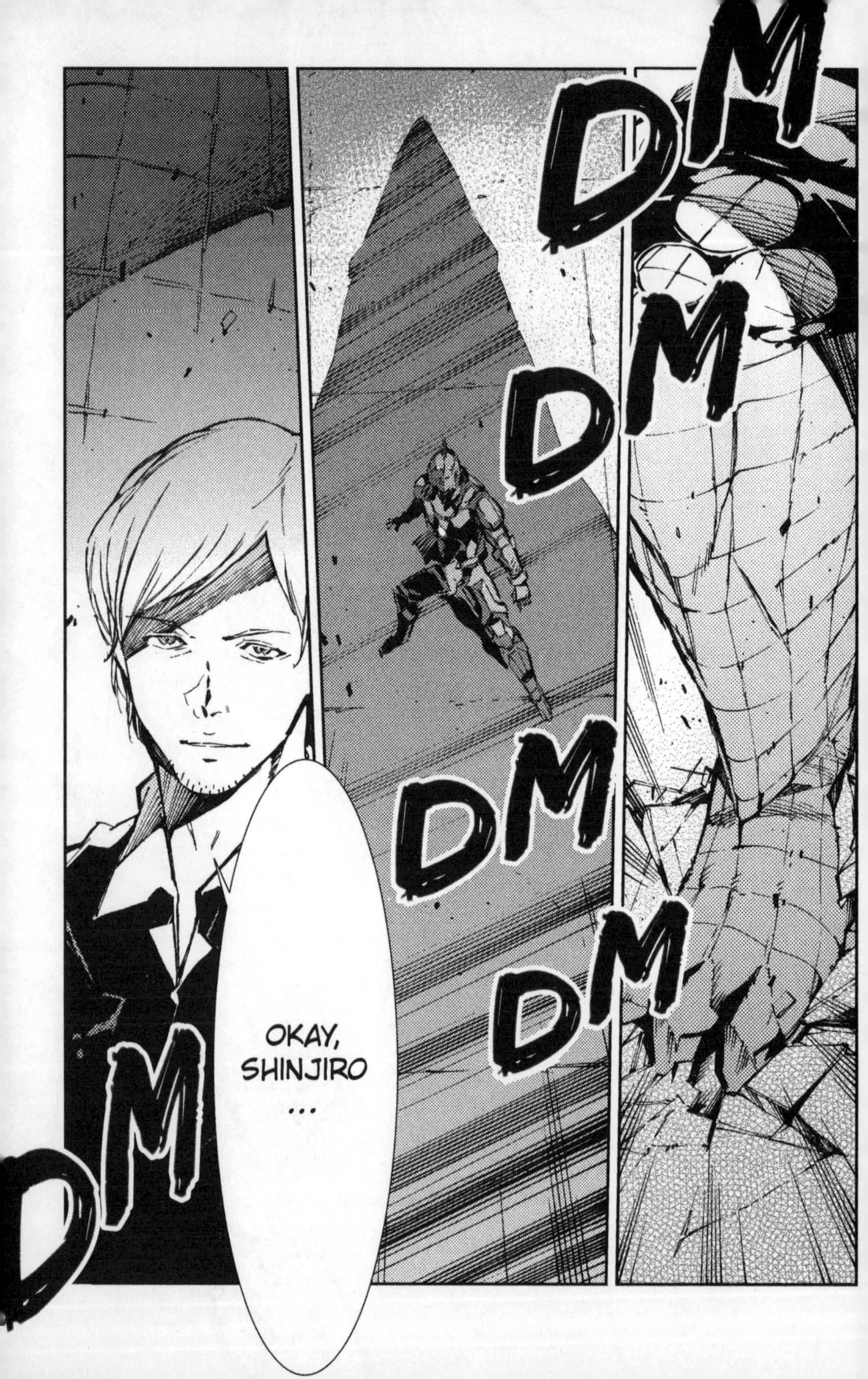
DM
DM
DM
DM
OKAY, SHINJIRO ...
DM

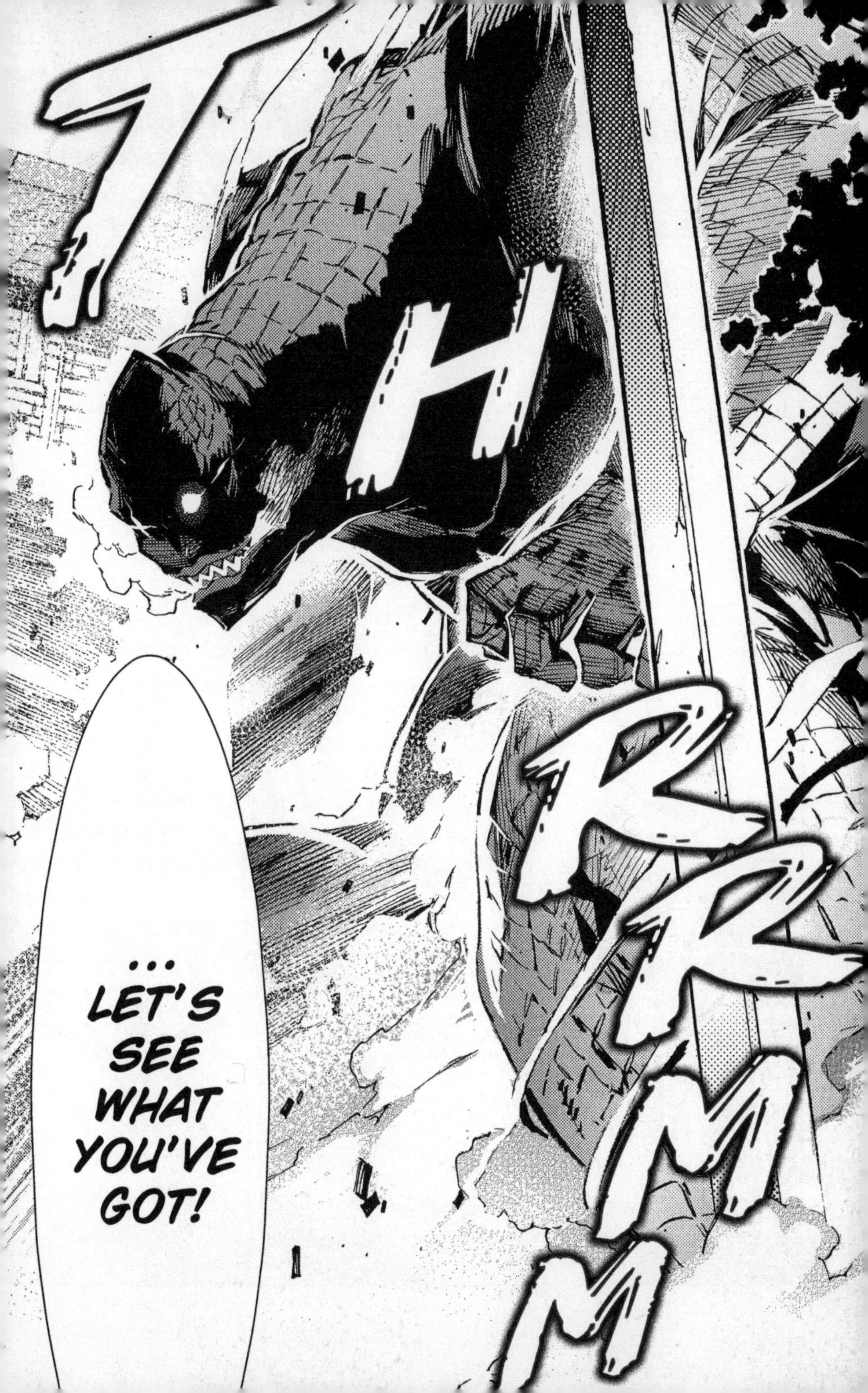
THH
RRMMM
...LET'S SEE WHAT YOU'VE GOT!

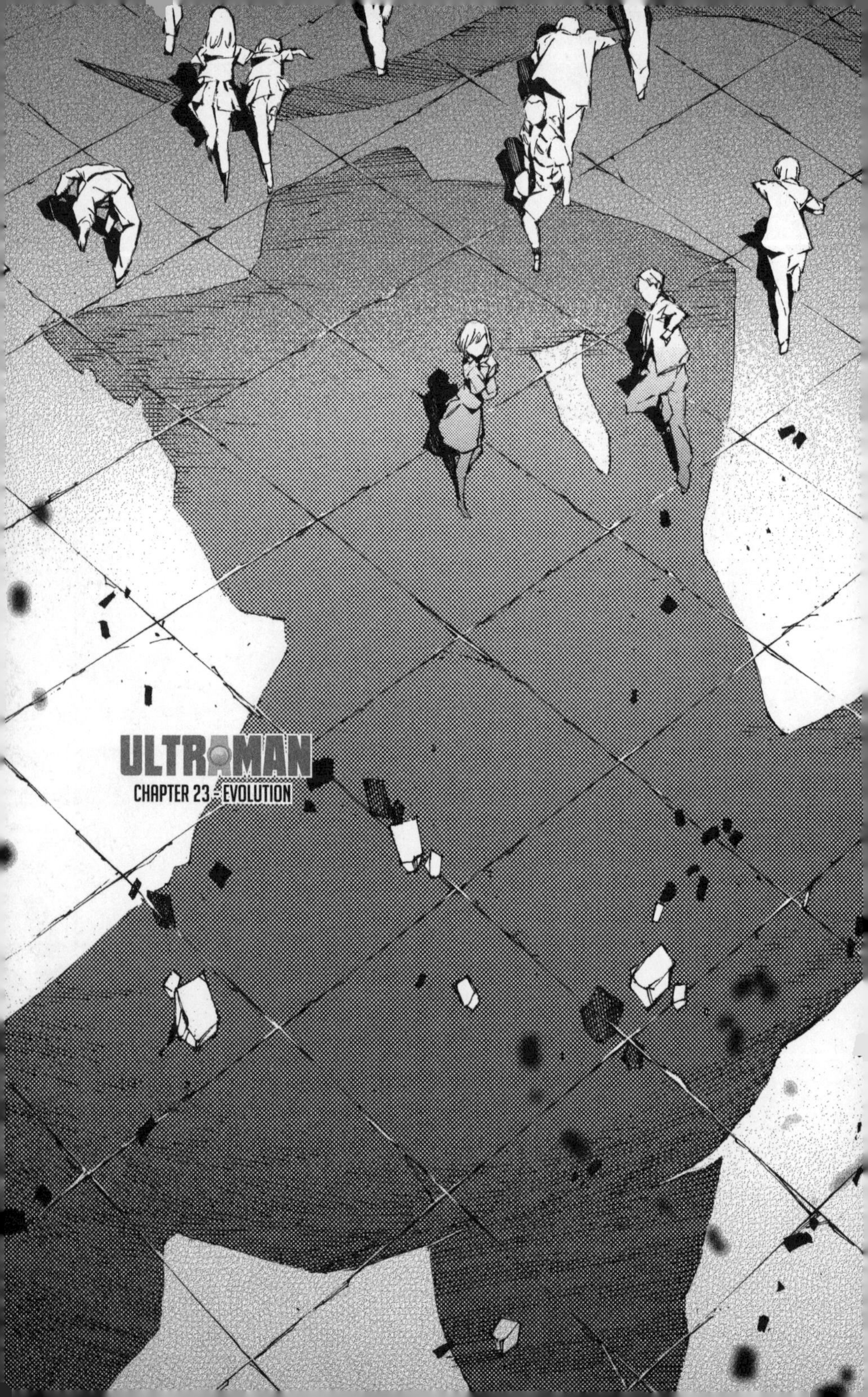
ULTRAMAN
CHAPTER 23: EVOLUTION

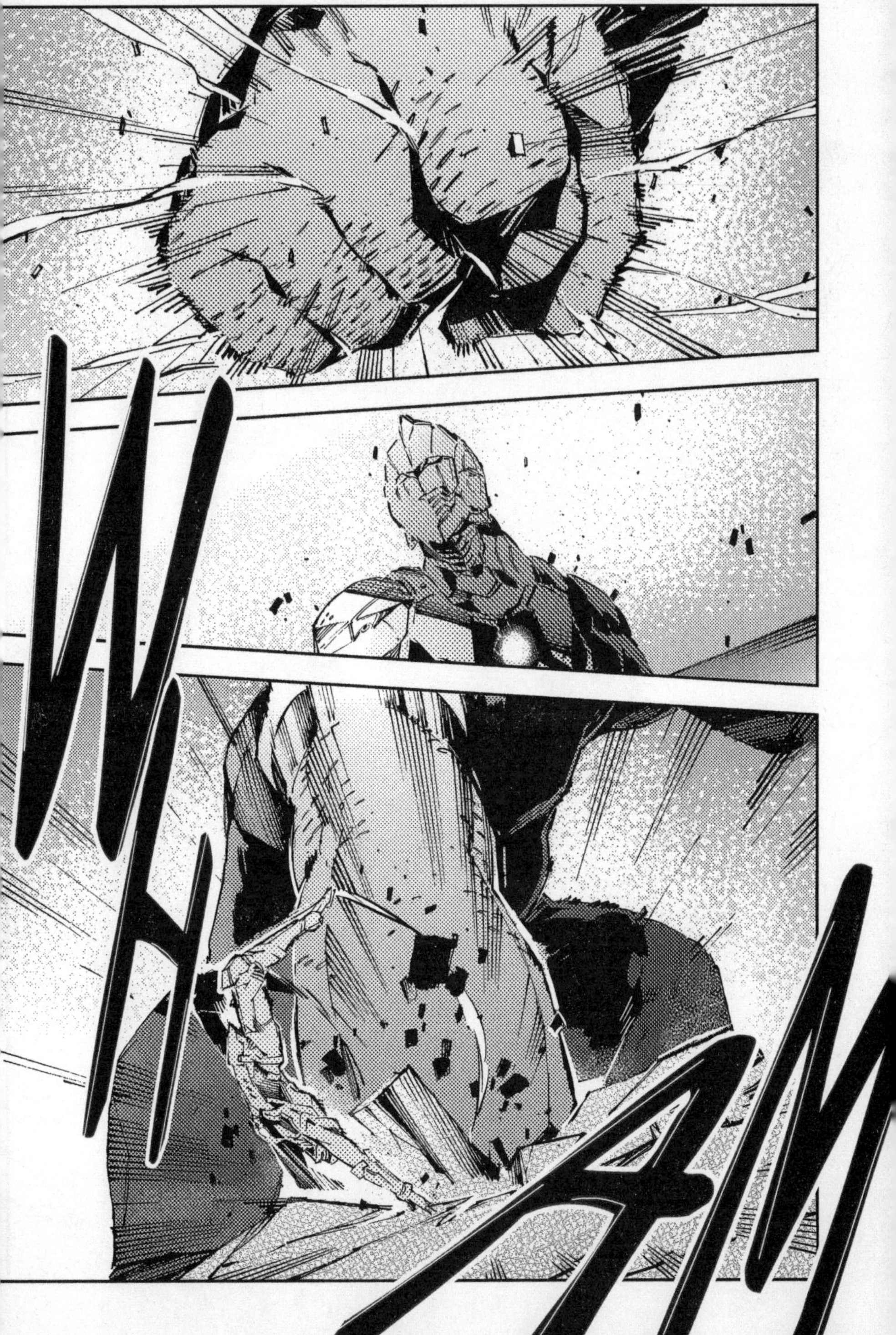
WHAM

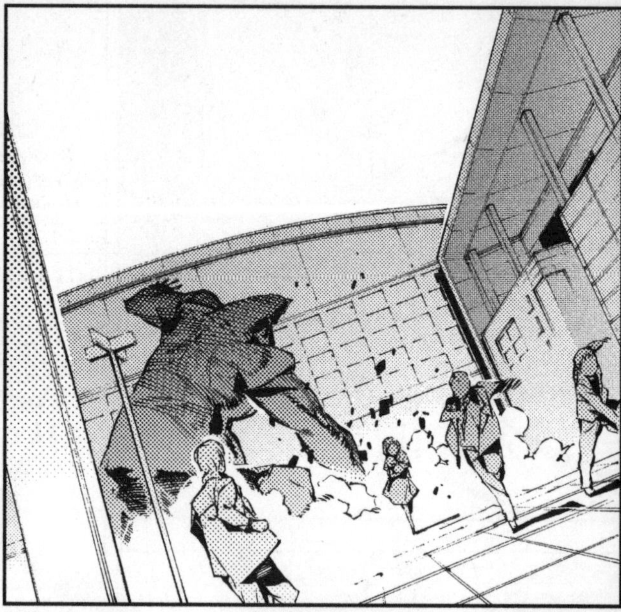

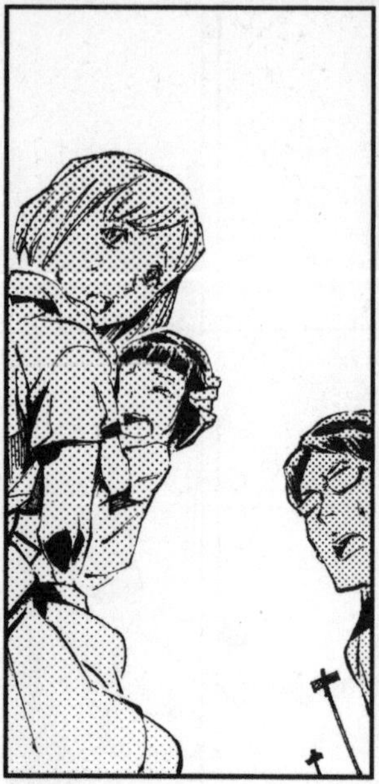

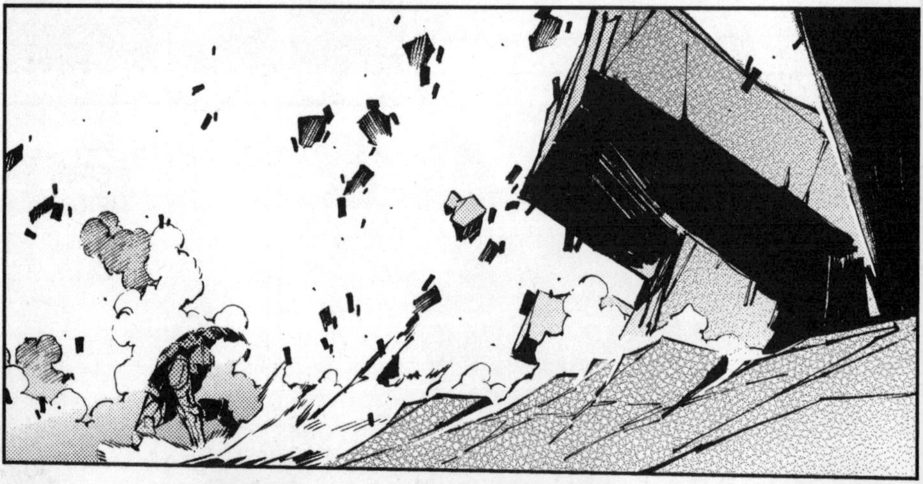

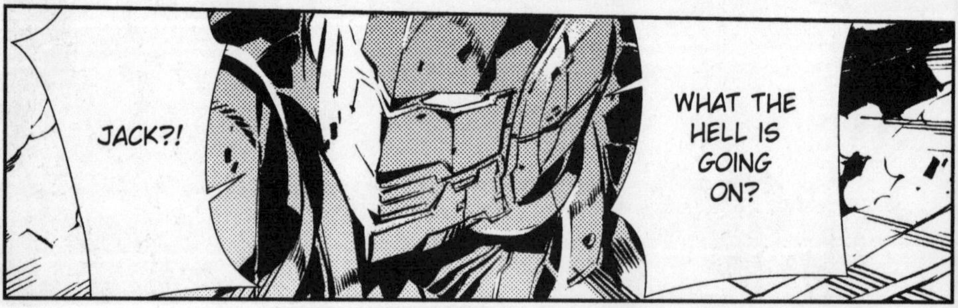
WHAT THE HELL IS GOING ON?
JACK?!

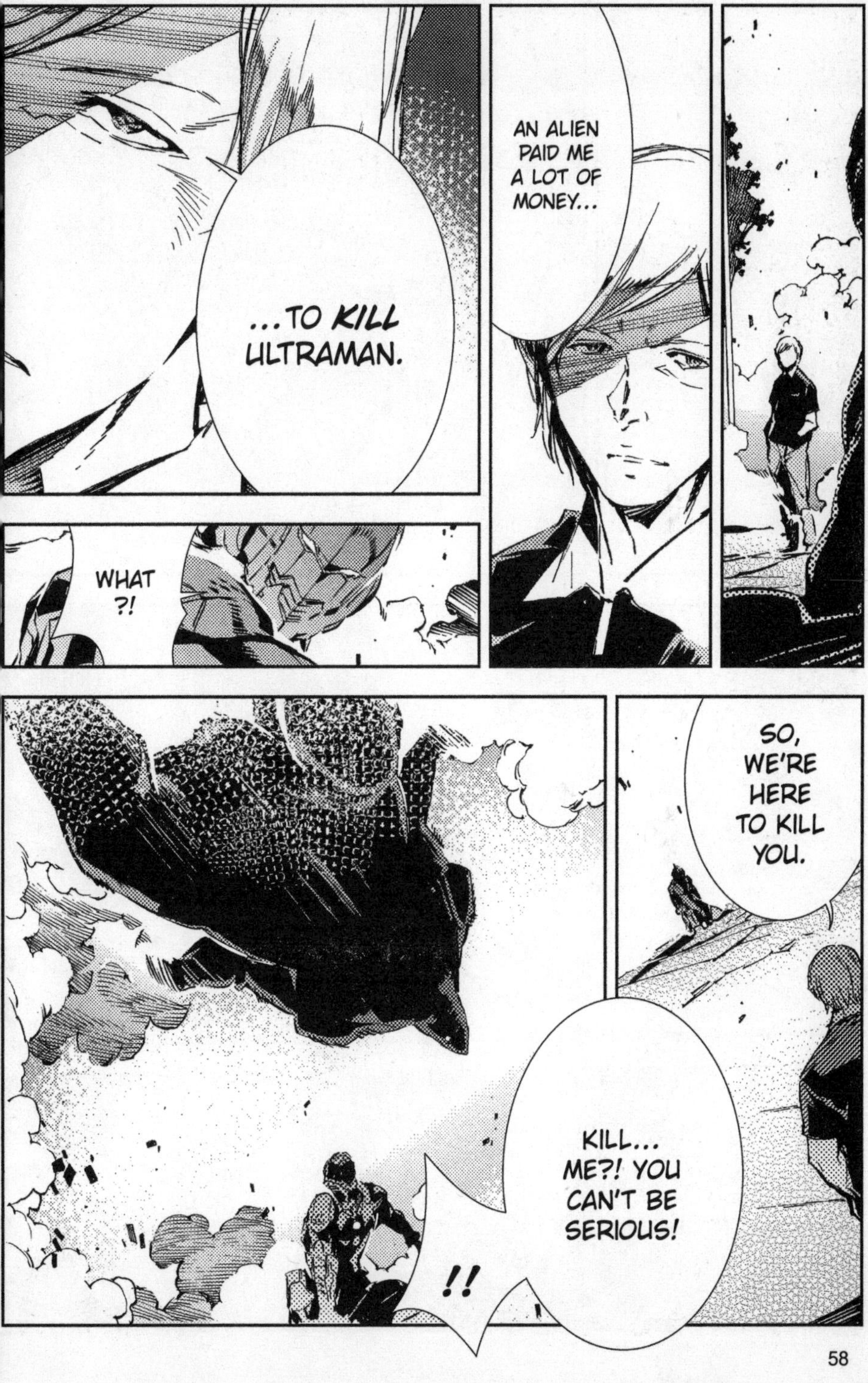
AN ALIEN PAID ME A LOT OF MONEY...
...TO KILL ULTRAMAN.
WHAT ?!
SO, WE'RE HERE TO KILL YOU.
KILL... ME?! YOU CAN'T BE SERIOUS!
!!

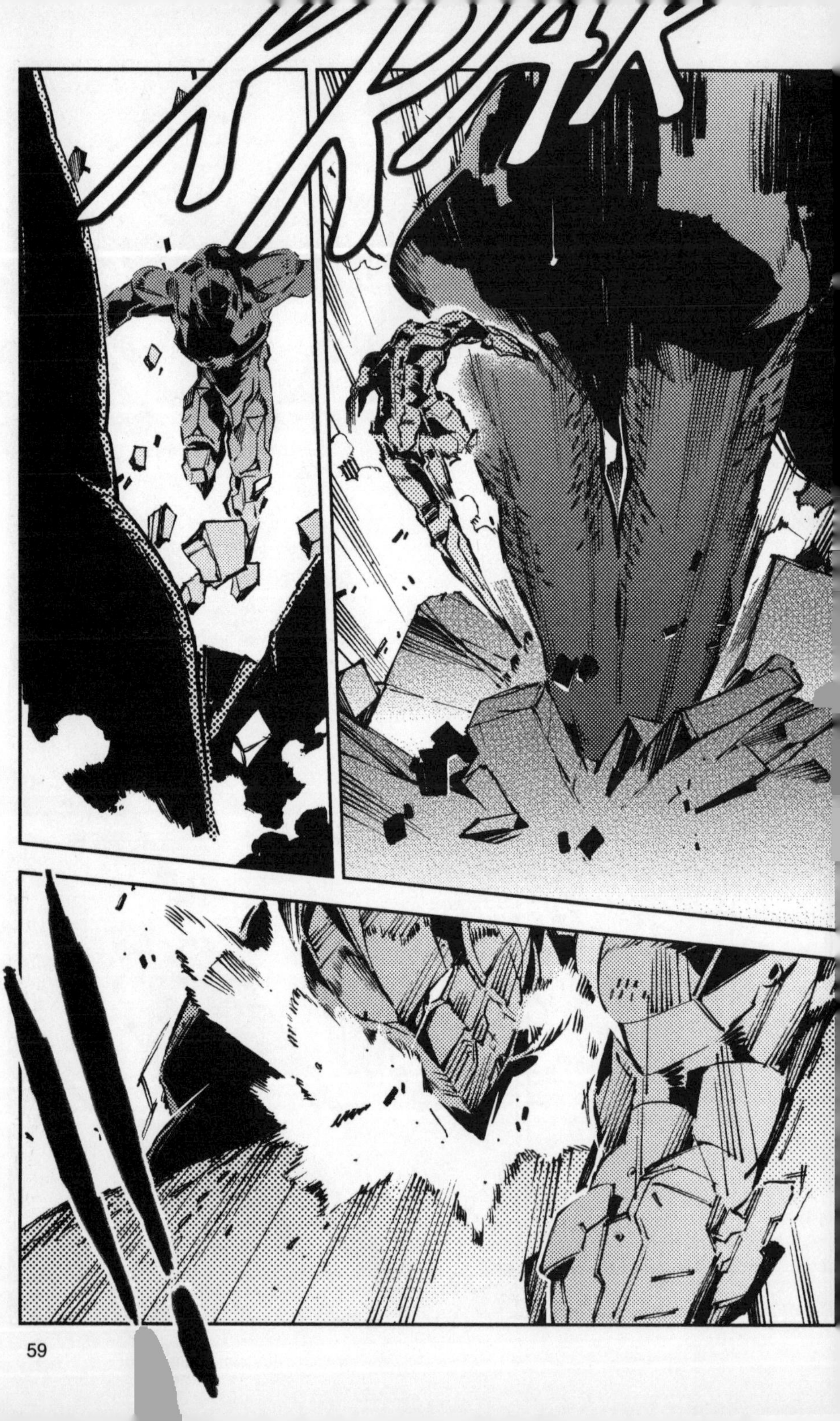

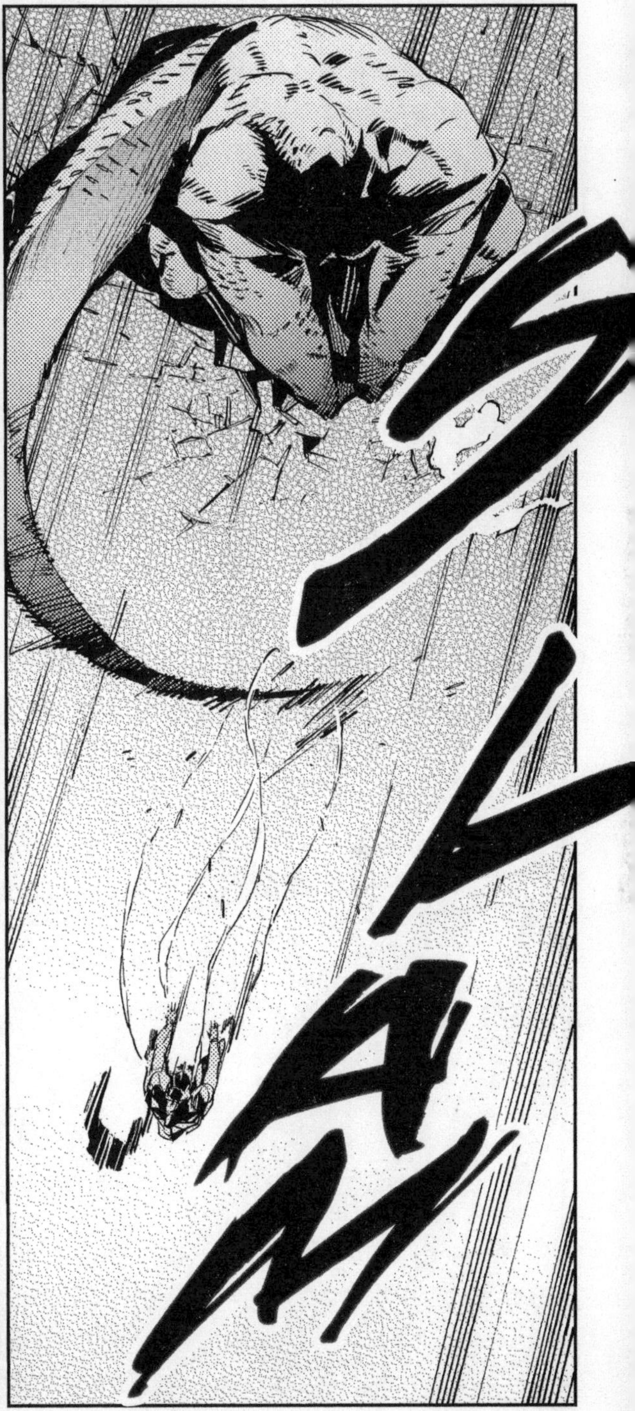
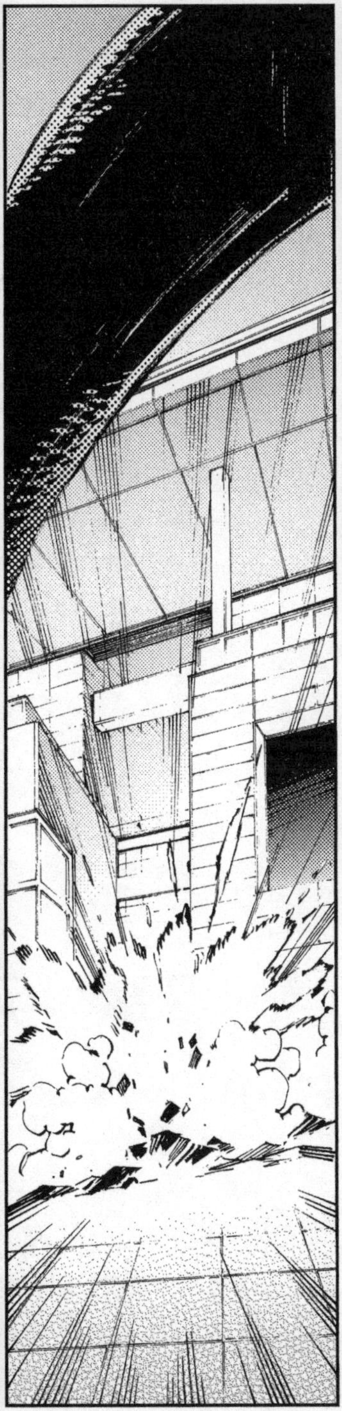

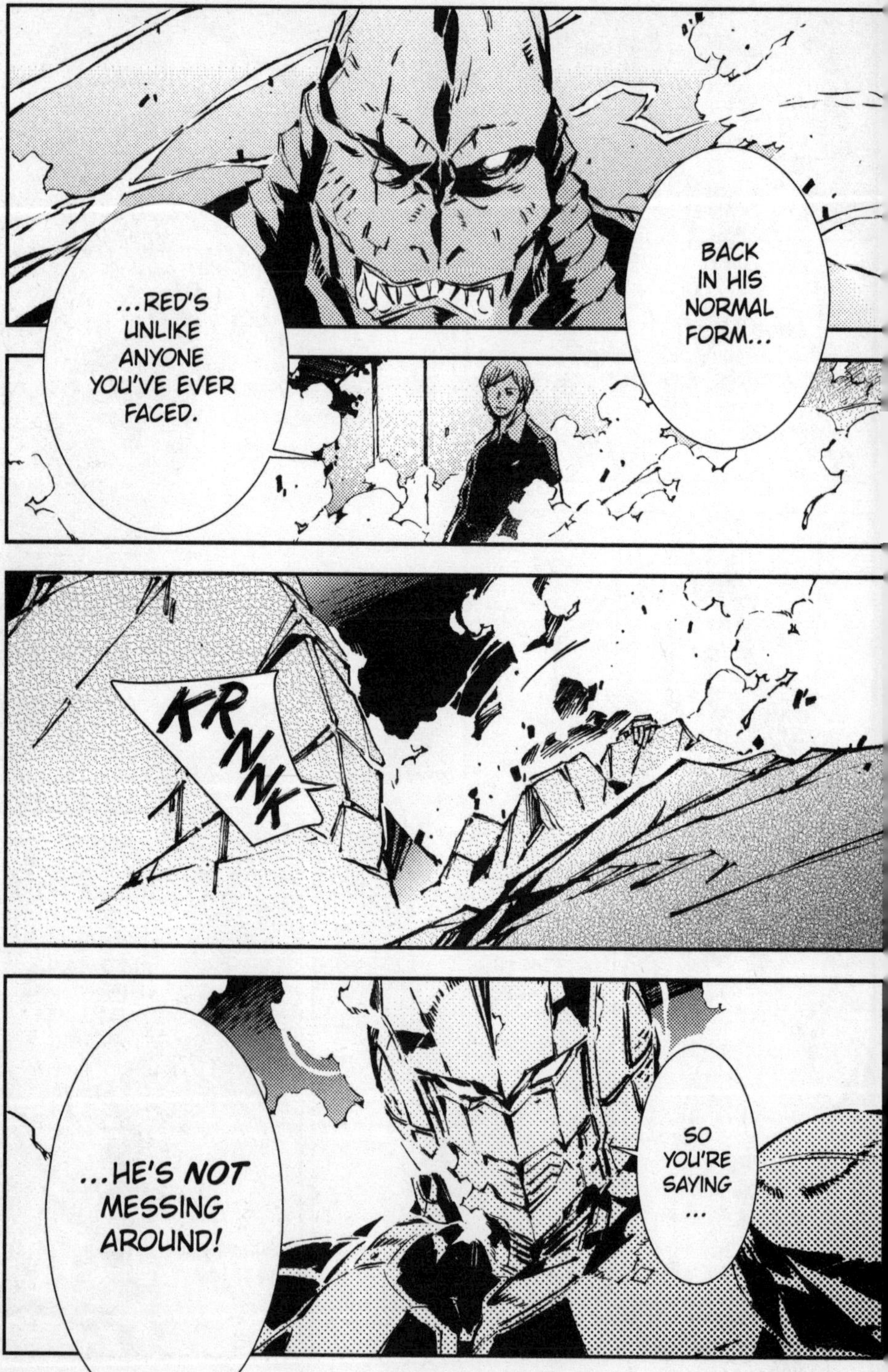
BACK IN HIS NORMAL FORM...
...RED'S UNLIKE ANYONE YOU'VE EVER FACED.
KRNNK
SO YOU'RE SAYING...
...HE'S *NOT* MESSING AROUND!

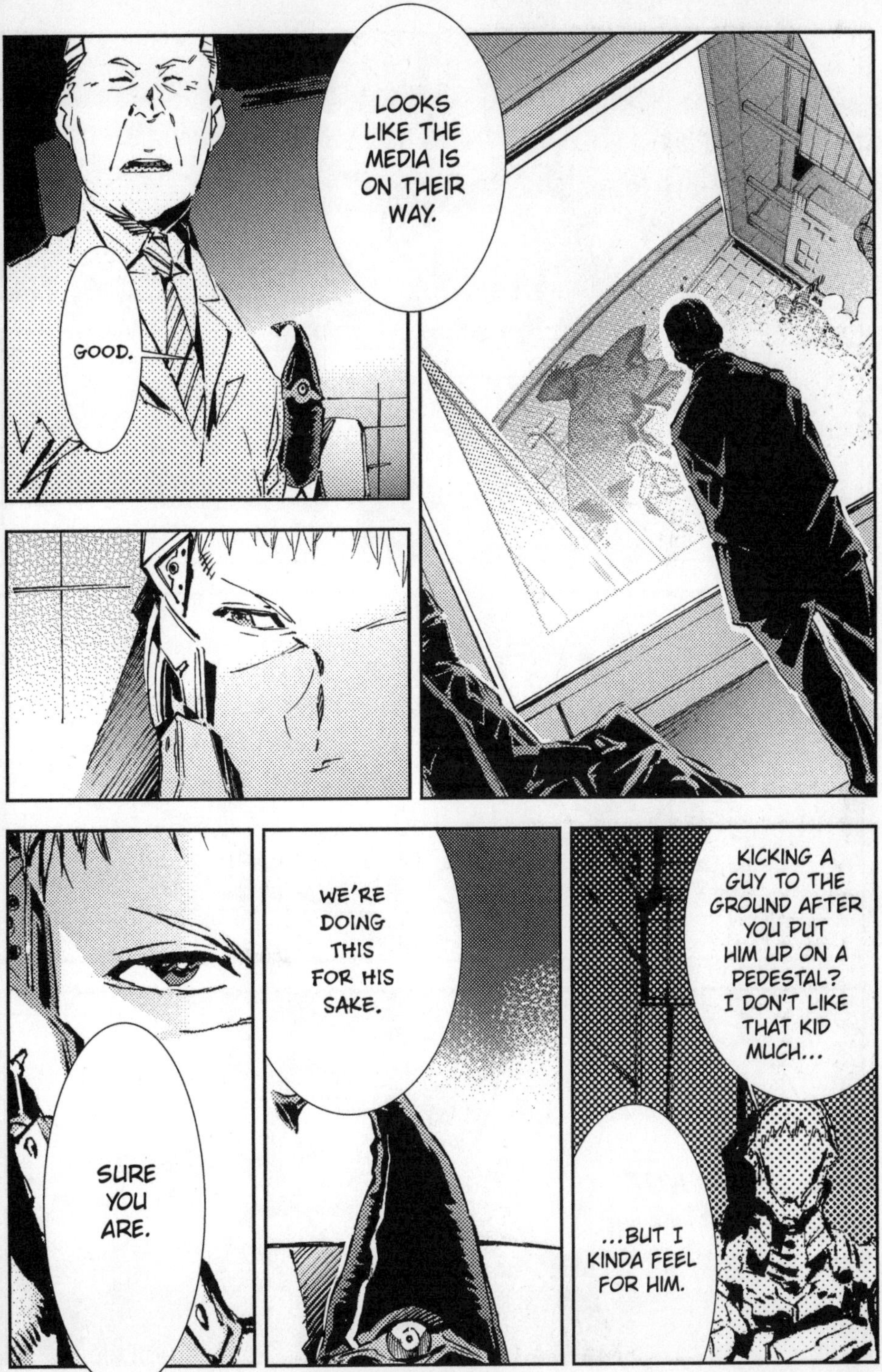
LOOKS LIKE THE MEDIA IS ON THEIR WAY.
GOOD.
KICKING A GUY TO THE GROUND AFTER YOU PUT HIM UP ON A PEDESTAL? I DON'T LIKE THAT KID MUCH...
...BUT I KINDA FEEL FOR HIM.
WE'RE DOING THIS FOR HIS SAKE.
SURE YOU ARE.

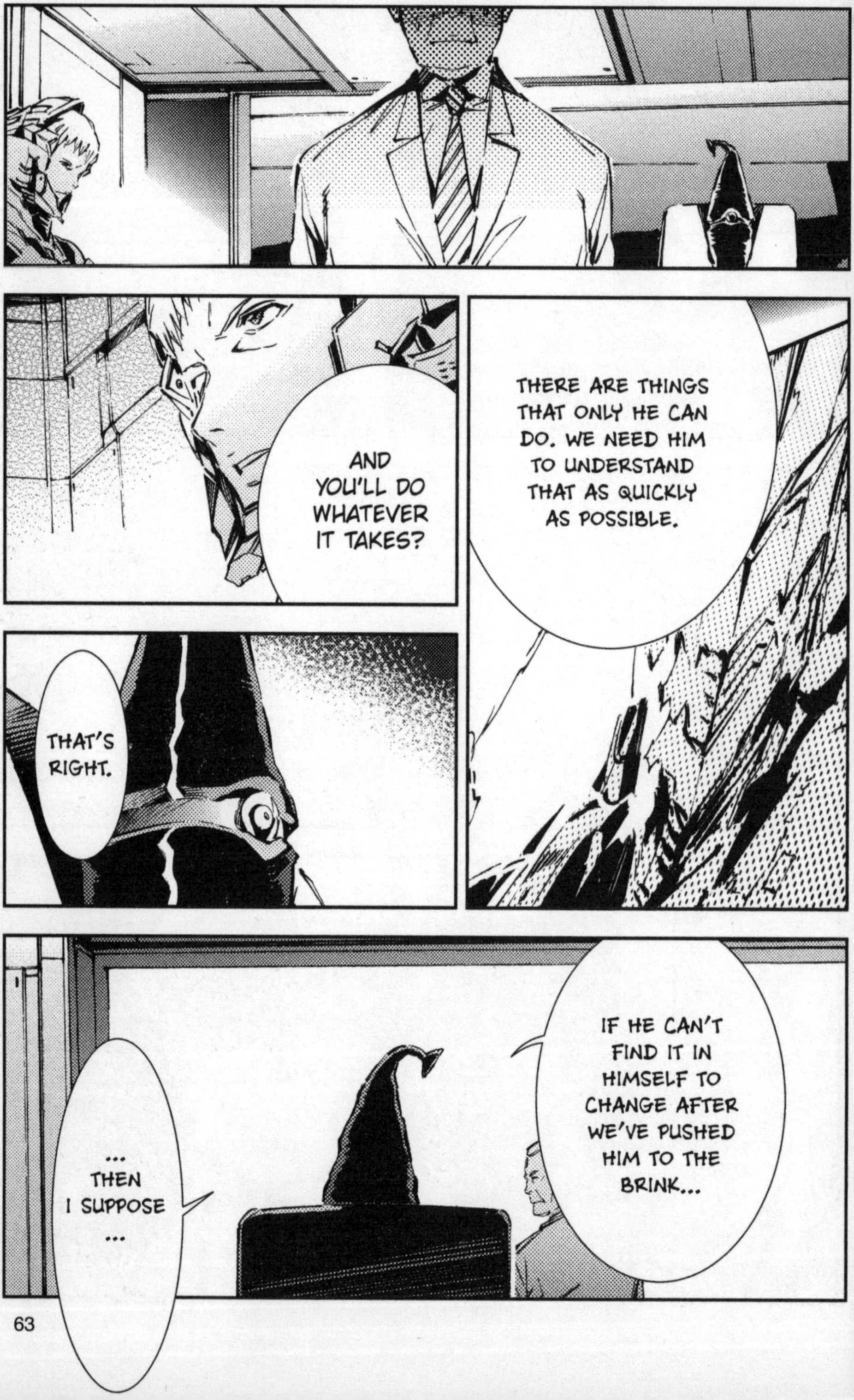
THERE ARE THINGS THAT ONLY HE CAN DO. WE NEED HIM TO UNDERSTAND THAT AS QUICKLY AS POSSIBLE.
AND YOU'LL DO WHATEVER IT TAKES?
THAT'S RIGHT.
IF HE CAN'T FIND IT IN HIMSELF TO CHANGE AFTER WE'VE PUSHED HIM TO THE BRINK...
... THEN I SUPPOSE ...

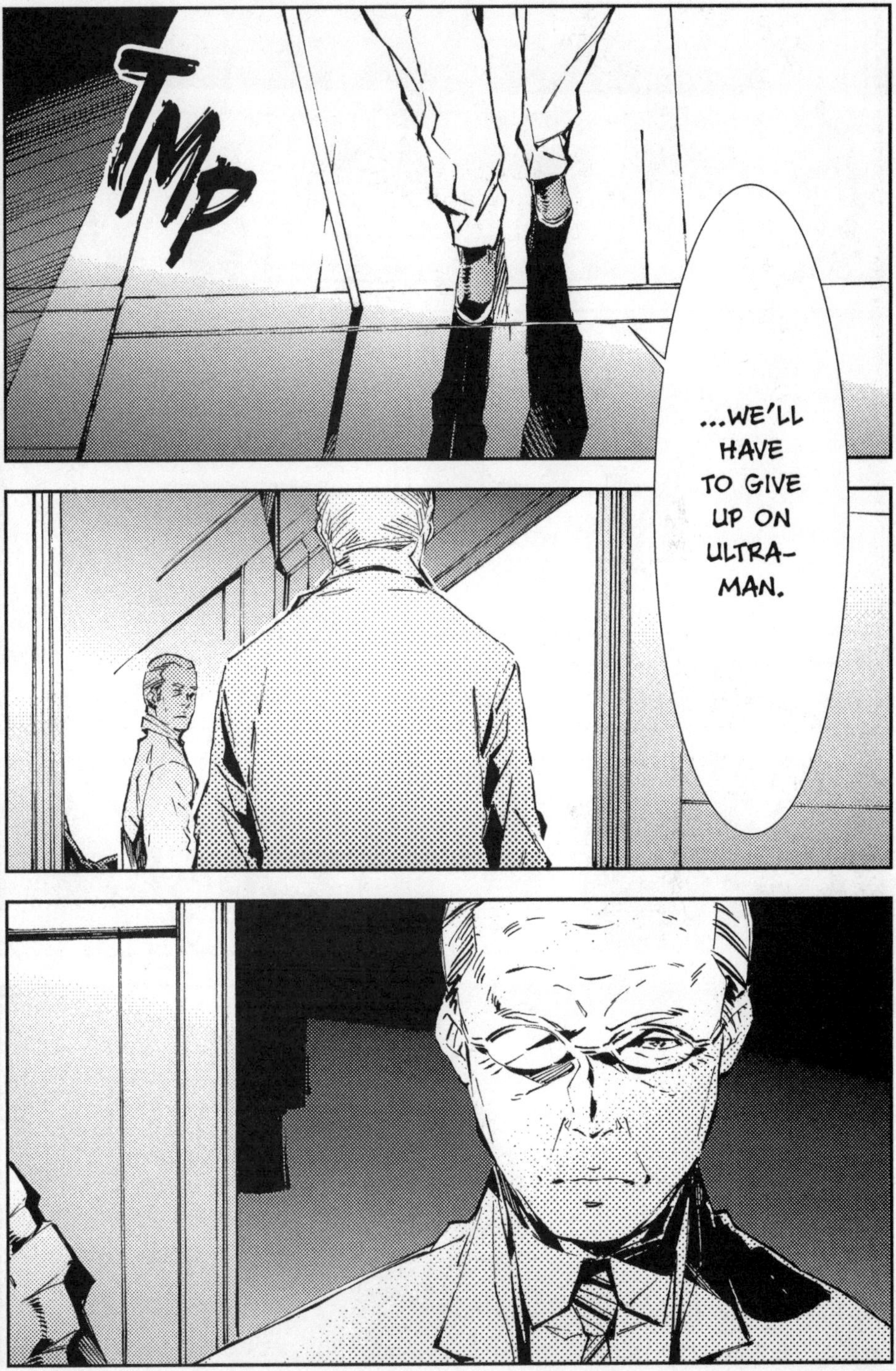
TMP
...WE'LL HAVE TO GIVE UP ON ULTRA-MAN.

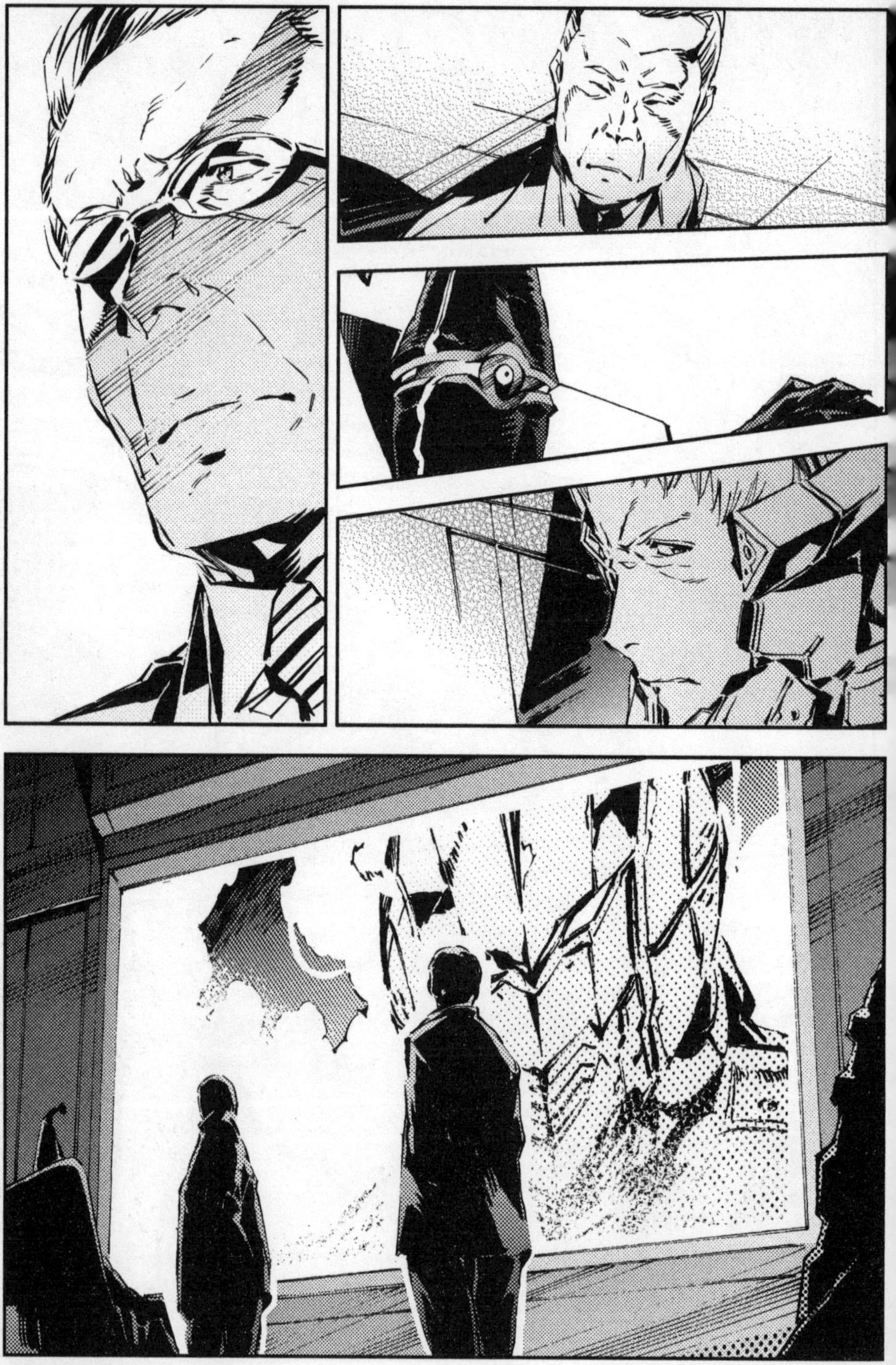

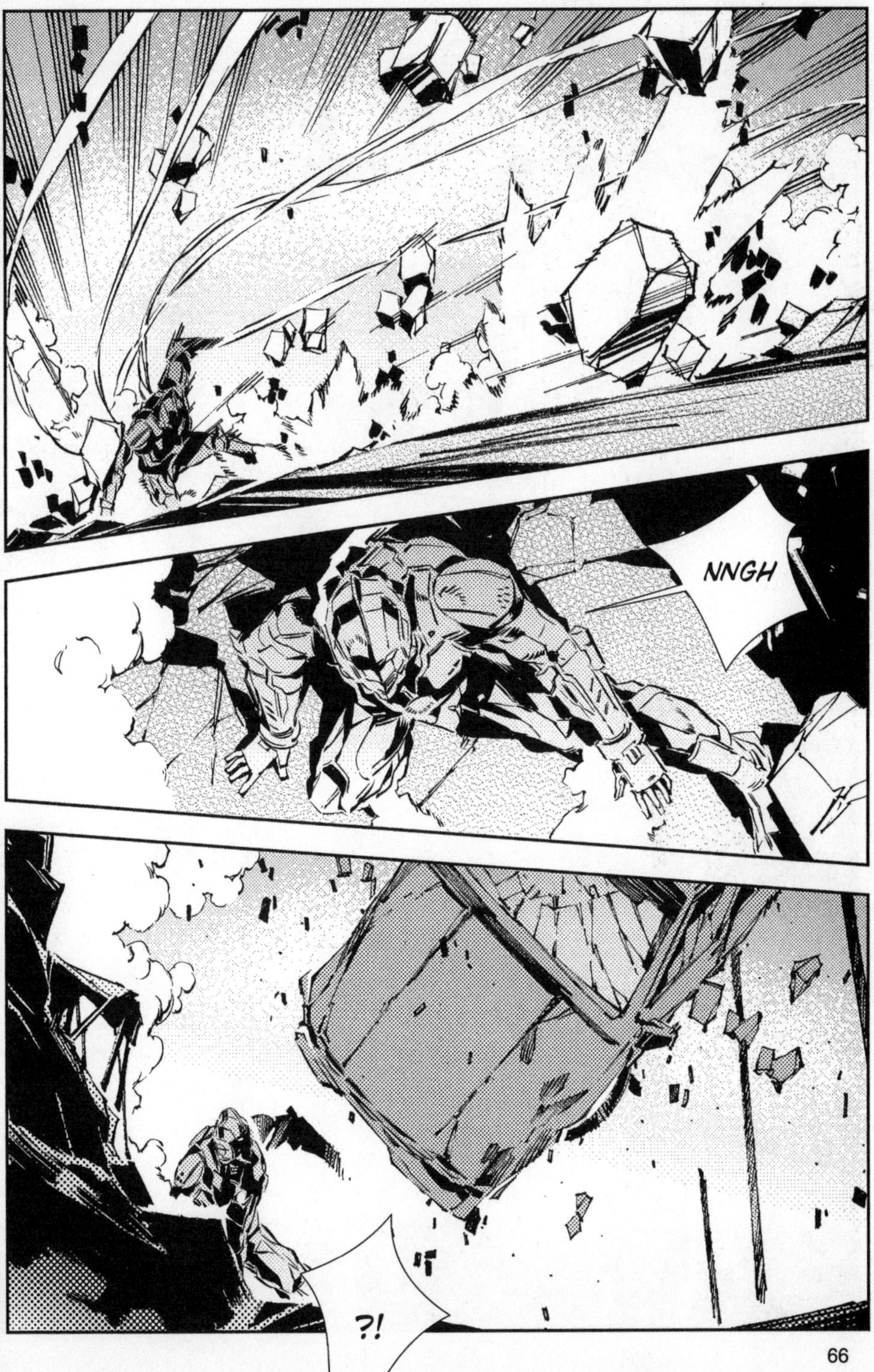
NNGH
?!

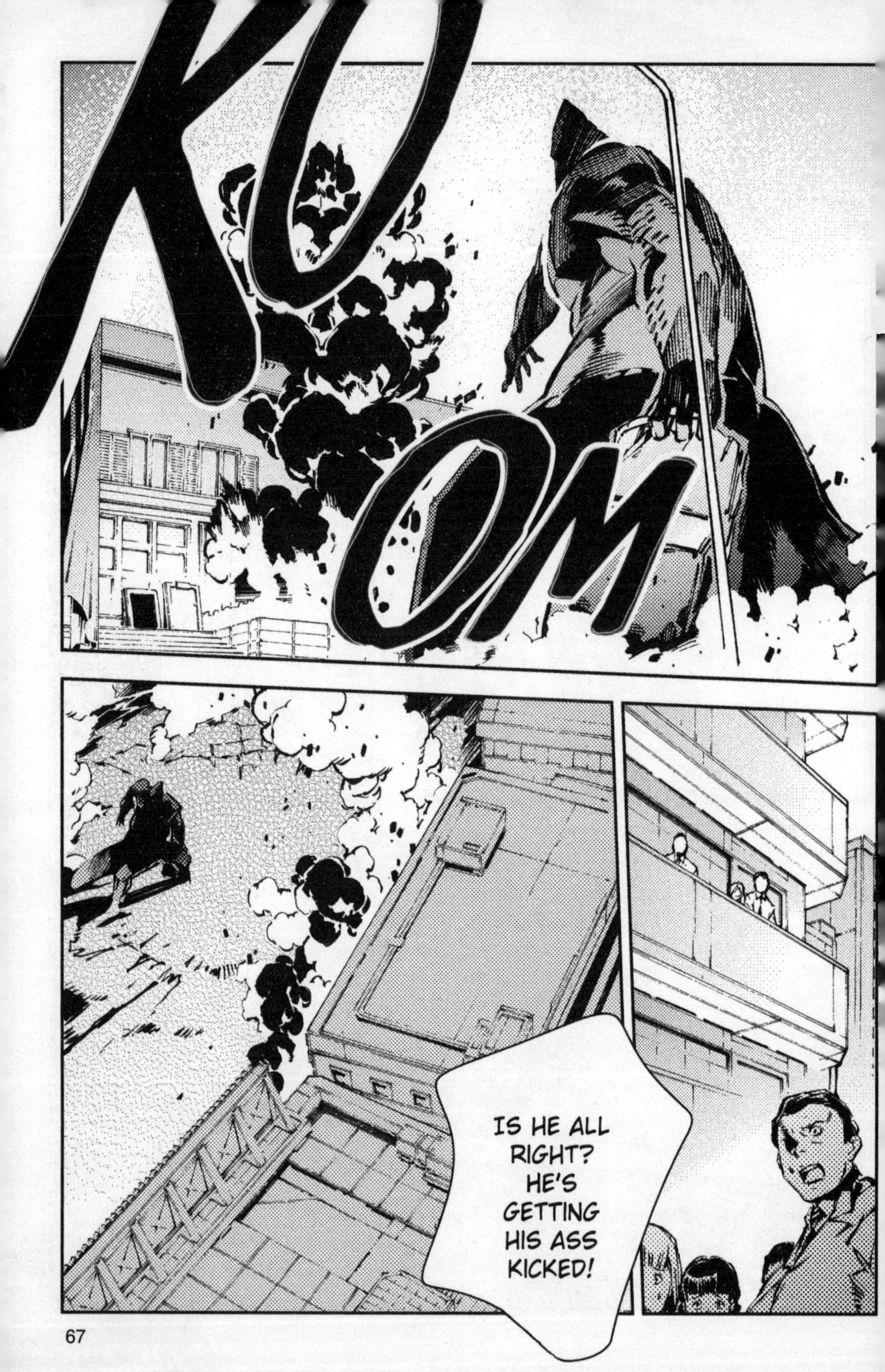
KU
OM
IS HE ALL RIGHT? HE'S GETTING HIS ASS KICKED!

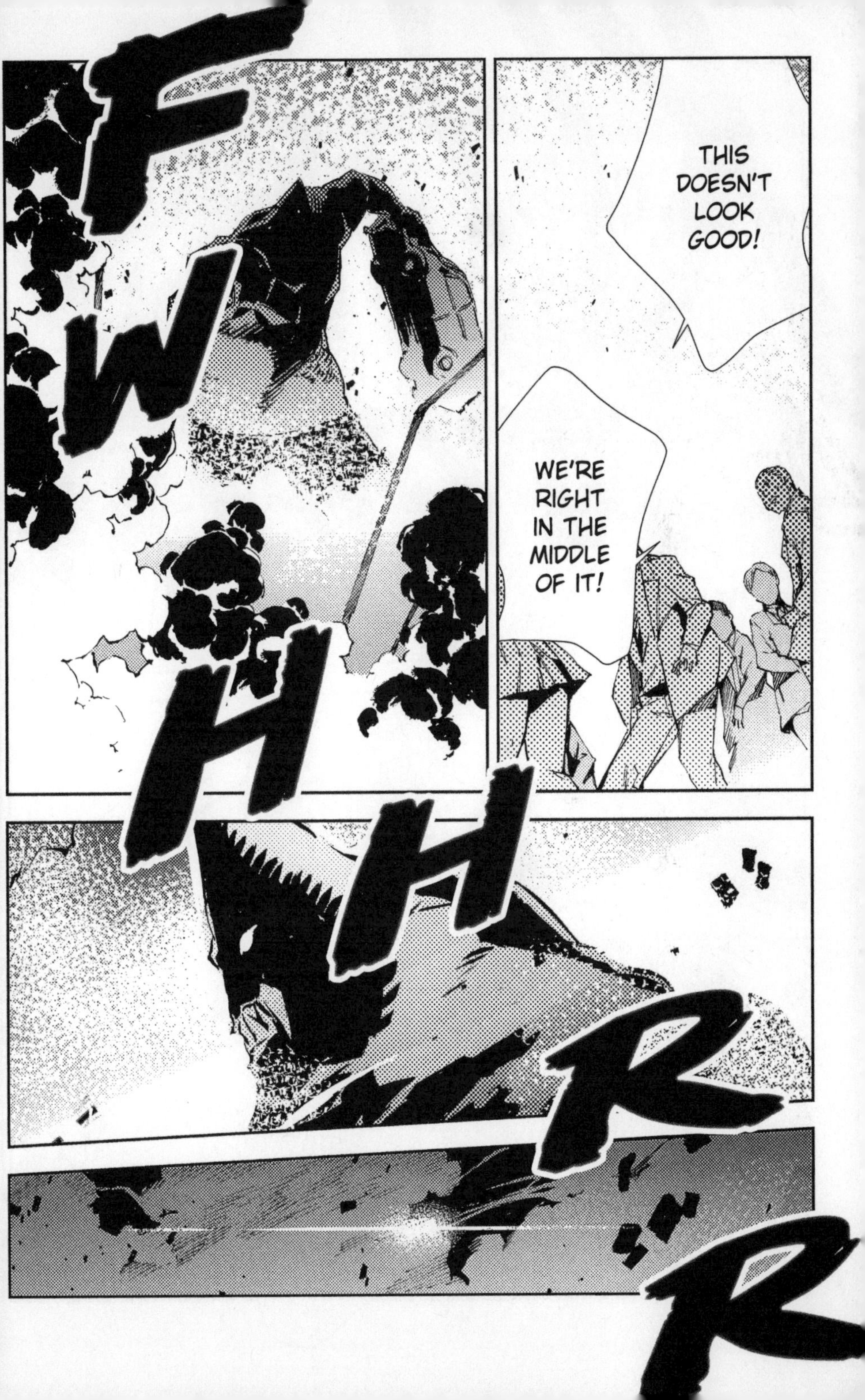
THIS DOESN'T LOOK GOOD!
WE'RE RIGHT IN THE MIDDLE OF IT!
FWHHRR

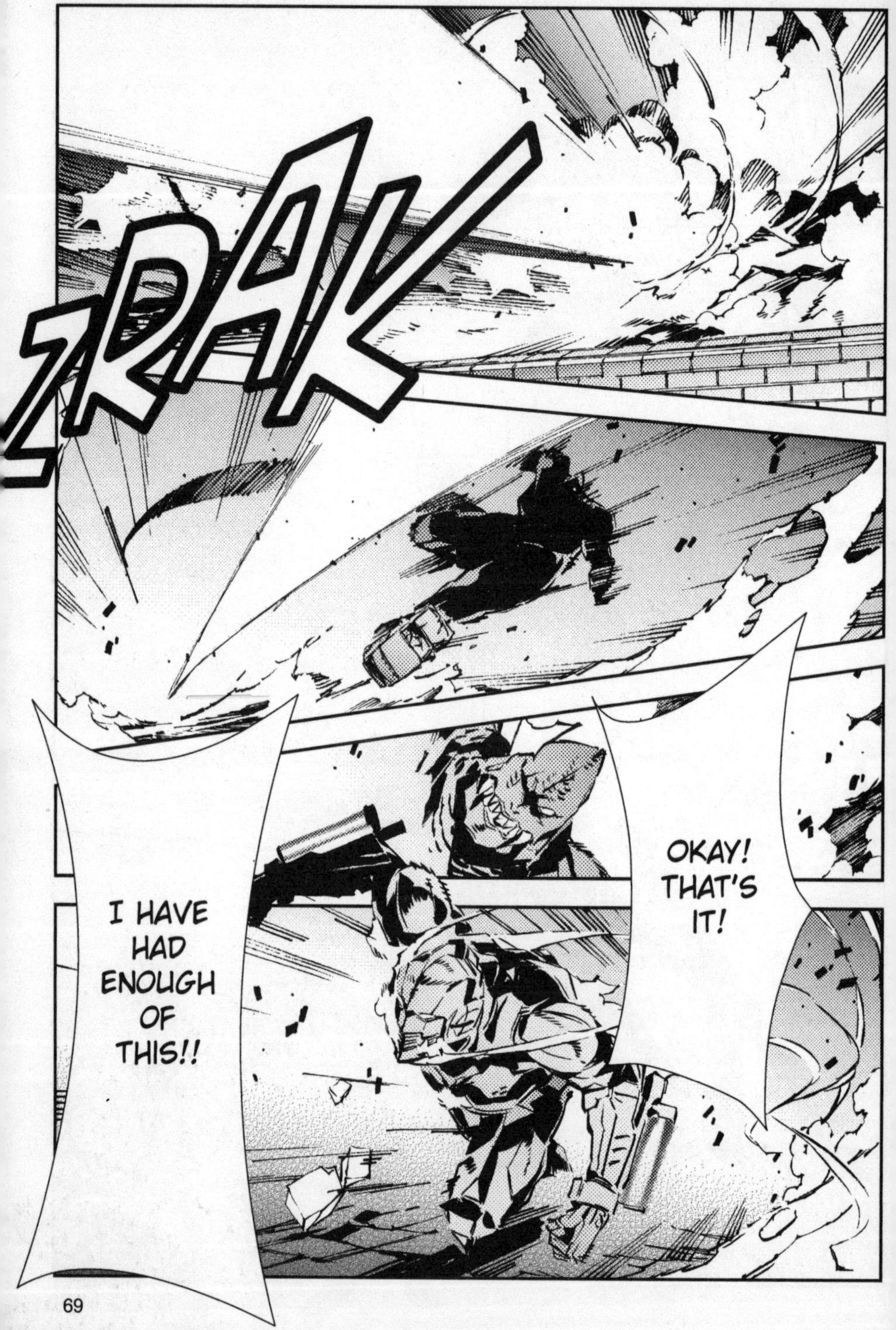
ZDAK
OKAY! THAT'S IT!
I HAVE HAD ENOUGH OF THIS!!

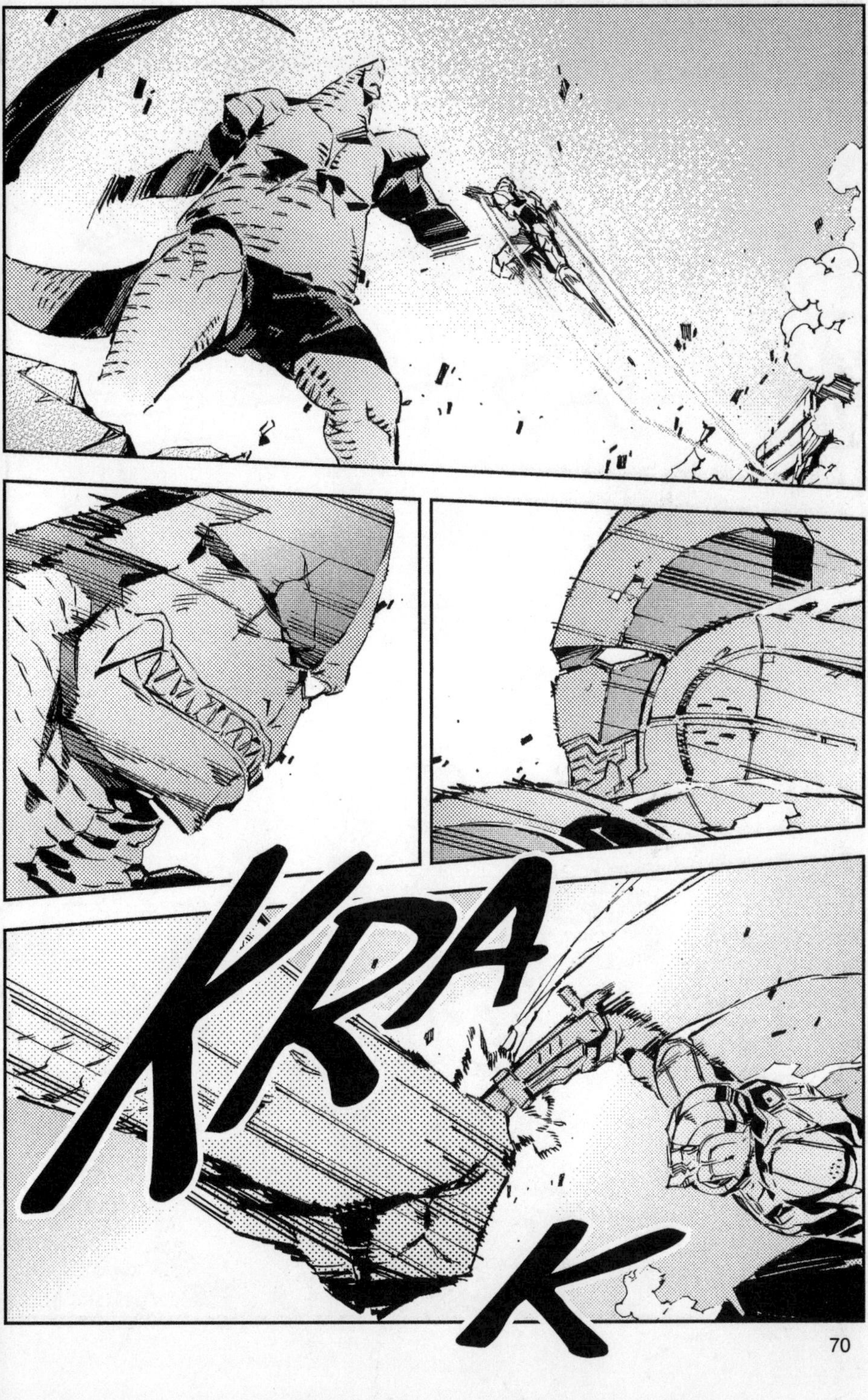
KRAAK

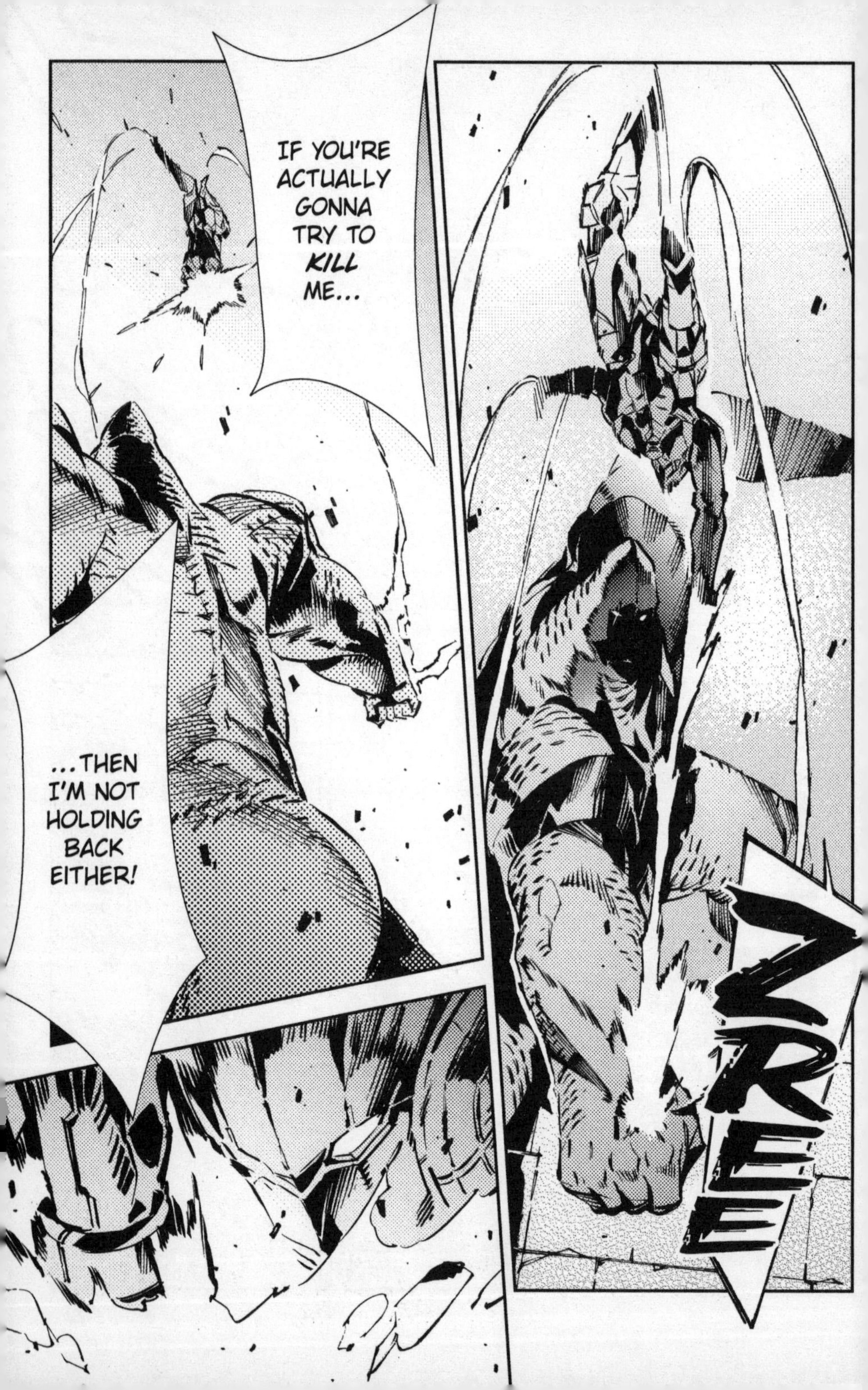
ZREEE
IF YOU'RE ACTUALLY GONNA TRY TO *KILL* ME...
...THEN I'M NOT HOLDING BACK EITHER!

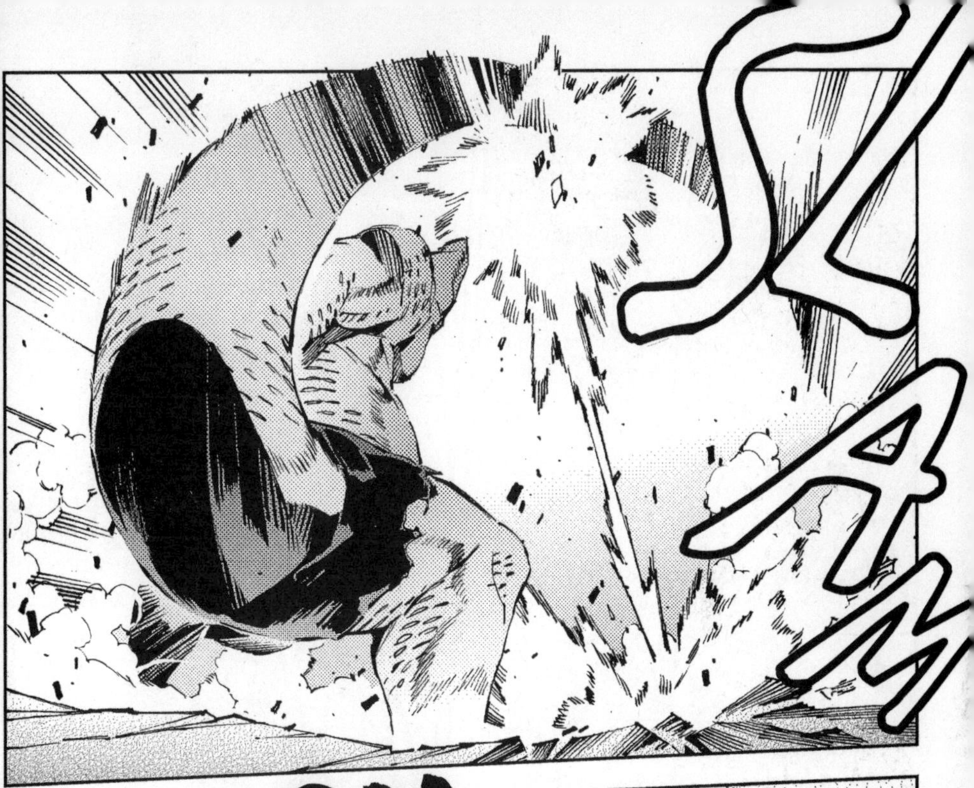
SLAM
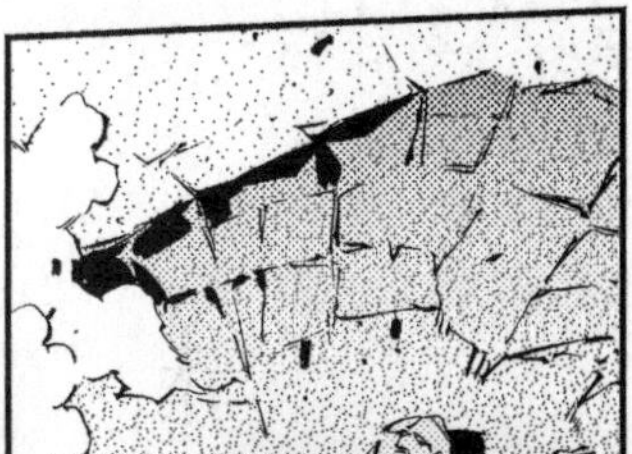
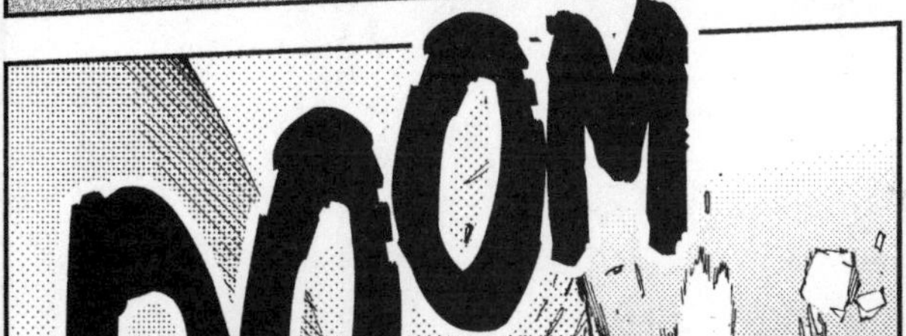
DOOM

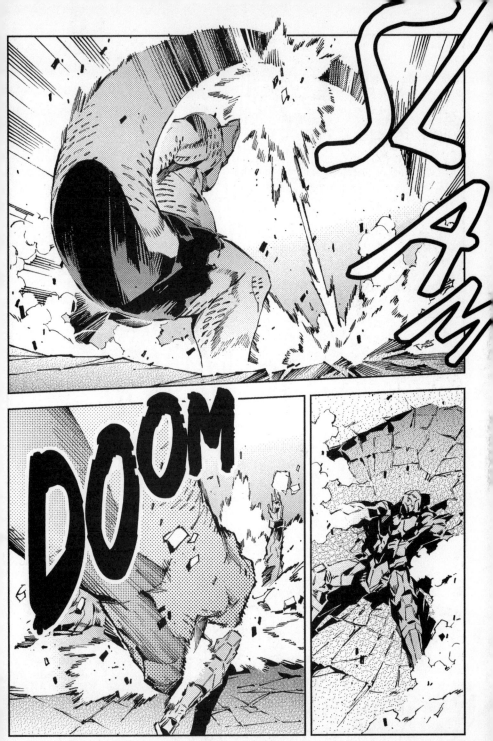

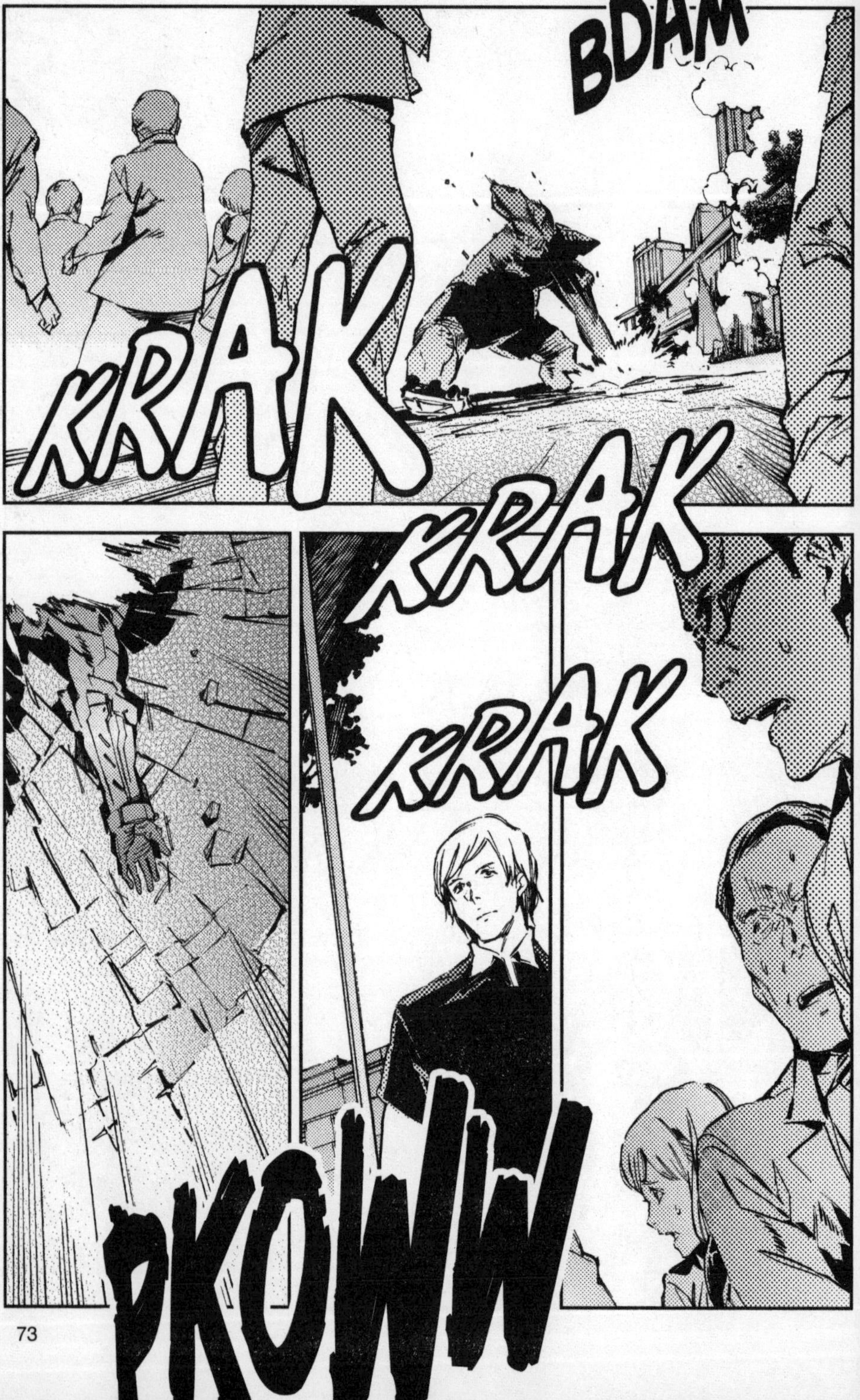
BDAM
KRAK
KRAK
KRAK
PKOWW

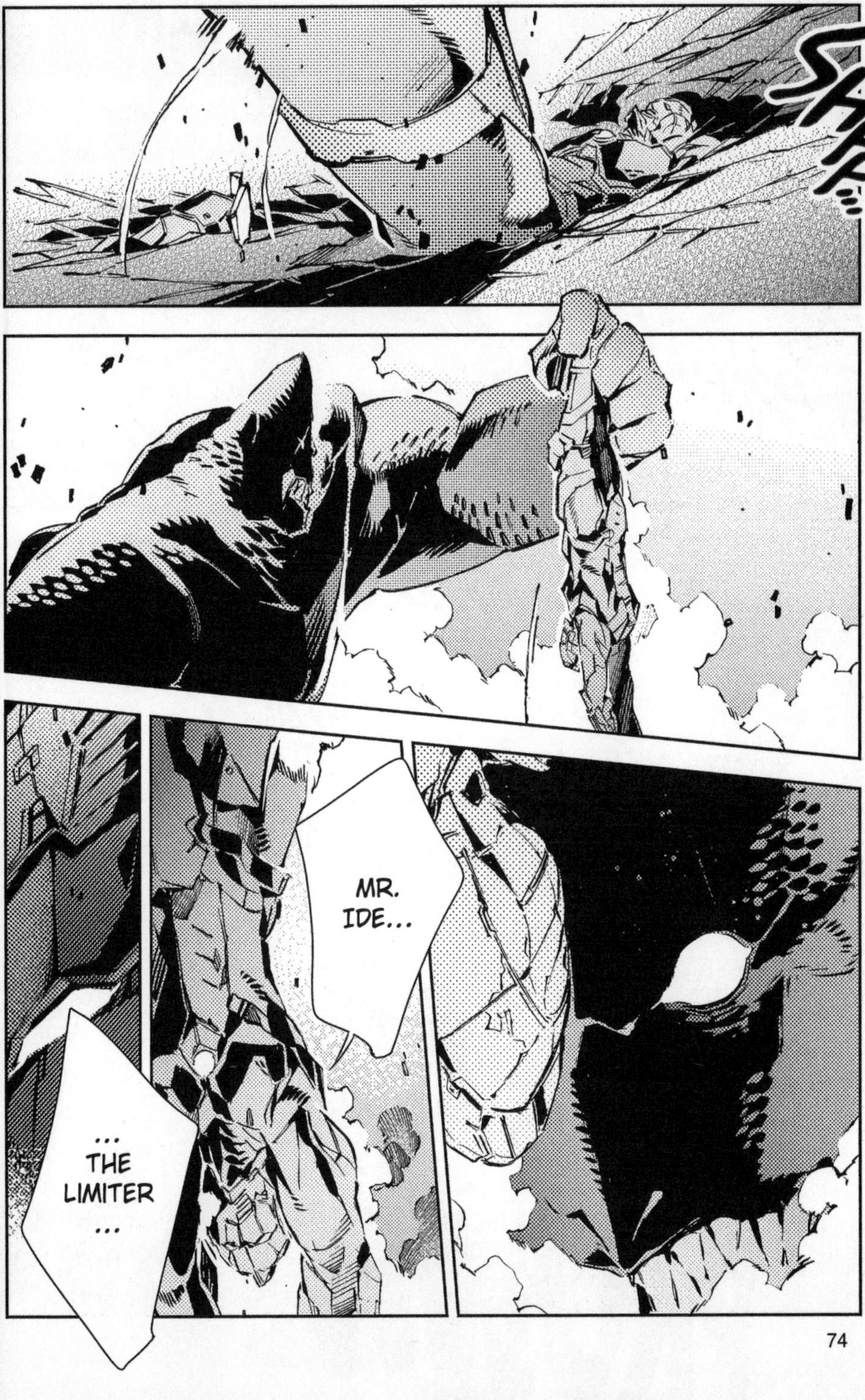
SHFFF...
MR. IDE...
...THE LIMITER...

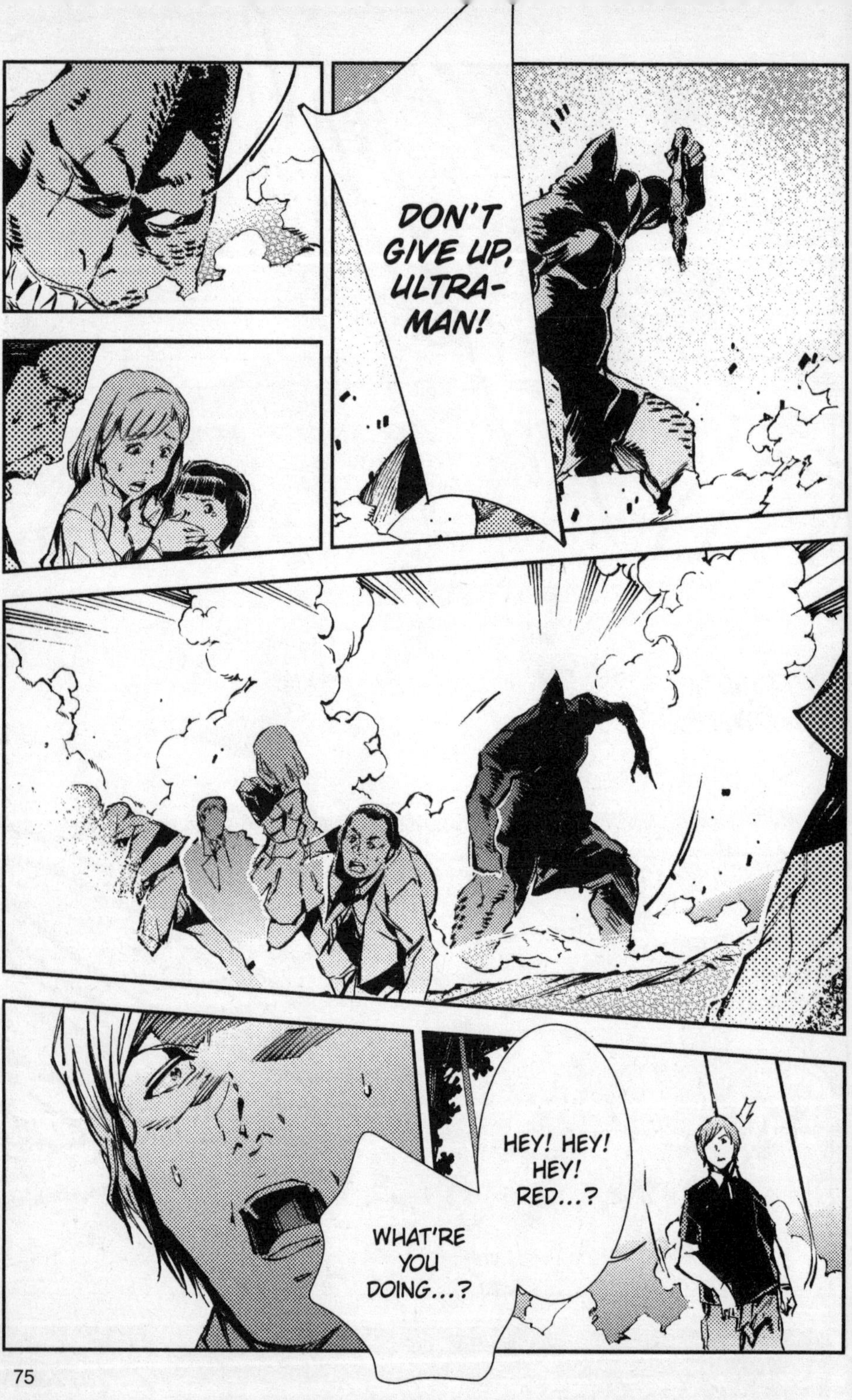
DON'T GIVE UP, ULTRA-MAN!
HEY! HEY! HEY! RED...?
WHAT'RE YOU DOING...?

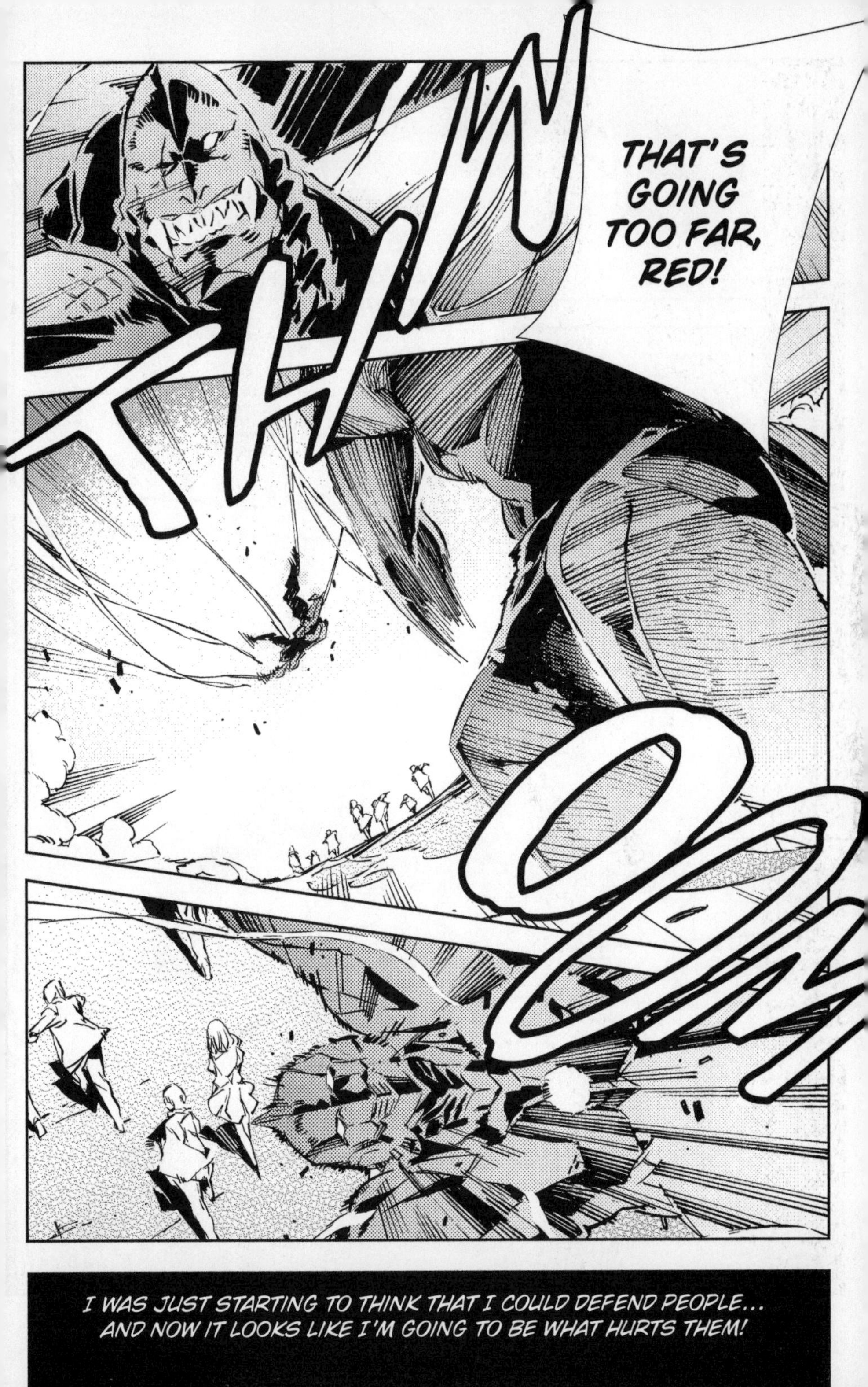
THAT'S GOING TOO FAR, RED!
THWOOM
I WAS JUST STARTING TO THINK THAT I COULD DEFEND PEOPLE...
AND NOW IT LOOKS LIKE I'M GOING TO BE WHAT HURTS THEM!

IF I
REALLY
CAN
BECOME
ULTRA-
MAN...
THEN
PLEASE
...

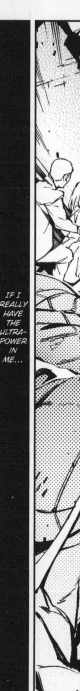

IF I
REALLY
HAVE
THE
ULTRA-
POWER
IN
ME...

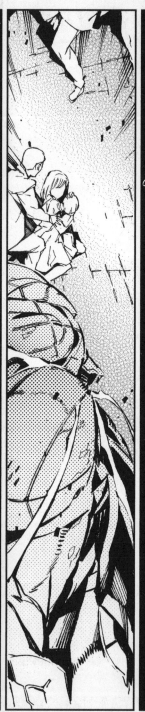

NO
WAY!
I'M
NOT
GOING
OUT
LIKE
THIS!

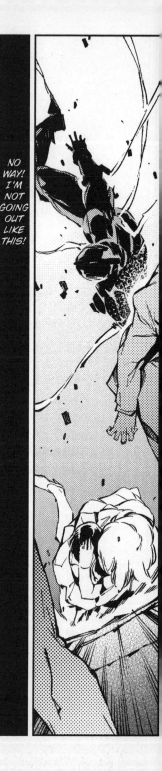

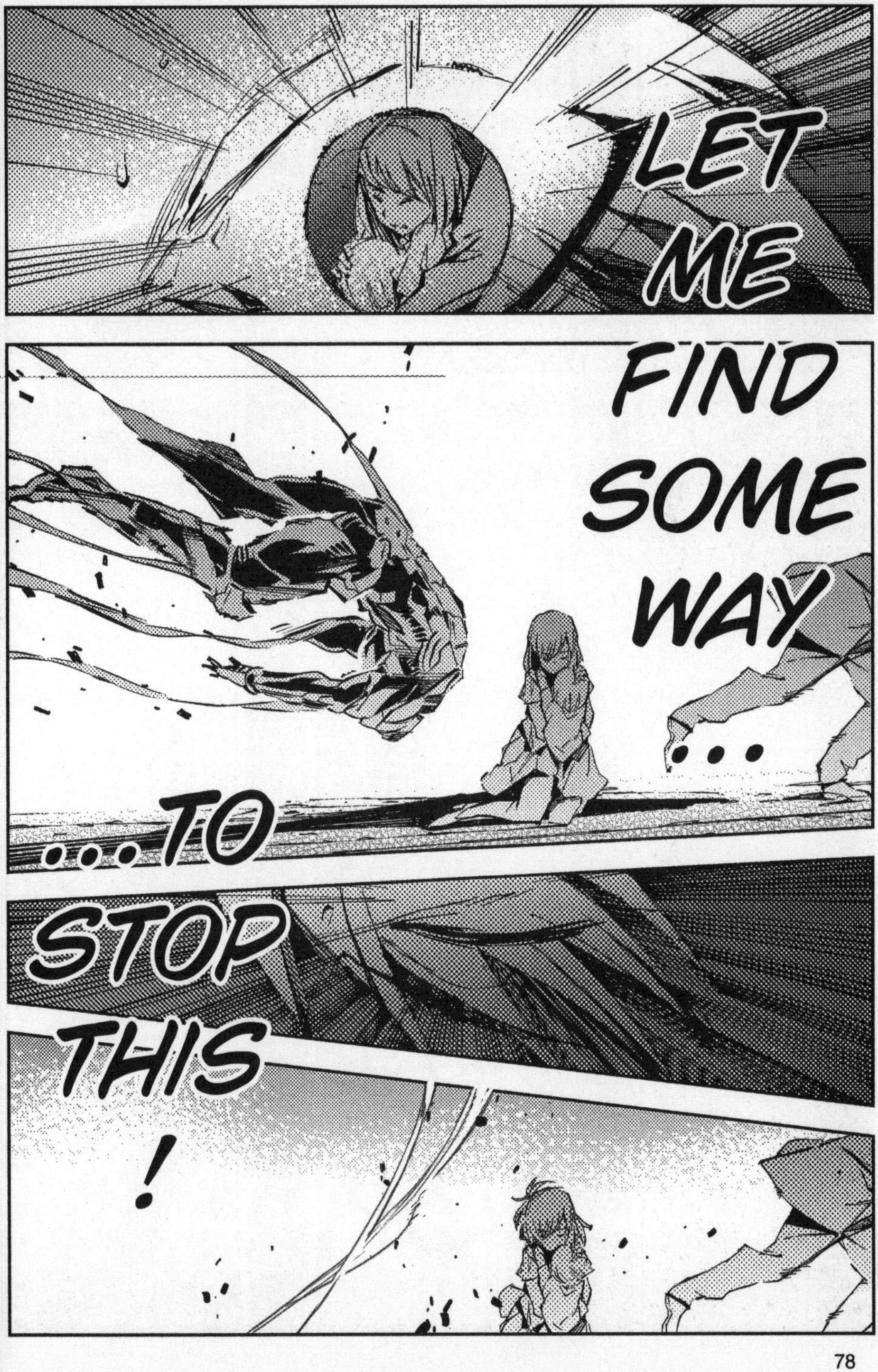
LET ME FIND SOME WAY...
...TO STOP THIS!

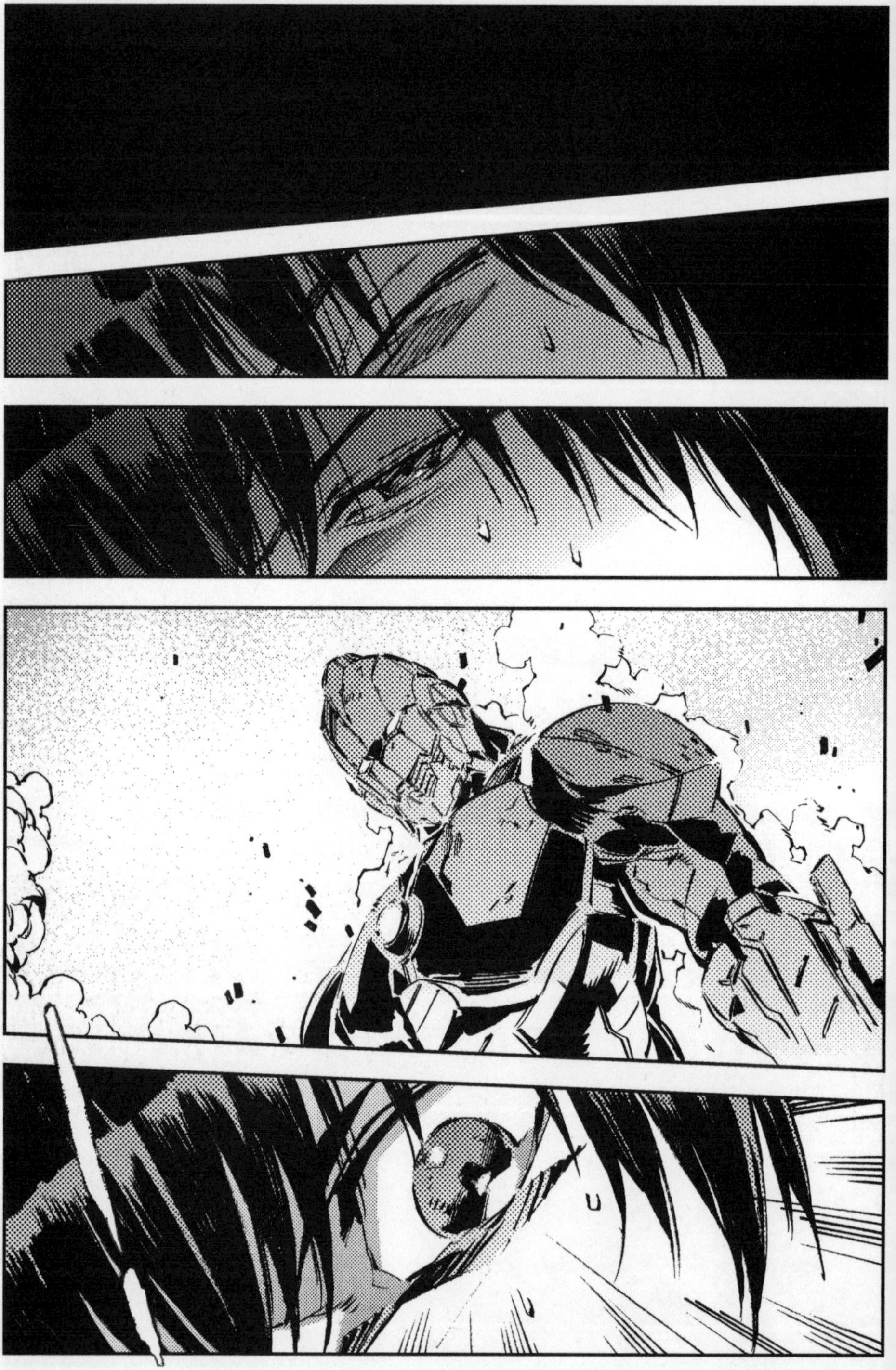

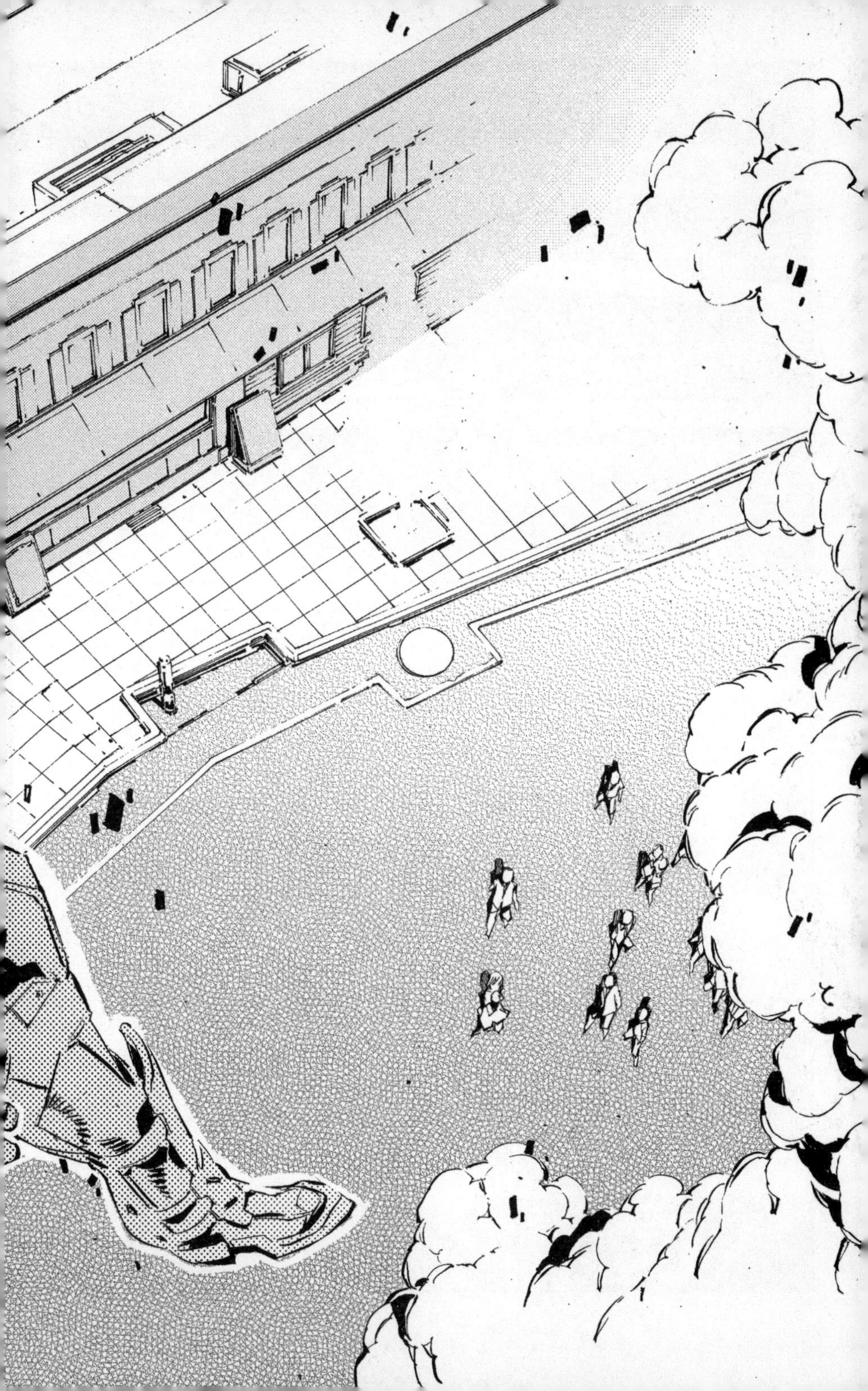

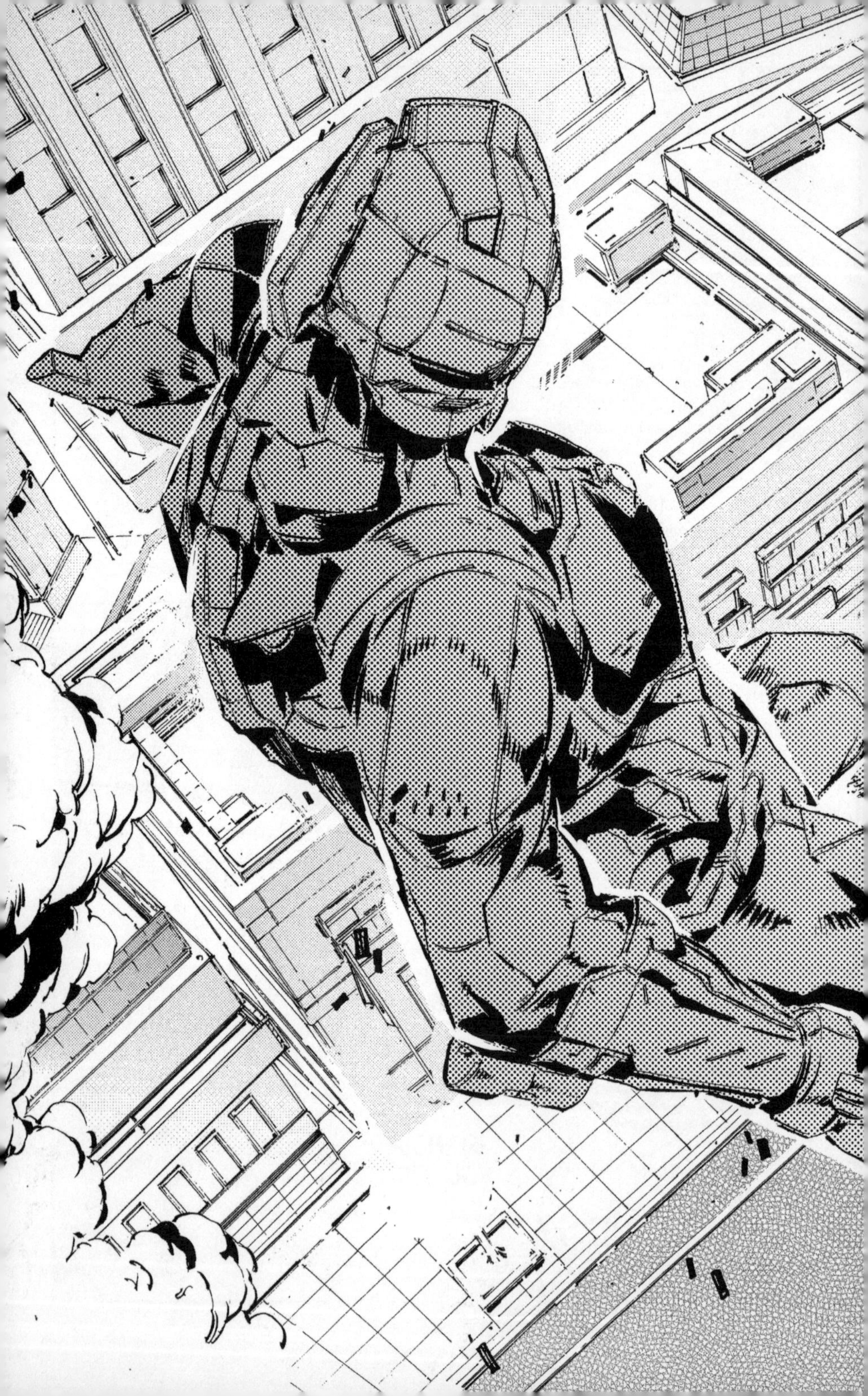

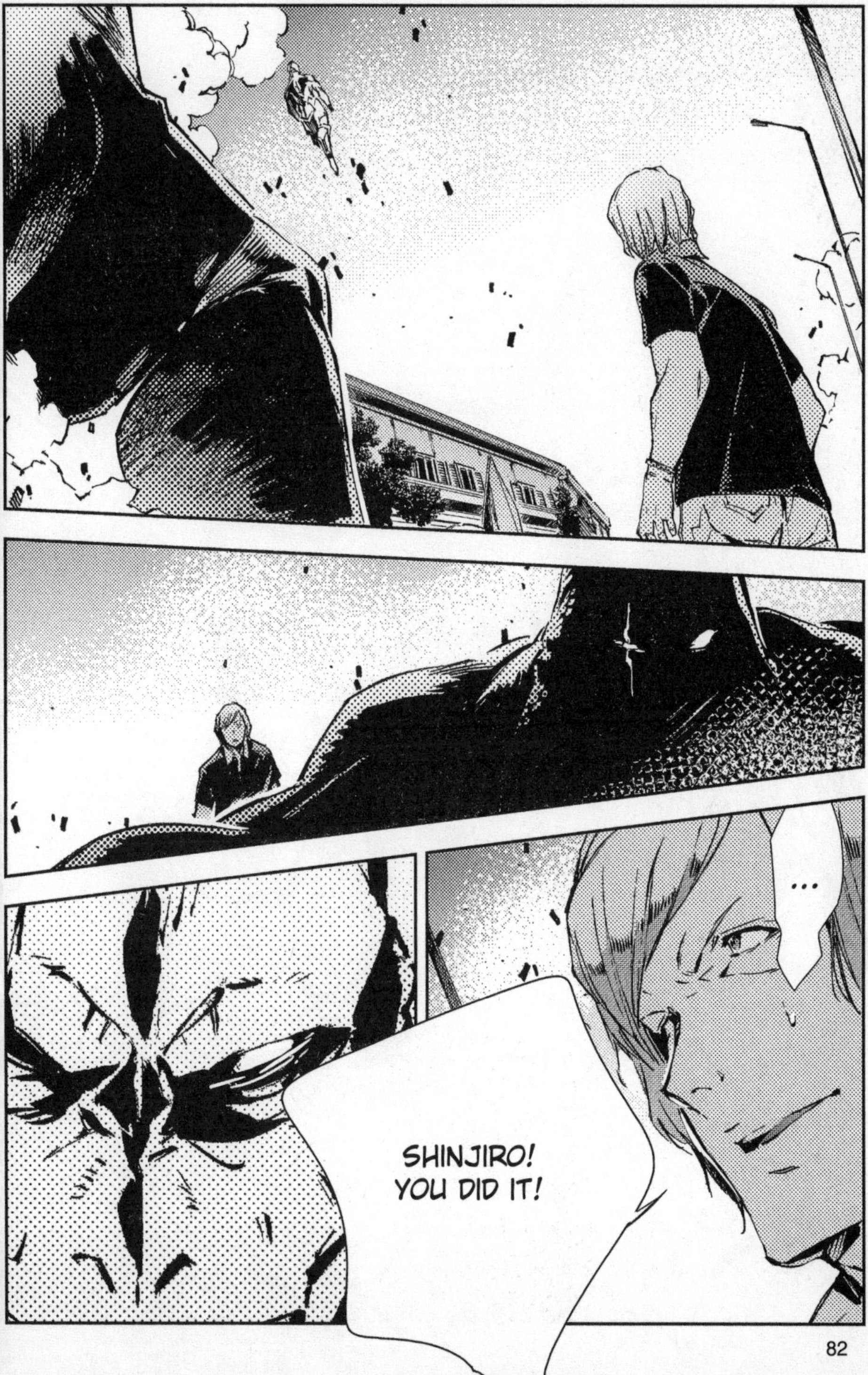
...
SHINJIRO! YOU DID IT!

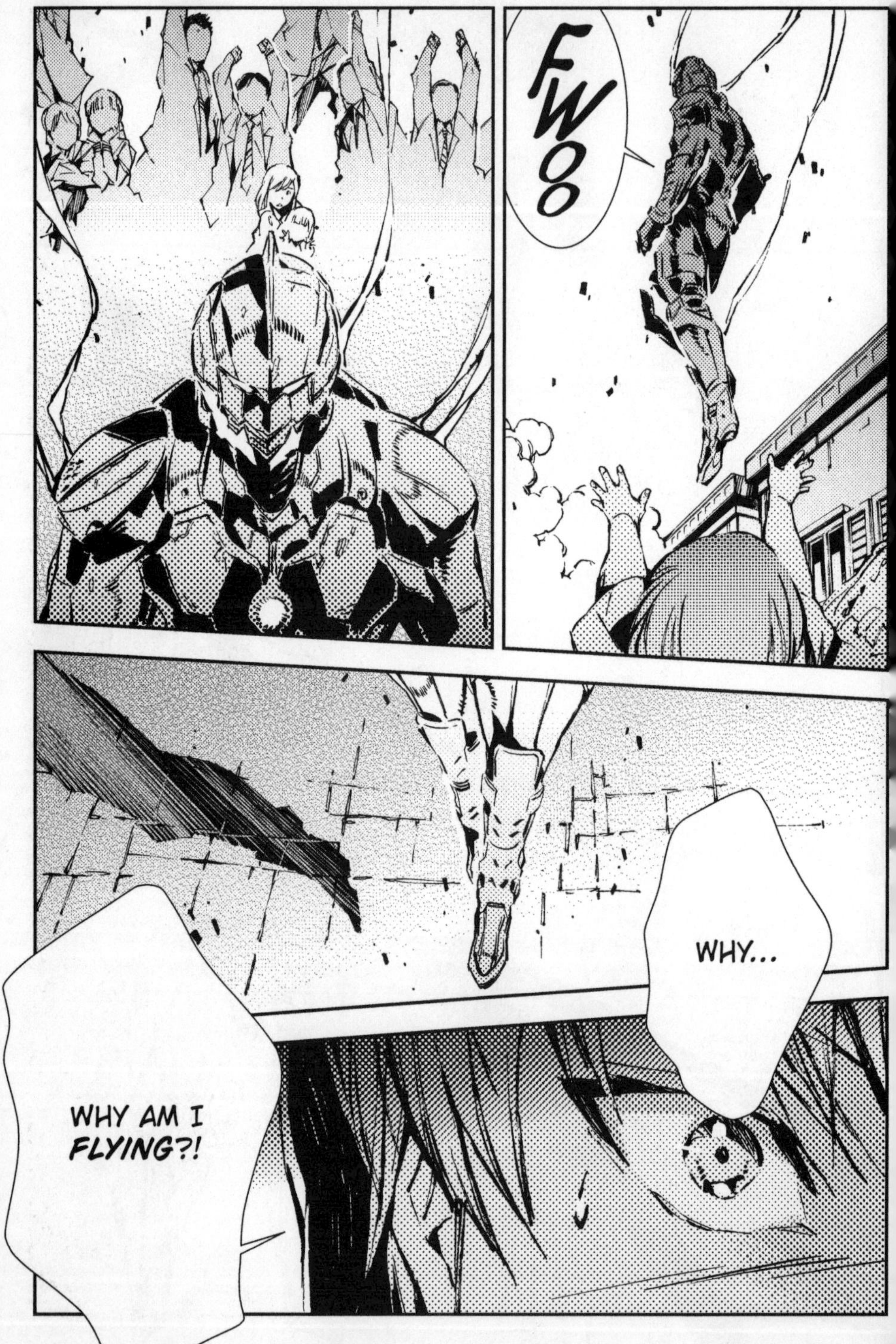
FWOO
WHY...
WHY AM I *FLYING?!*

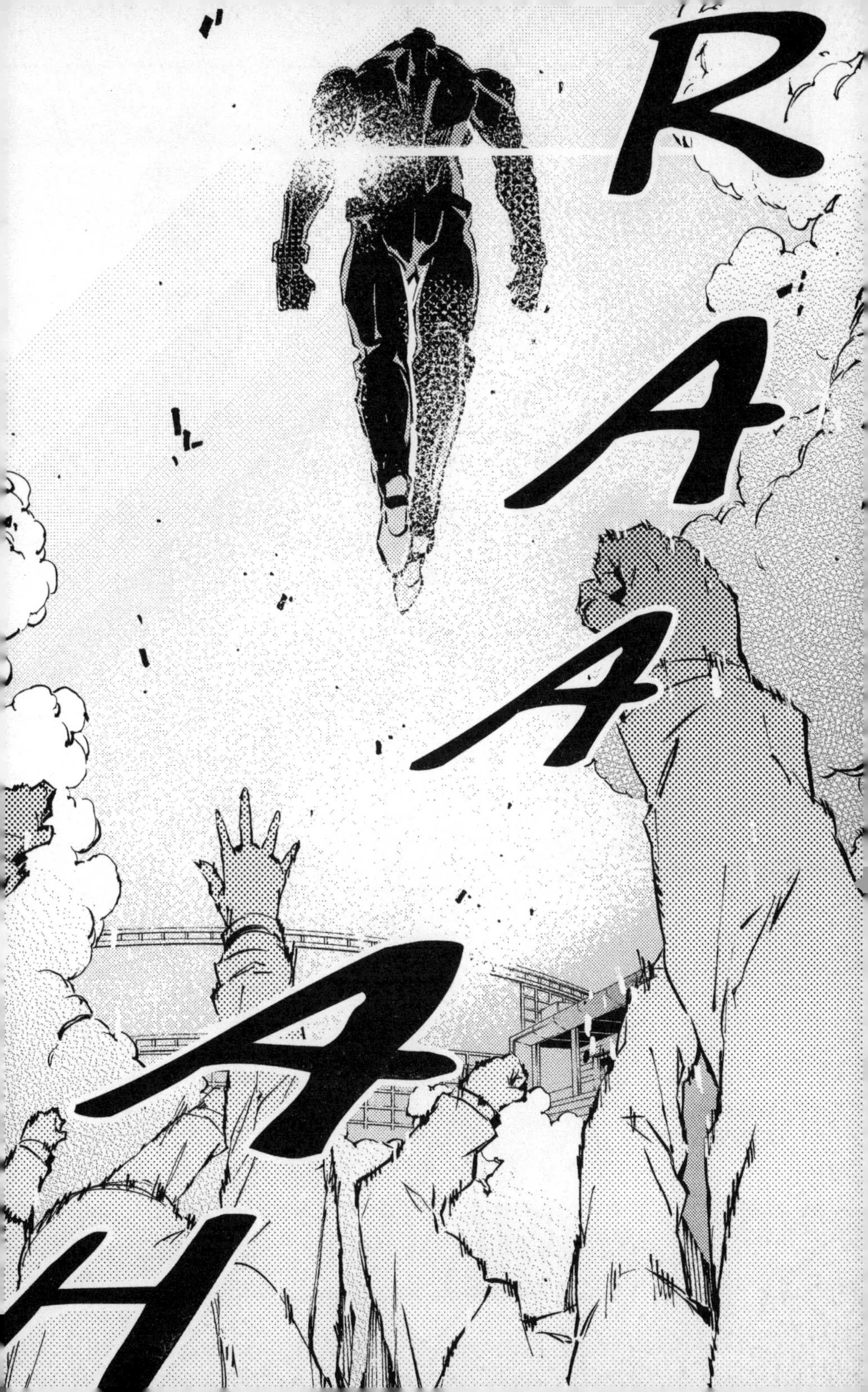
RAAAH

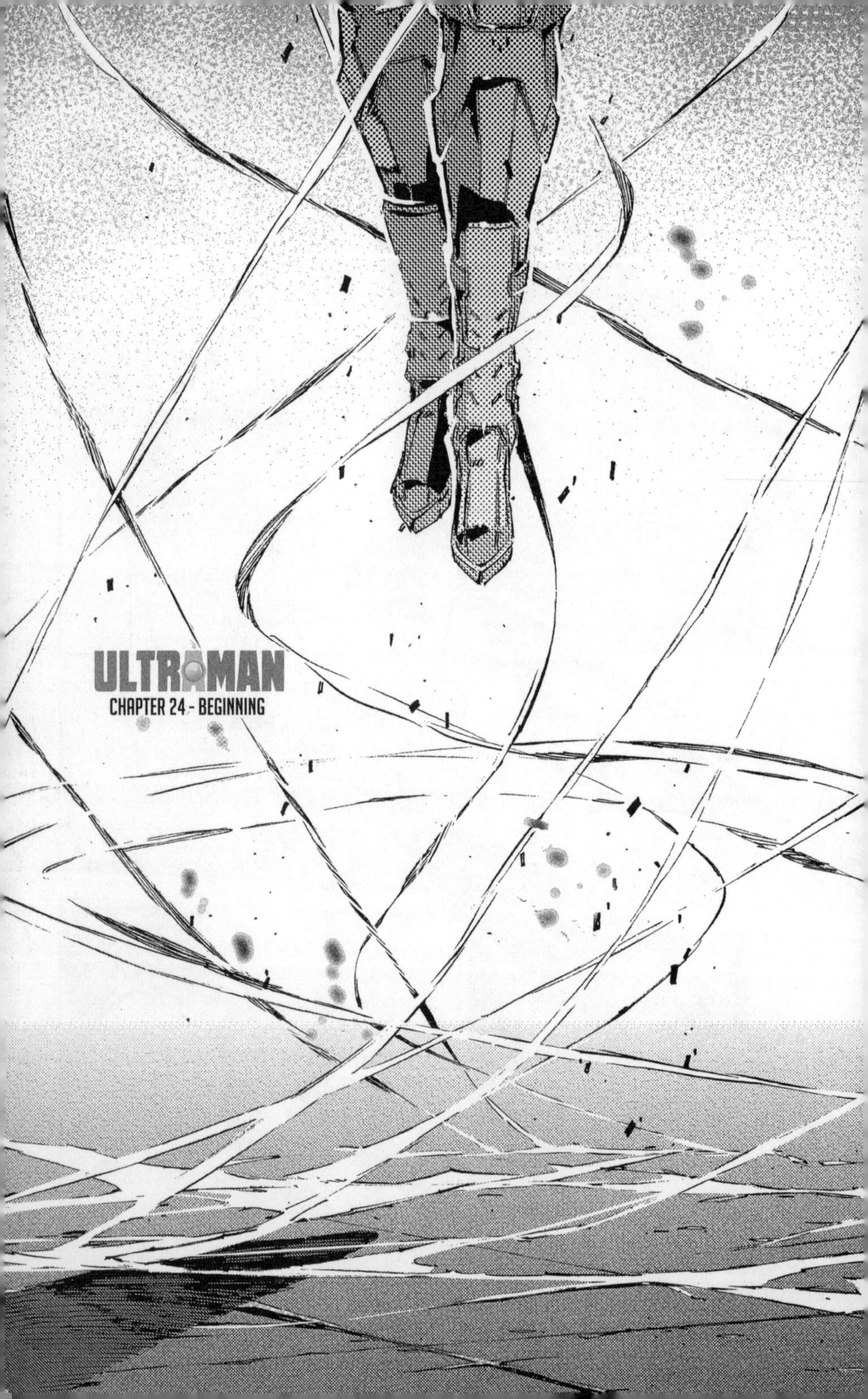
ULTRAMAN
CHAPTER 24 - BEGINNING

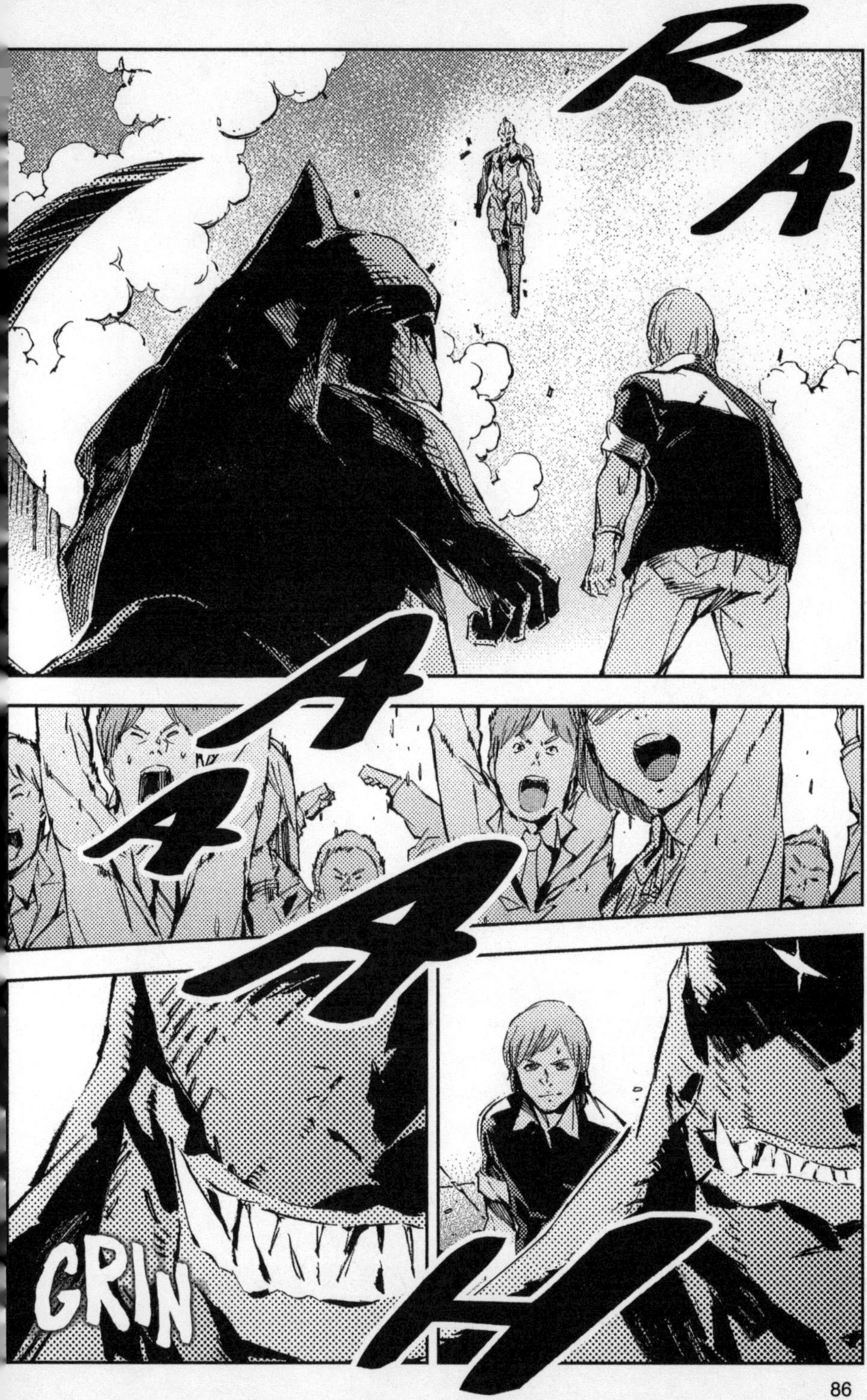
RAAAAH
GRIN

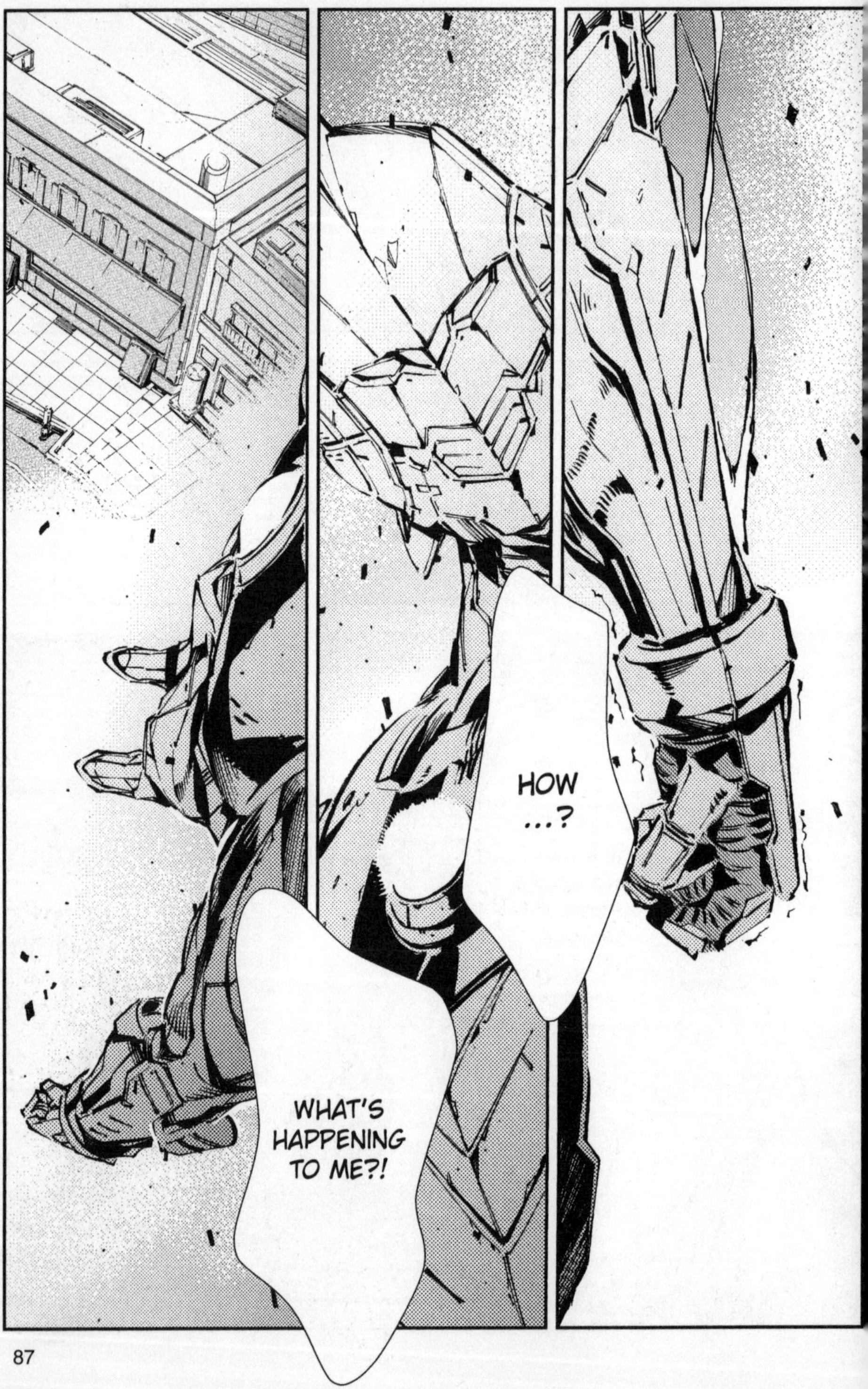
HOW ...?
WHAT'S HAPPENING TO ME?!

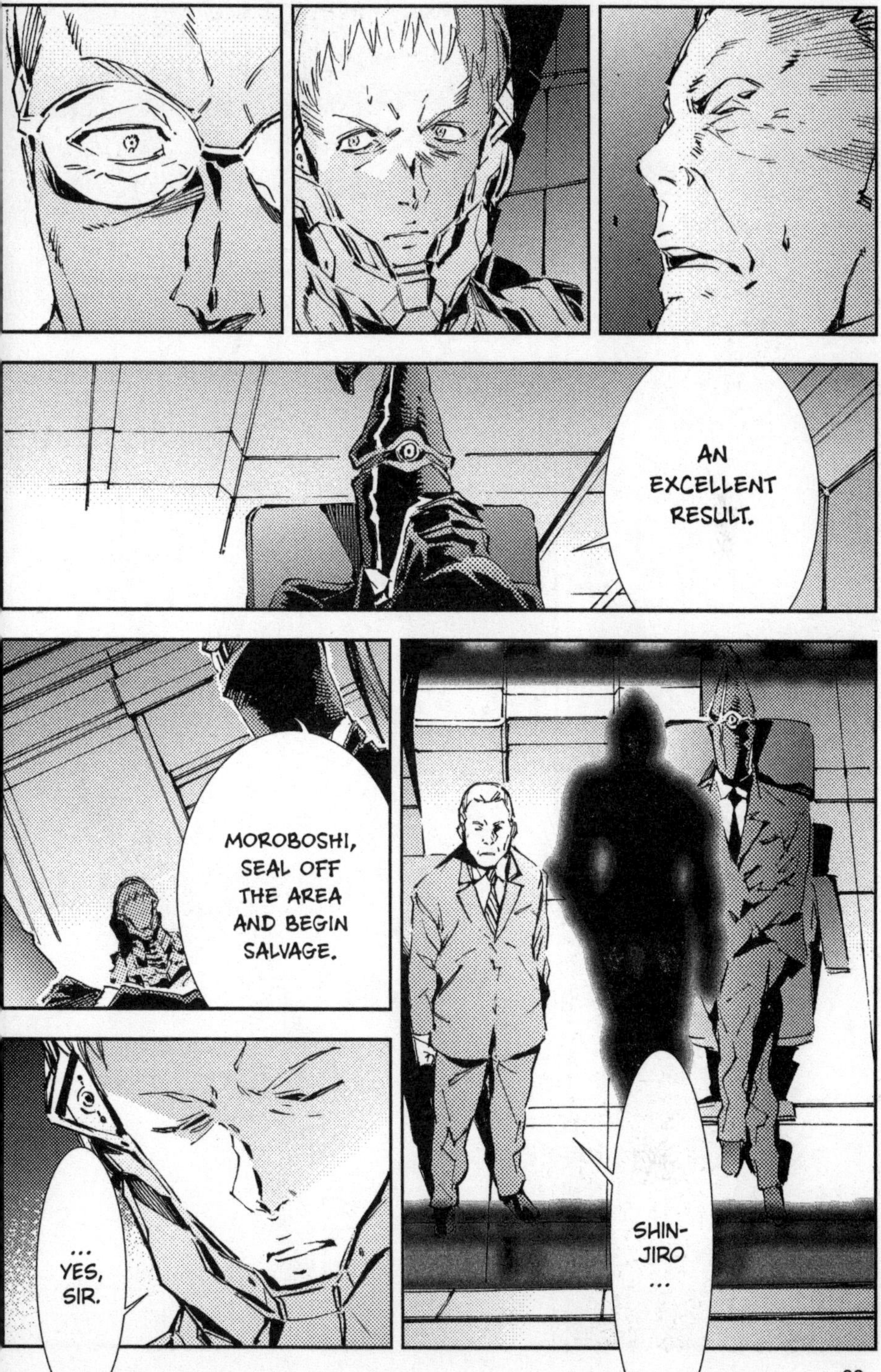
AN EXCELLENT RESULT.
SHIN-JIRO...
MOROBOSHI, SEAL OFF THE AREA AND BEGIN SALVAGE.
... YES, SIR.

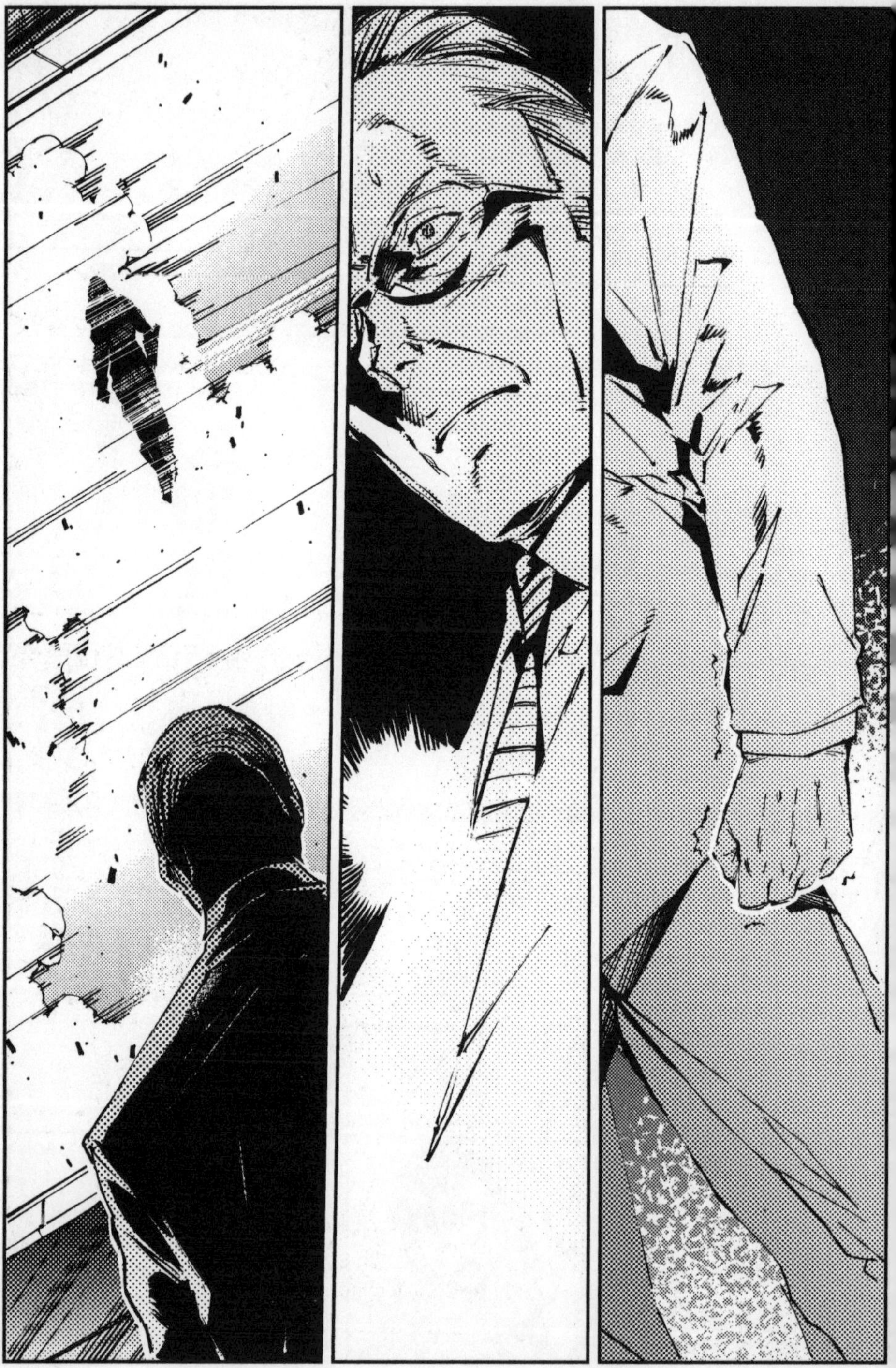

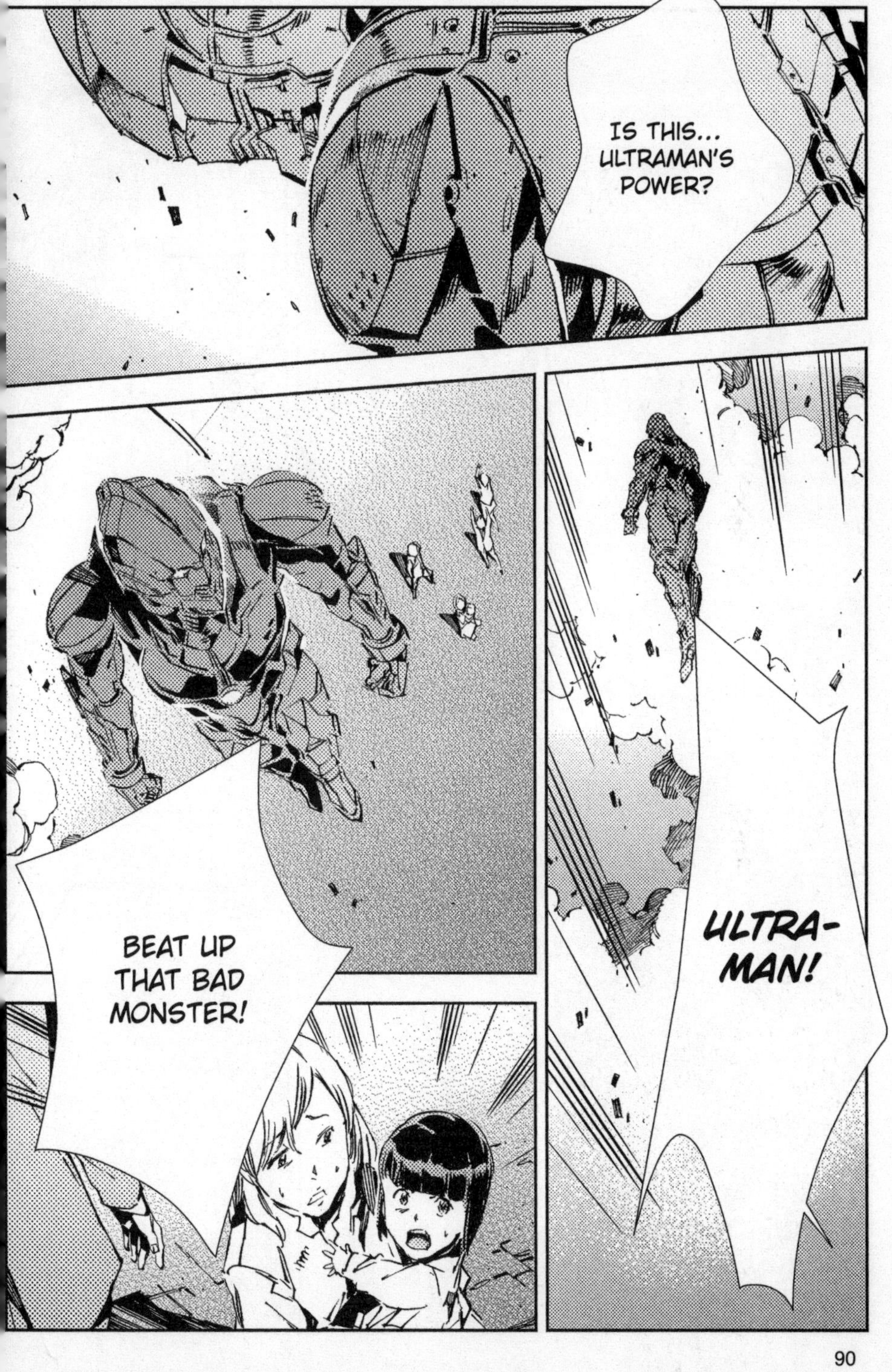
IS THIS... ULTRAMAN'S POWER?
ULTRA-MAN!
BEAT UP THAT BAD MONSTER!

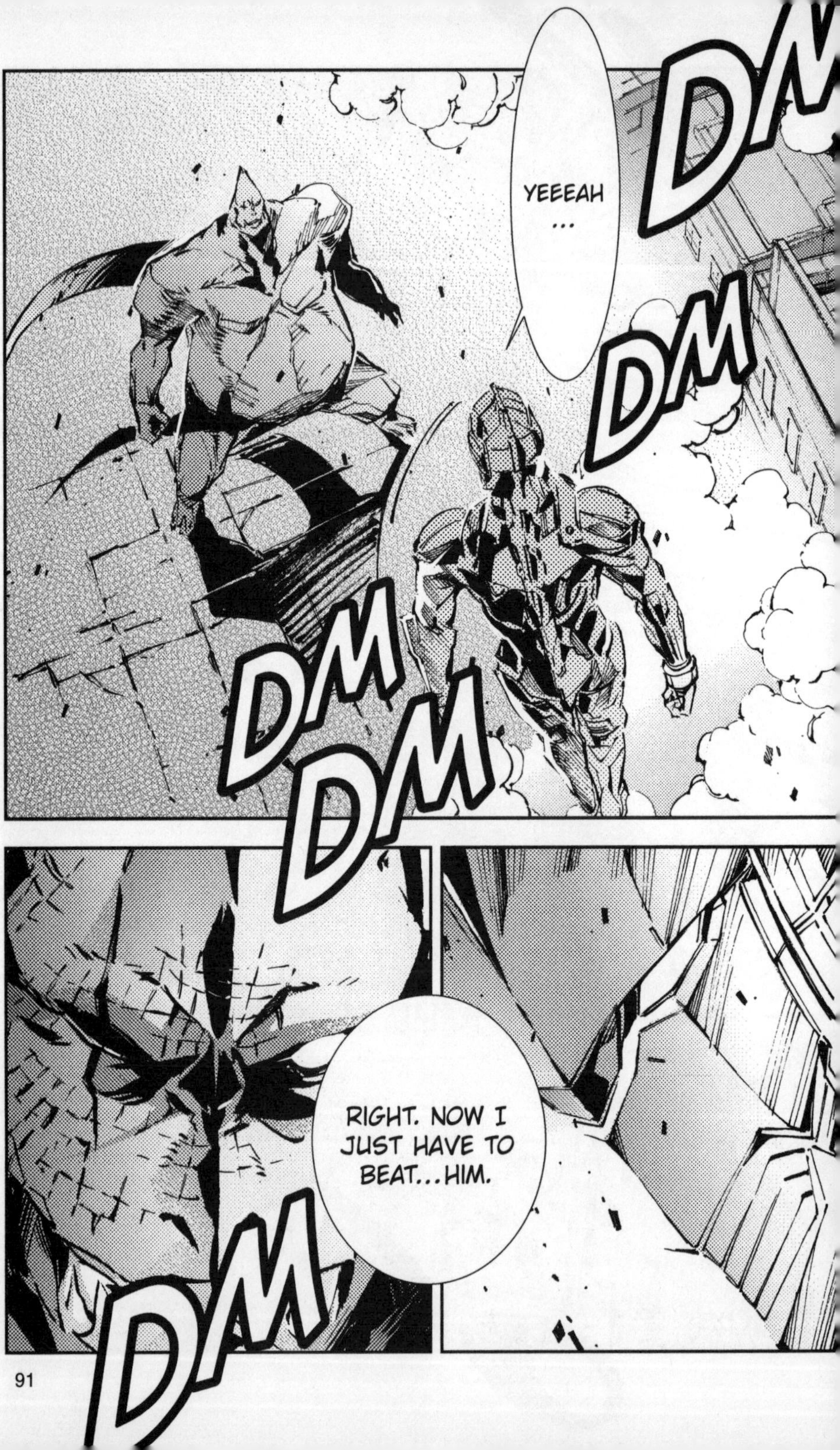
YEEEAH ...
DM
DM
DM
RIGHT. NOW I JUST HAVE TO BEAT...HIM.
DM

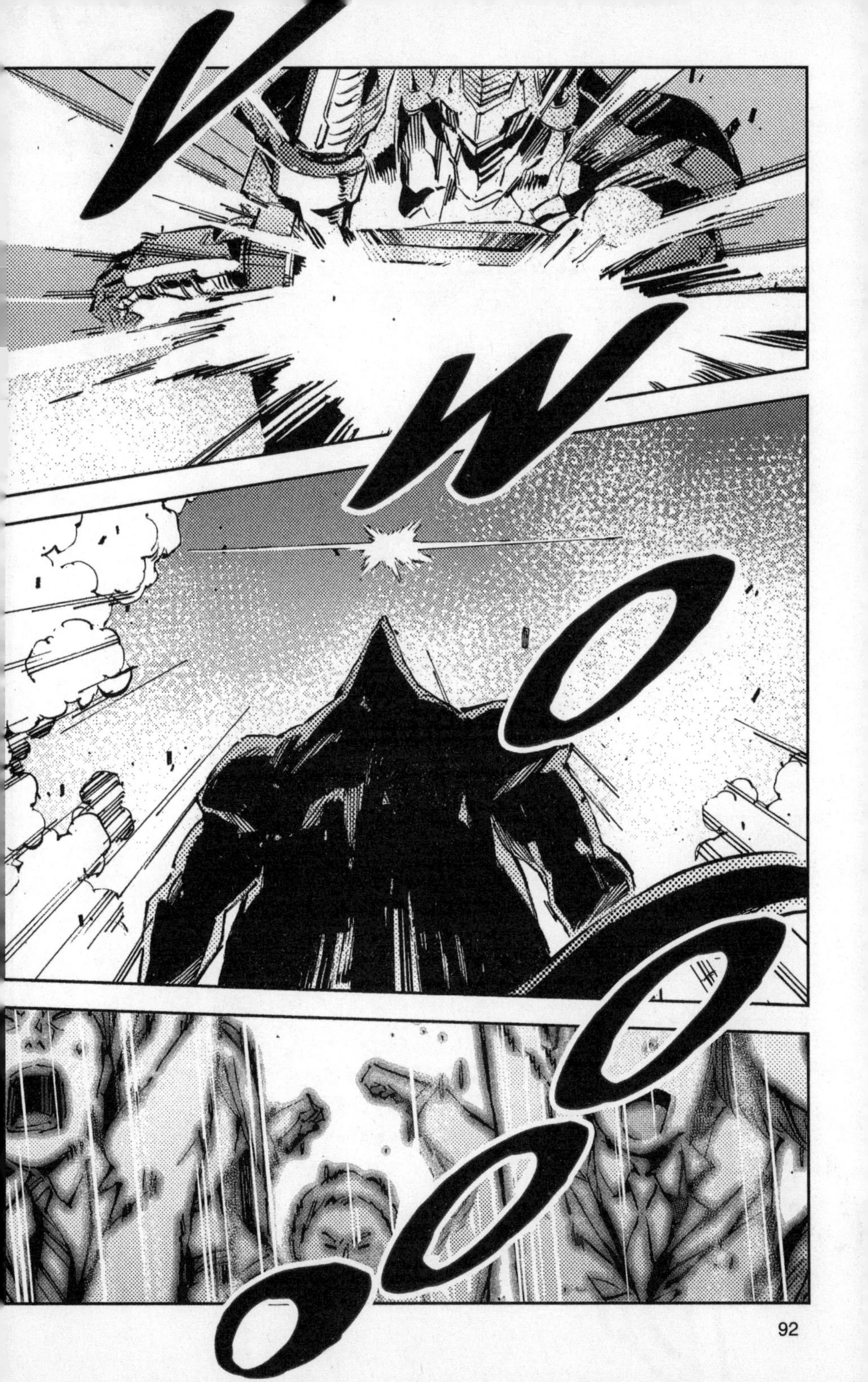
VWOOOOOO

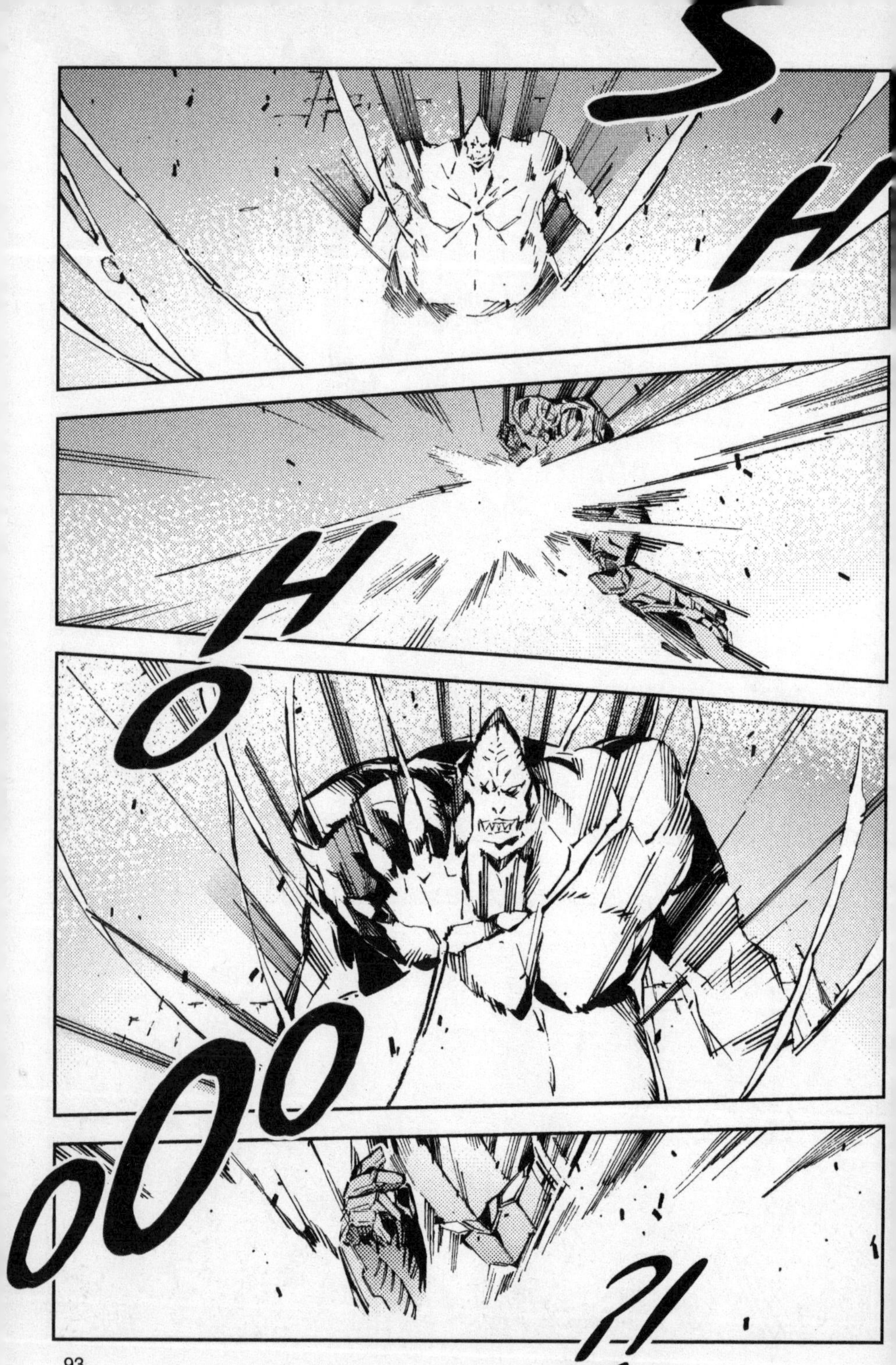
SHHOOOOO
?!!

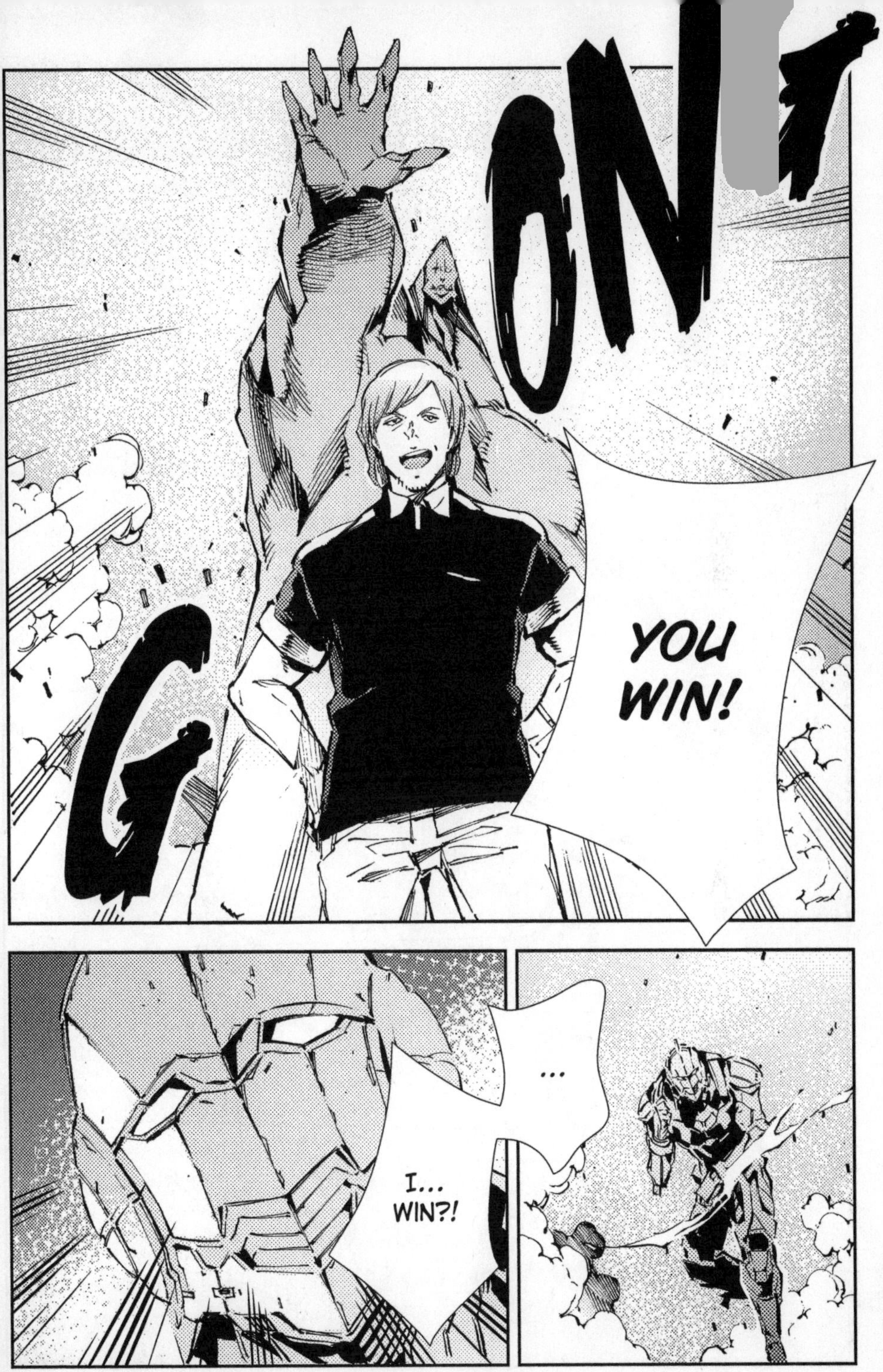
GON
YOU WIN!
...
I... WIN?!

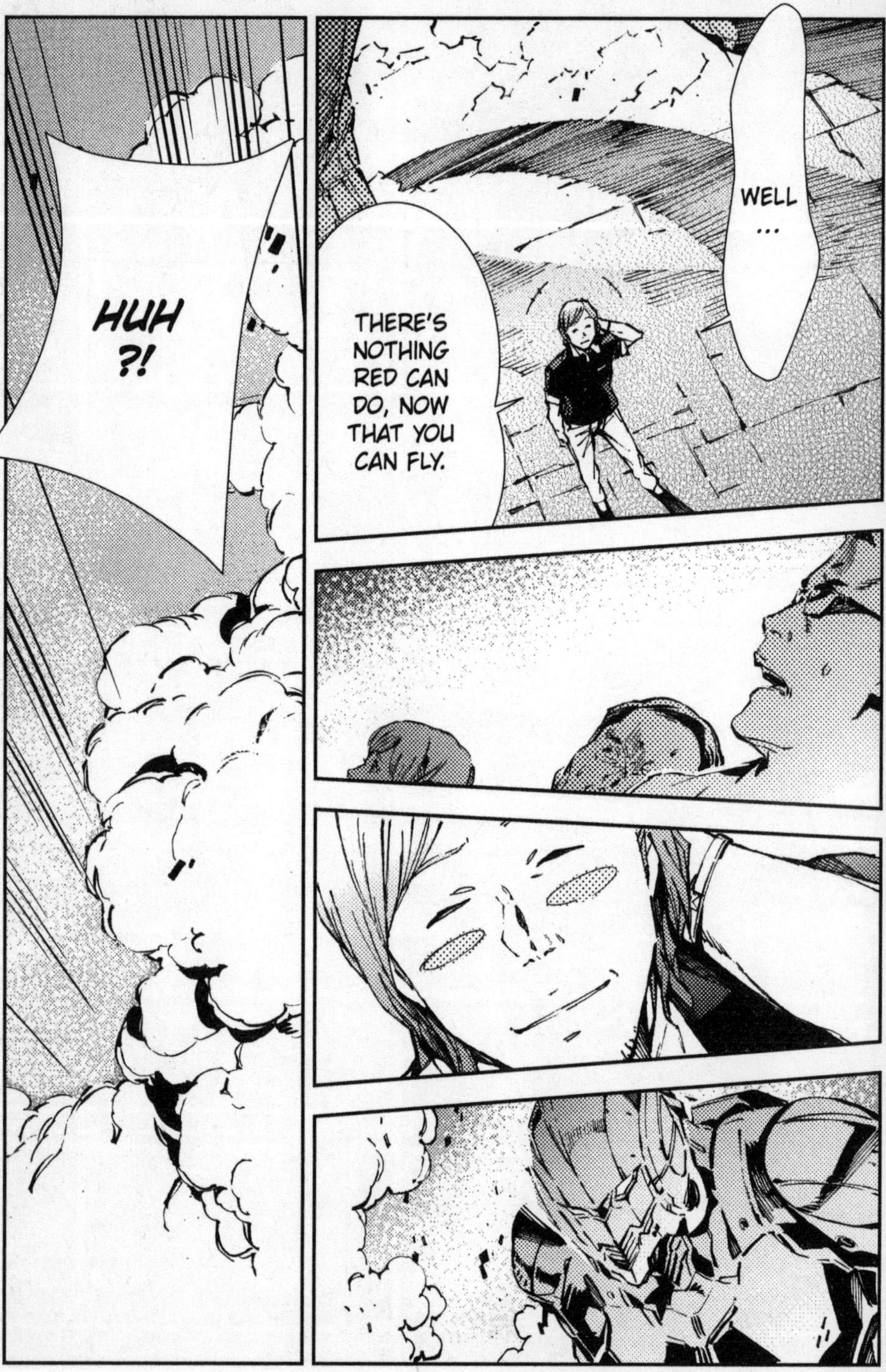
WELL ...
THERE'S NOTHING RED CAN DO, NOW THAT YOU CAN FLY.
HUH ?!

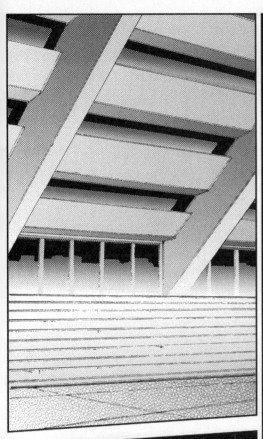

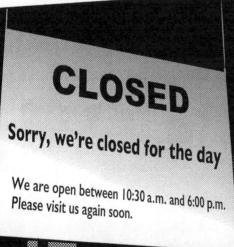

CLOSED

Sorry, we're closed for the day

We are open between 10:30 a.m. and 6:00 p.m.
Please visit us again soon.

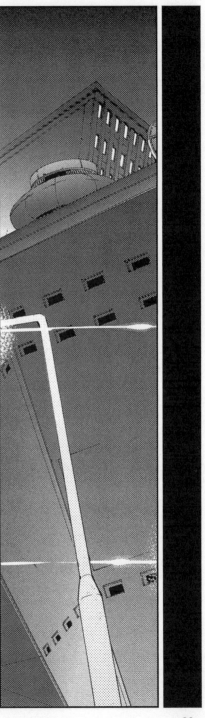

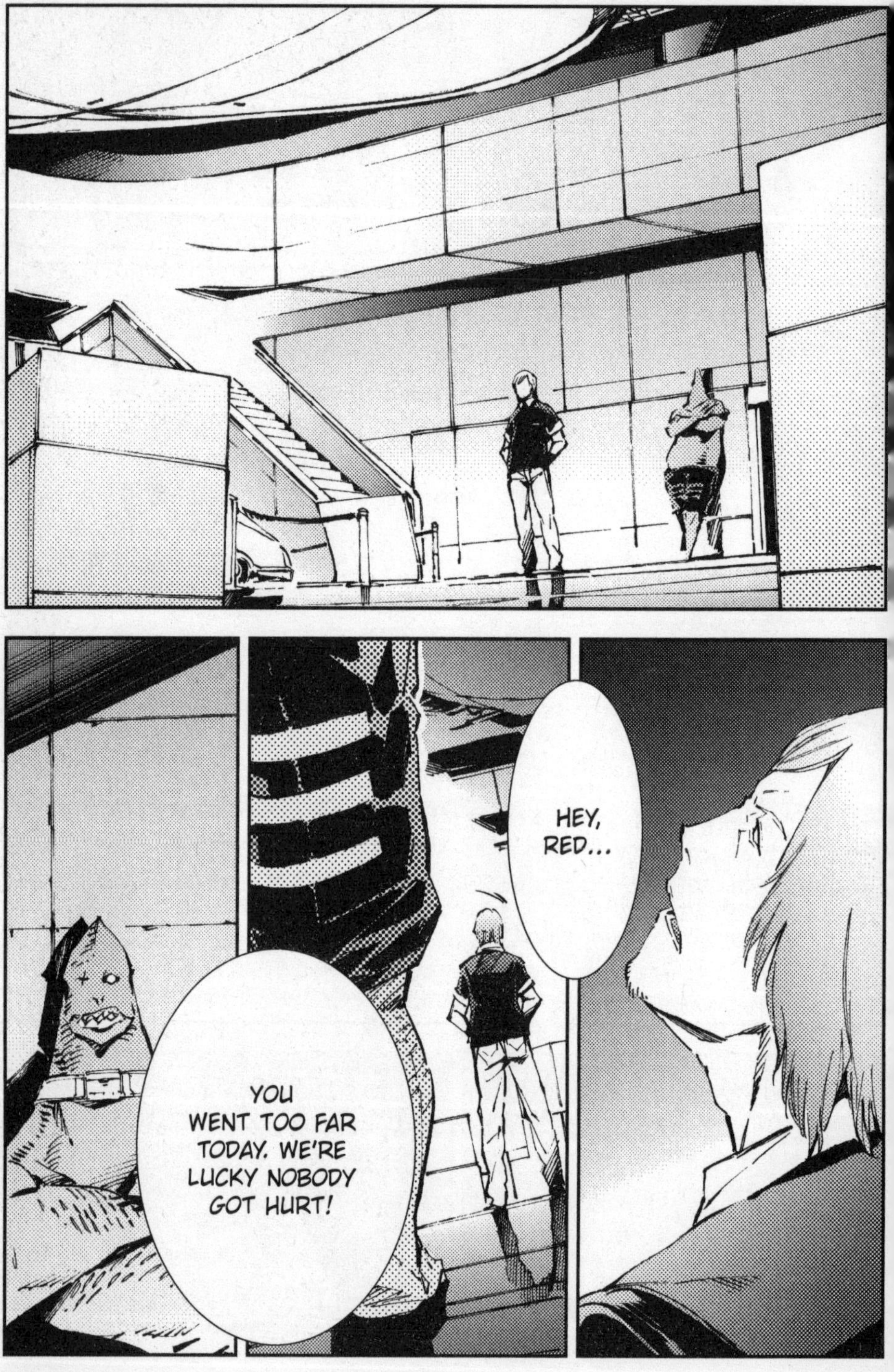
HEY, RED...
YOU WENT TOO FAR TODAY. WE'RE LUCKY NOBODY GOT HURT!

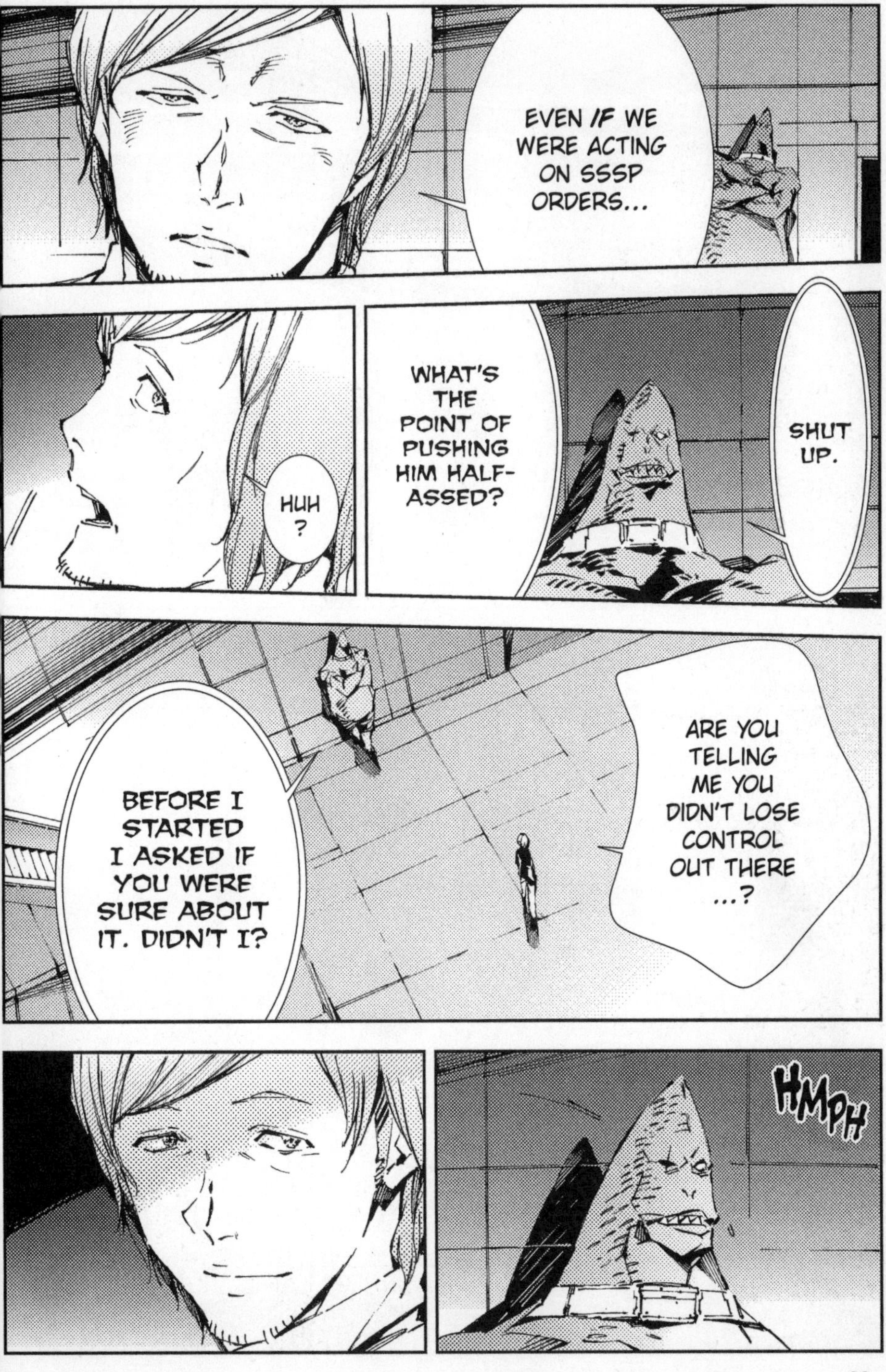
EVEN *IF* WE WERE ACTING ON SSSP ORDERS...
SHUT UP.
WHAT'S THE POINT OF PUSHING HIM HALF-ASSED?
HUH?
ARE YOU TELLING ME YOU DIDN'T LOSE CONTROL OUT THERE ...?
BEFORE I STARTED I ASKED IF YOU WERE SURE ABOUT IT. DIDN'T I?
HMPH

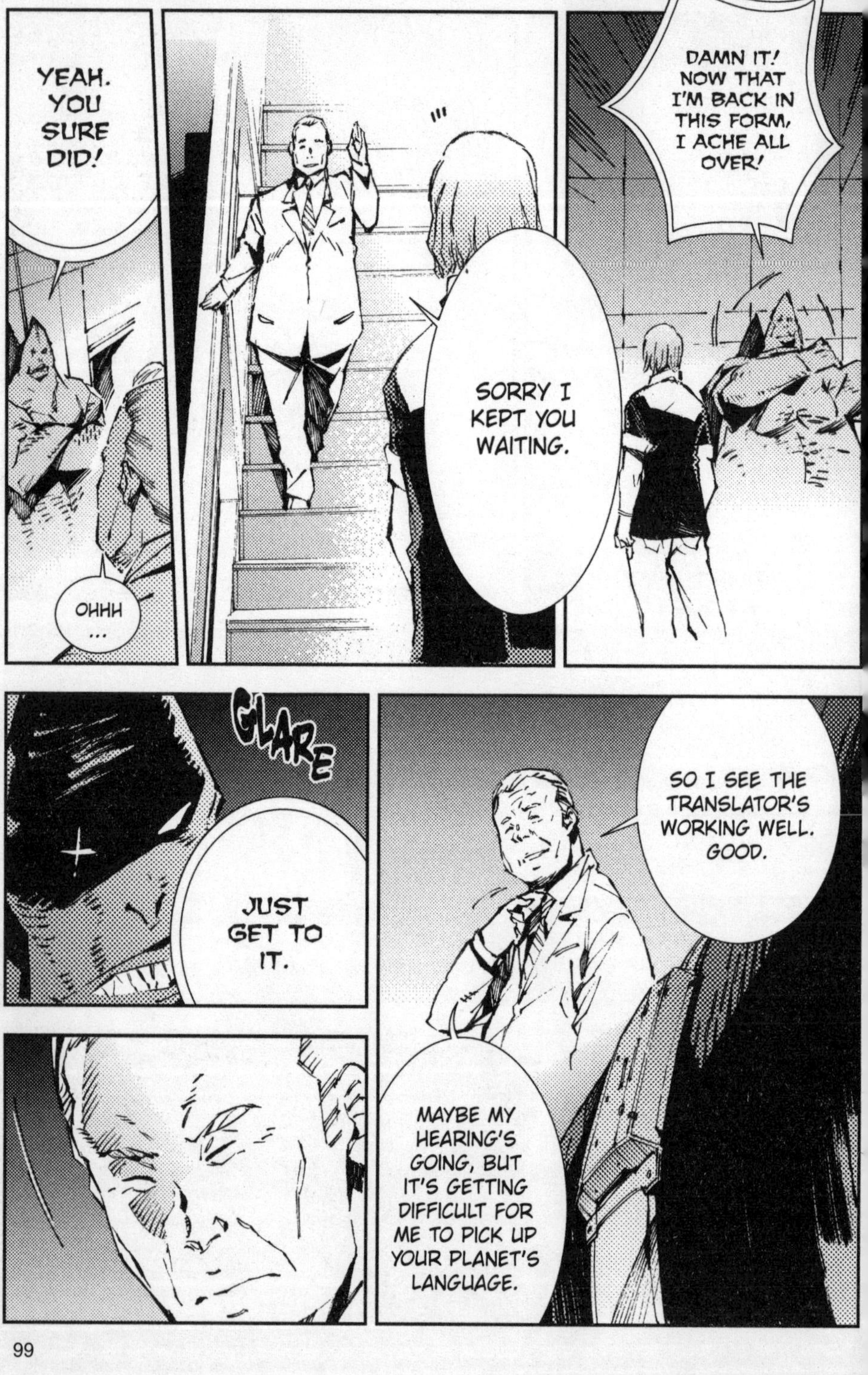
DAMN IT! NOW THAT I'M BACK IN THIS FORM, I ACHE ALL OVER!
'''
SORRY I KEPT YOU WAITING.
YEAH. YOU SURE DID!
OHHH ...
SO I SEE THE TRANSLATOR'S WORKING WELL. GOOD.
GLARE
JUST GET TO IT.
MAYBE MY HEARING'S GOING, BUT IT'S GETTING DIFFICULT FOR ME TO PICK UP YOUR PLANET'S LANGUAGE.

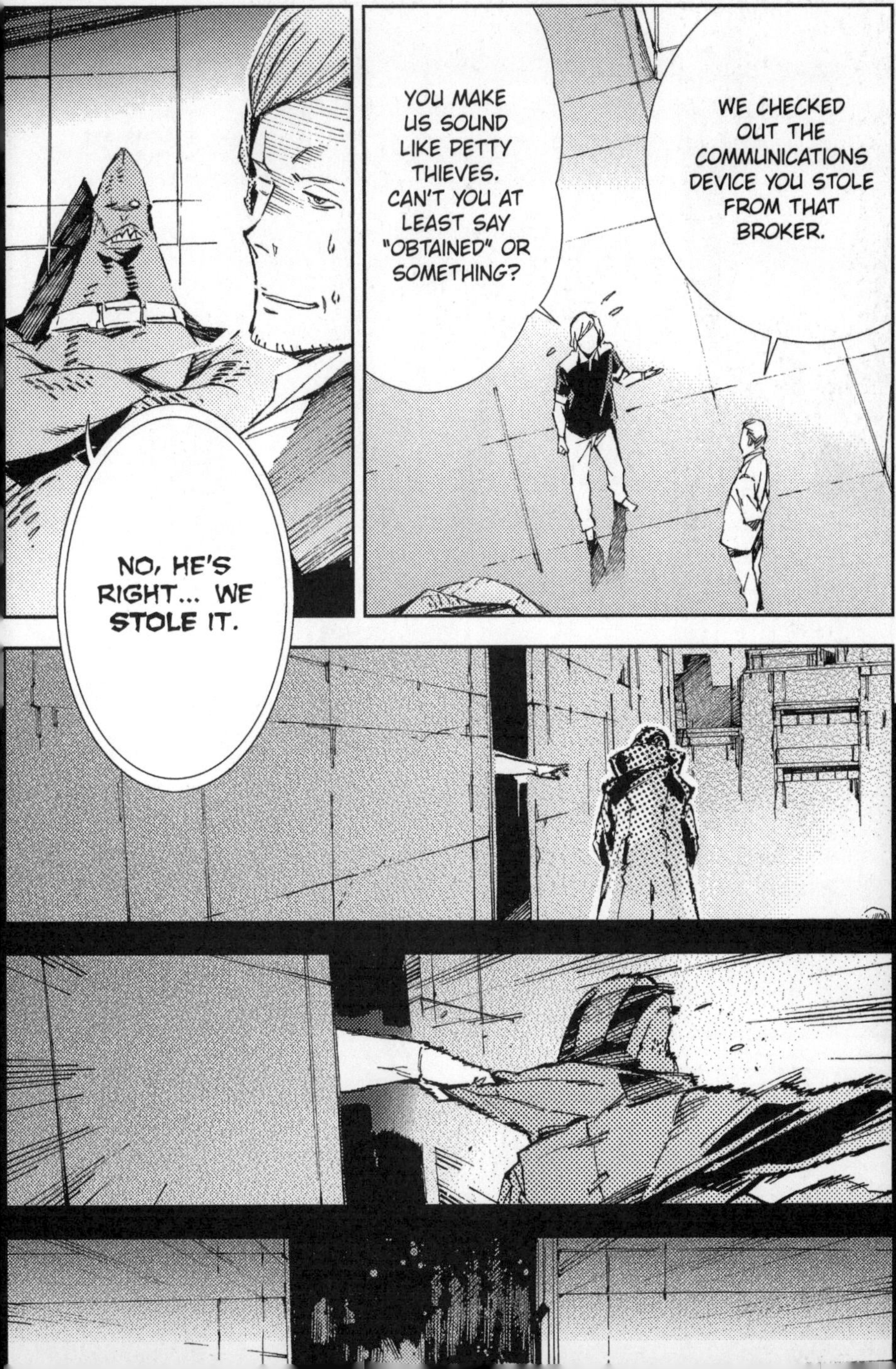
WE CHECKED OUT THE COMMUNICATIONS DEVICE YOU STOLE FROM THAT BROKER.
YOU MAKE US SOUND LIKE PETTY THIEVES. CAN'T YOU AT LEAST SAY "OBTAINED" OR SOMETHING?
NO, HE'S RIGHT... WE STOLE IT.

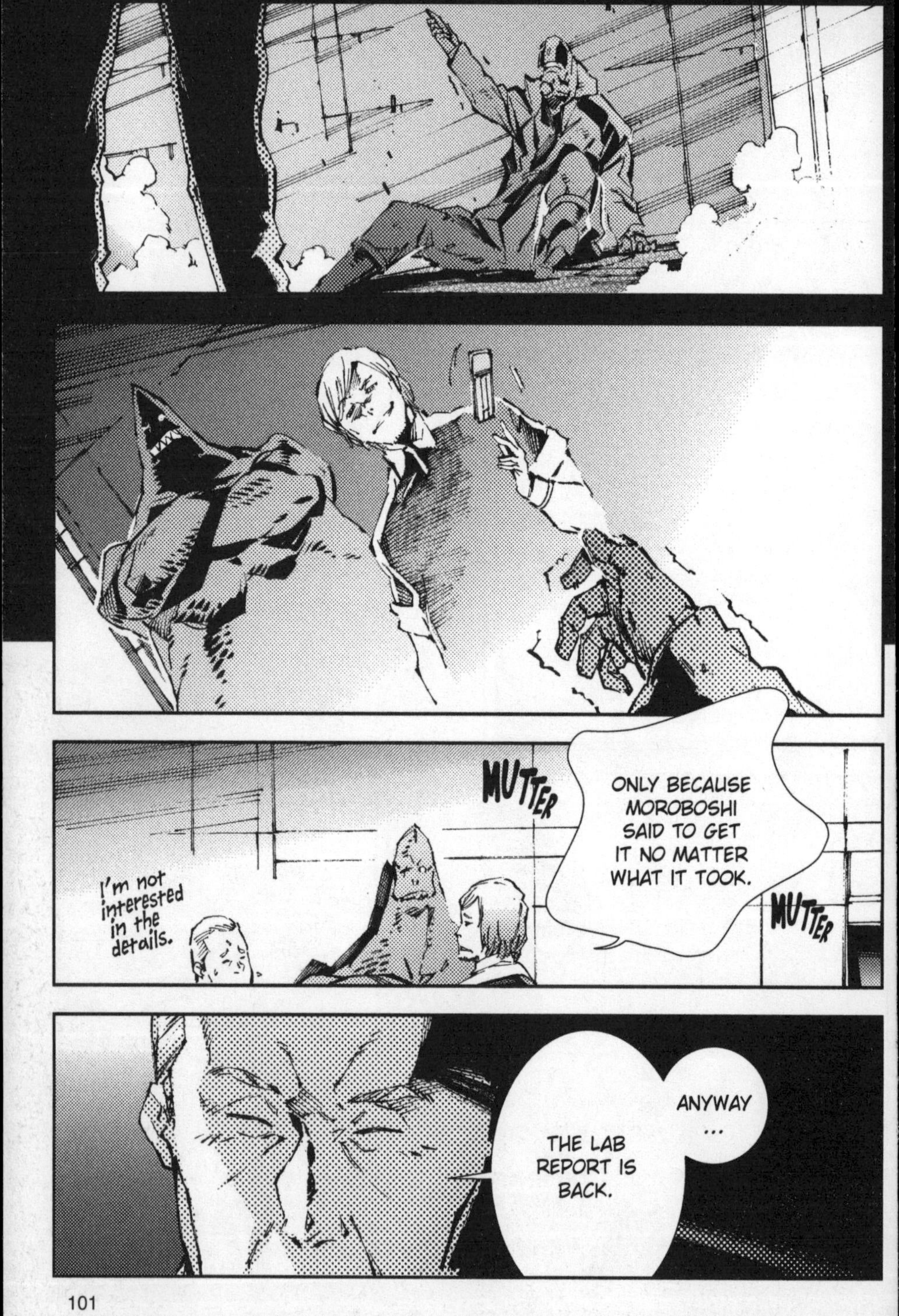
MUTTER
ONLY BECAUSE MOROBOSHI SAID TO GET IT NO MATTER WHAT IT TOOK.
MUTTER
I'm not interested in the details.
ANYWAY ...
THE LAB REPORT IS BACK.

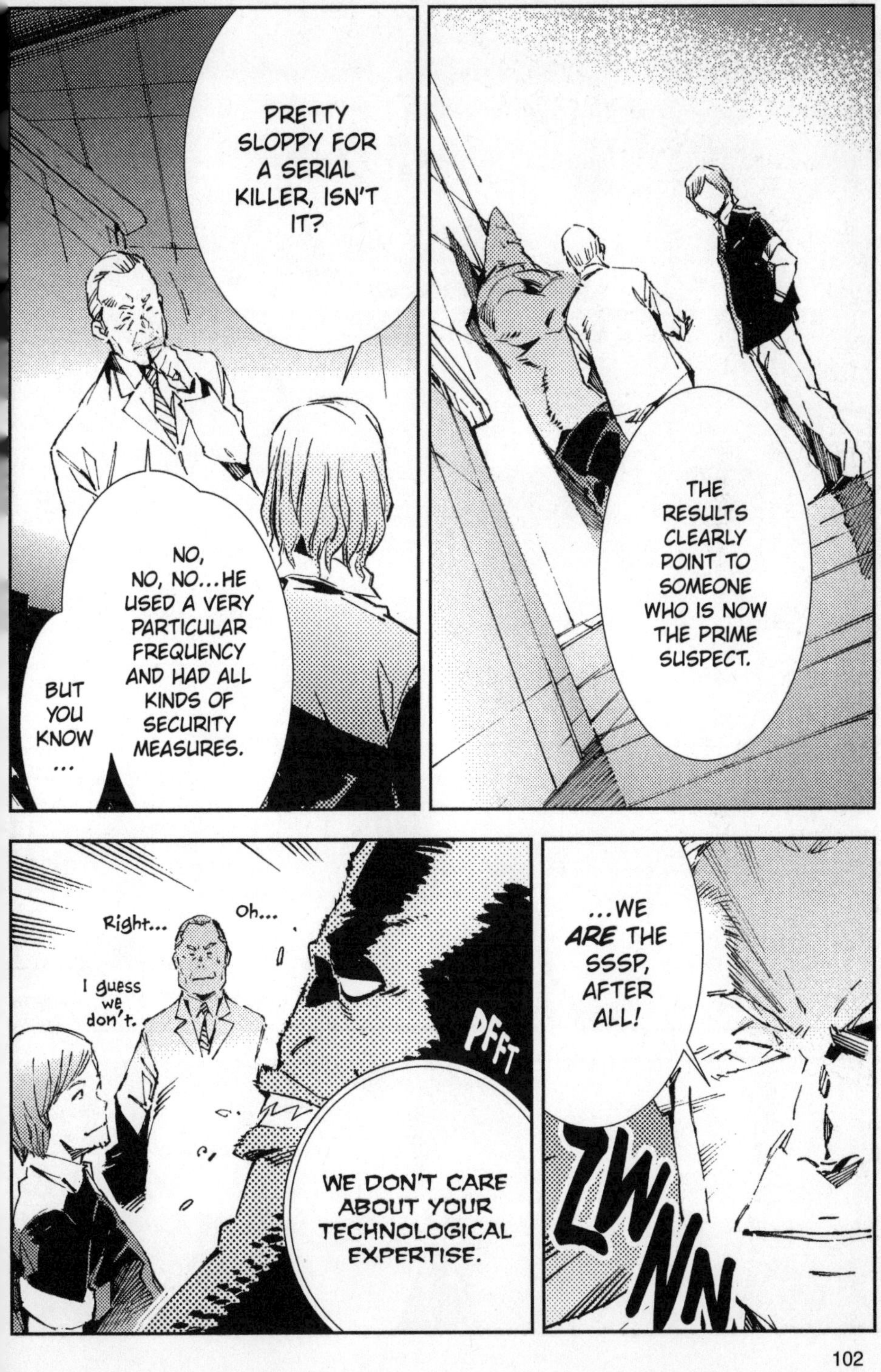
THE RESULTS CLEARLY POINT TO SOMEONE WHO IS NOW THE PRIME SUSPECT.
PRETTY SLOPPY FOR A SERIAL KILLER, ISN'T IT?
NO, NO, NO...HE USED A VERY PARTICULAR FREQUENCY AND HAD ALL KINDS OF SECURITY MEASURES.
BUT YOU KNOW...
...WE ARE THE SSSP, AFTER ALL!
ZWNNN
PFFT
Oh...
Right...
I guess we don't.
WE DON'T CARE ABOUT YOUR TECHNOLOGICAL EXPERTISE.

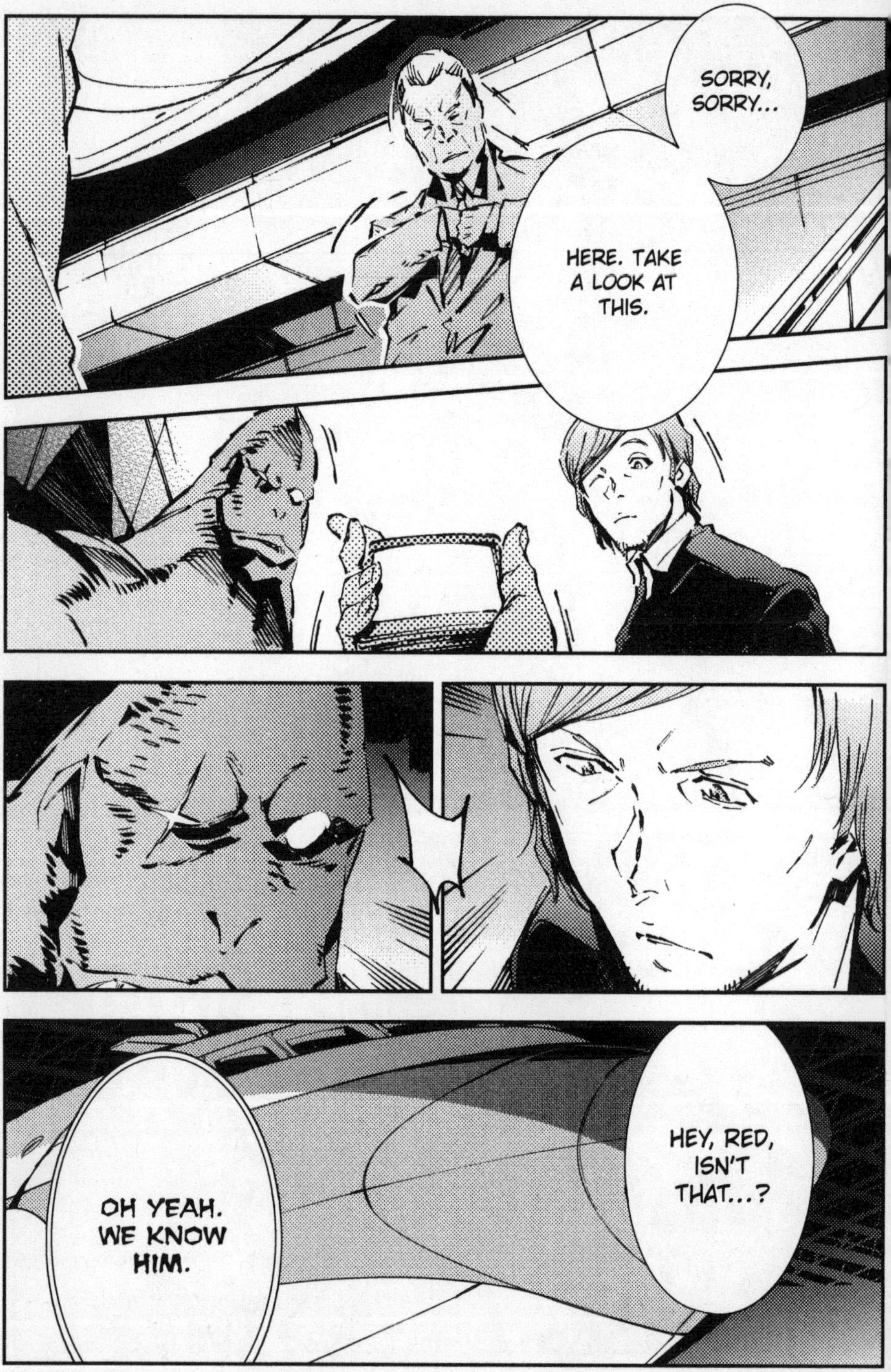
SORRY, SORRY...
HERE. TAKE A LOOK AT THIS.
HEY, RED, ISN'T THAT...?
OH YEAH. WE KNOW HIM.

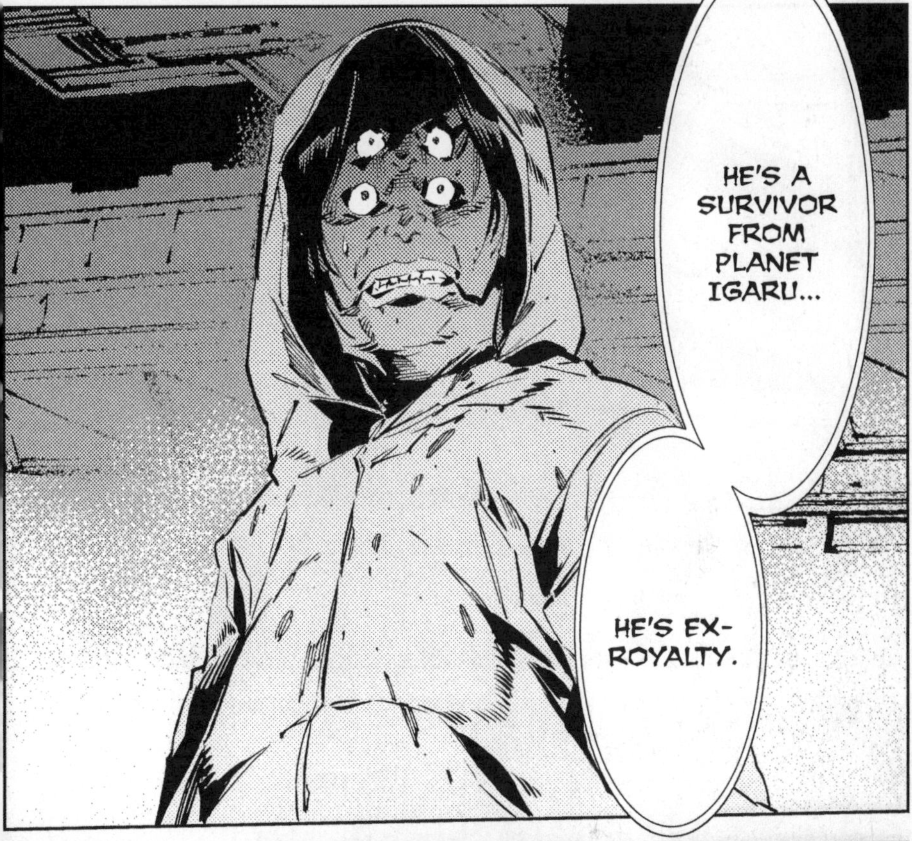
HE'S A SURVIVOR FROM PLANET IGARU...
HE'S EX-ROYALTY.
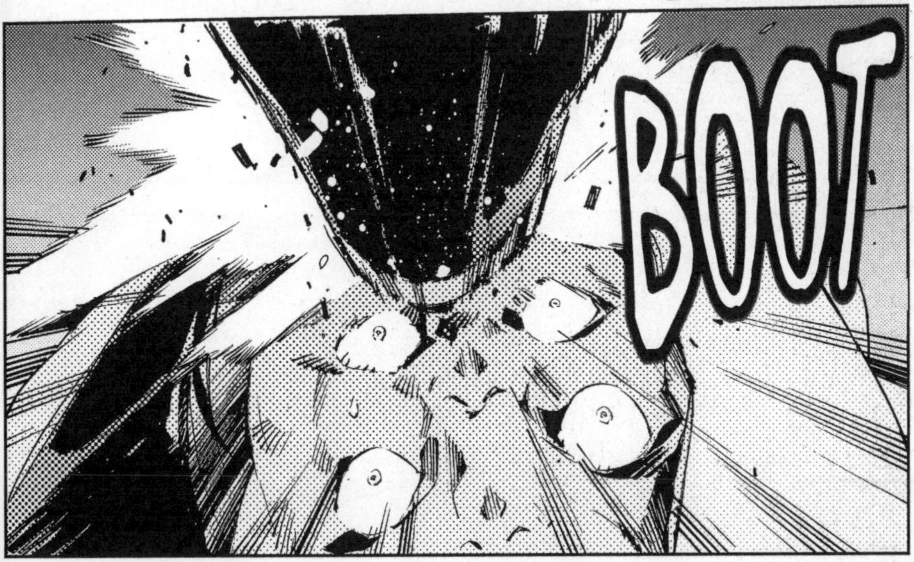
BOOT

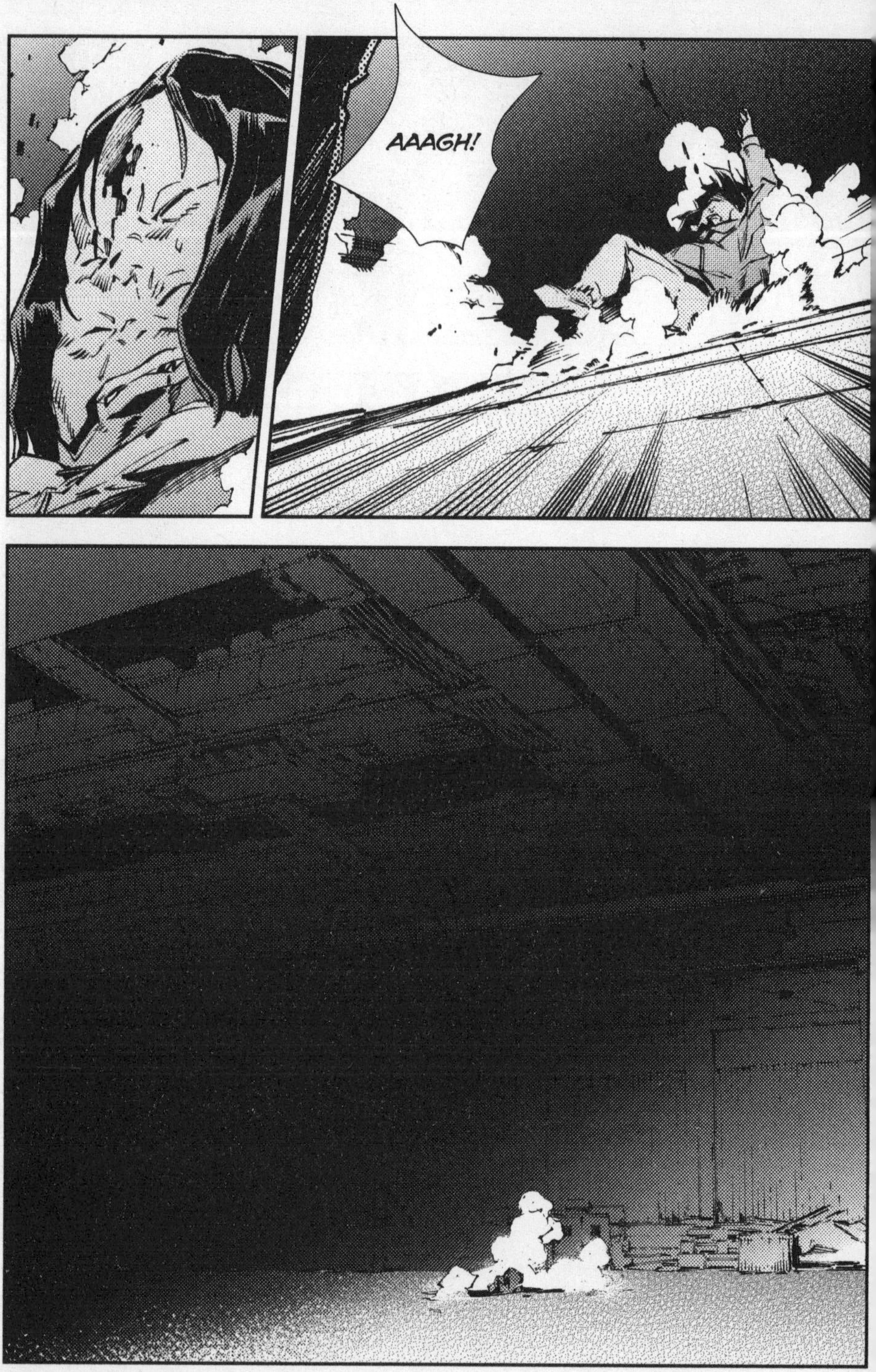
AAAGH!

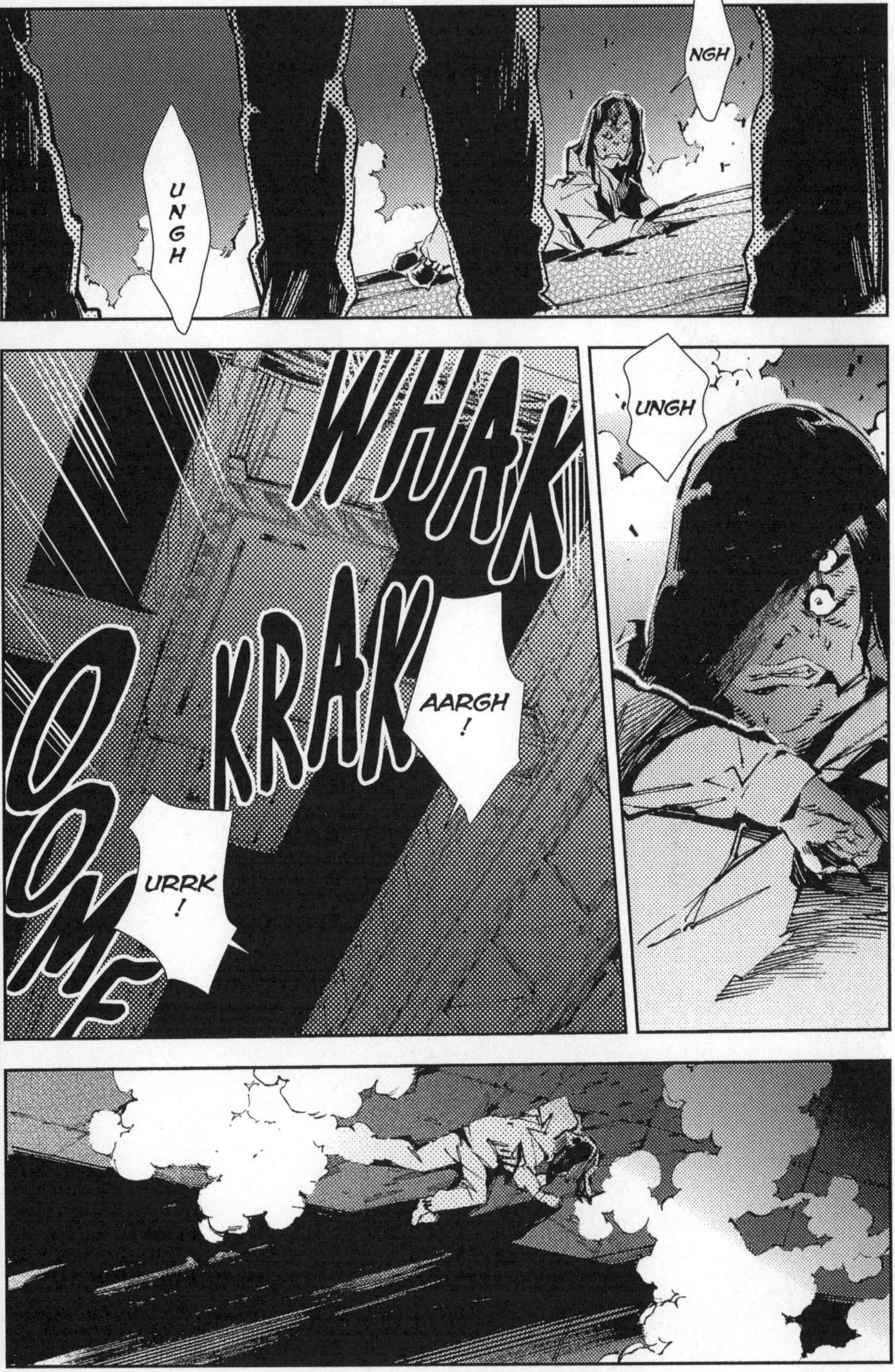
NGH
UNGH
UNGH
WHAK
AARGH!
KRAK
OOMF
URRK!

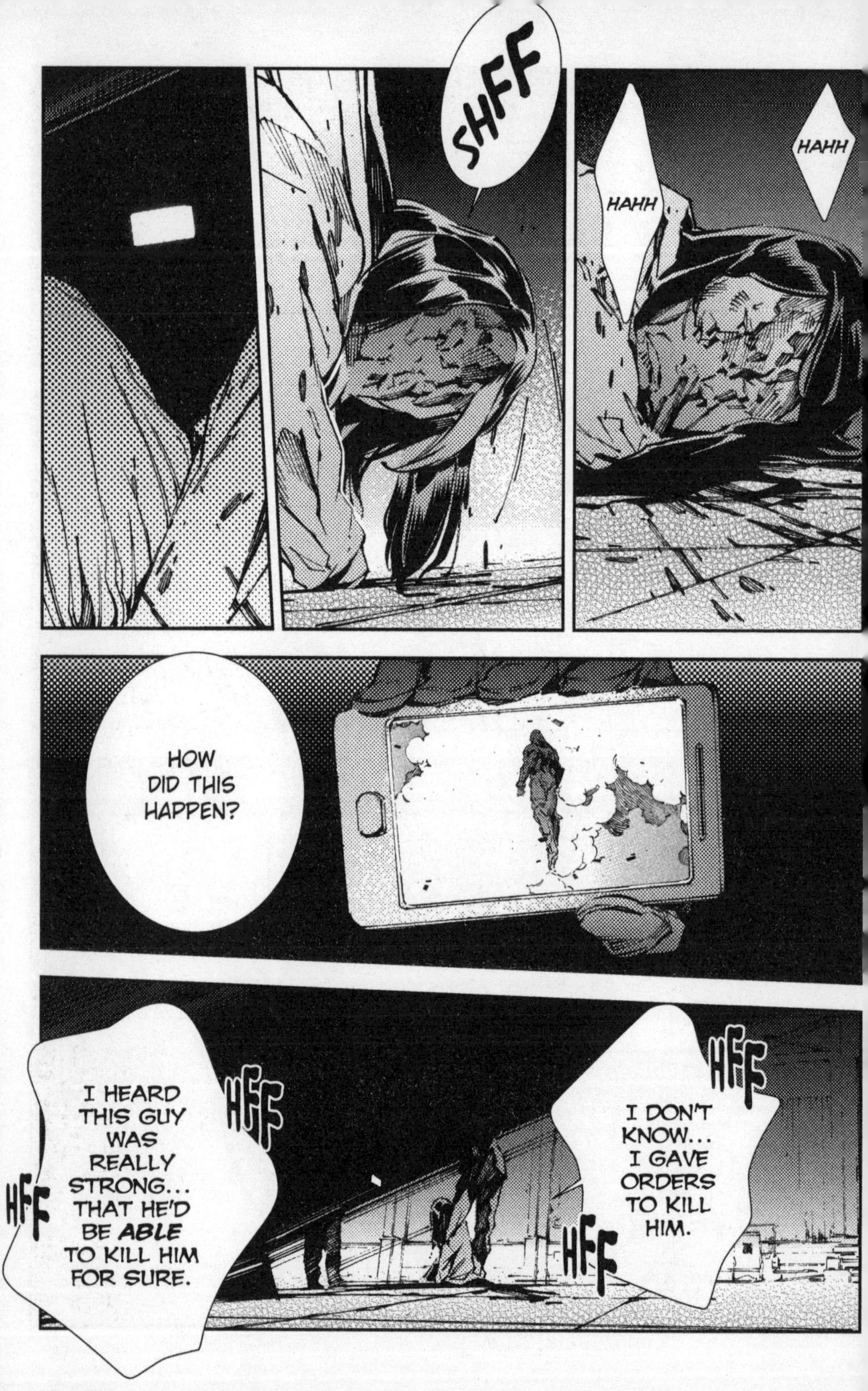
HAHH
HAHH
SHFF
HOW DID THIS HAPPEN?
HFF
I DON'T KNOW… I GAVE ORDERS TO KILL HIM.
HFF
HFF
I HEARD THIS GUY WAS REALLY STRONG… THAT HE'D BE *ABLE* TO KILL HIM FOR SURE.
HFF

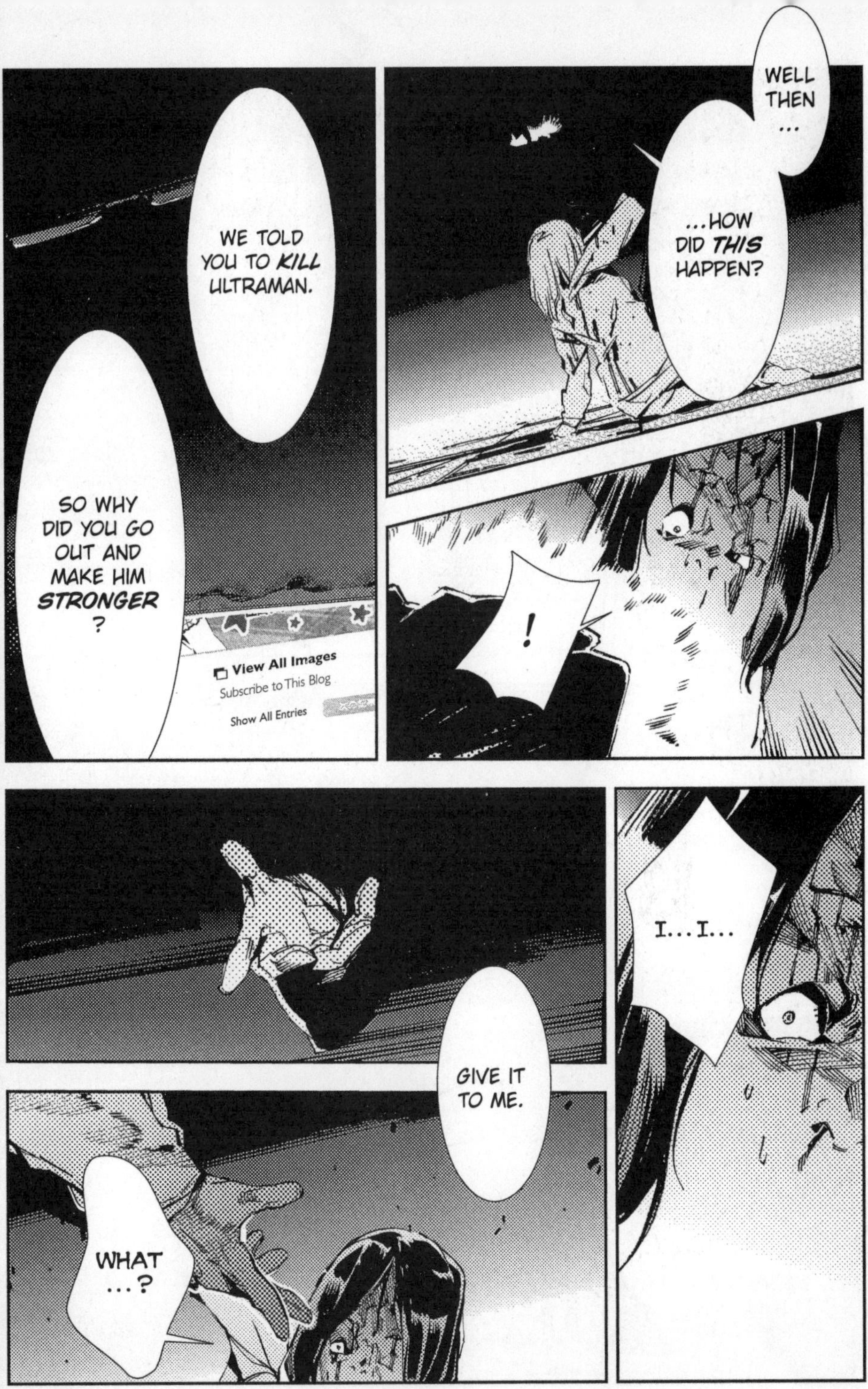
WELL THEN ...
...HOW DID *THIS* HAPPEN?
!
WE TOLD YOU TO *KILL* ULTRAMAN.
SO WHY DID YOU GO OUT AND MAKE HIM *STRONGER* ?
View All Images
Subscribe to This Blog
Show All Entries
I... I...
GIVE IT TO ME.
WHAT ...?

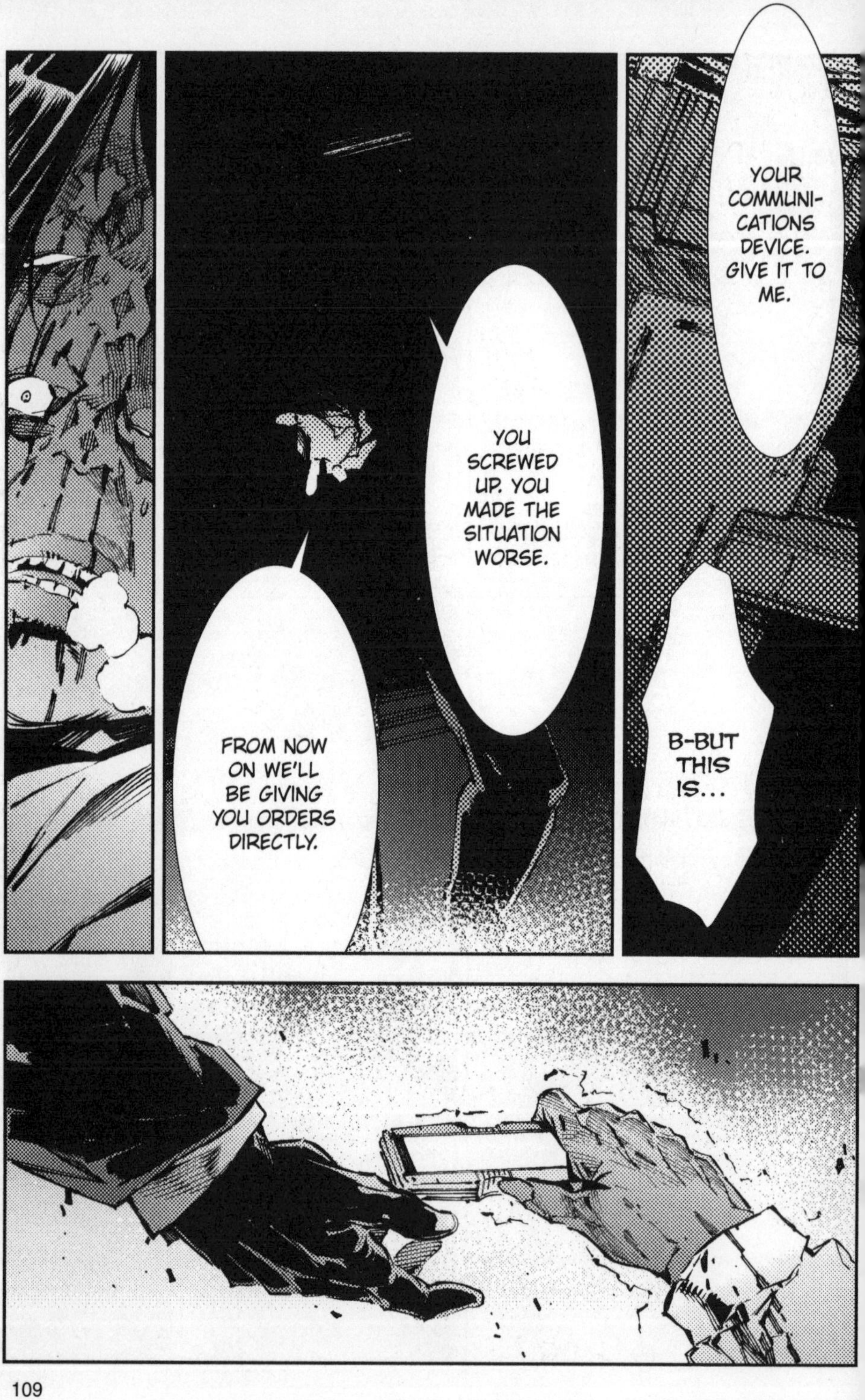
YOUR COMMUNI-CATIONS DEVICE. GIVE IT TO ME.
B-BUT THIS IS...
YOU SCREWED UP. YOU MADE THE SITUATION WORSE.
FROM NOW ON WE'LL BE GIVING YOU ORDERS DIRECTLY.

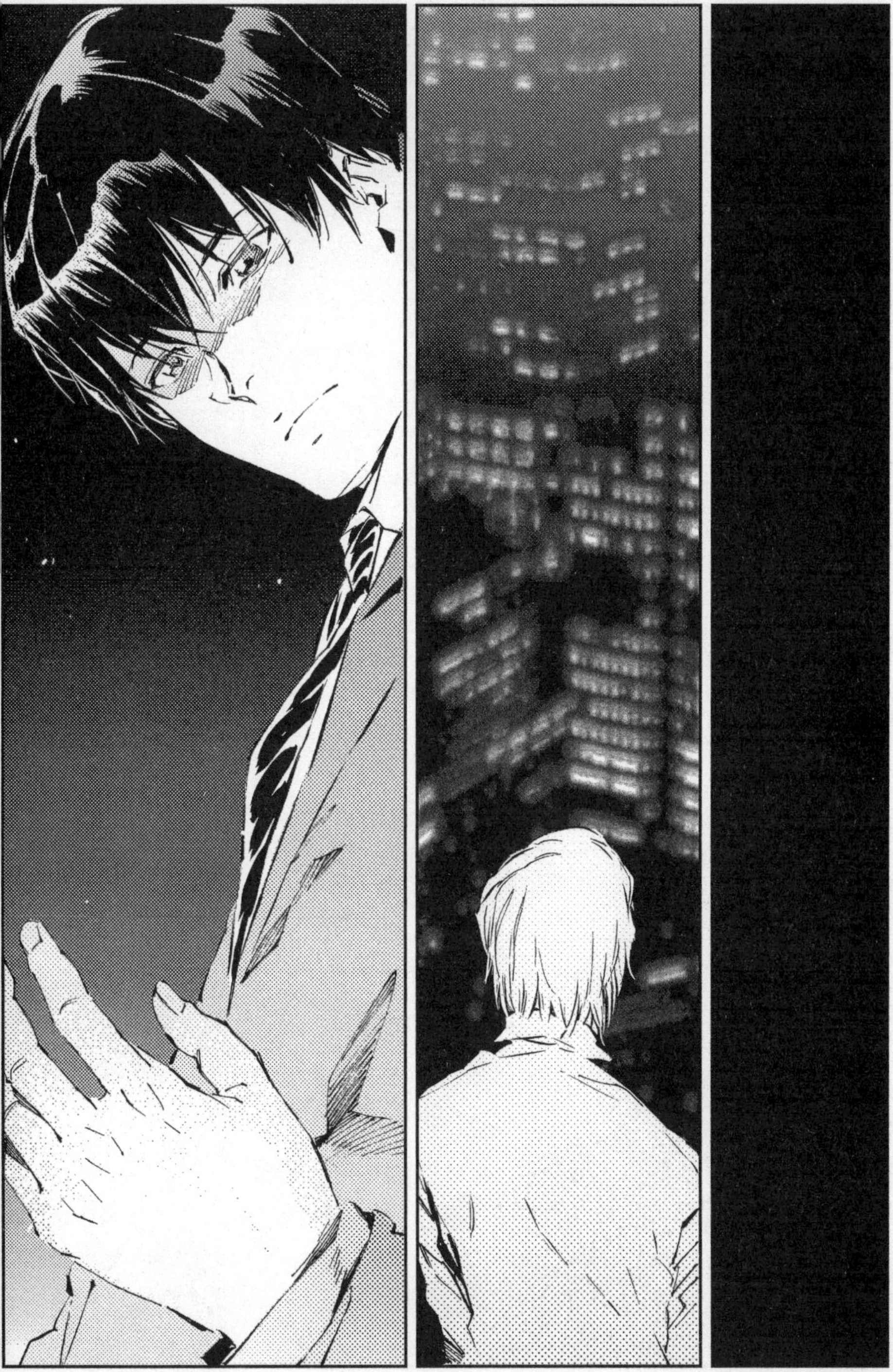

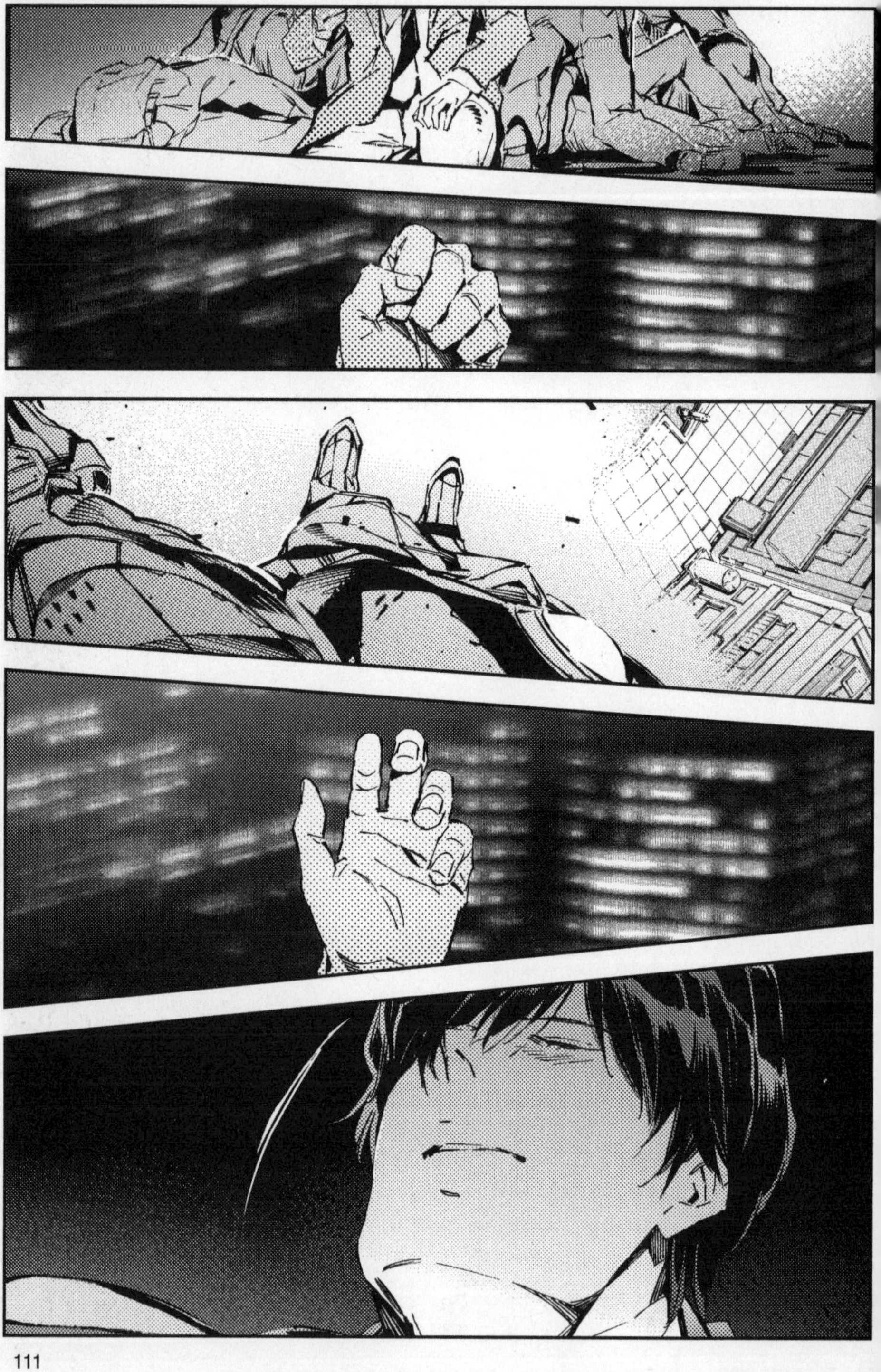

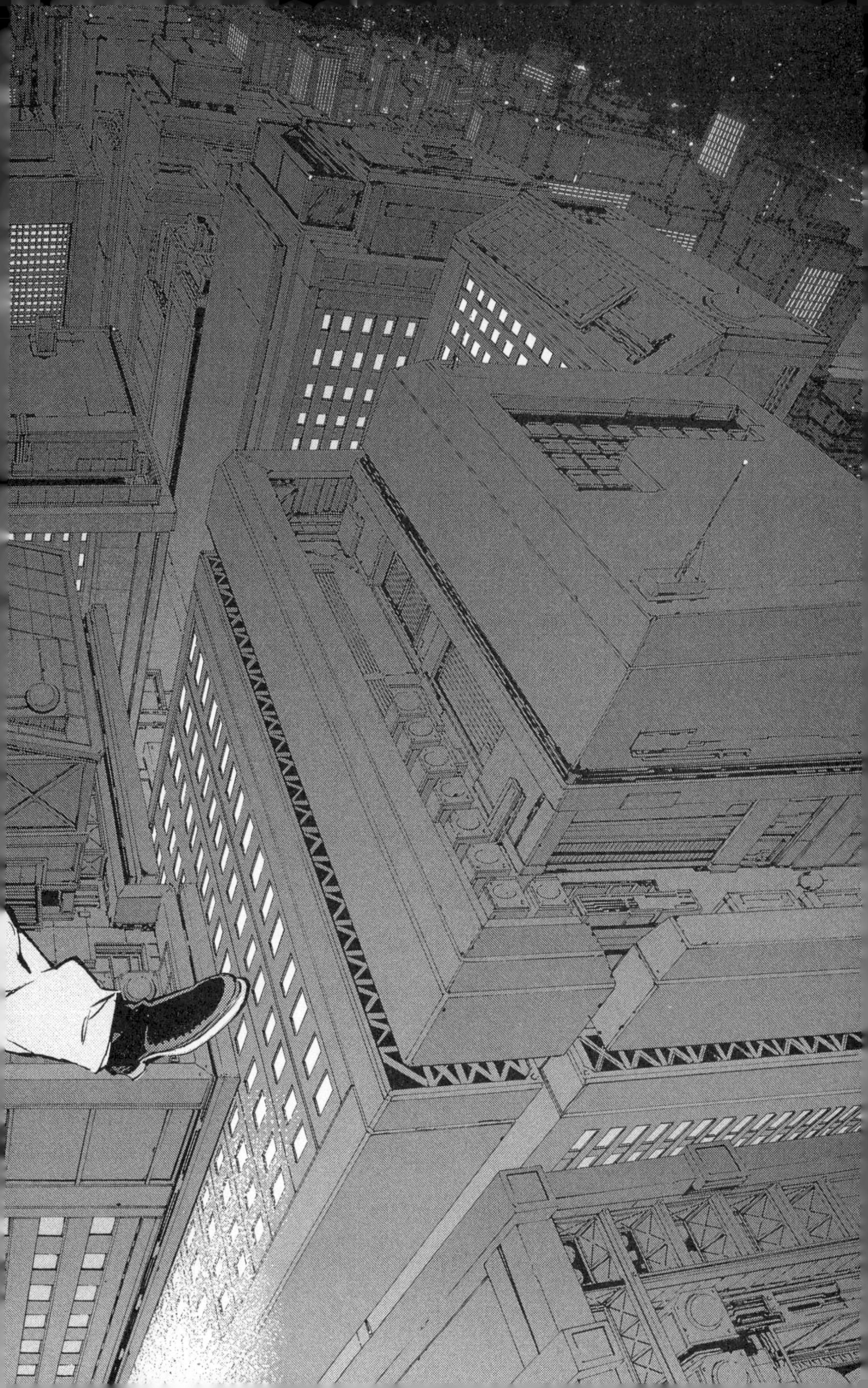

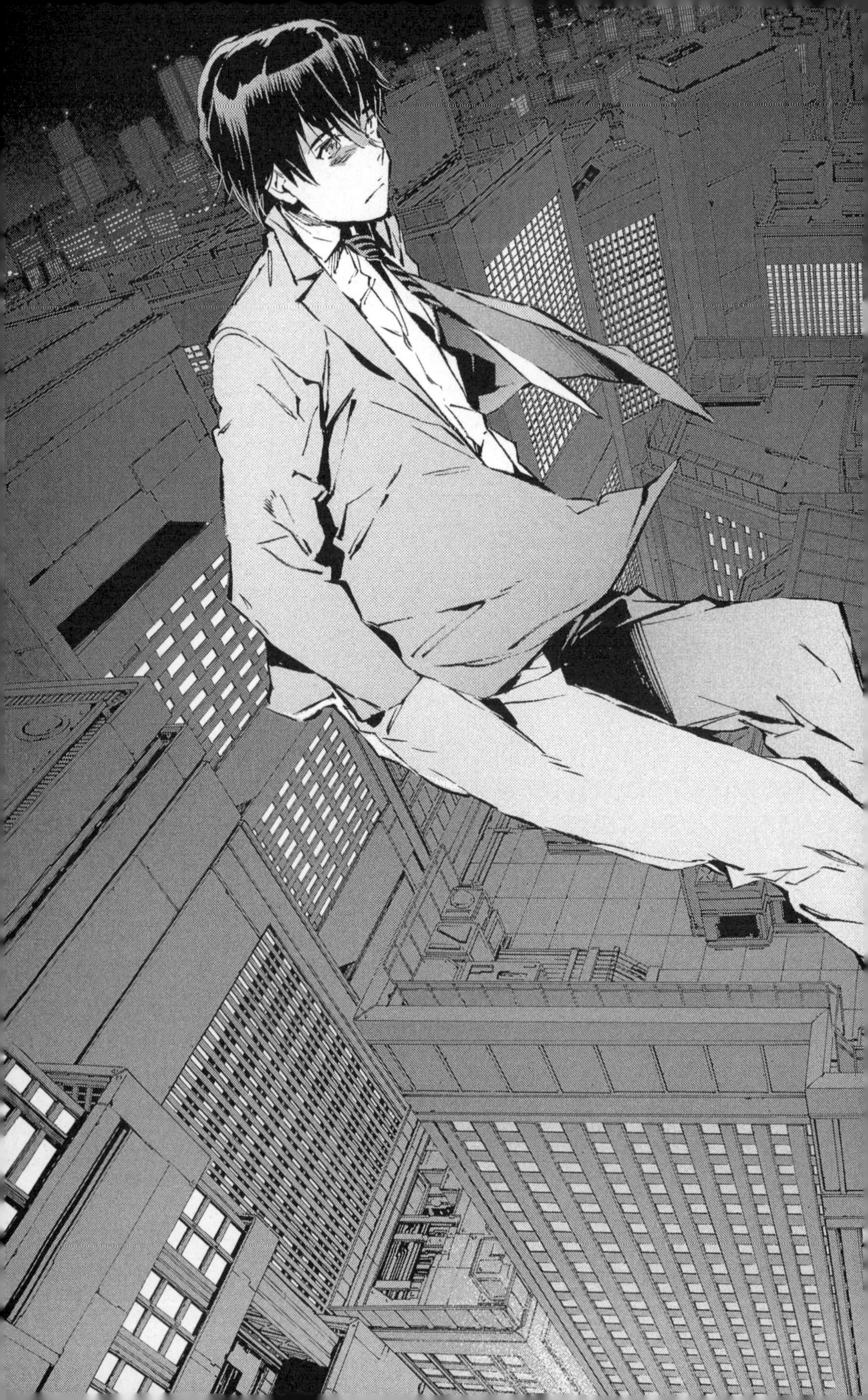

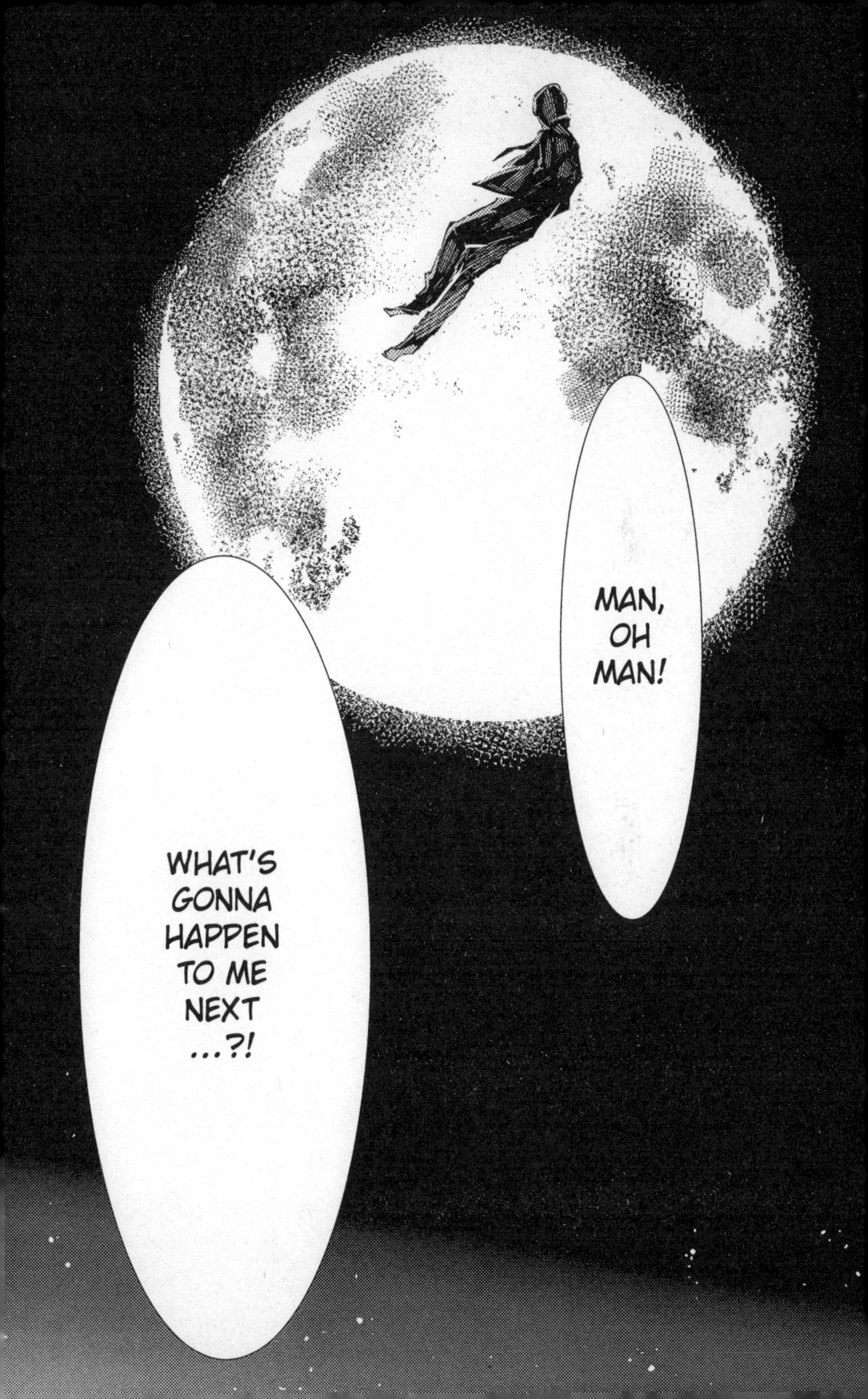
MAN, OH MAN!
WHAT'S GONNA HAPPEN TO ME NEXT ...?!

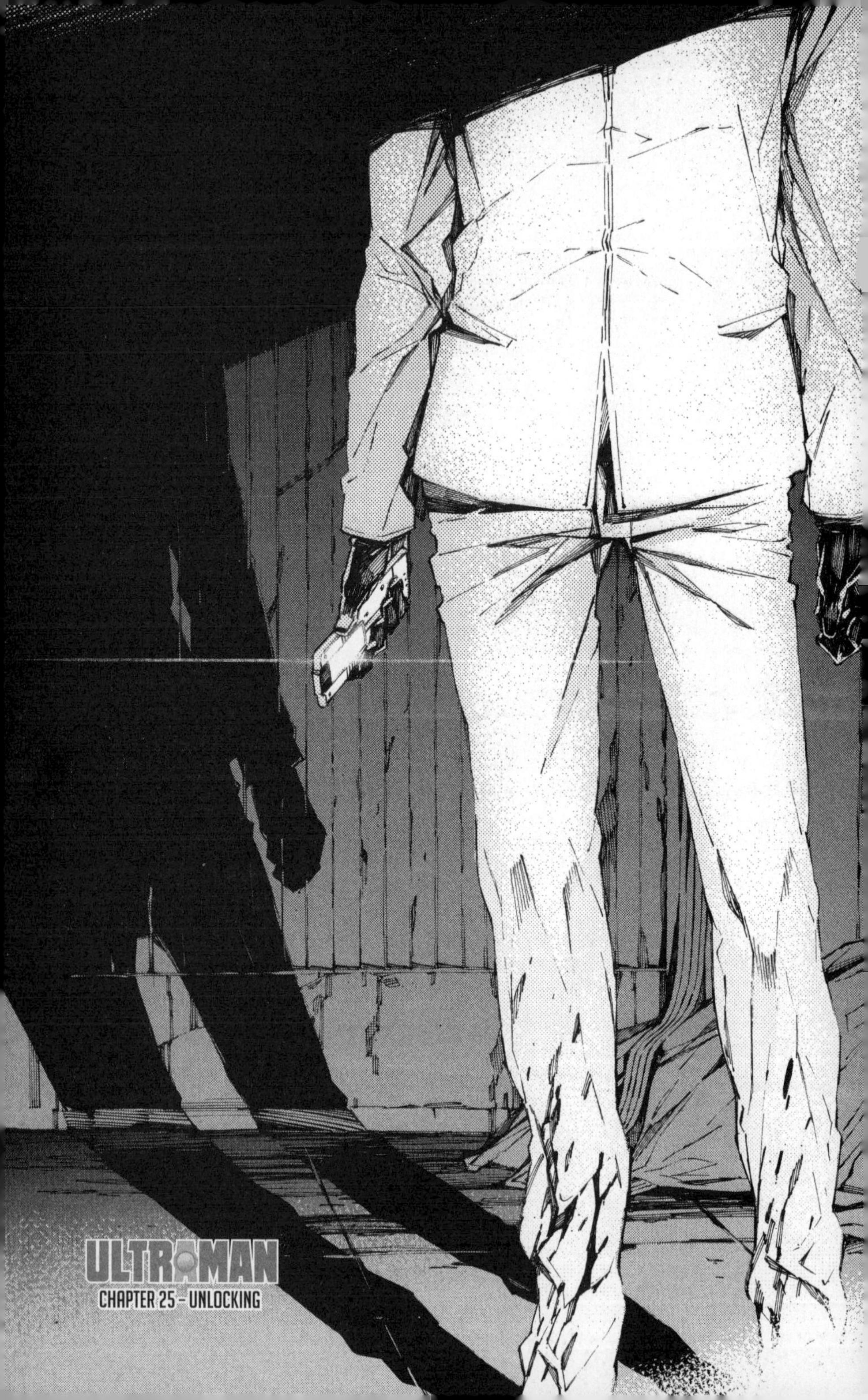
ULTRAMAN
CHAPTER 25 - UNLOCKING

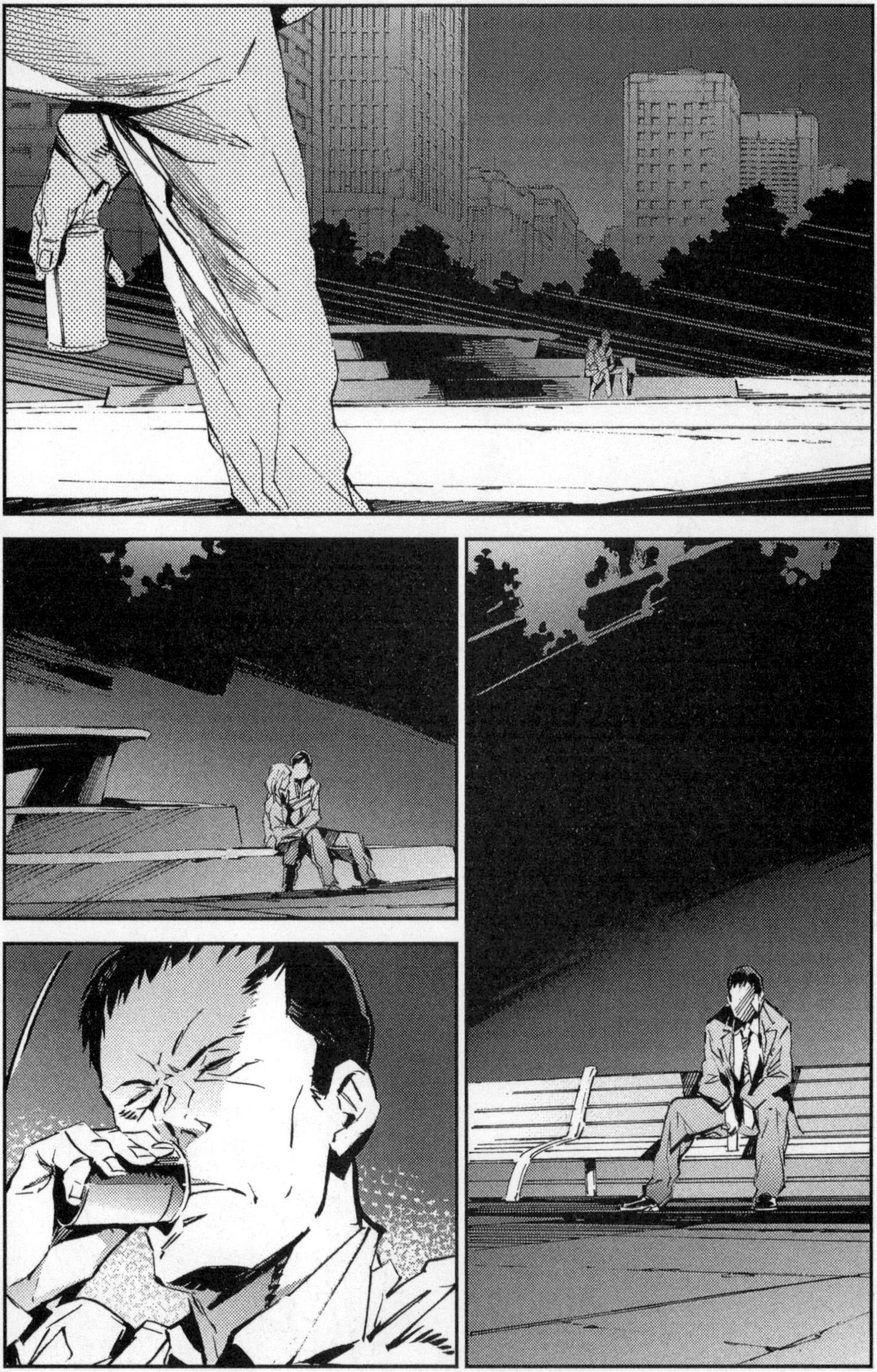

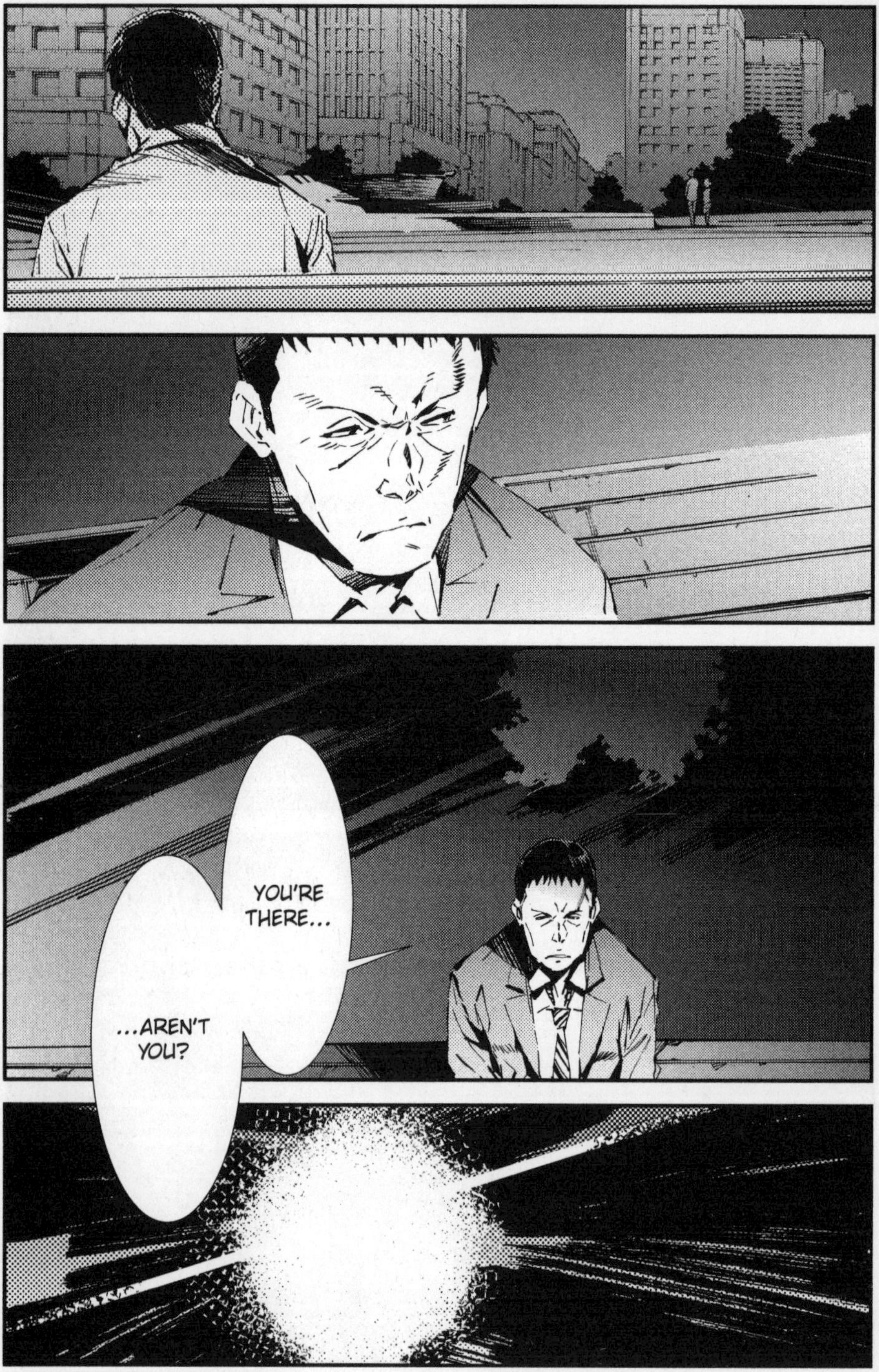
YOU'RE THERE...
...AREN'T YOU?

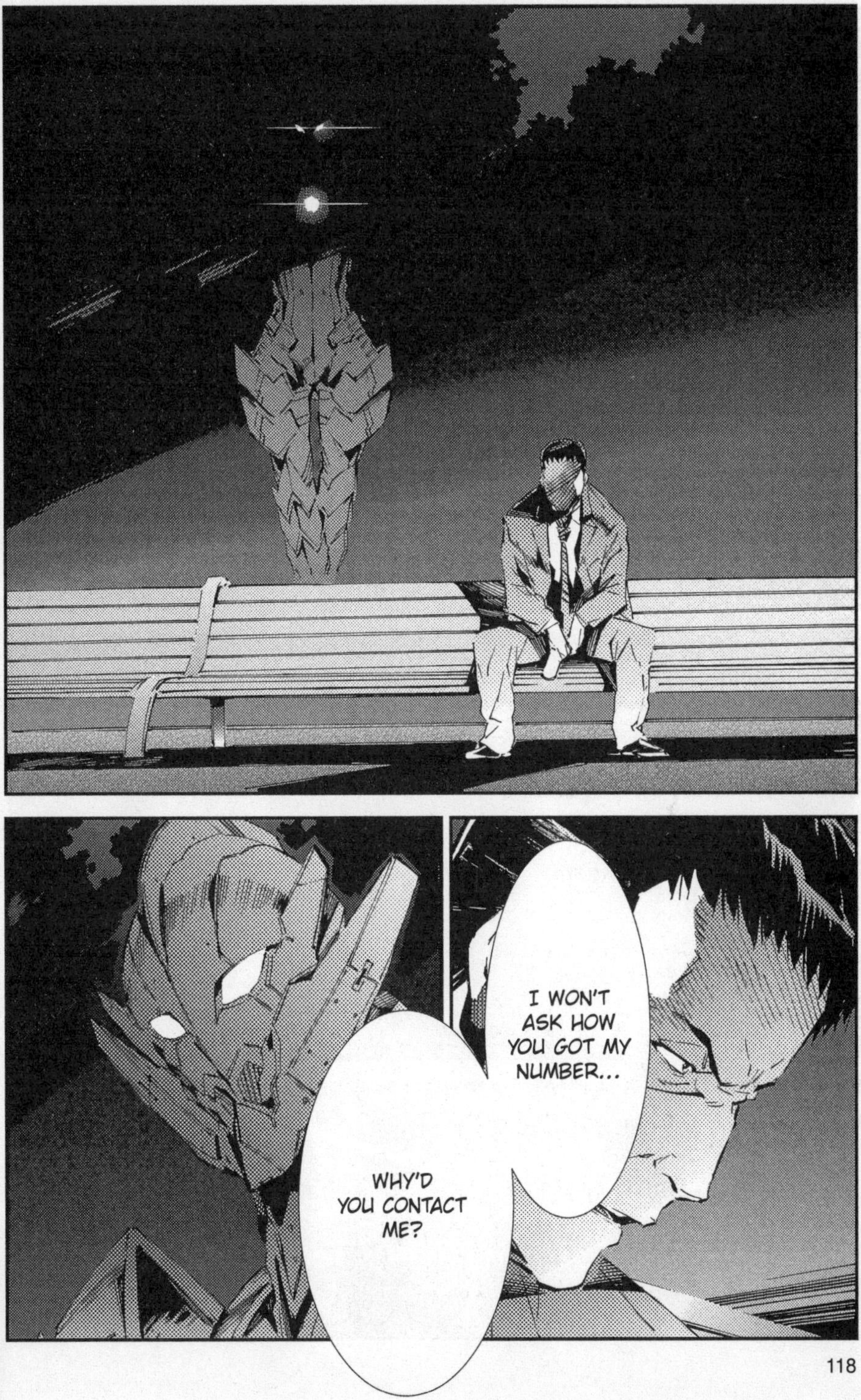
I WON'T ASK HOW YOU GOT MY NUMBER...
WHY'D YOU CONTACT ME?

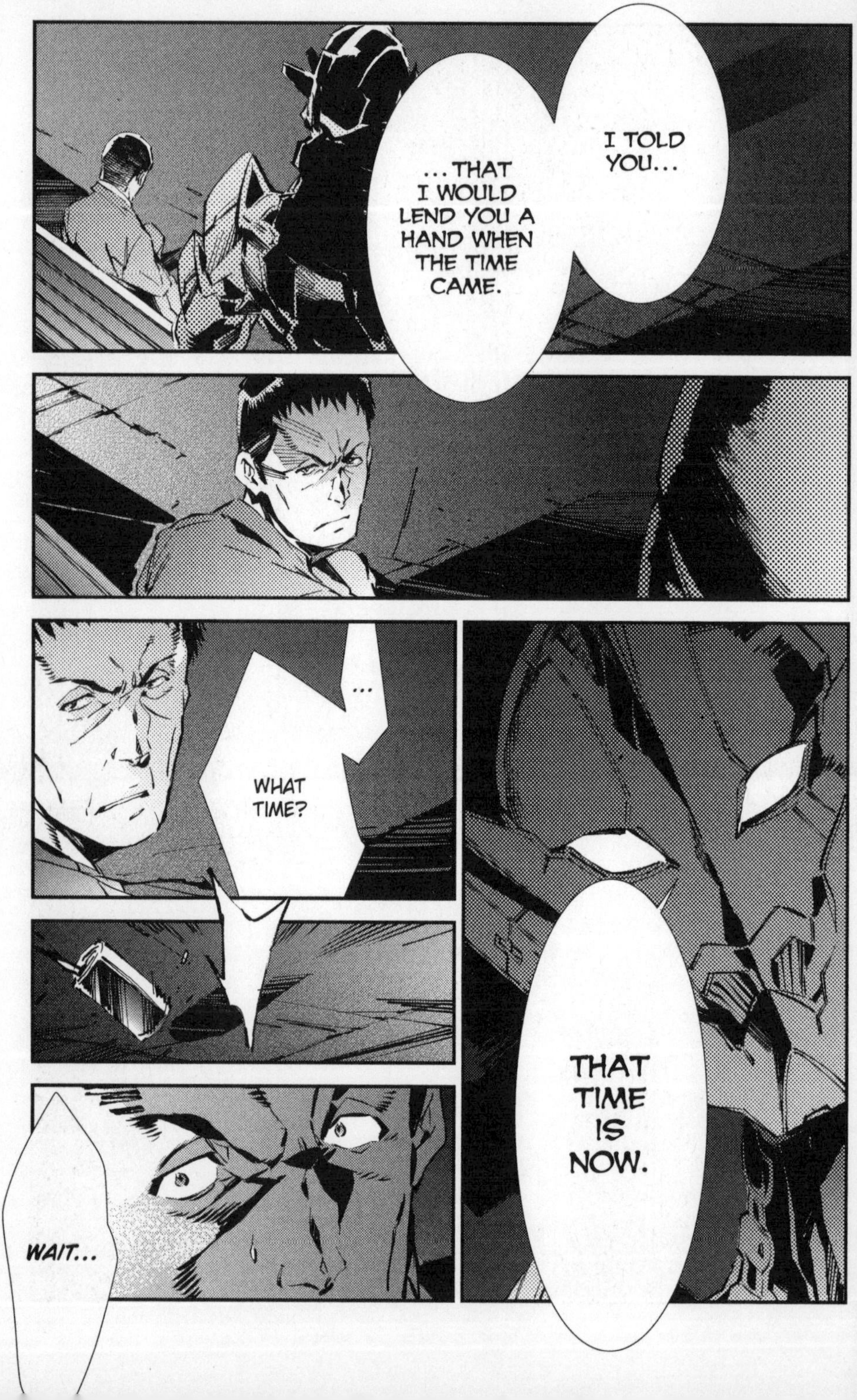
I TOLD YOU...
...THAT I WOULD LEND YOU A HAND WHEN THE TIME CAME.
...
WHAT TIME?
THAT TIME IS NOW.
WAIT...

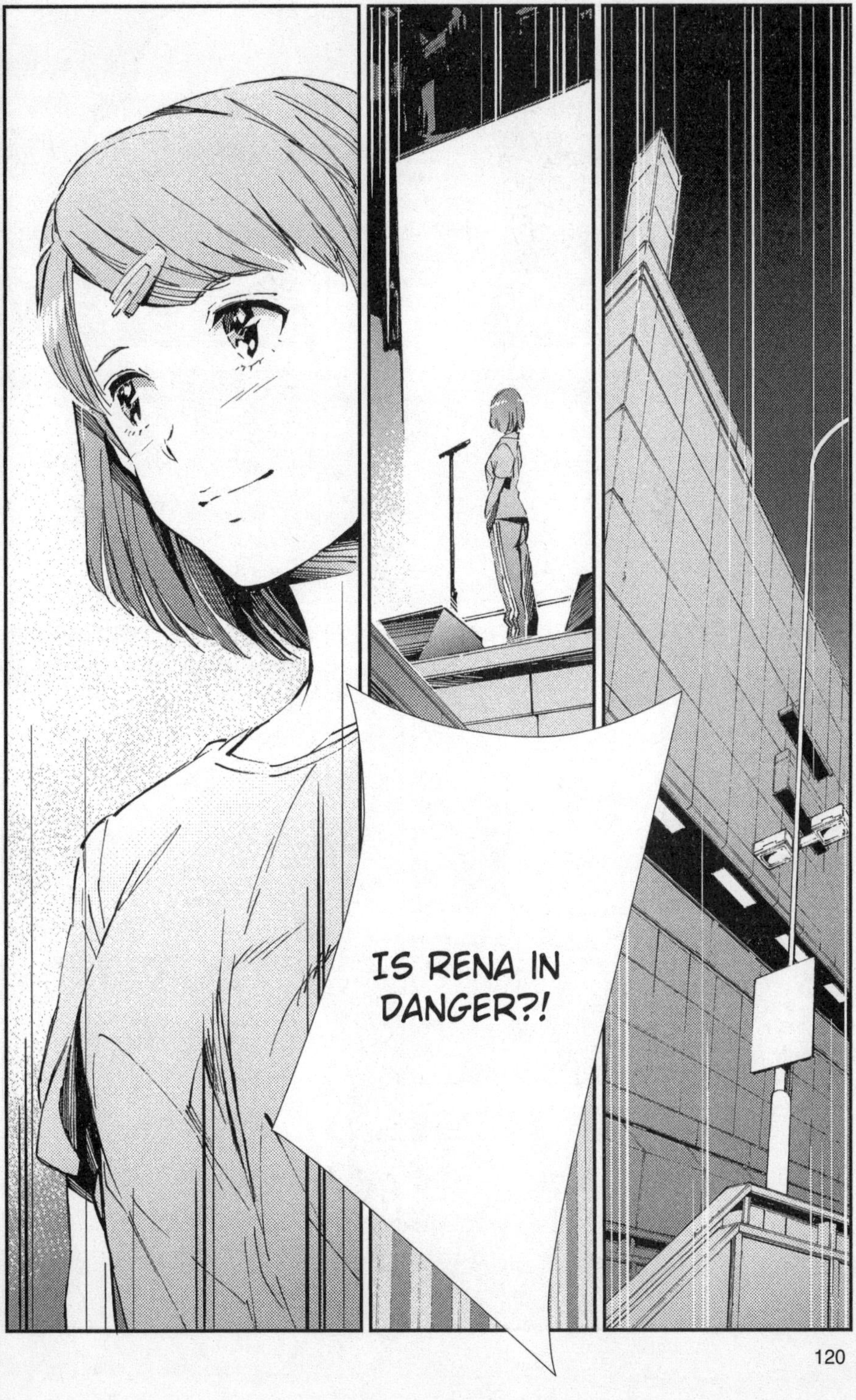
IS RENA IN DANGER?!

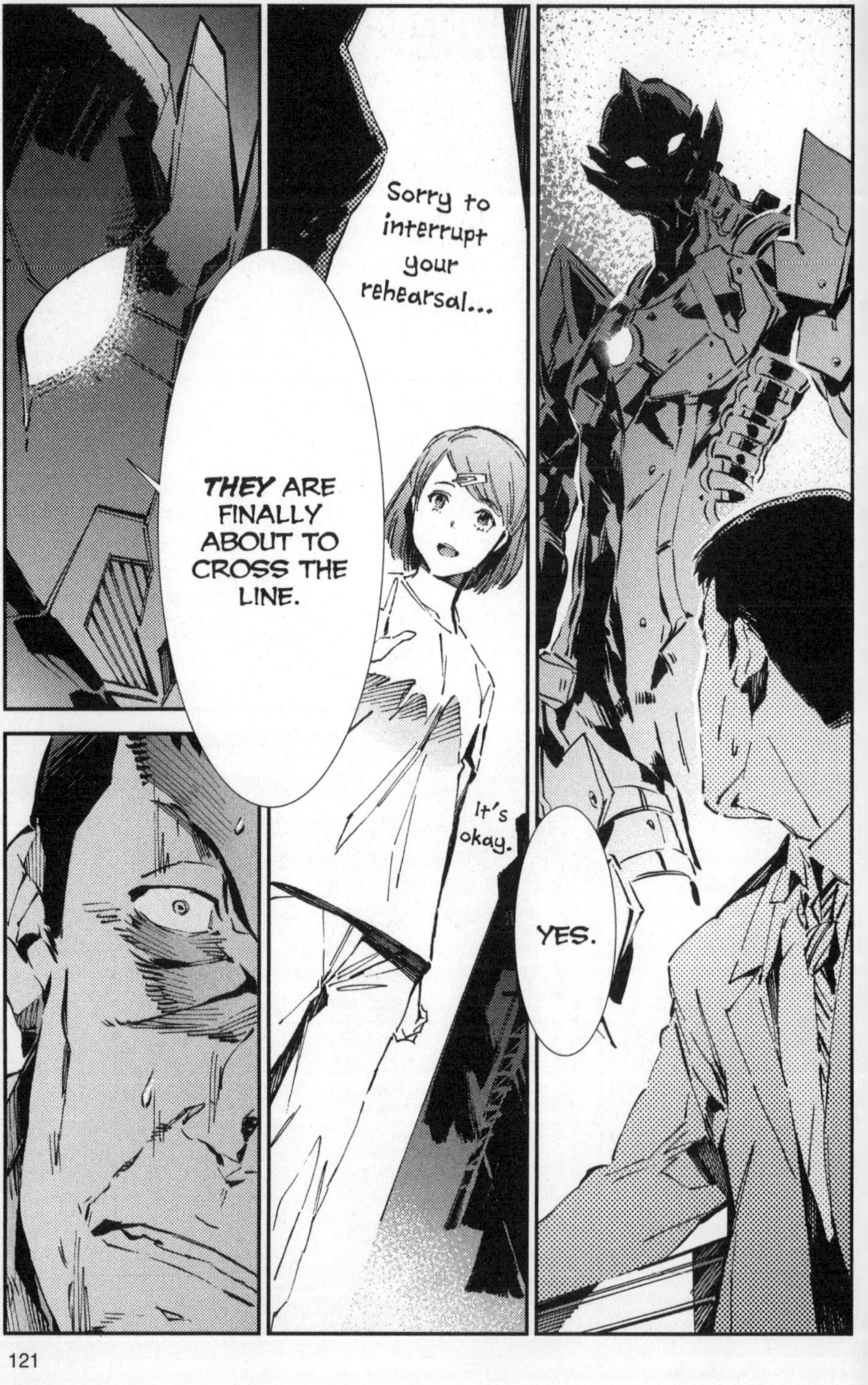
YES.
Sorry to interrupt your rehearsal...
THEY ARE FINALLY ABOUT TO CROSS THE LINE.
It's okay.

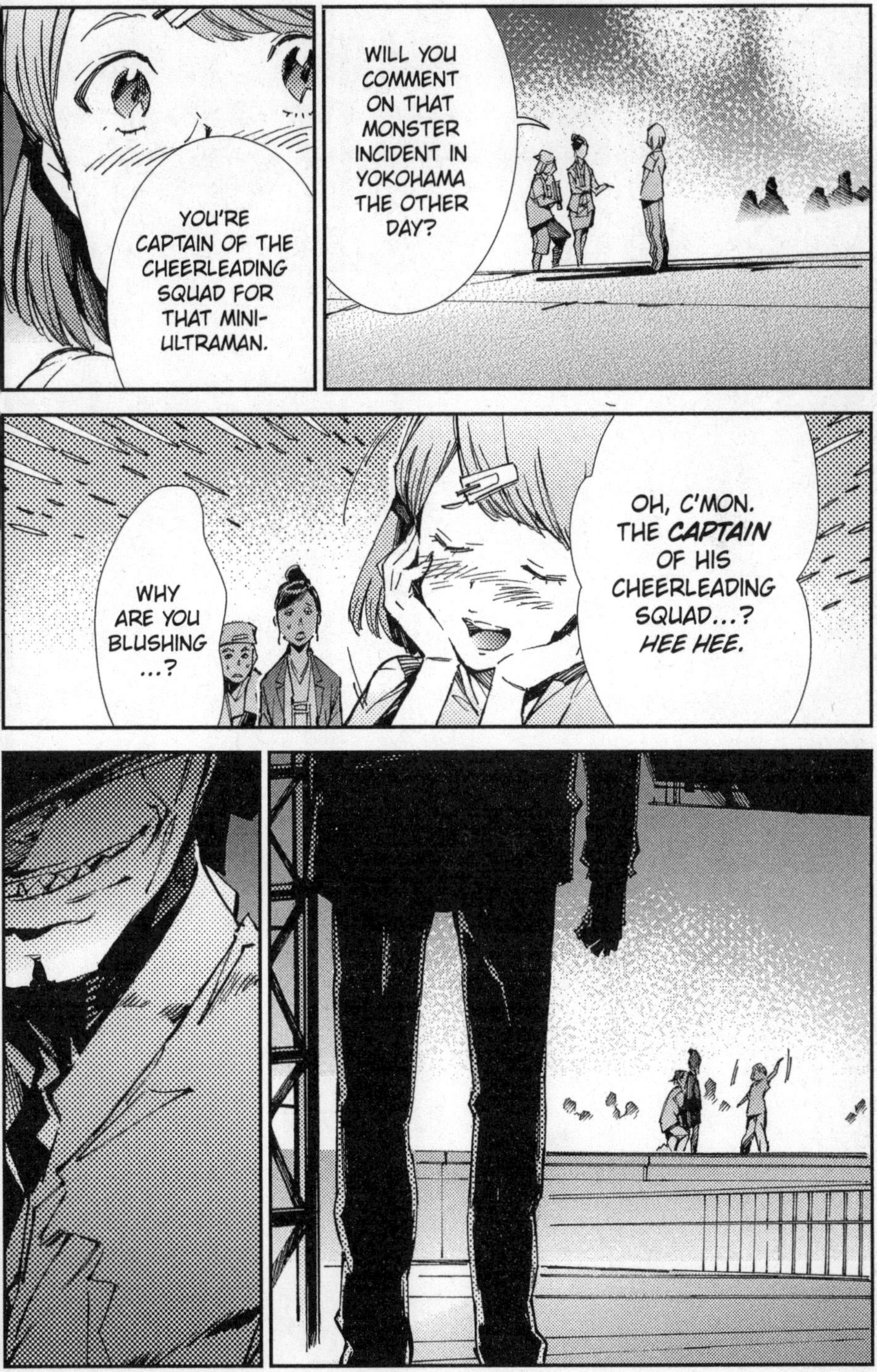
WILL YOU COMMENT ON THAT MONSTER INCIDENT IN YOKOHAMA THE OTHER DAY?
YOU'RE CAPTAIN OF THE CHEERLEADING SQUAD FOR THAT MINI-ULTRAMAN.
OH, C'MON. THE *CAPTAIN* OF HIS CHEERLEADING SQUAD...? *HEE HEE.*
WHY ARE YOU BLUSHING ...?

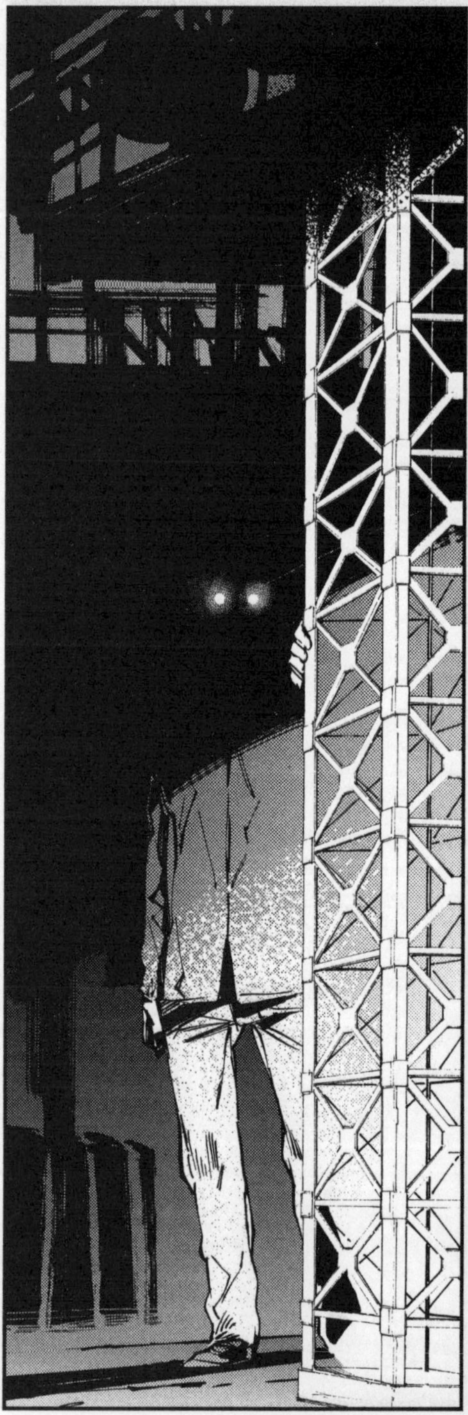
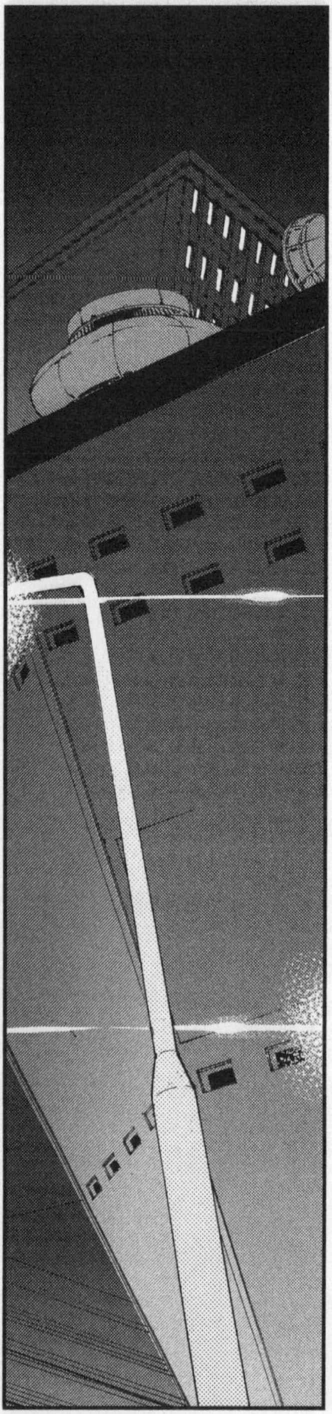

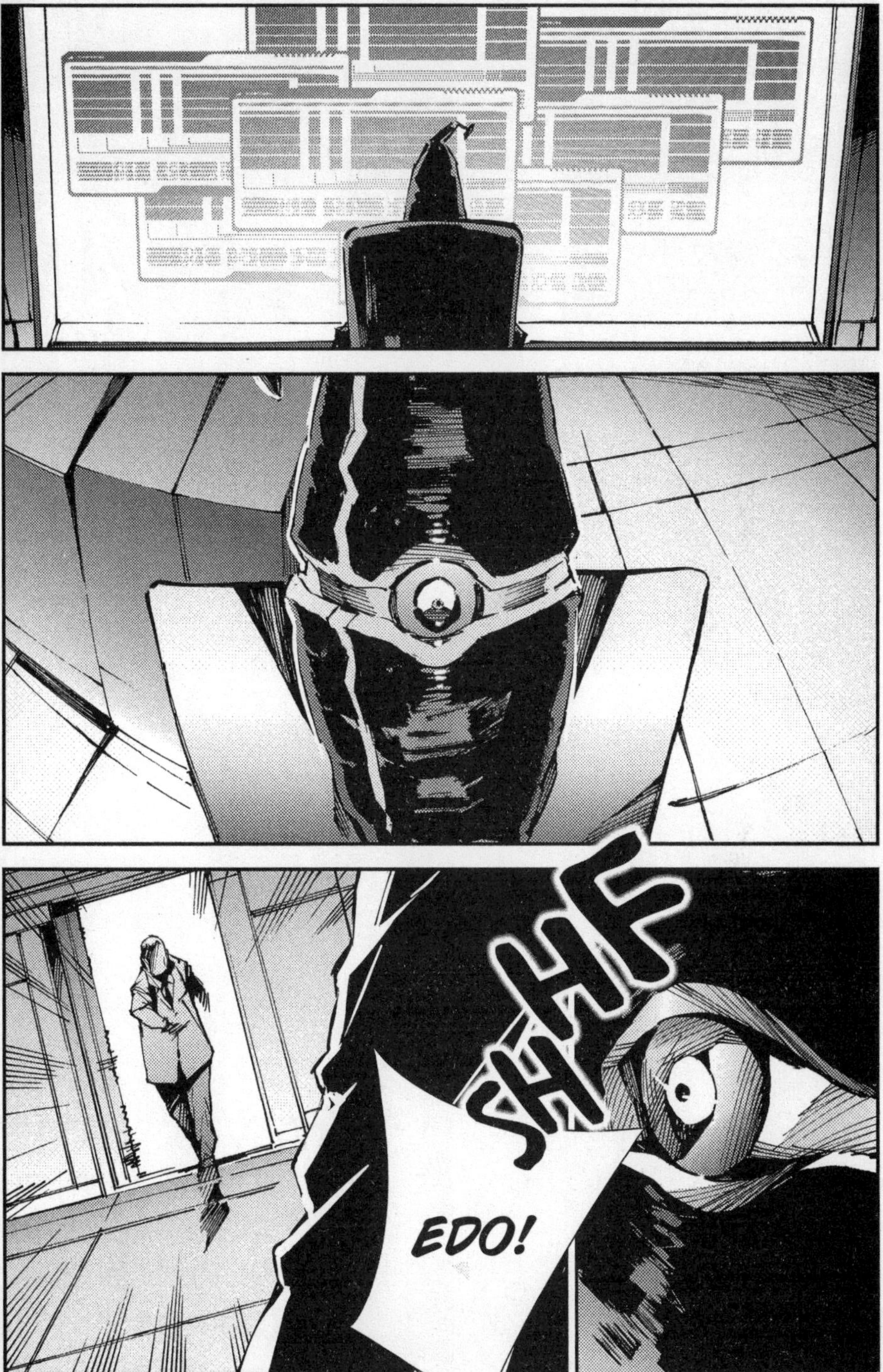
SHHF
EDO!

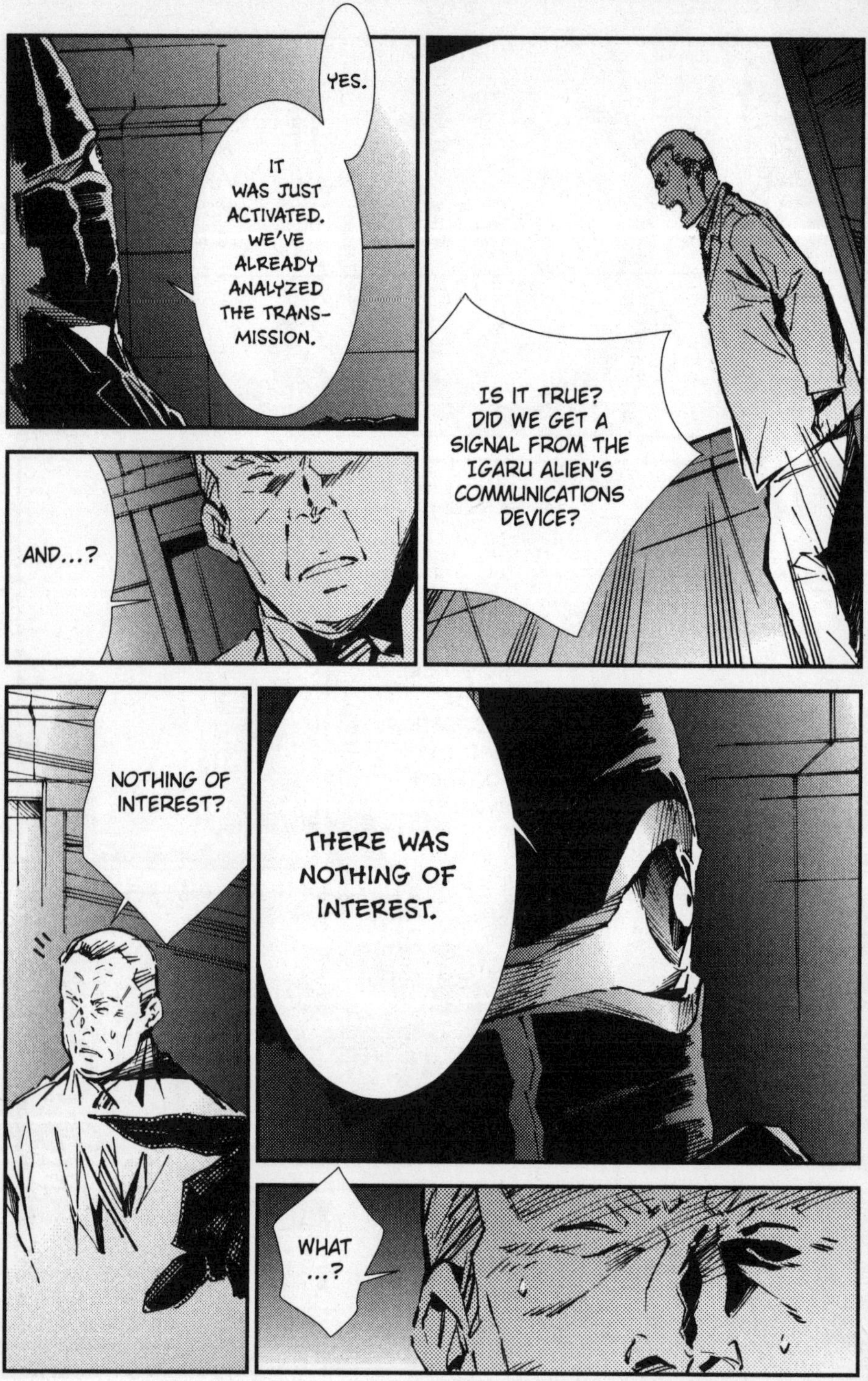
IS IT TRUE? DID WE GET A SIGNAL FROM THE IGARU ALIEN'S COMMUNICATIONS DEVICE?
YES.
IT WAS JUST ACTIVATED. WE'VE ALREADY ANALYZED THE TRANS-MISSION.
AND...?
THERE WAS NOTHING OF INTEREST.
NOTHING OF INTEREST?
WHAT ...?

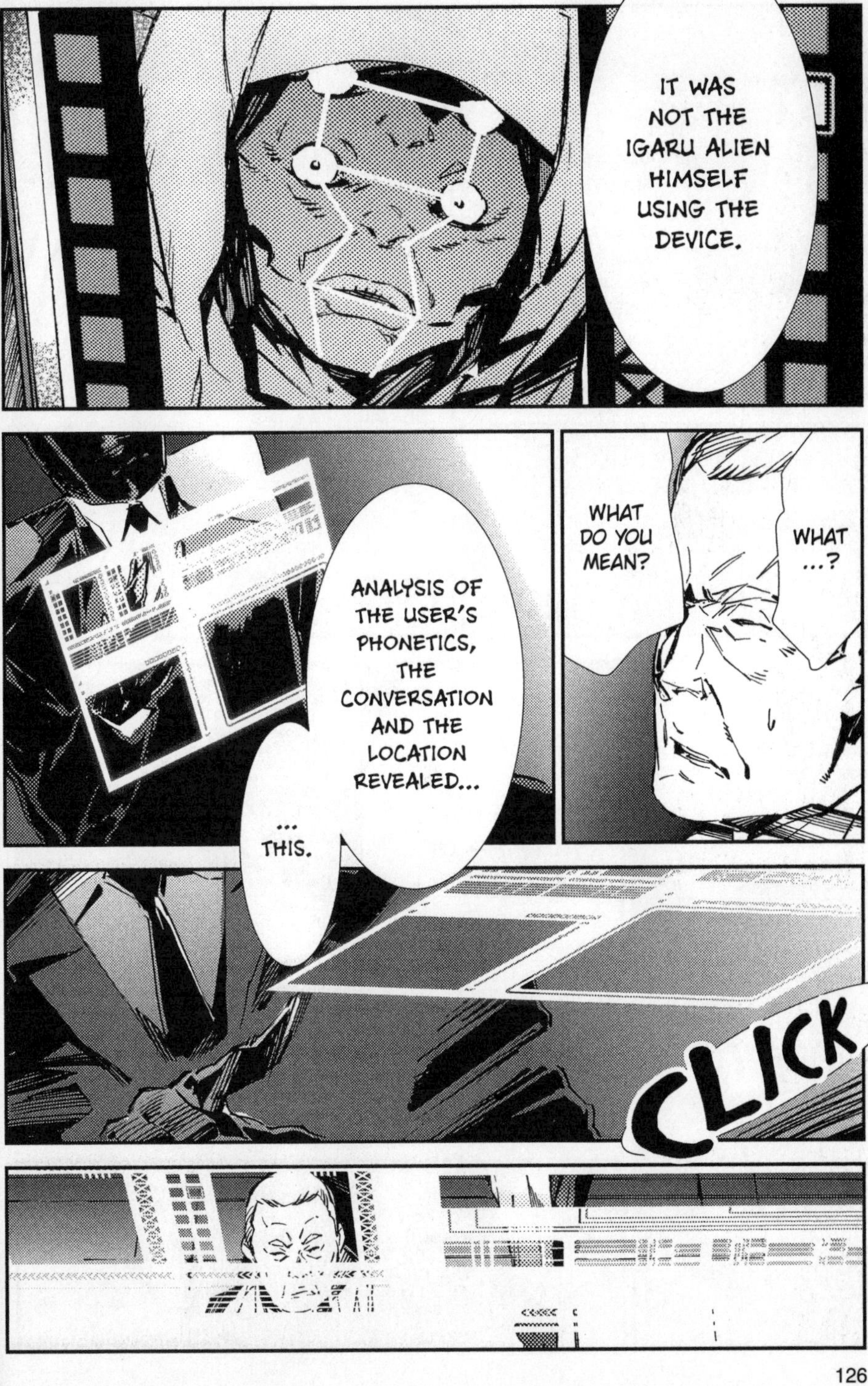
IT WAS NOT THE IGARU ALIEN HIMSELF USING THE DEVICE.
WHAT ...?
WHAT DO YOU MEAN?
ANALYSIS OF THE USER'S PHONETICS, THE CONVERSATION AND THE LOCATION REVEALED...
... THIS.
CLICK

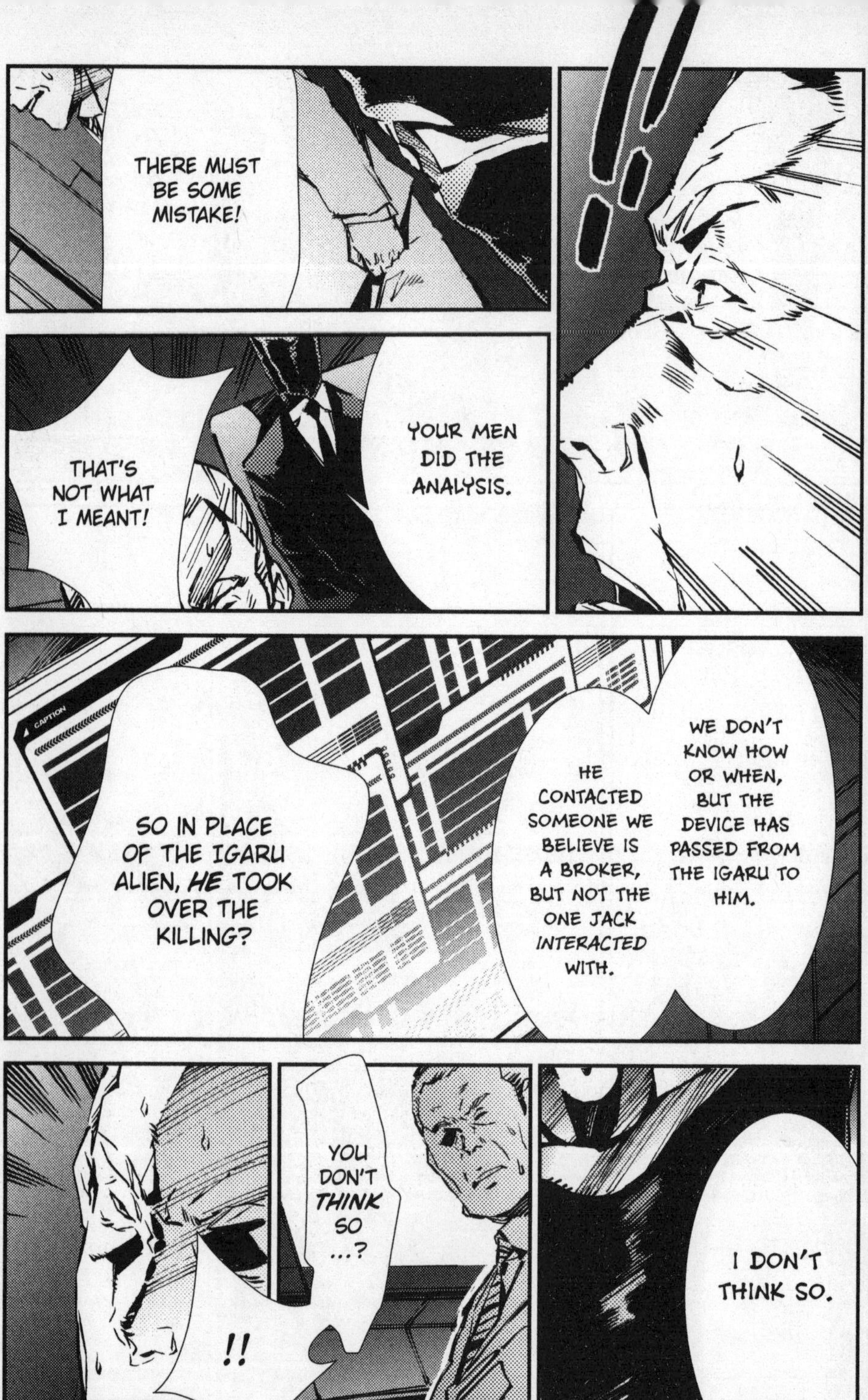
THERE MUST BE SOME MISTAKE!
YOUR MEN DID THE ANALYSIS.
THAT'S NOT WHAT I MEANT!
WE DON'T KNOW HOW OR WHEN, BUT THE DEVICE HAS PASSED FROM THE IGARU TO HIM.
HE CONTACTED SOMEONE WE BELIEVE IS A BROKER, BUT NOT THE ONE JACK *INTERACTED* WITH.
SO IN PLACE OF THE IGARU ALIEN, ***HE*** TOOK OVER THE KILLING?
CAPTION
I DON'T THINK SO.
YOU DON'T ***THINK*** SO ...?
!!

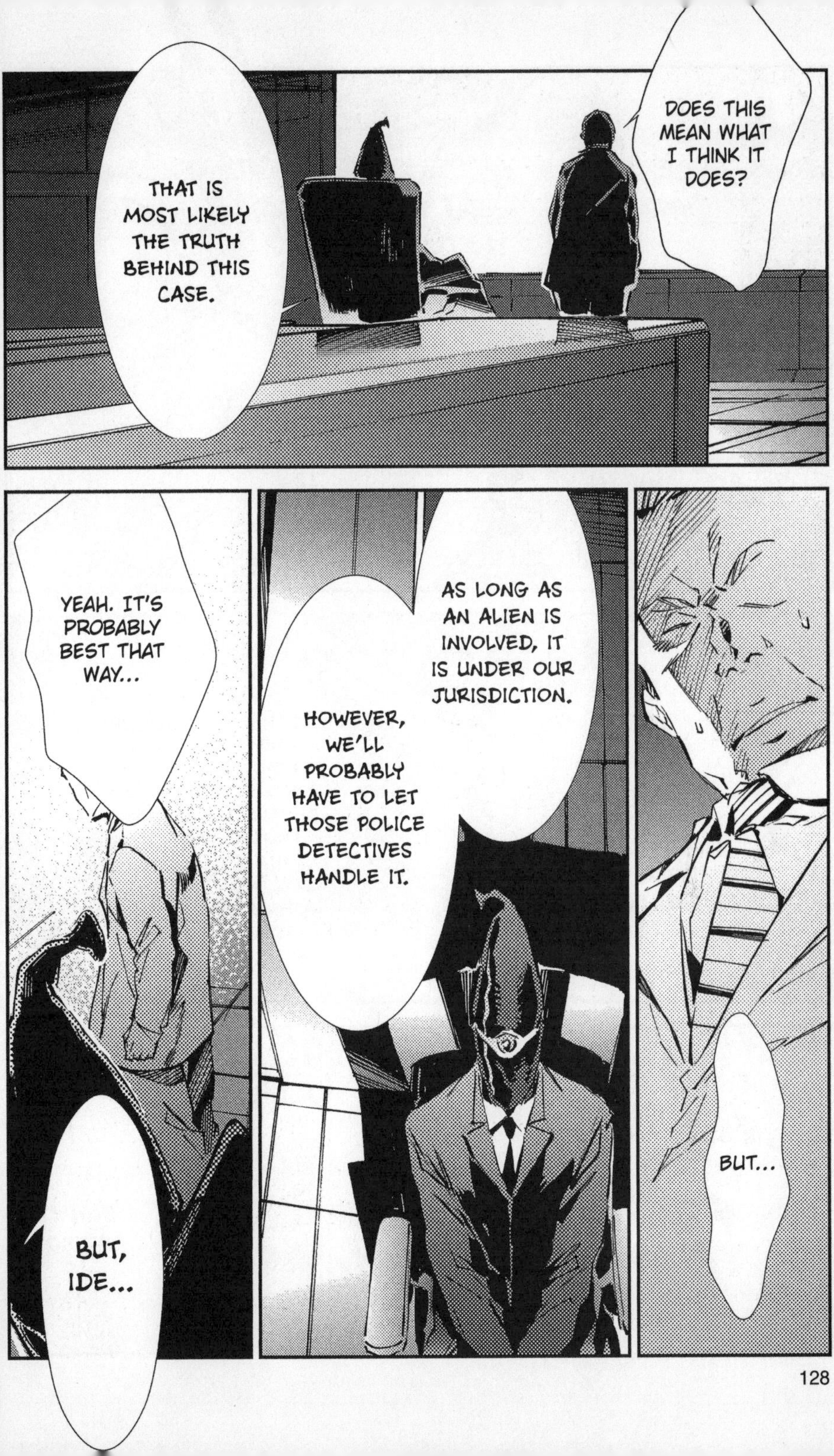
DOES THIS MEAN WHAT I THINK IT DOES?
THAT IS MOST LIKELY THE TRUTH BEHIND THIS CASE.
BUT...
AS LONG AS AN ALIEN IS INVOLVED, IT IS UNDER OUR JURISDICTION.
HOWEVER, WE'LL PROBABLY HAVE TO LET THOSE POLICE DETECTIVES HANDLE IT.
YEAH. IT'S PROBABLY BEST THAT WAY...
BUT, IDE...

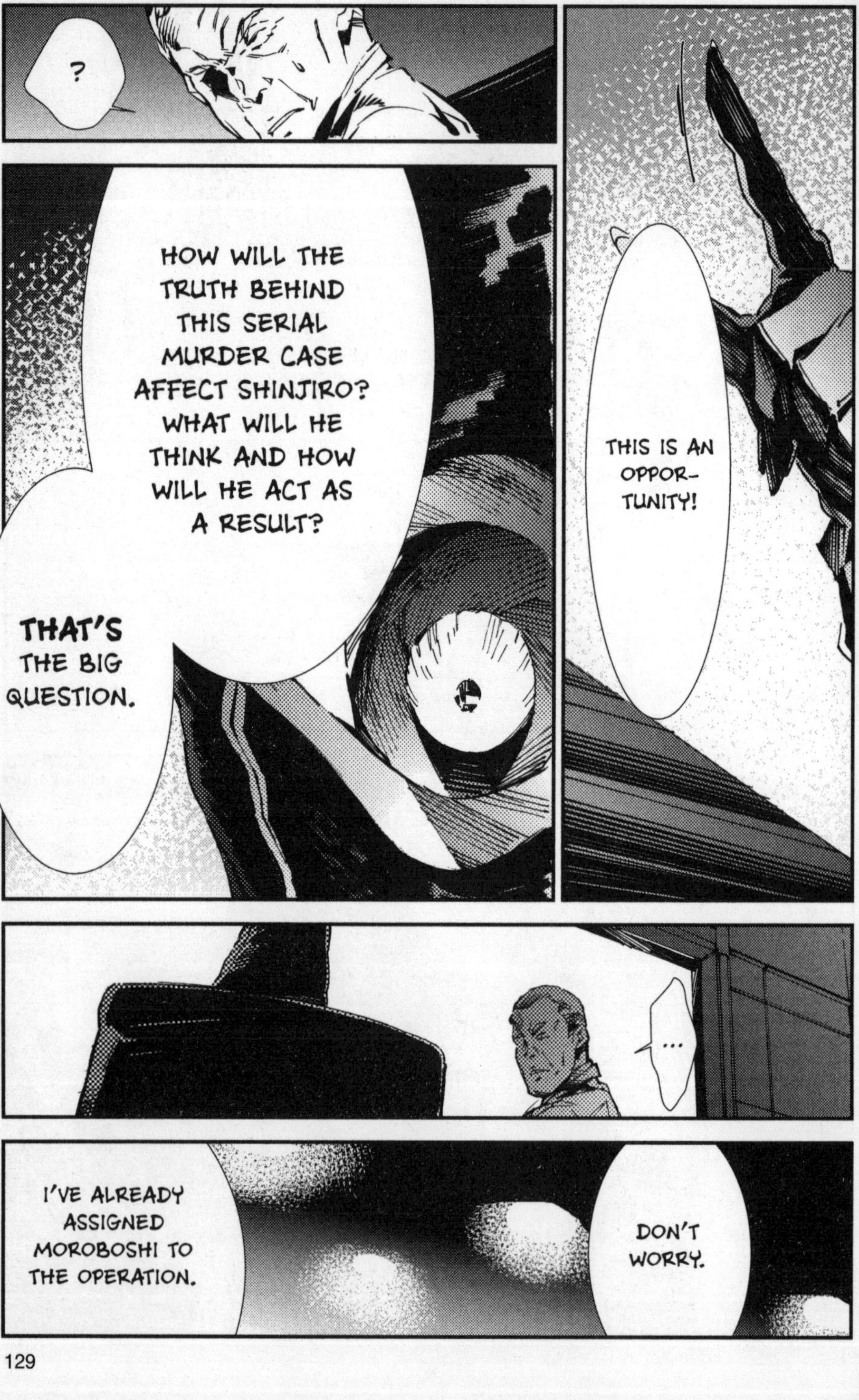
THIS IS AN OPPORTUNITY!
?
HOW WILL THE TRUTH BEHIND THIS SERIAL MURDER CASE AFFECT SHINJIRO? WHAT WILL HE THINK AND HOW WILL HE ACT AS A RESULT?
THAT'S THE BIG QUESTION.
...
DON'T WORRY.
I'VE ALREADY ASSIGNED MOROBOSHI TO THE OPERATION.

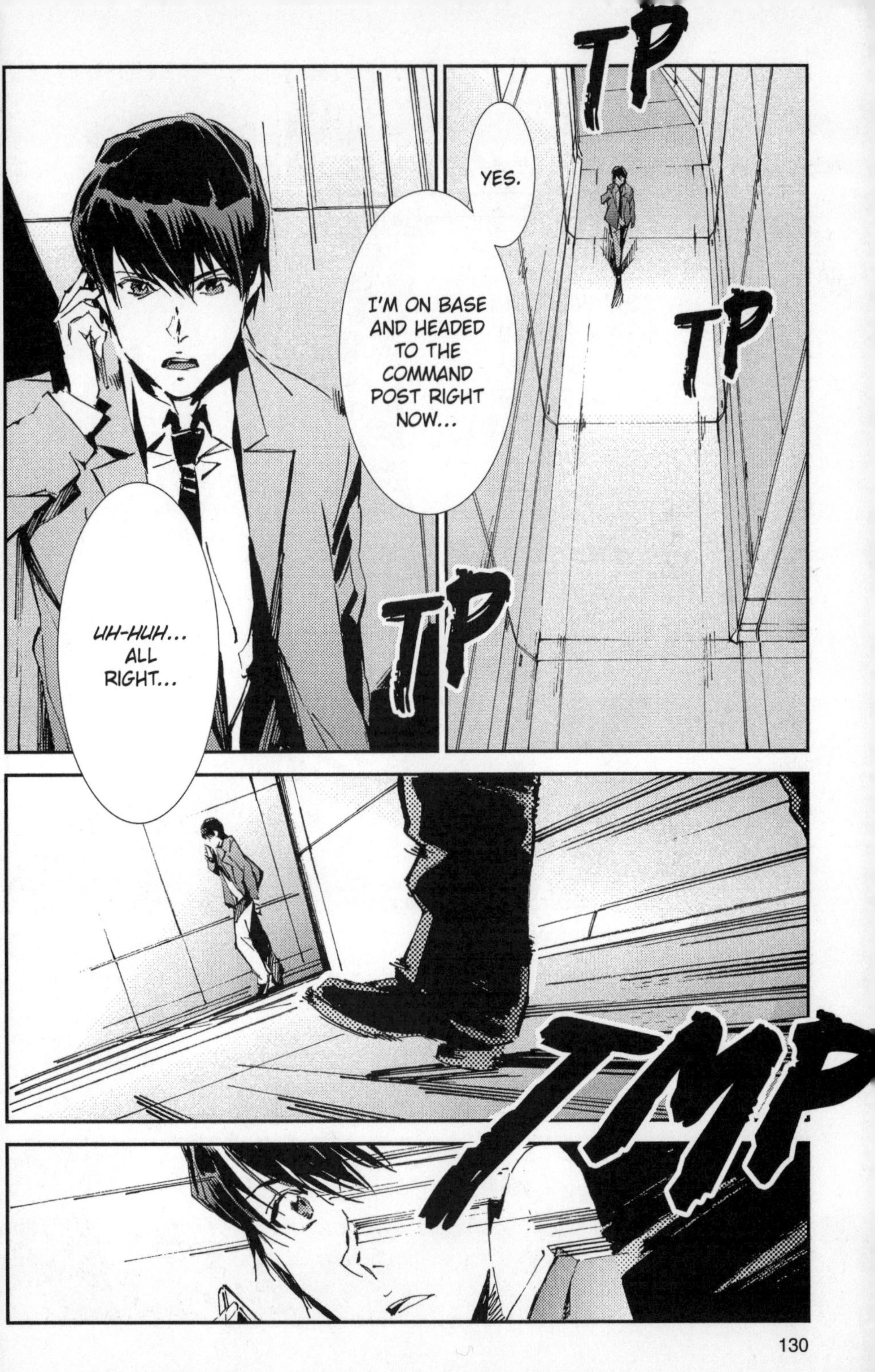
TP
YES.
I'M ON BASE AND HEADED TO THE COMMAND POST RIGHT NOW...
TP
TP
UH-HUH... ALL RIGHT...
TMP

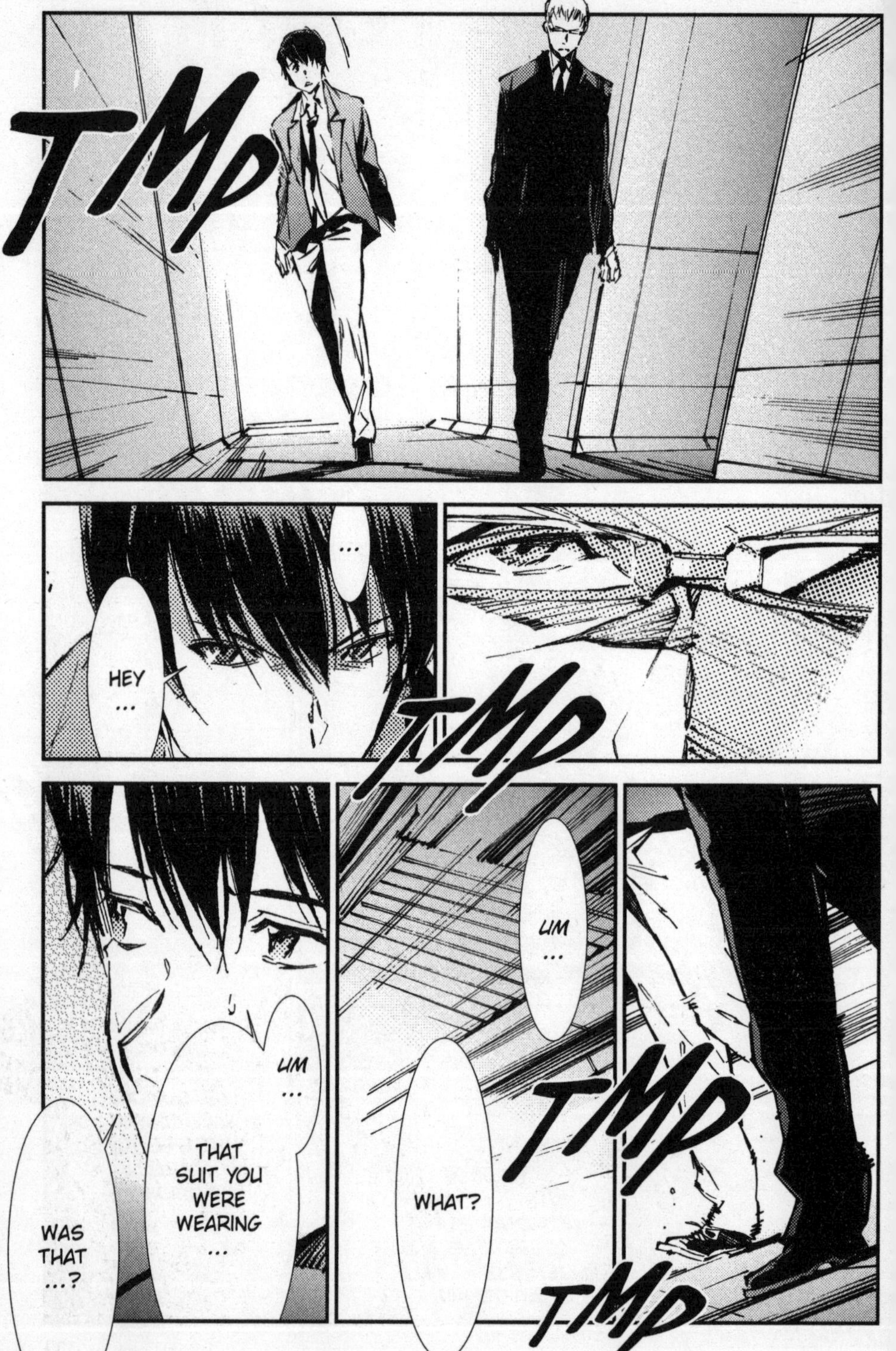
TMP
TMP
...
HEY ...
TMP
TMP
UM ...
WHAT?
UM ...
THAT SUIT YOU WERE WEARING ...
WAS THAT ...?

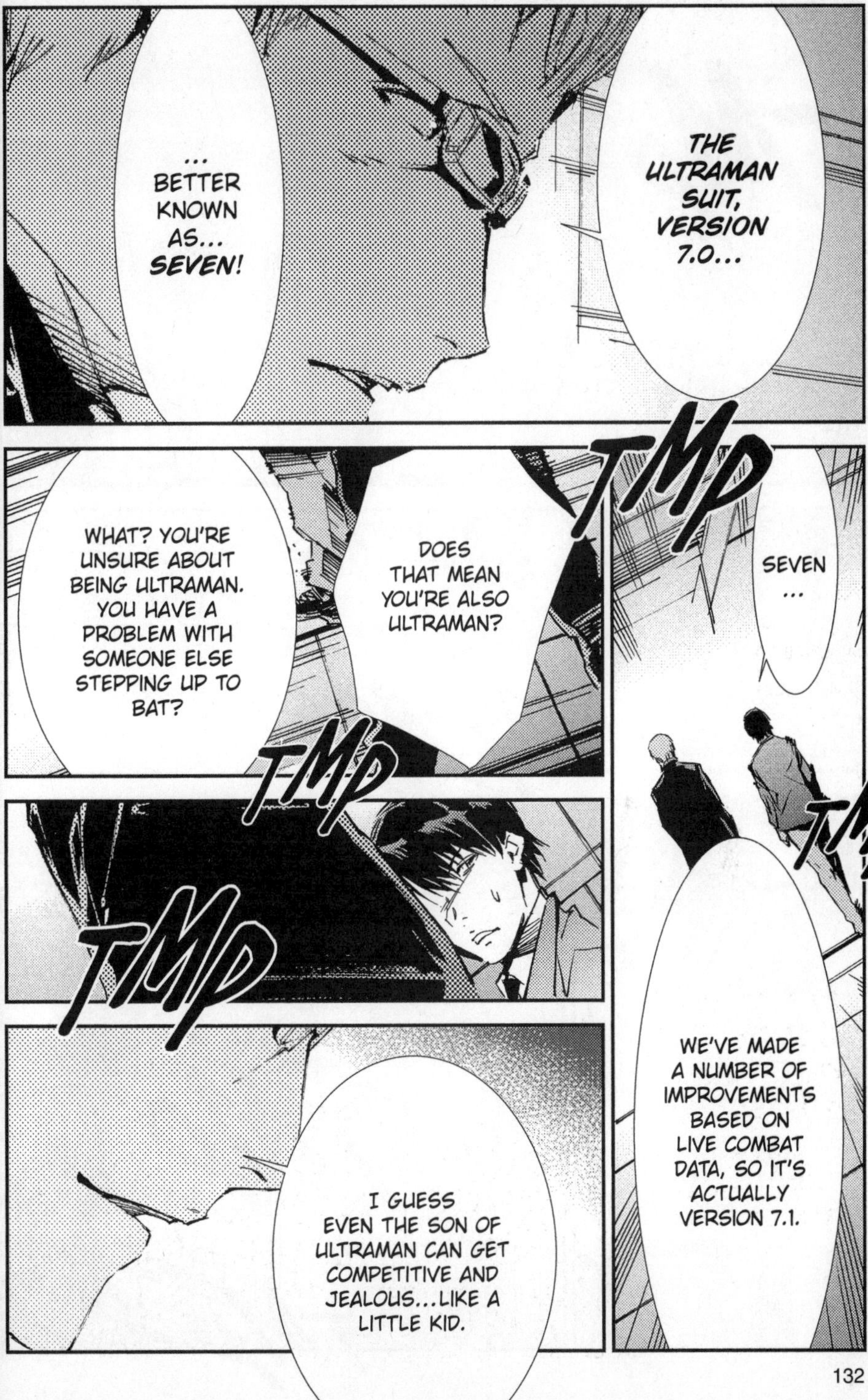
THE ULTRAMAN SUIT, VERSION 7.0...
... BETTER KNOWN AS... SEVEN!
TMP
SEVEN ...
TMP
WE'VE MADE A NUMBER OF IMPROVEMENTS BASED ON LIVE COMBAT DATA, SO IT'S ACTUALLY VERSION 7.1.
DOES THAT MEAN YOU'RE ALSO ULTRAMAN?
WHAT? YOU'RE UNSURE ABOUT BEING ULTRAMAN. YOU HAVE A PROBLEM WITH SOMEONE ELSE STEPPING UP TO BAT?
TMP
TMP
I GUESS EVEN THE SON OF ULTRAMAN CAN GET COMPETITIVE AND JEALOUS...LIKE A LITTLE KID.

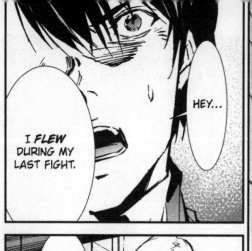

HEY...

I *FLEW* DURING MY LAST FIGHT.

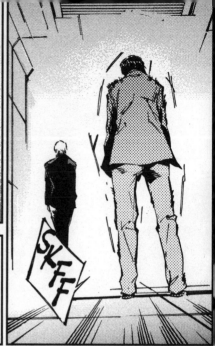

SKFF

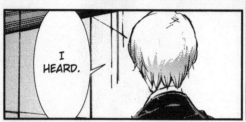

I HEARD.

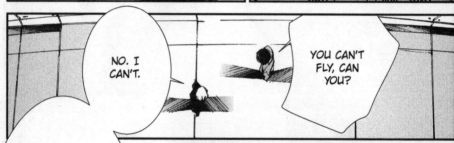

NO. I CAN'T.

YOU CAN'T FLY, CAN YOU?

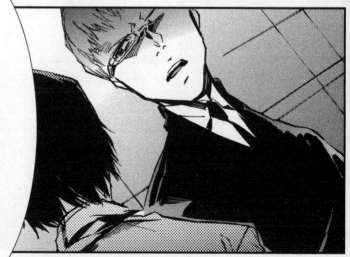

BUT I CAN *POSITIVELY* KILL THOSE GODDAMNED ALIENS WITHOUT HESITATION.

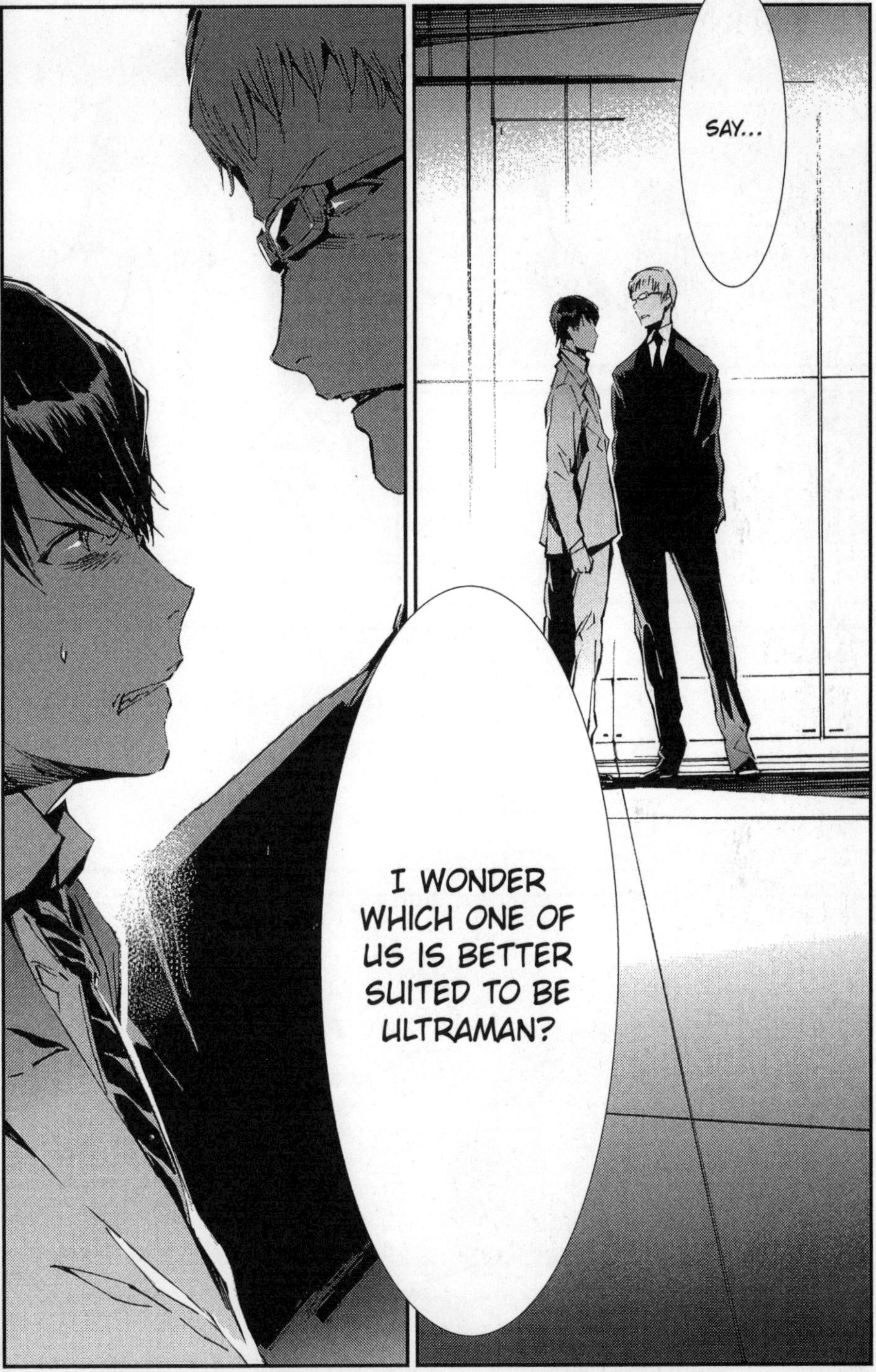
SAY...
I WONDER WHICH ONE OF US IS BETTER SUITED TO BE ULTRAMAN?

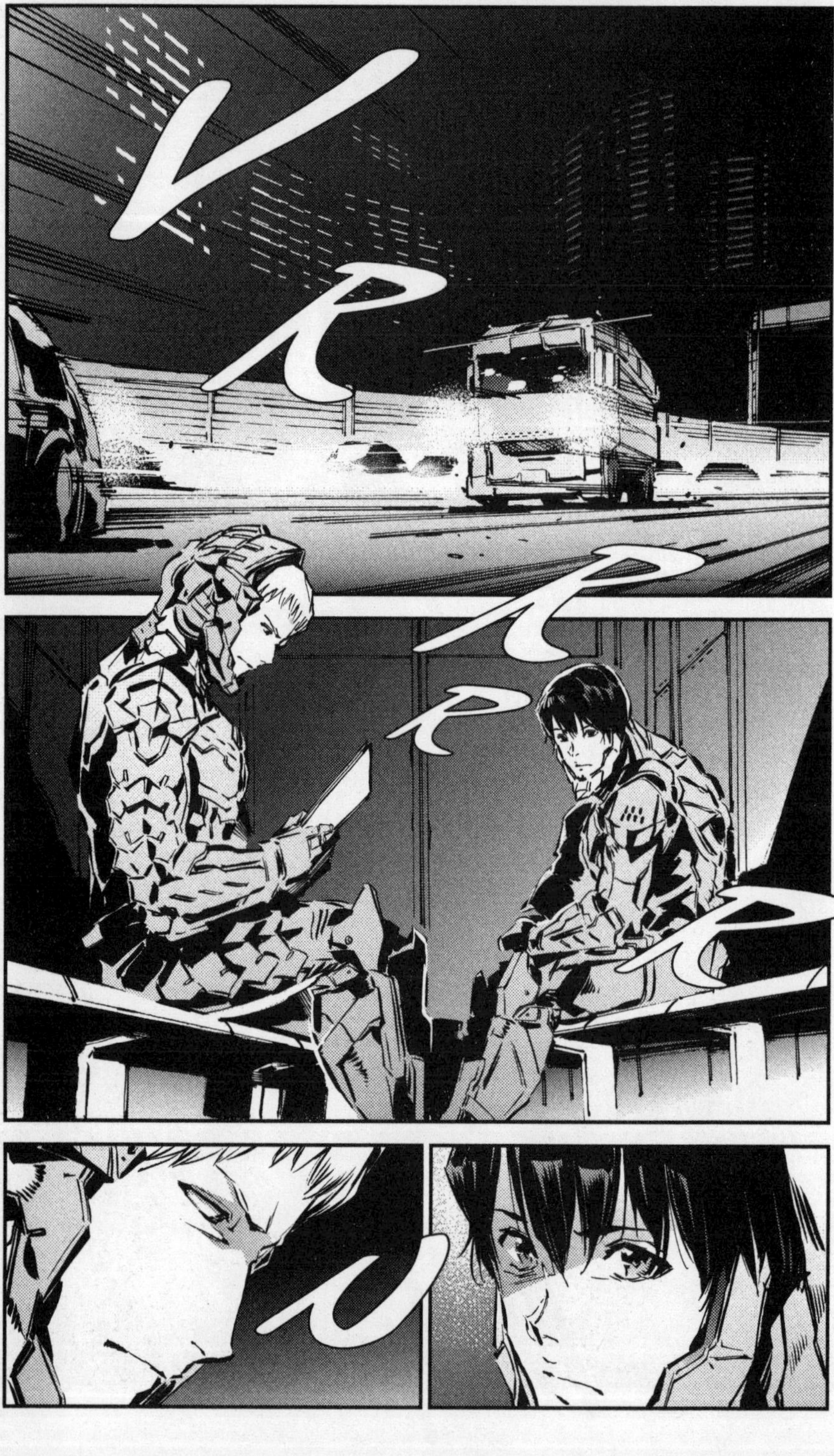
VRRRR

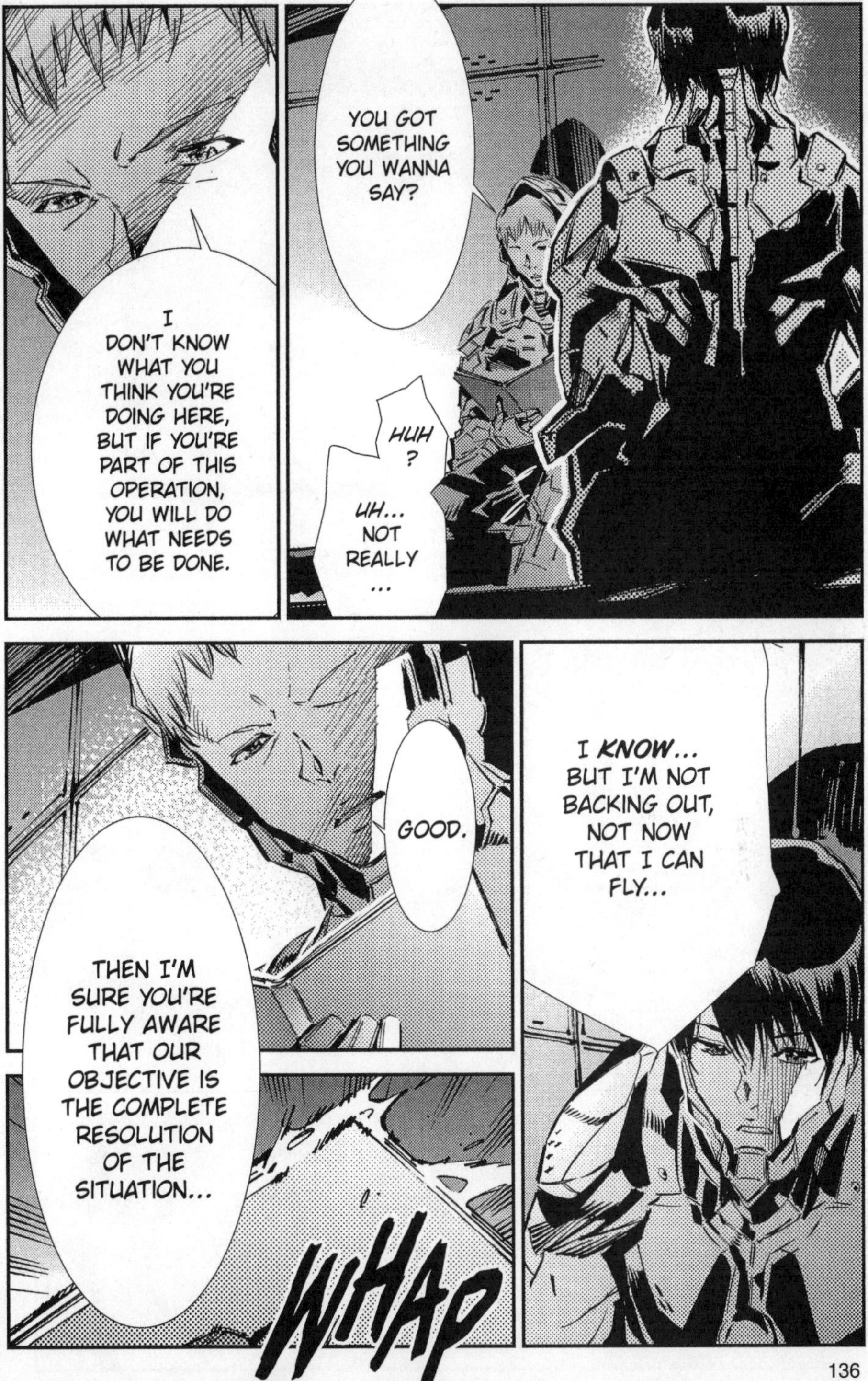
YOU GOT SOMETHING YOU WANNA SAY?
HUH?
UH... NOT REALLY...
I DON'T KNOW WHAT YOU THINK YOU'RE DOING HERE, BUT IF YOU'RE PART OF THIS OPERATION, YOU WILL DO WHAT NEEDS TO BE DONE.
I *KNOW*... BUT I'M NOT BACKING OUT, NOT NOW THAT I CAN FLY...
GOOD.
THEN I'M SURE YOU'RE FULLY AWARE THAT OUR OBJECTIVE IS THE COMPLETE RESOLUTION OF THE SITUATION...
WHAP

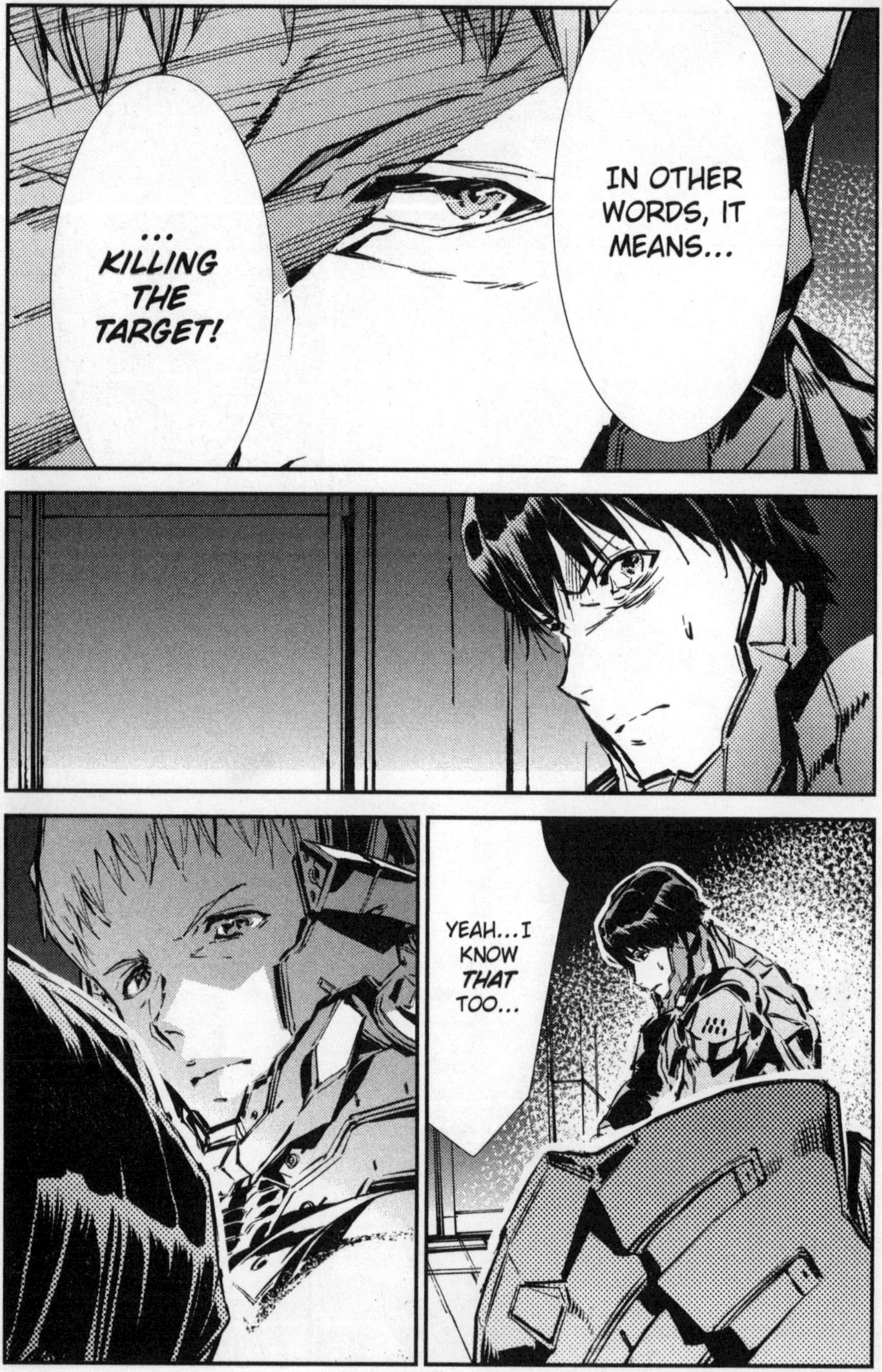
IN OTHER WORDS, IT MEANS...
... *KILLING THE TARGET!*
YEAH...I KNOW *THAT* TOO...

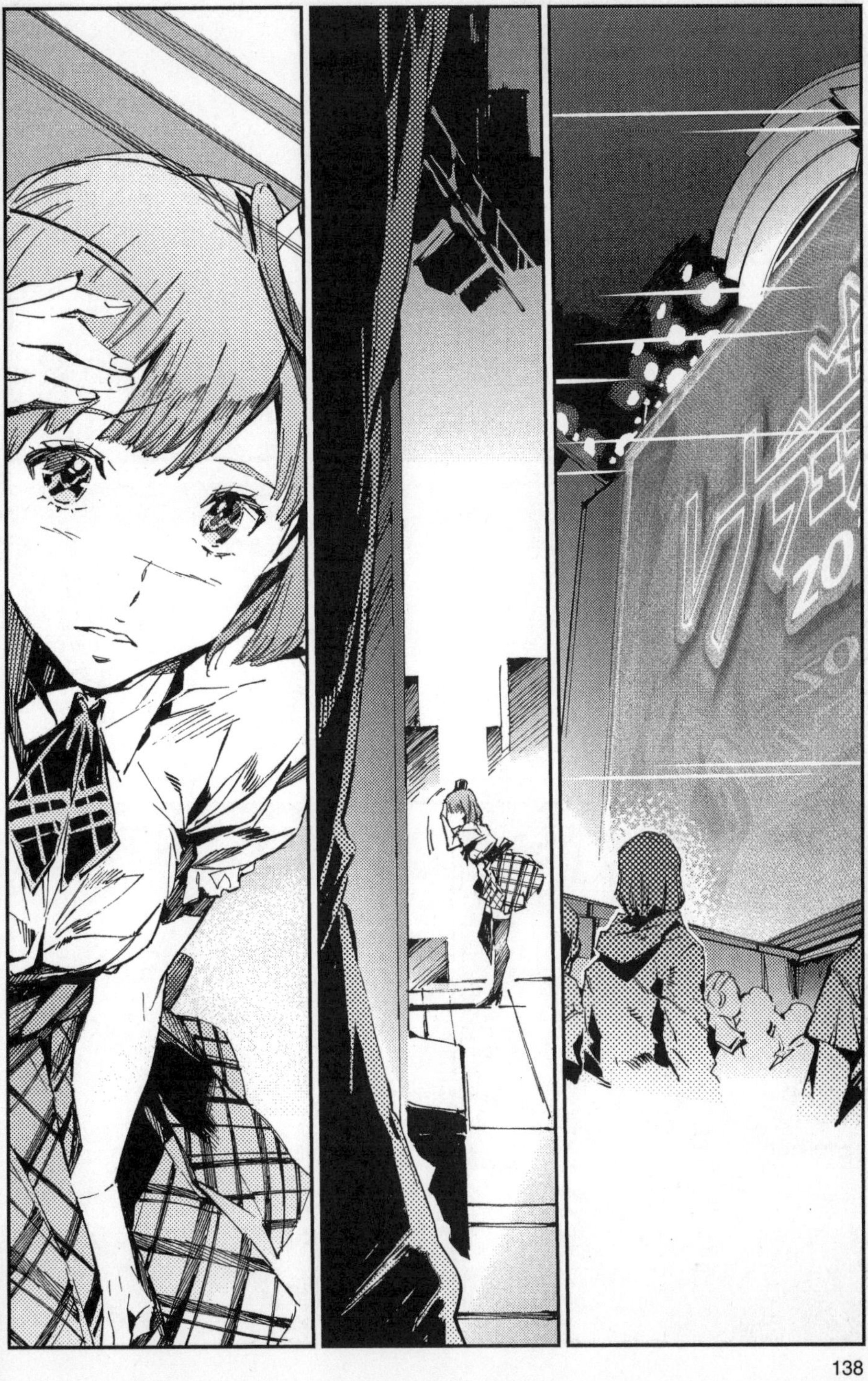

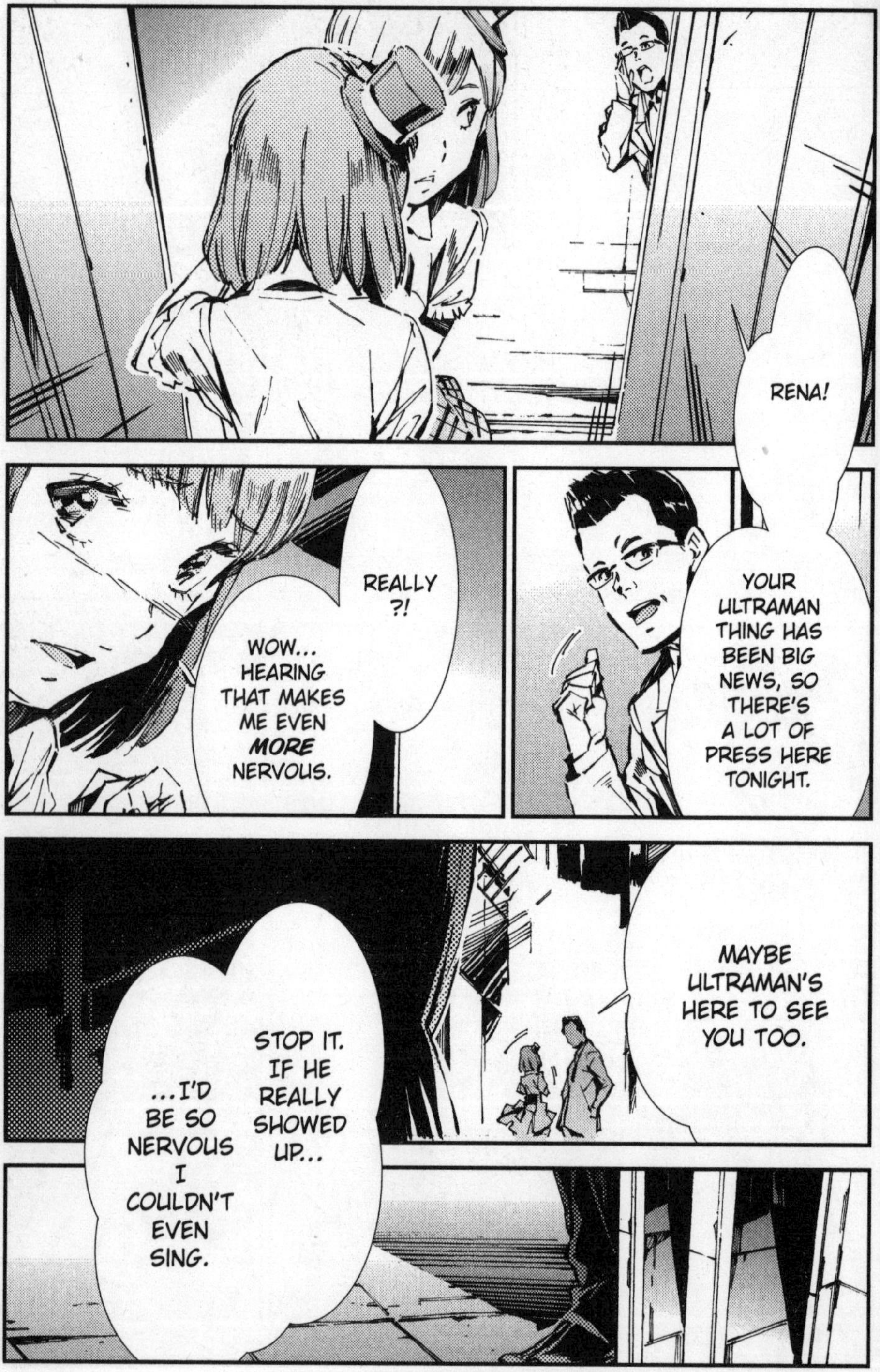
RENA!
YOUR ULTRAMAN THING HAS BEEN BIG NEWS, SO THERE'S A LOT OF PRESS HERE TONIGHT.
REALLY ?!
WOW... HEARING THAT MAKES ME EVEN *MORE* NERVOUS.
MAYBE ULTRAMAN'S HERE TO SEE YOU TOO.
STOP IT. IF HE REALLY SHOWED UP...
...I'D BE SO NERVOUS I COULDN'T EVEN SING.

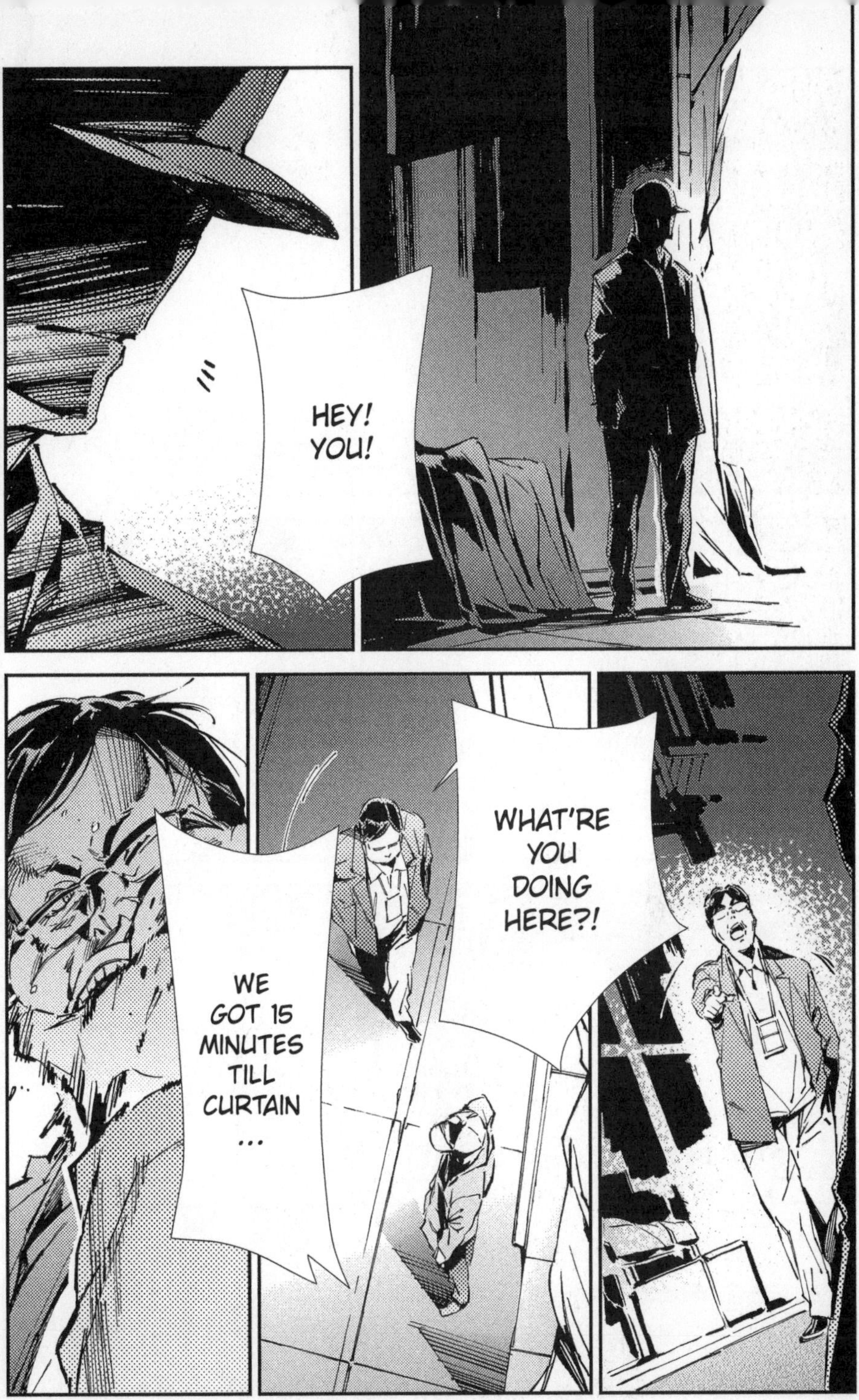
HEY! YOU!
WHAT'RE YOU DOING HERE?!
WE GOT 15 MINUTES TILL CURTAIN ...

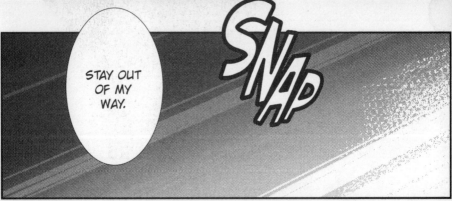

STAY OUT OF MY WAY.

SNAP

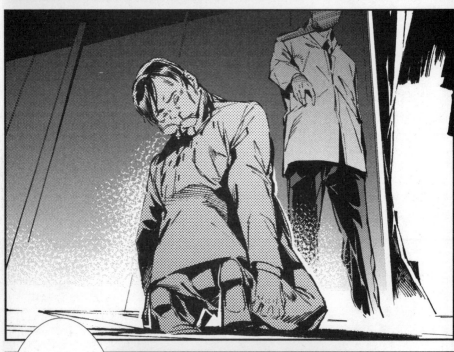

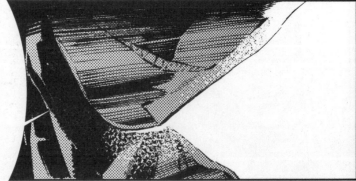

NOW... LET'S GET THIS SHOW ON THE ROAD.

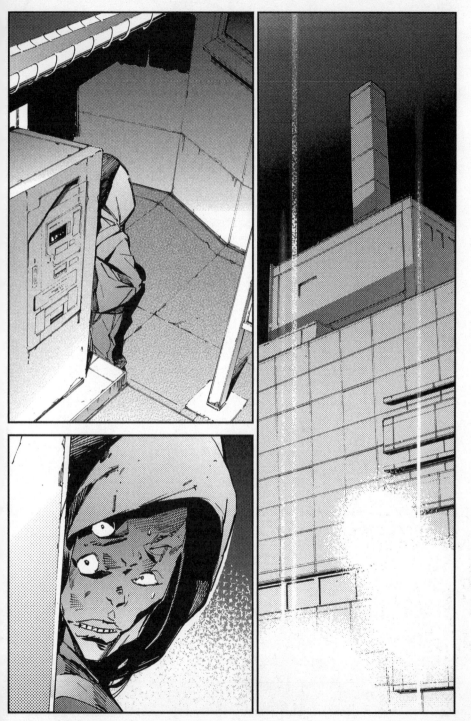

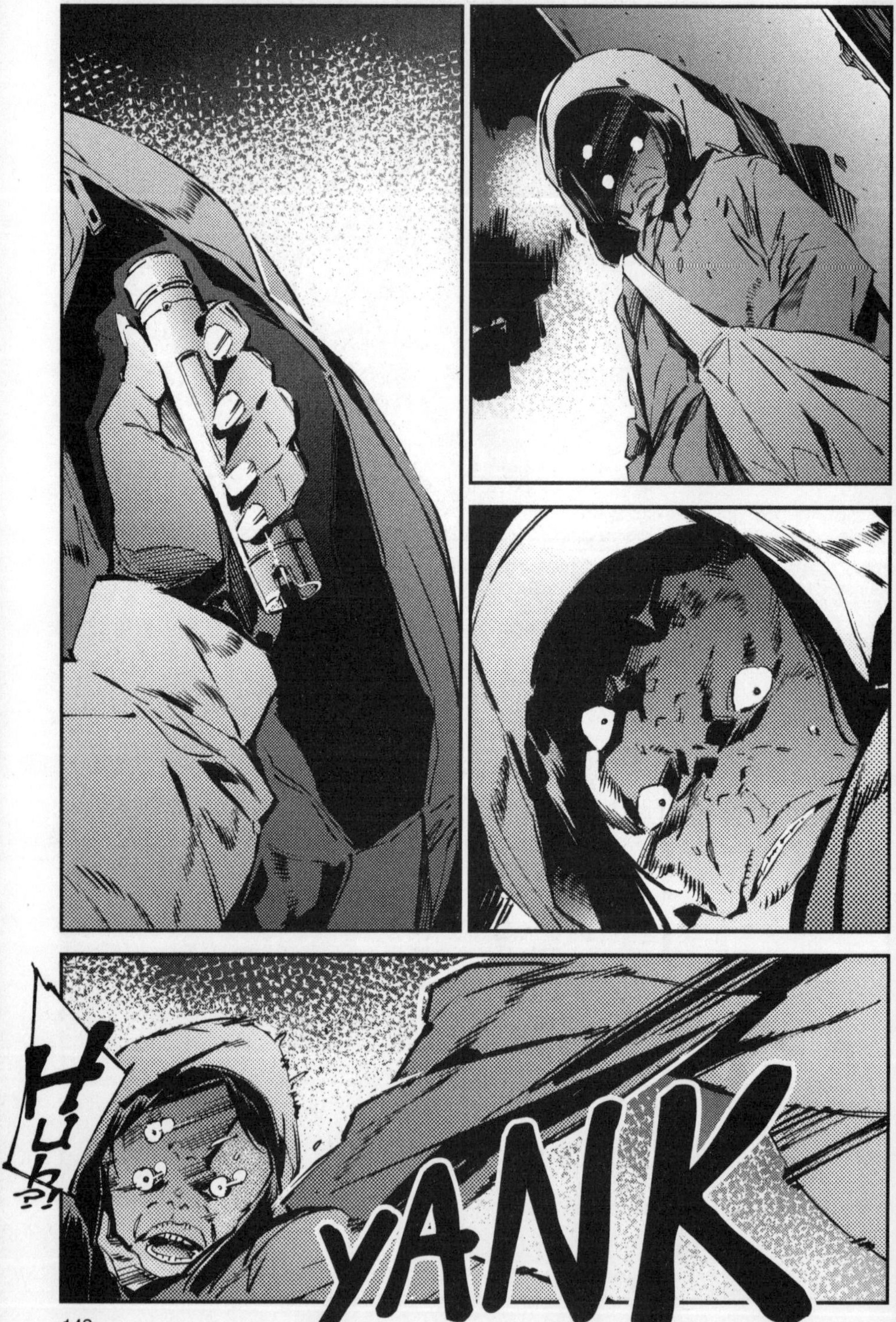
YANK
Huh?!

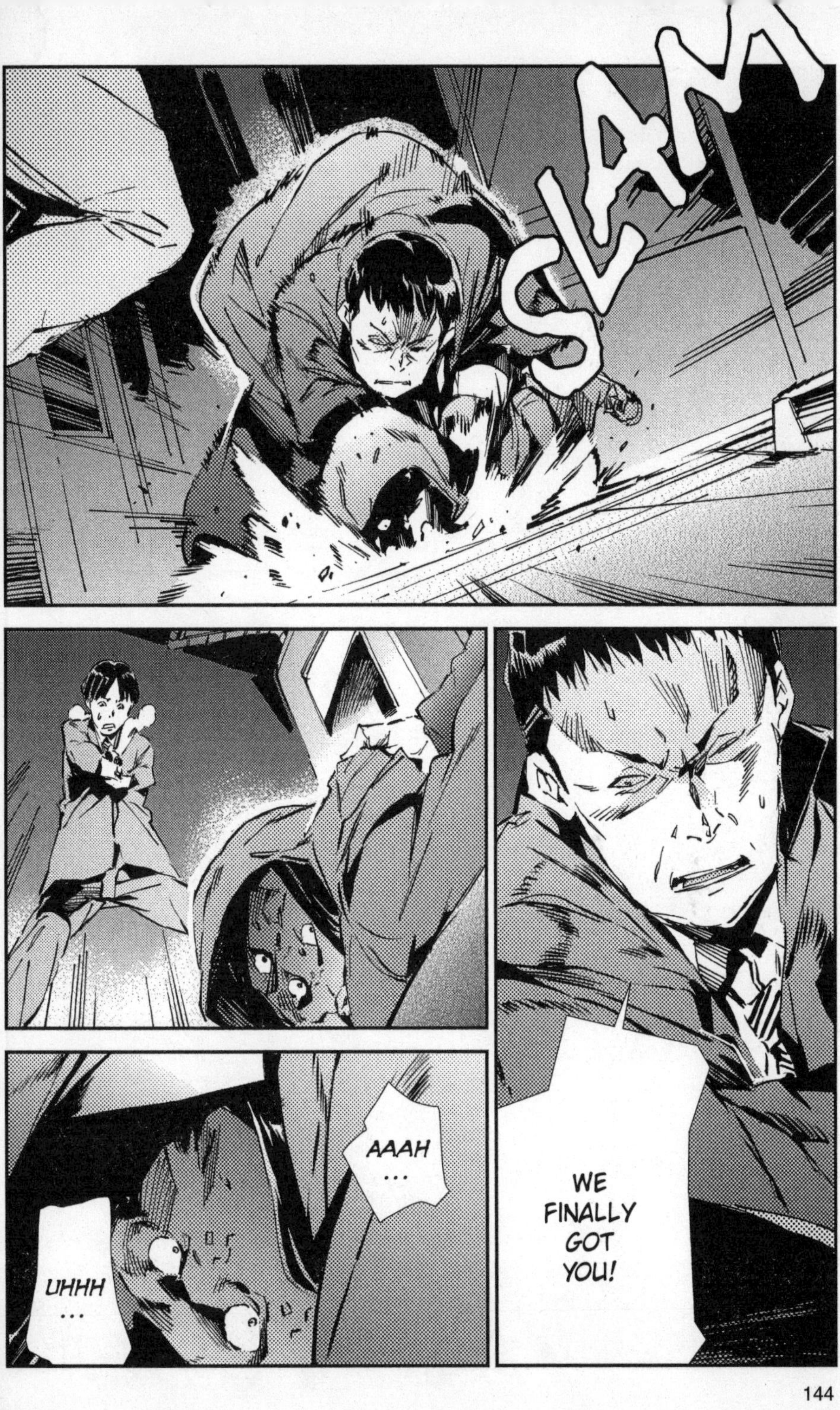
SLAM
WE FINALLY GOT YOU!
AAAH ...
UHHH ...

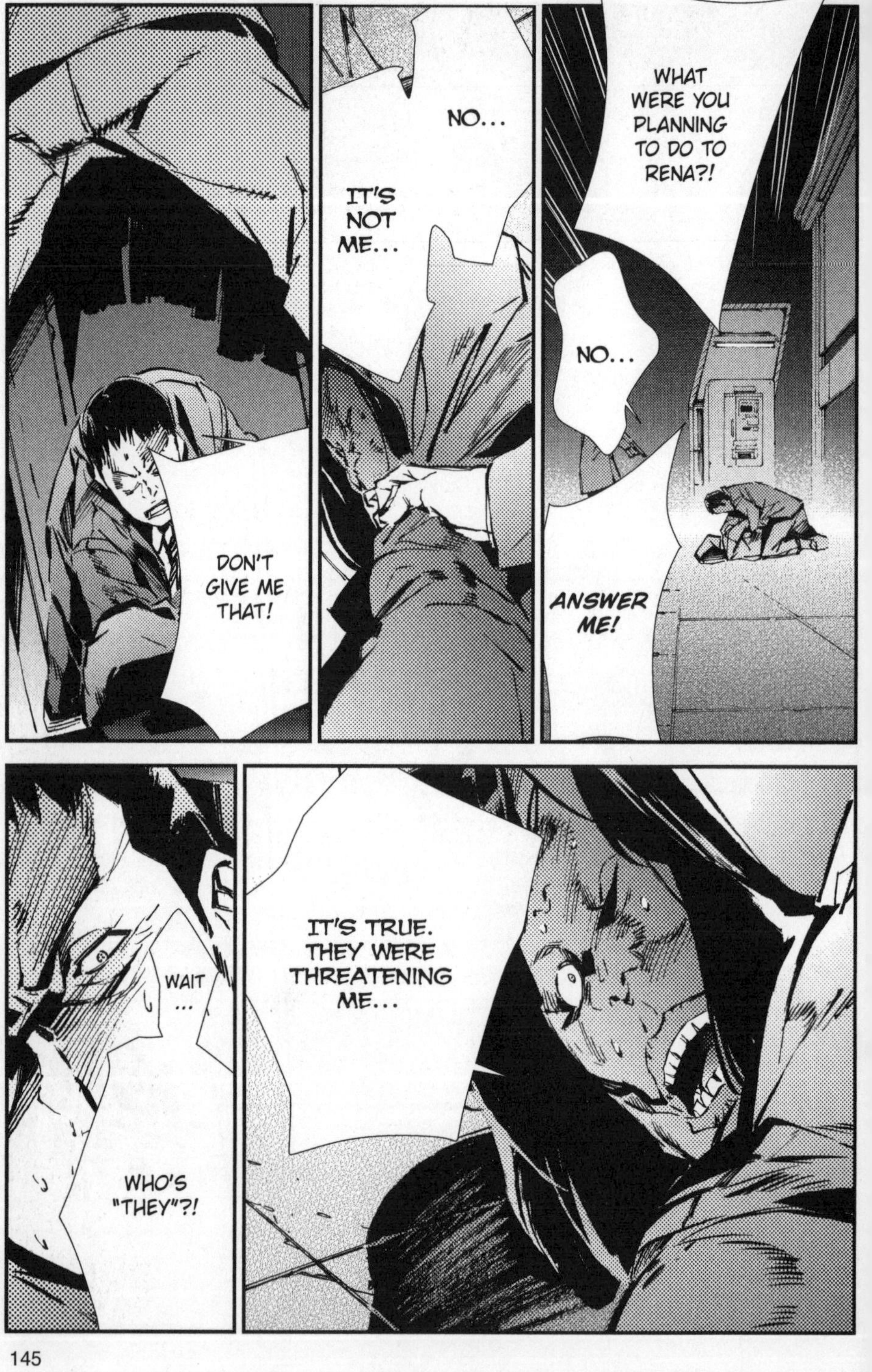
WHAT WERE YOU PLANNING TO DO TO RENA?!
NO...
ANSWER ME!
NO...
IT'S NOT ME...
DON'T GIVE ME THAT!
IT'S TRUE. THEY WERE THREATENING ME...
WAIT ...
WHO'S "THEY"?!

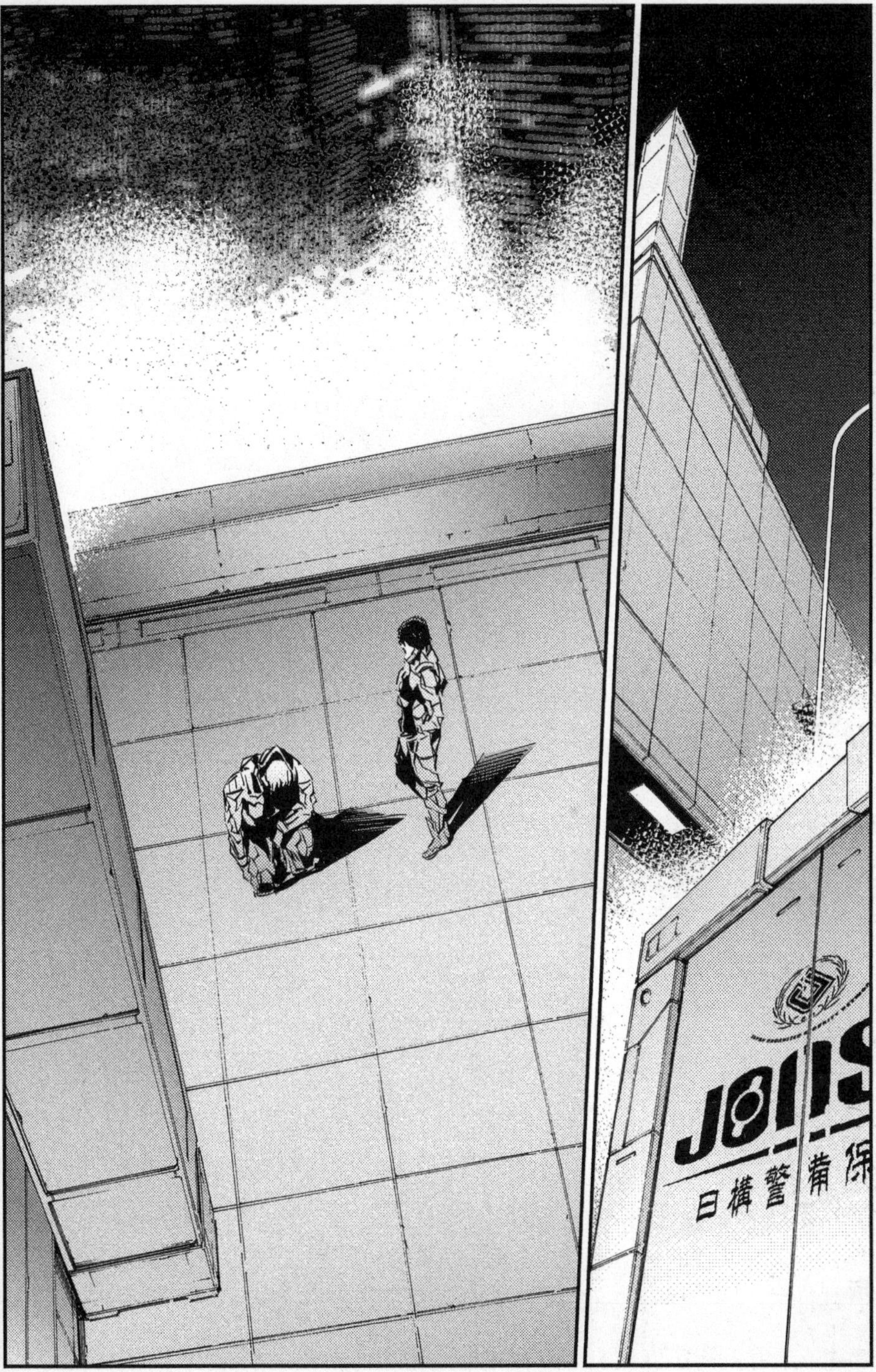
日構警備保

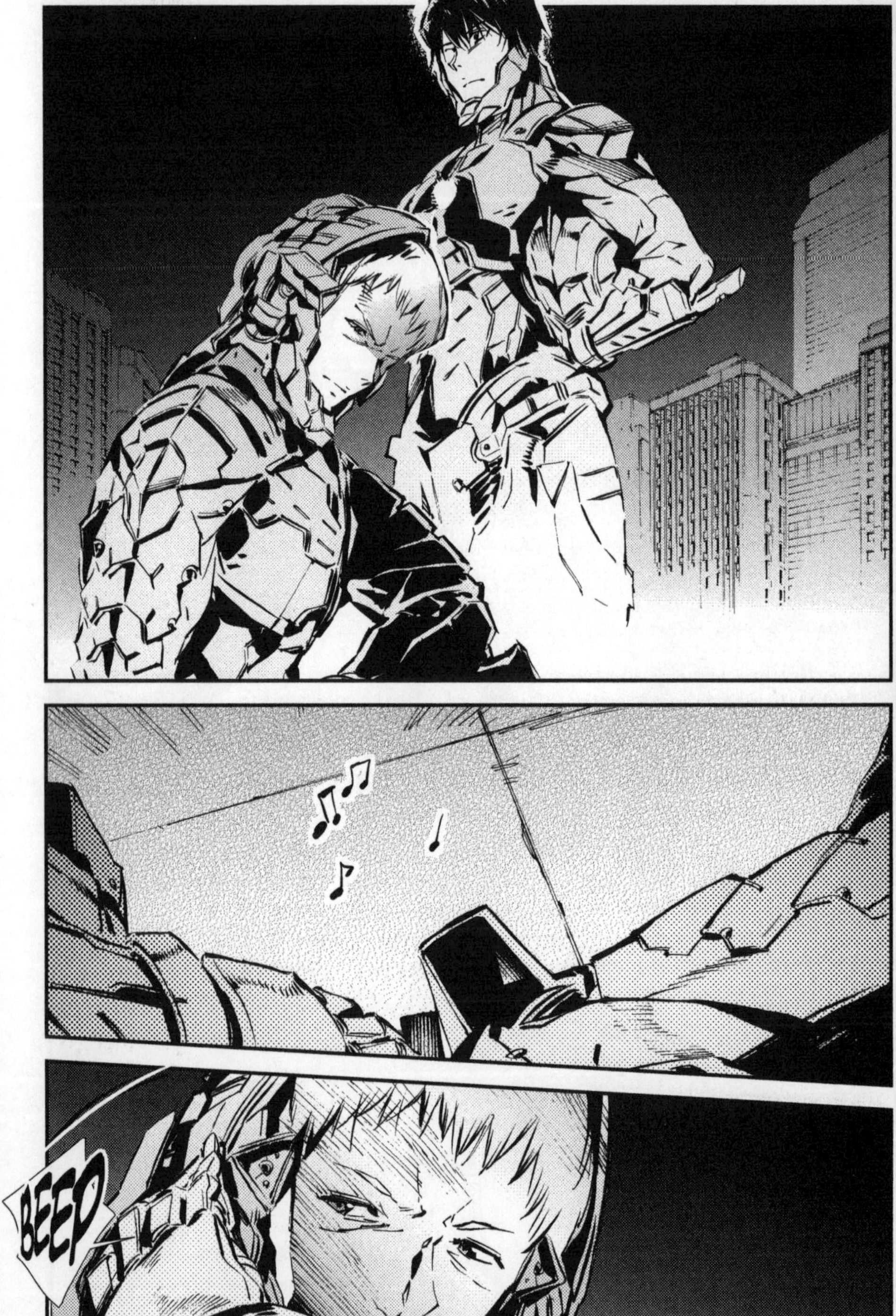
BEEP

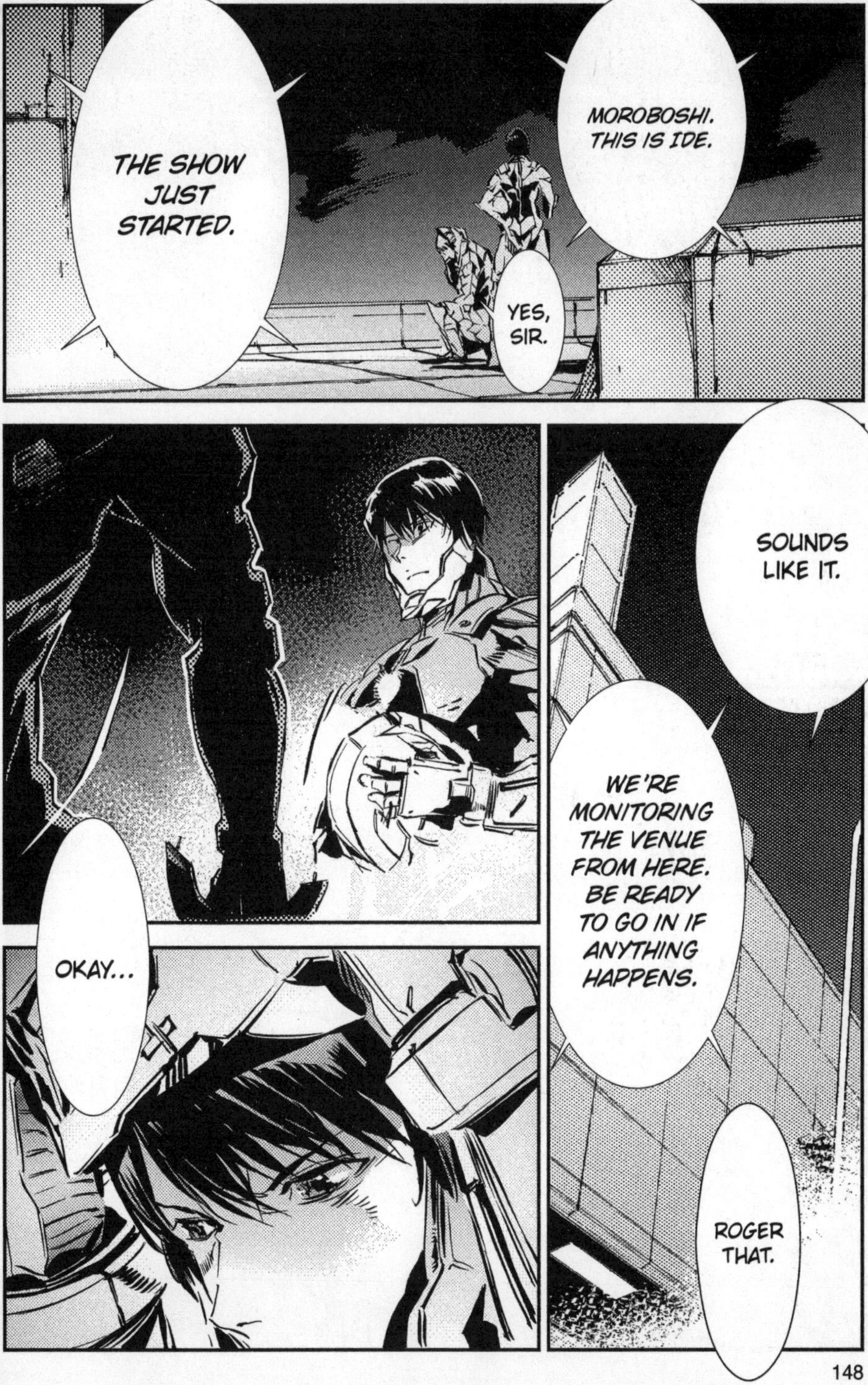
MOROBOSHI. THIS IS IDE.
YES, SIR.
THE SHOW JUST STARTED.
SOUNDS LIKE IT.
WE'RE MONITORING THE VENUE FROM HERE. BE READY TO GO IN IF ANYTHING HAPPENS.
ROGER THAT.
OKAY...

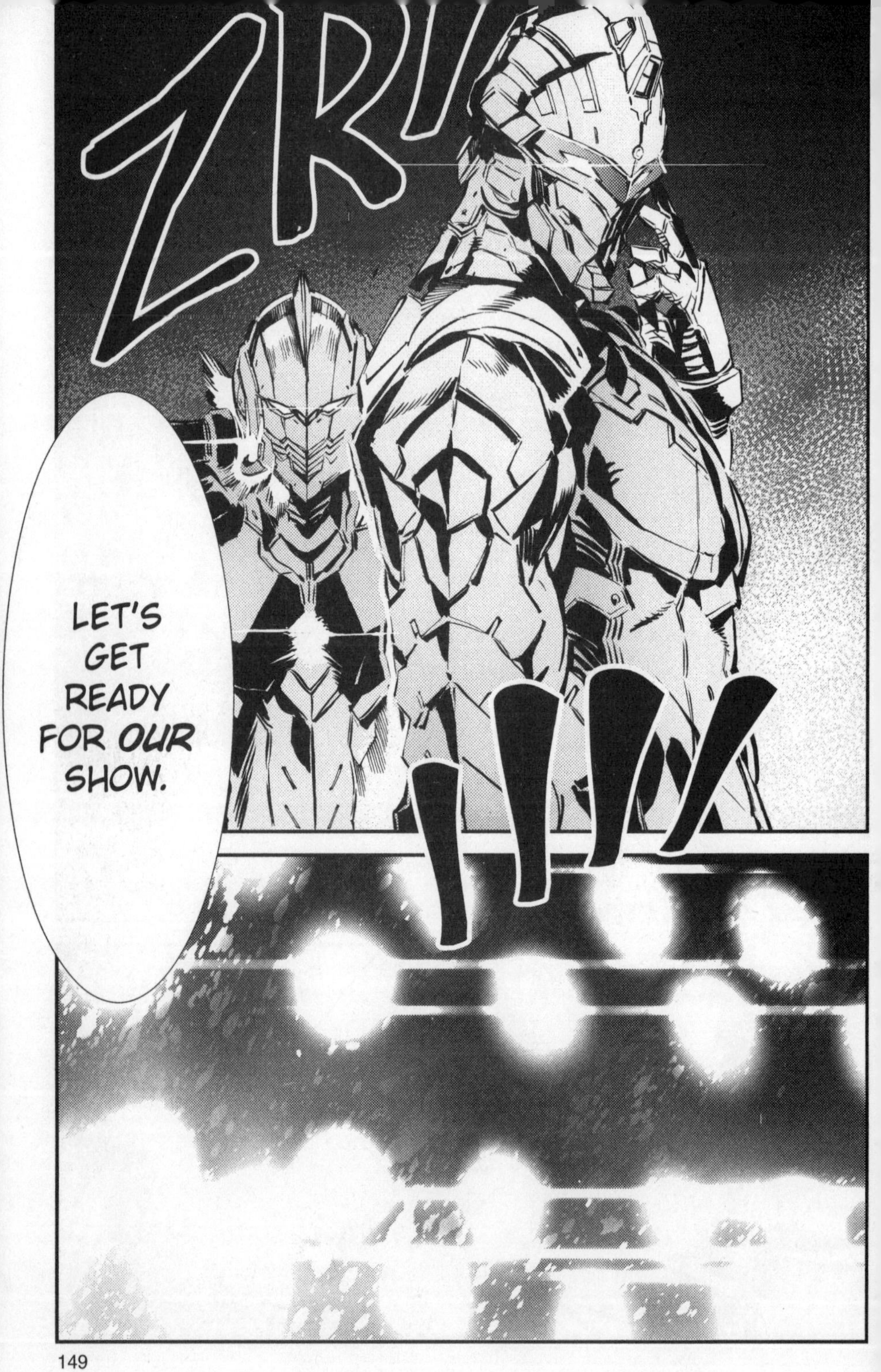
ZRU
LET'S GET READY FOR OUR SHOW.

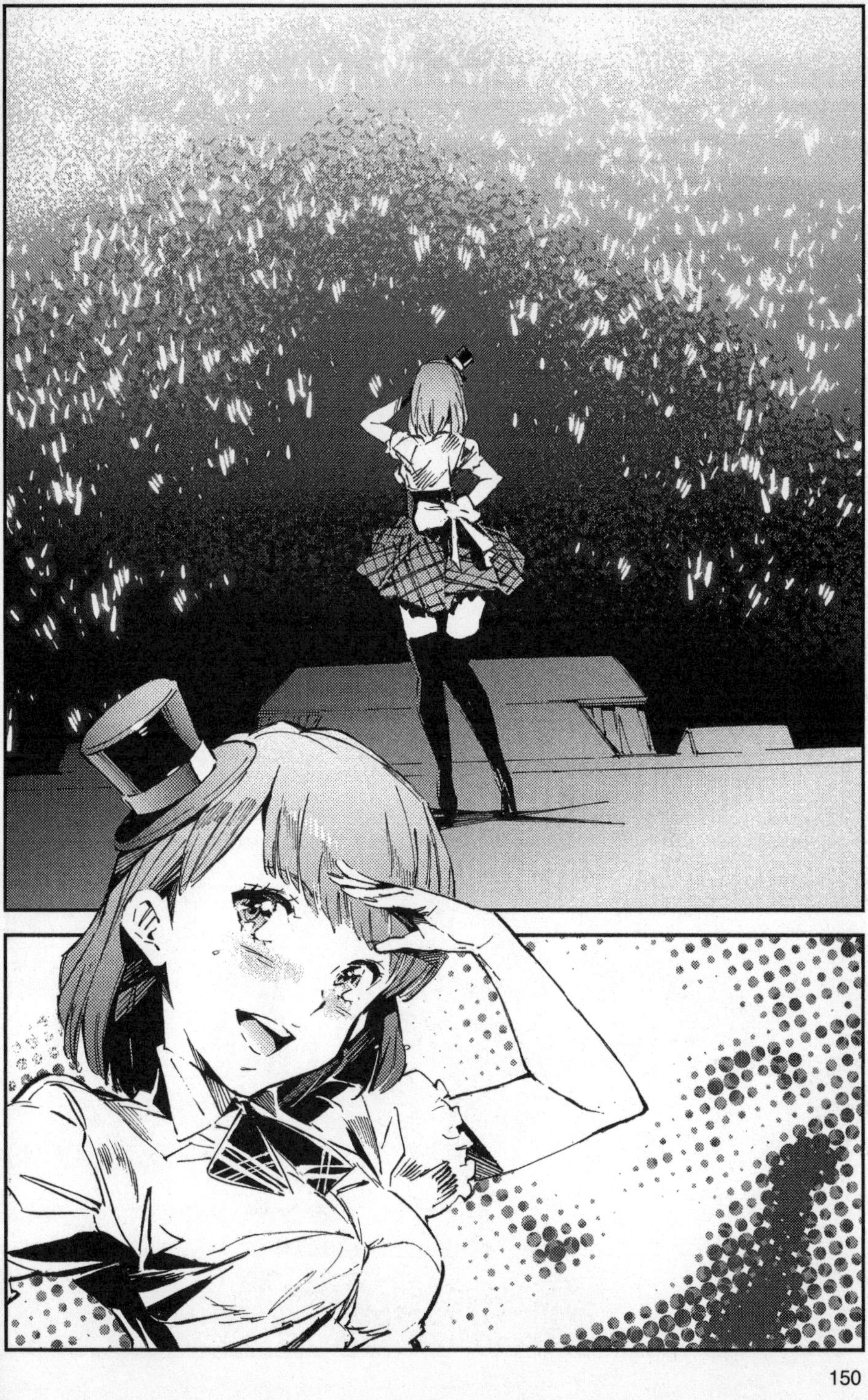

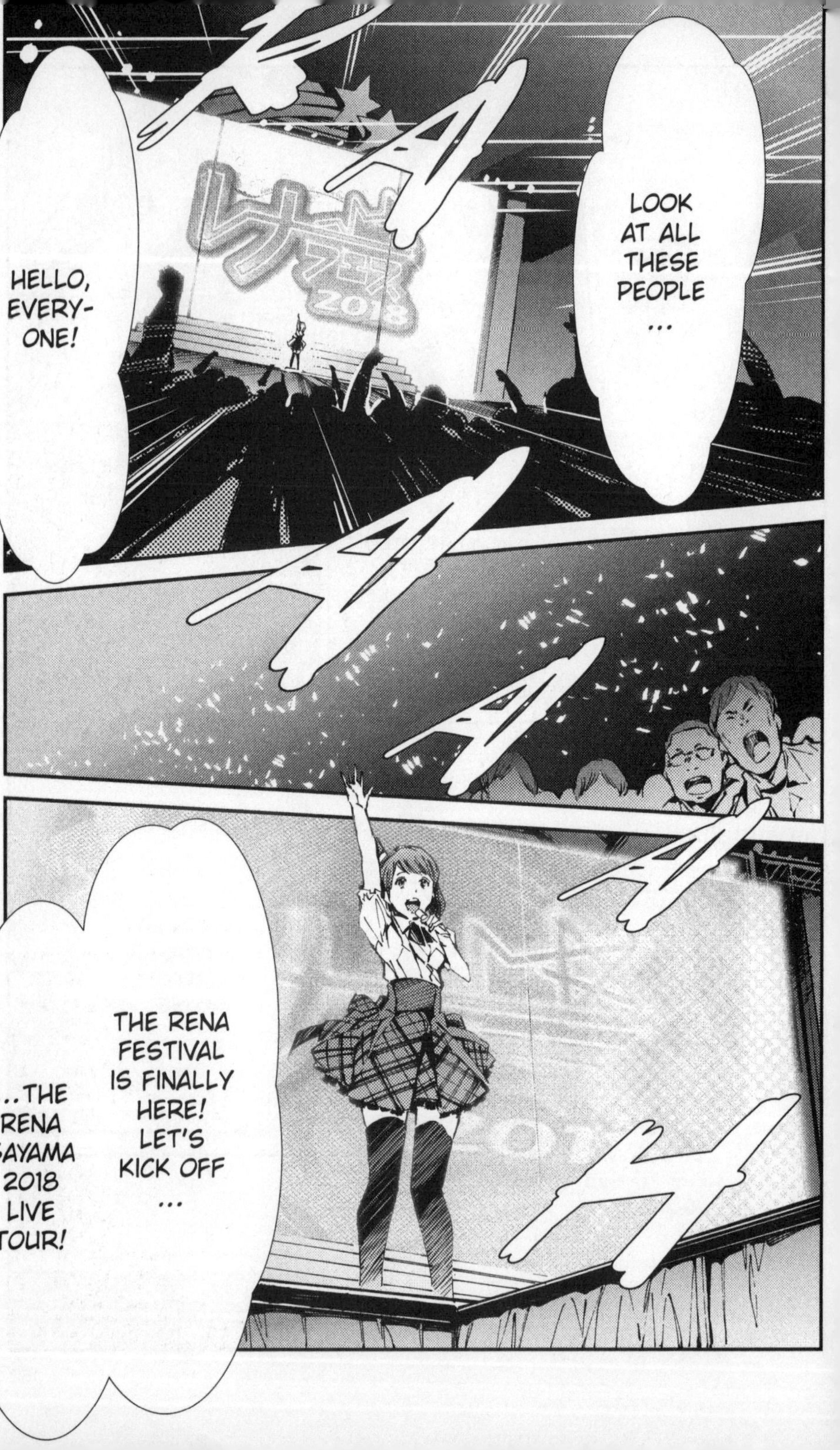
LOOK AT ALL THESE PEOPLE...
HELLO, EVERY-ONE!
THE RENA FESTIVAL IS FINALLY HERE! LET'S KICK OFF...
...THE RENA SAYAMA 2018 LIVE TOUR!

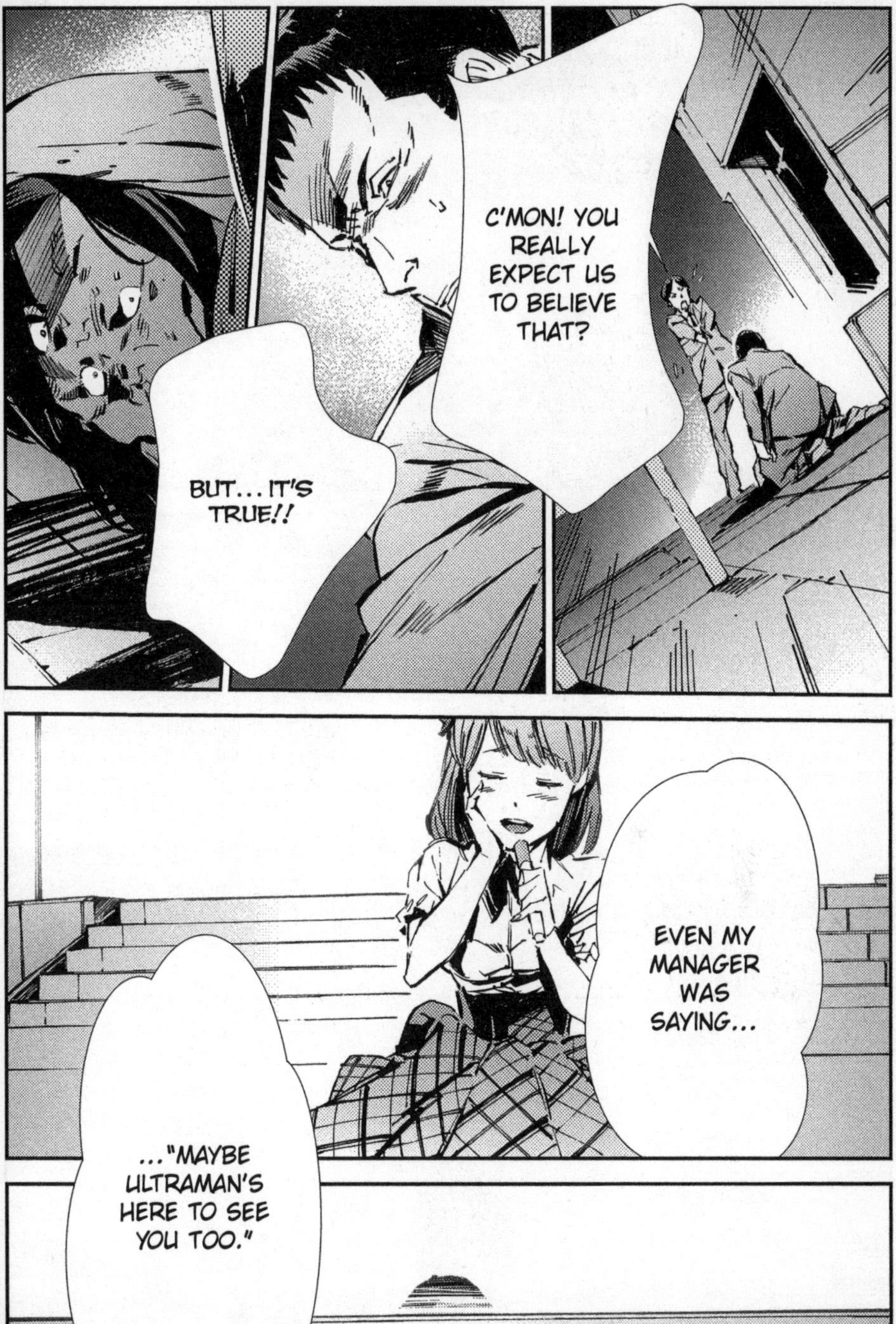
C'MON! YOU REALLY EXPECT US TO BELIEVE THAT?
BUT... IT'S TRUE!!
EVEN MY MANAGER WAS SAYING...
..."MAYBE ULTRAMAN'S HERE TO SEE YOU TOO."

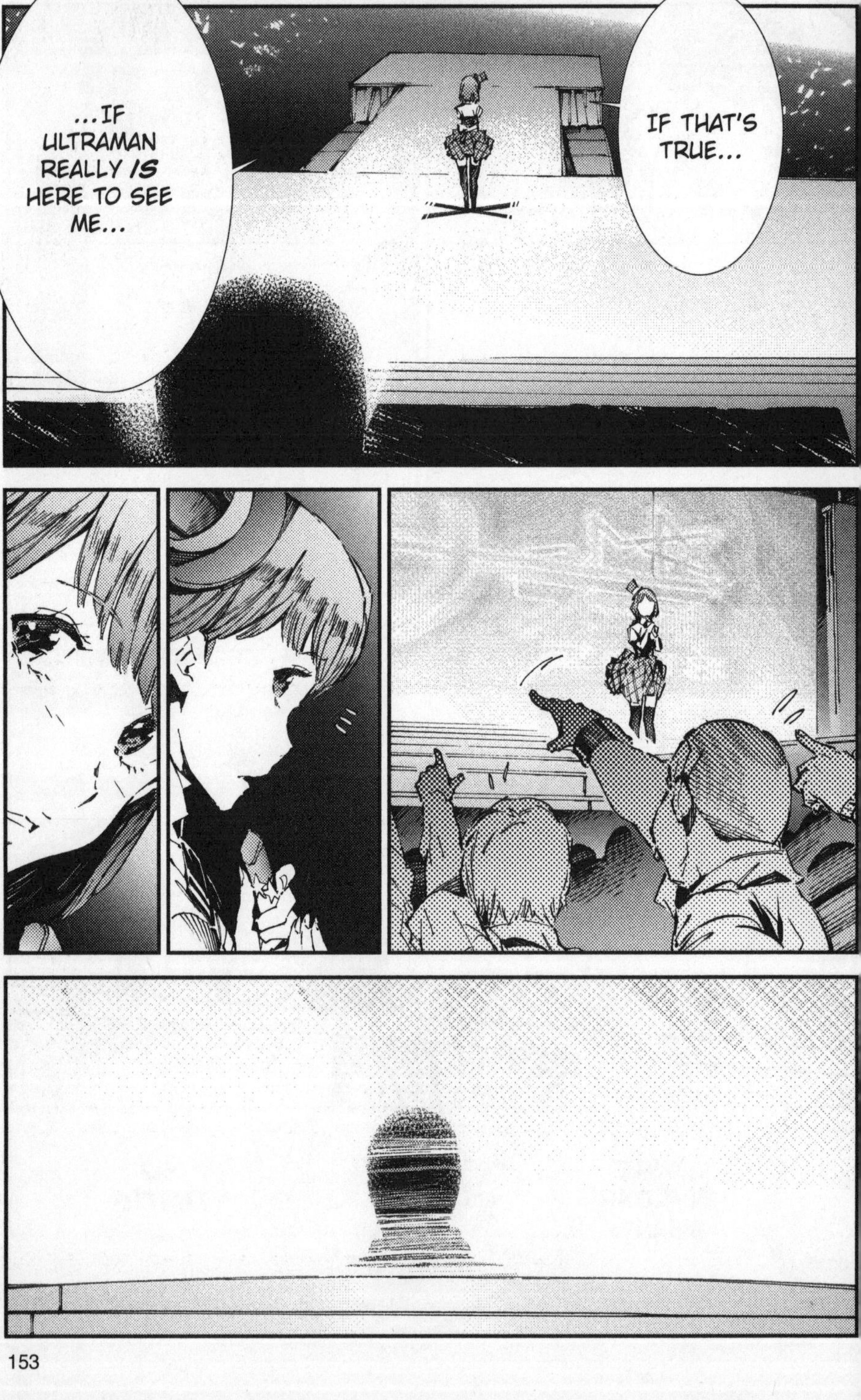
IF THAT'S TRUE...
...IF ULTRAMAN REALLY *IS* HERE TO SEE ME...

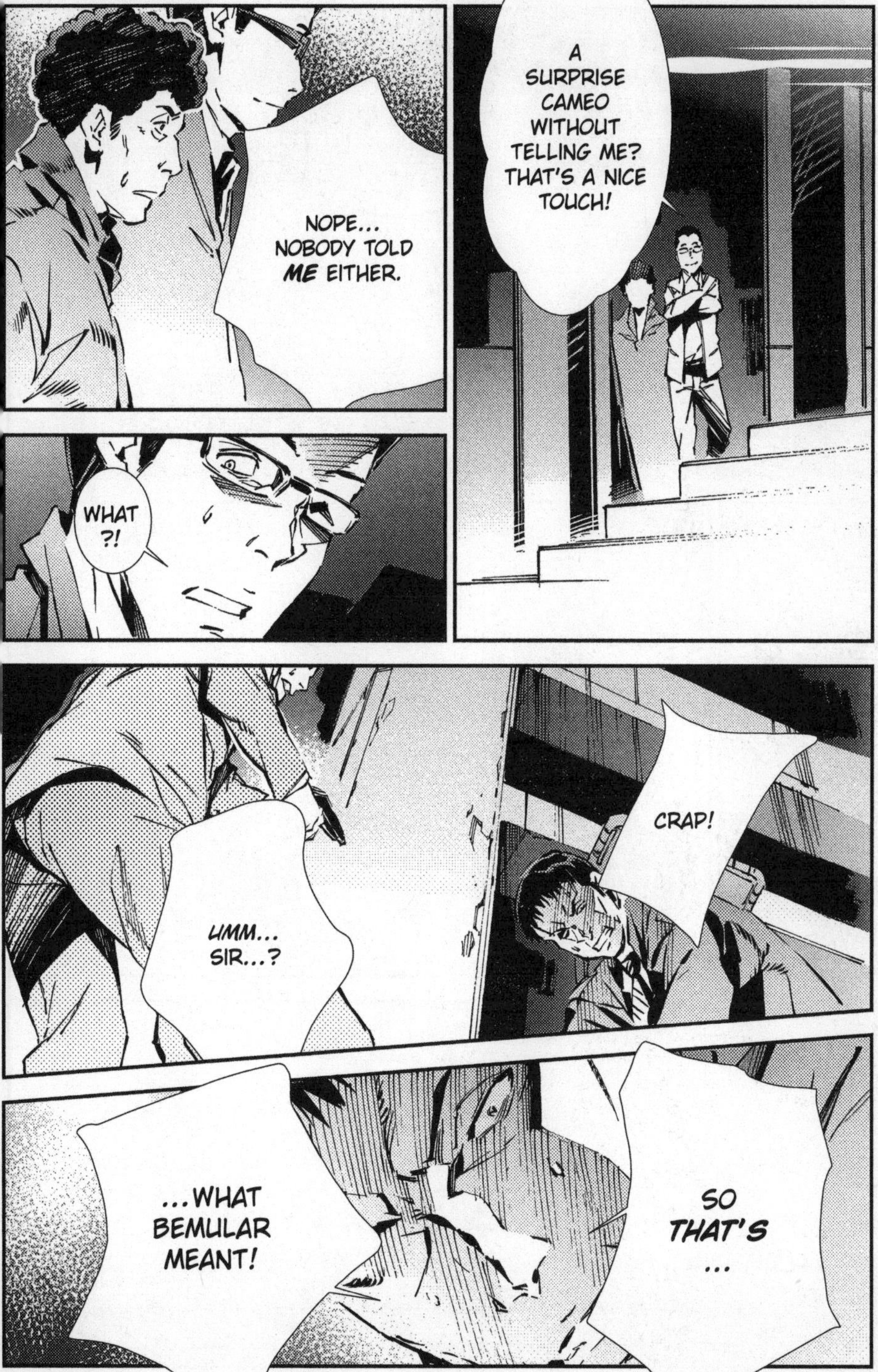
A SURPRISE CAMEO WITHOUT TELLING ME? THAT'S A NICE TOUCH!
NOPE... NOBODY TOLD ME EITHER.
WHAT ?!
CRAP!
UMM... SIR...?
SO THAT'S ...
...WHAT BEMULAR MEANT!

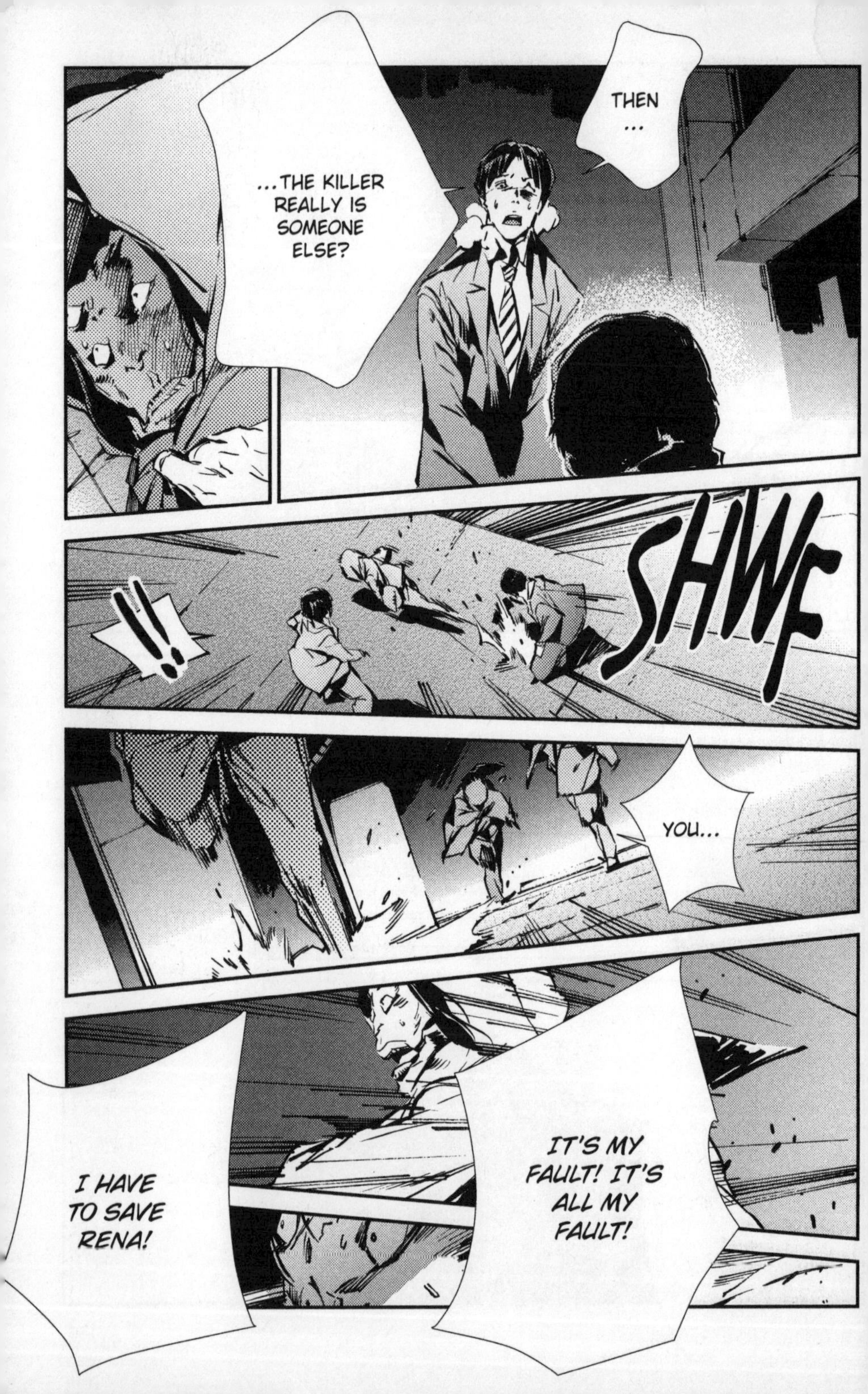
THEN ...
...THE KILLER REALLY IS SOMEONE ELSE?
SHWF
!!
YOU...
IT'S MY FAULT! IT'S ALL MY FAULT!
I HAVE TO SAVE RENA!

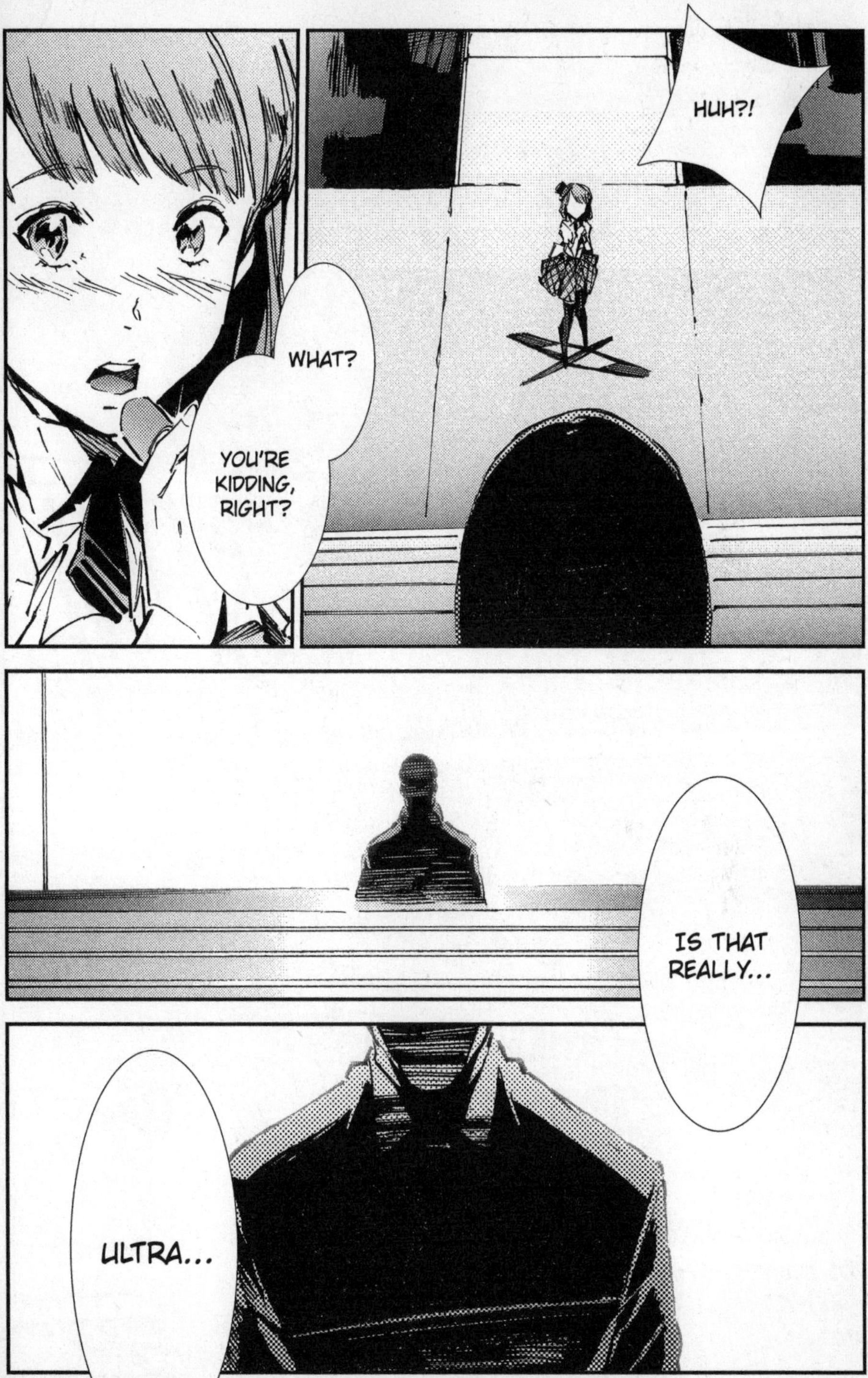
HUH?!
WHAT?
YOU'RE KIDDING, RIGHT?
IS THAT REALLY...
ULTRA...

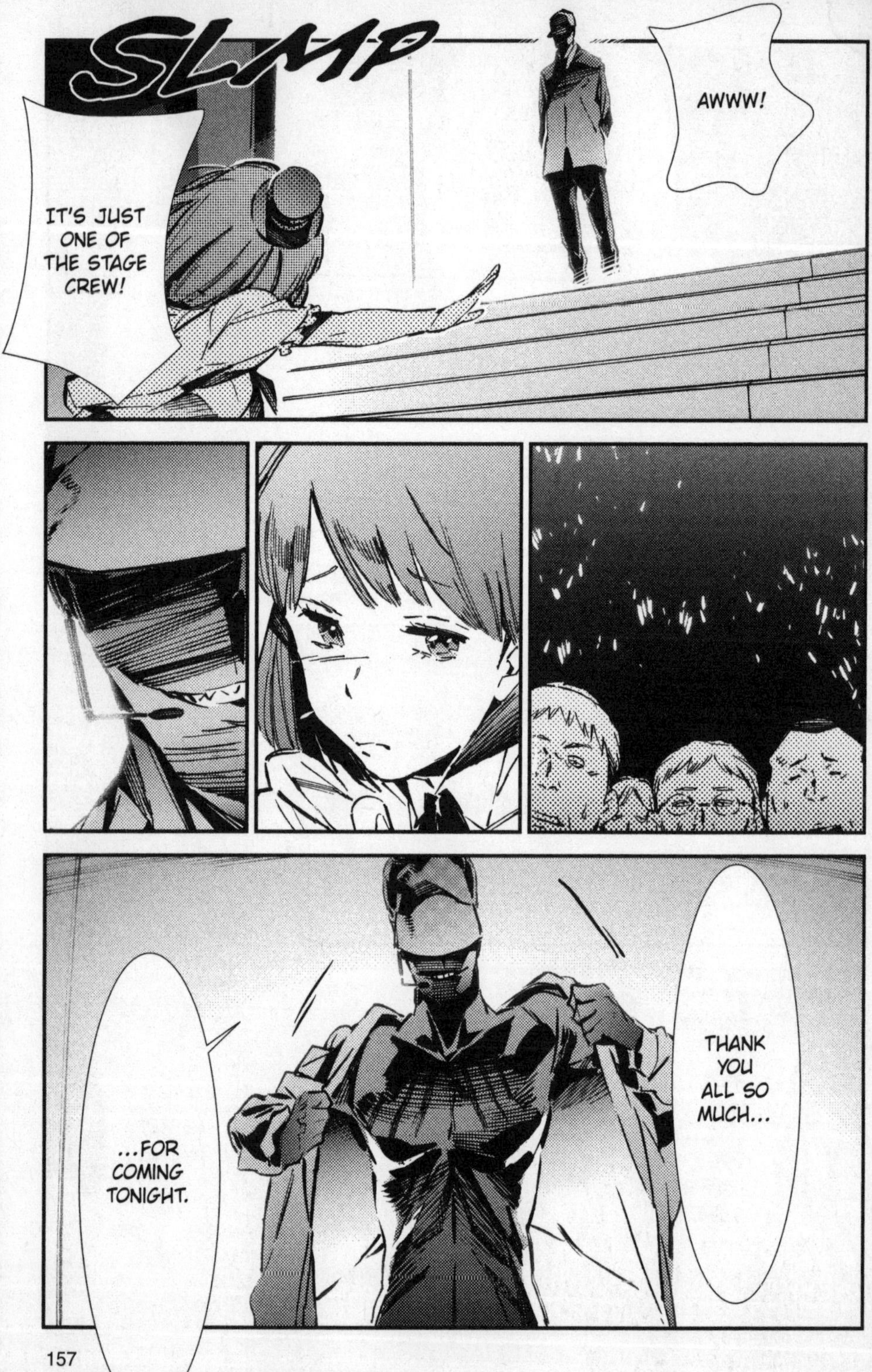
SLMP
AWWW!
IT'S JUST ONE OF THE STAGE CREW!
THANK YOU ALL SO MUCH...
...FOR COMING TONIGHT.

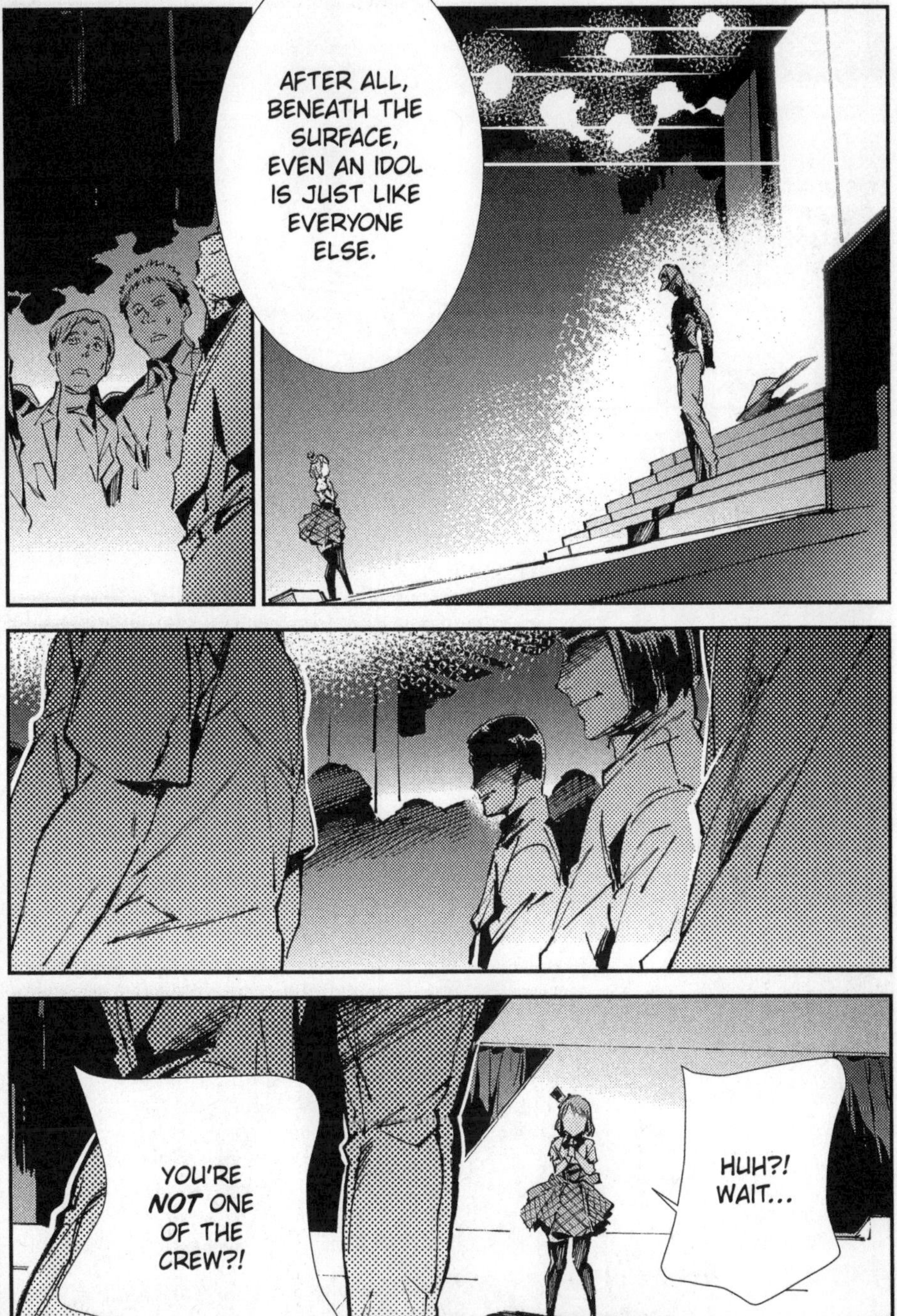
AFTER ALL, BENEATH THE SURFACE, EVEN AN IDOL IS JUST LIKE EVERYONE ELSE.
HUH?! WAIT...
YOU'RE *NOT* ONE OF THE CREW?!

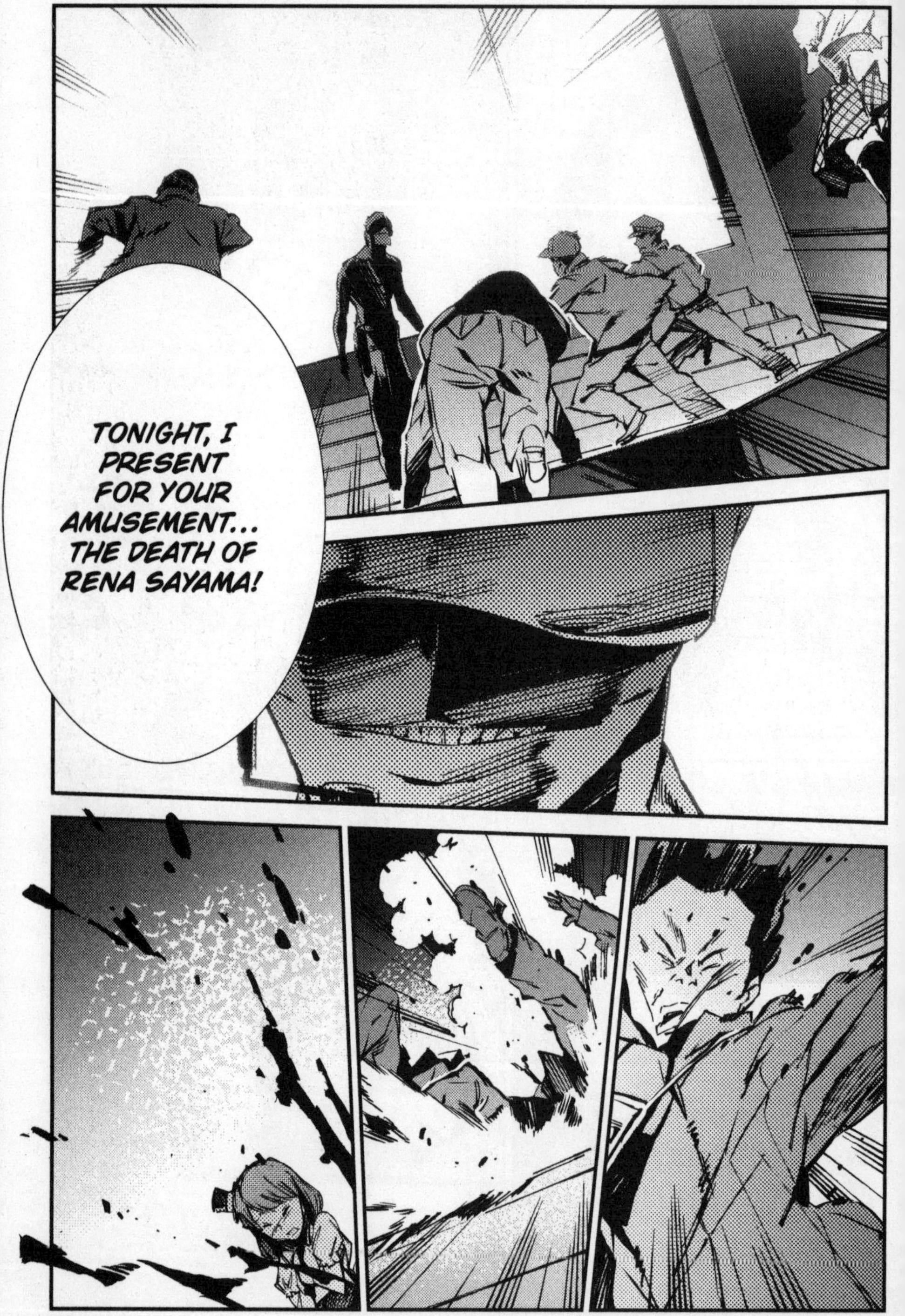
TONIGHT, I PRESENT FOR YOUR AMUSEMENT... THE DEATH OF RENA SAYAMA!

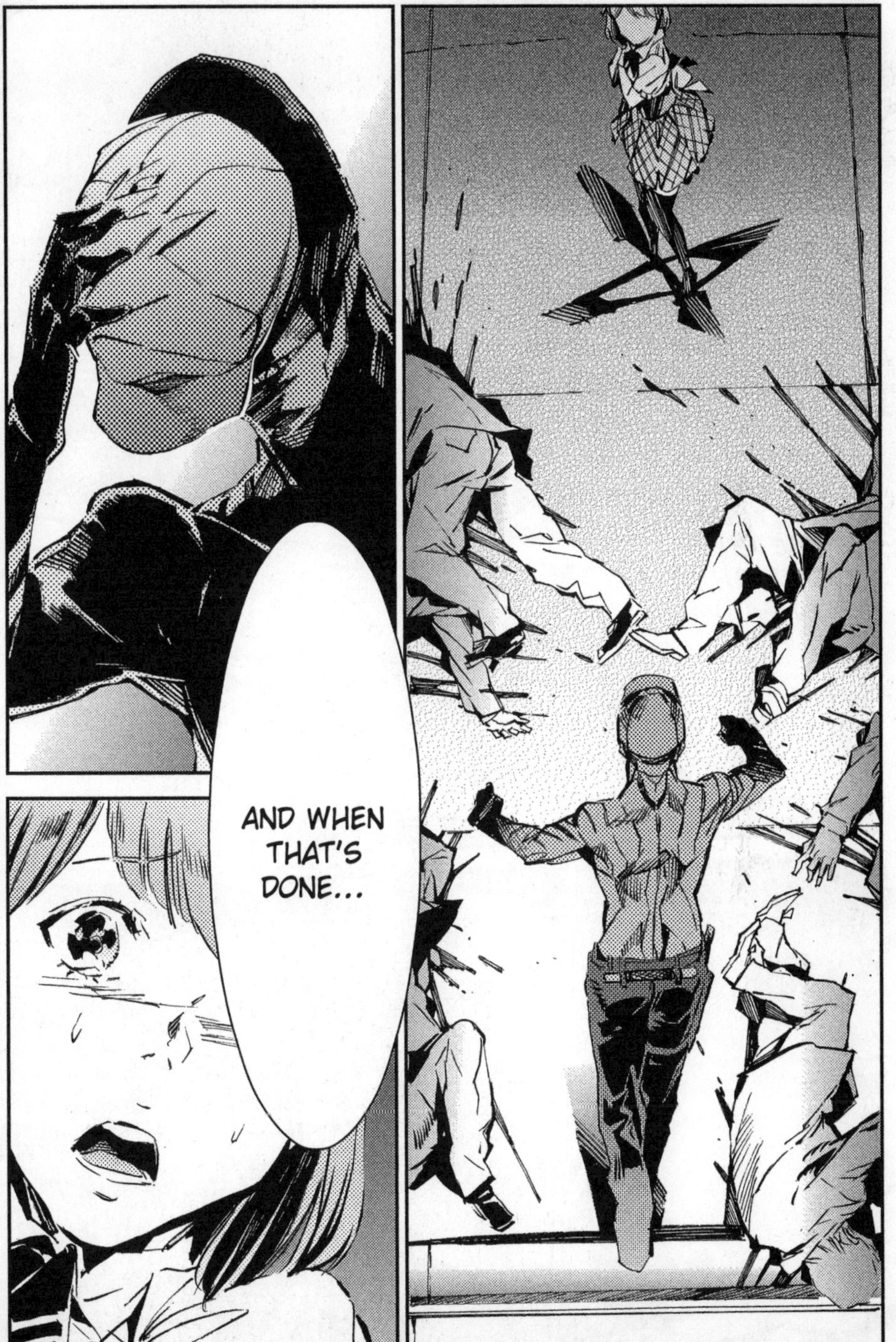
AND WHEN THAT'S DONE...

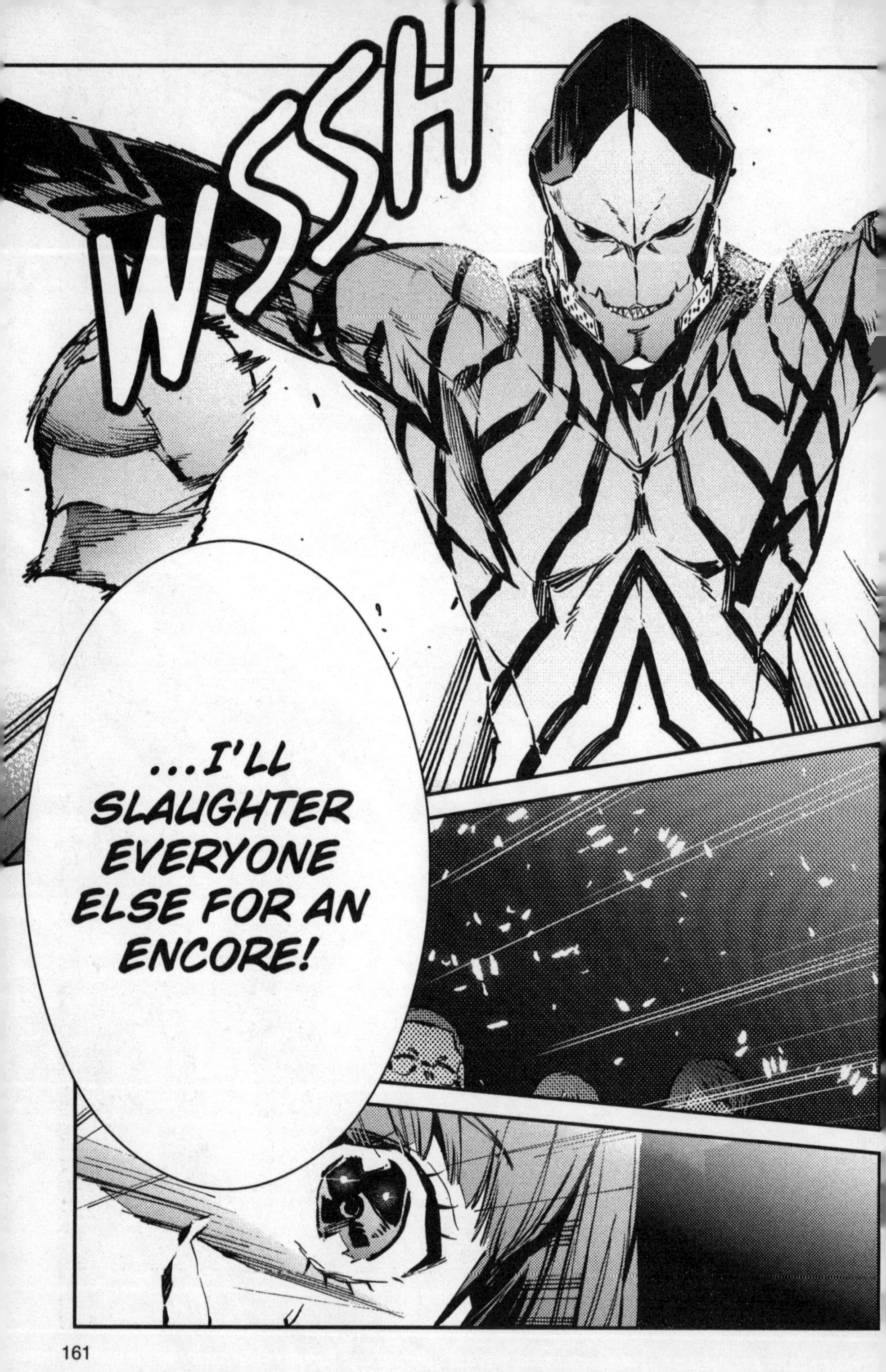
WSSH
...I'LL SLAUGHTER EVERYONE ELSE FOR AN ENCORE!

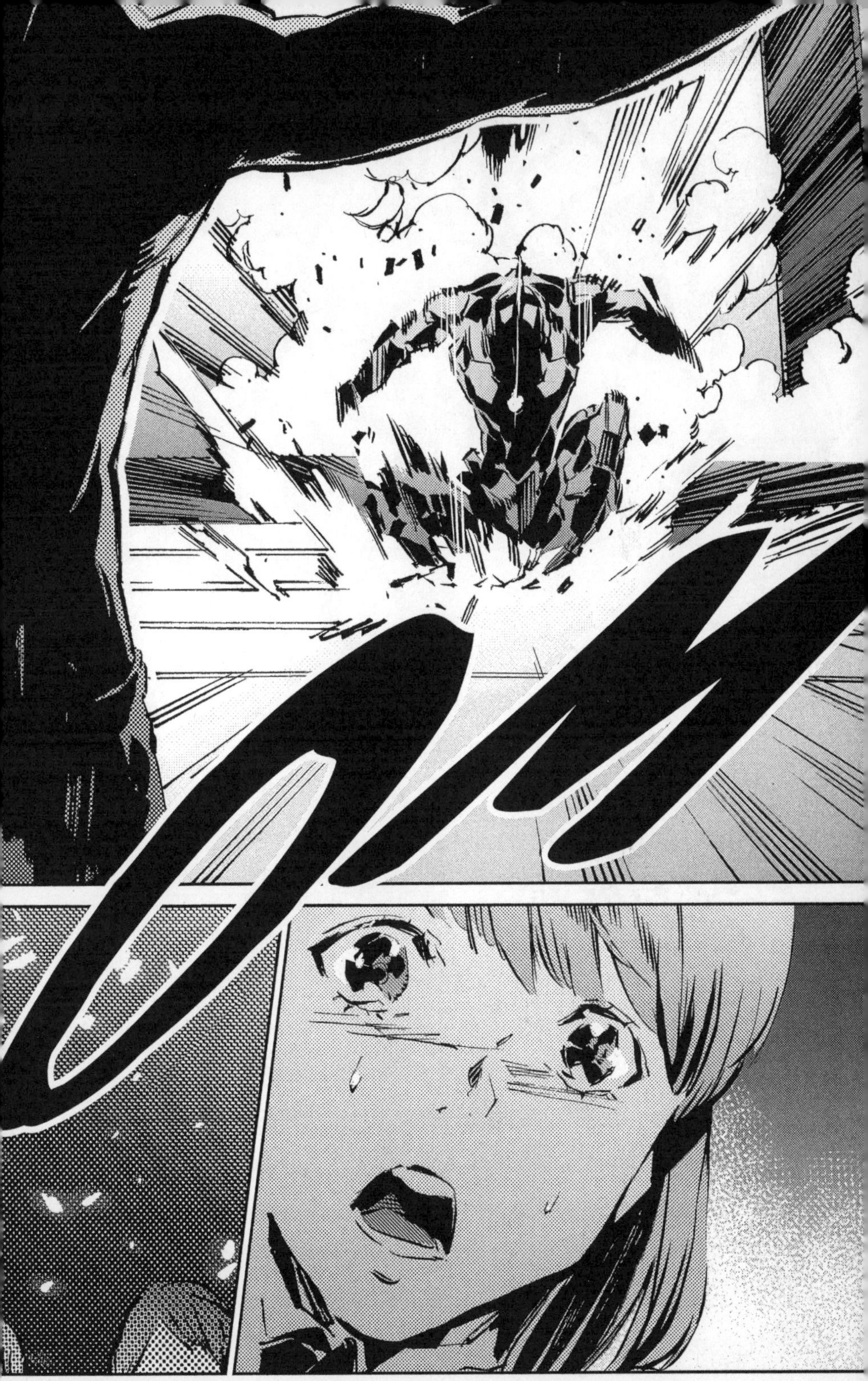

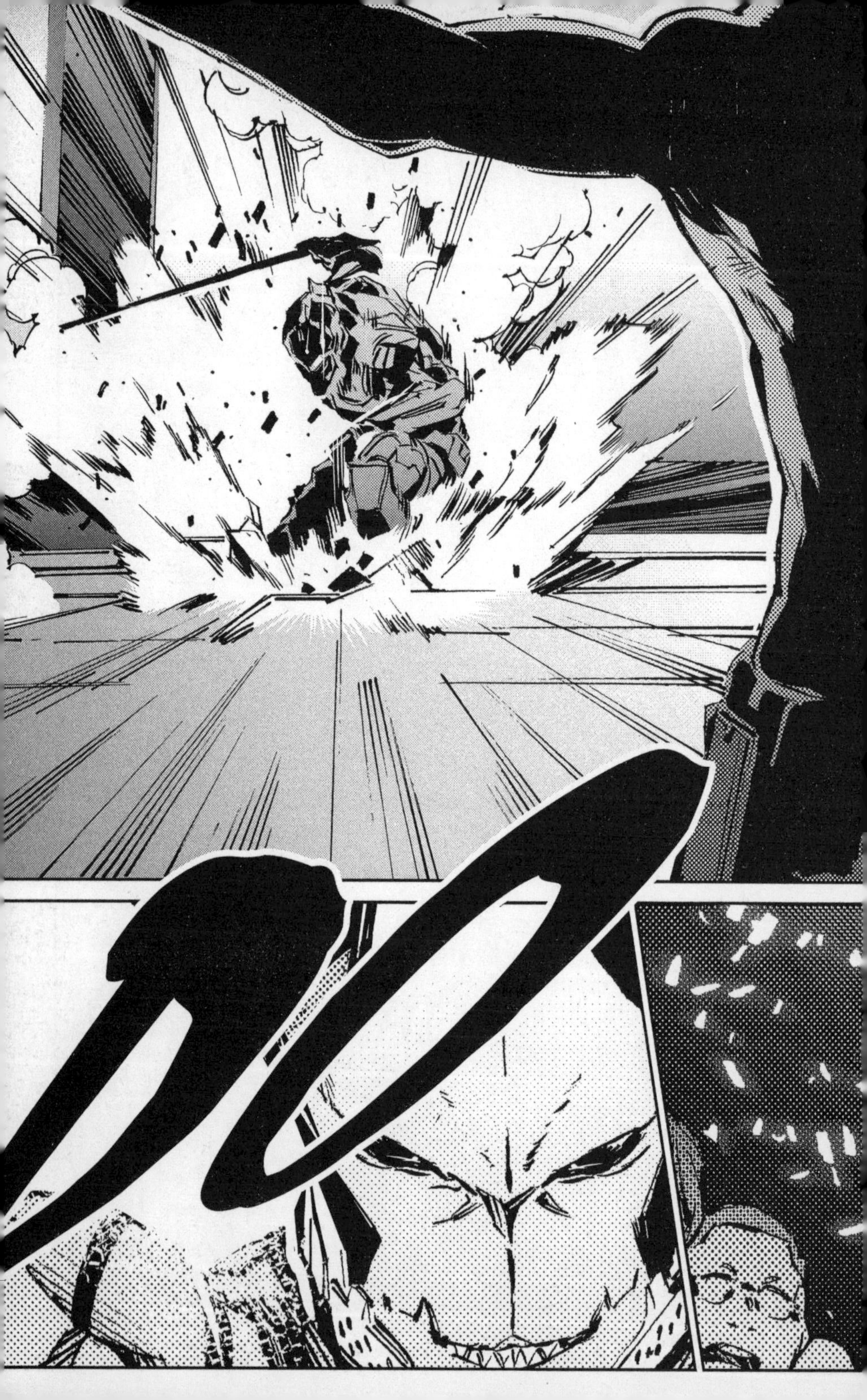

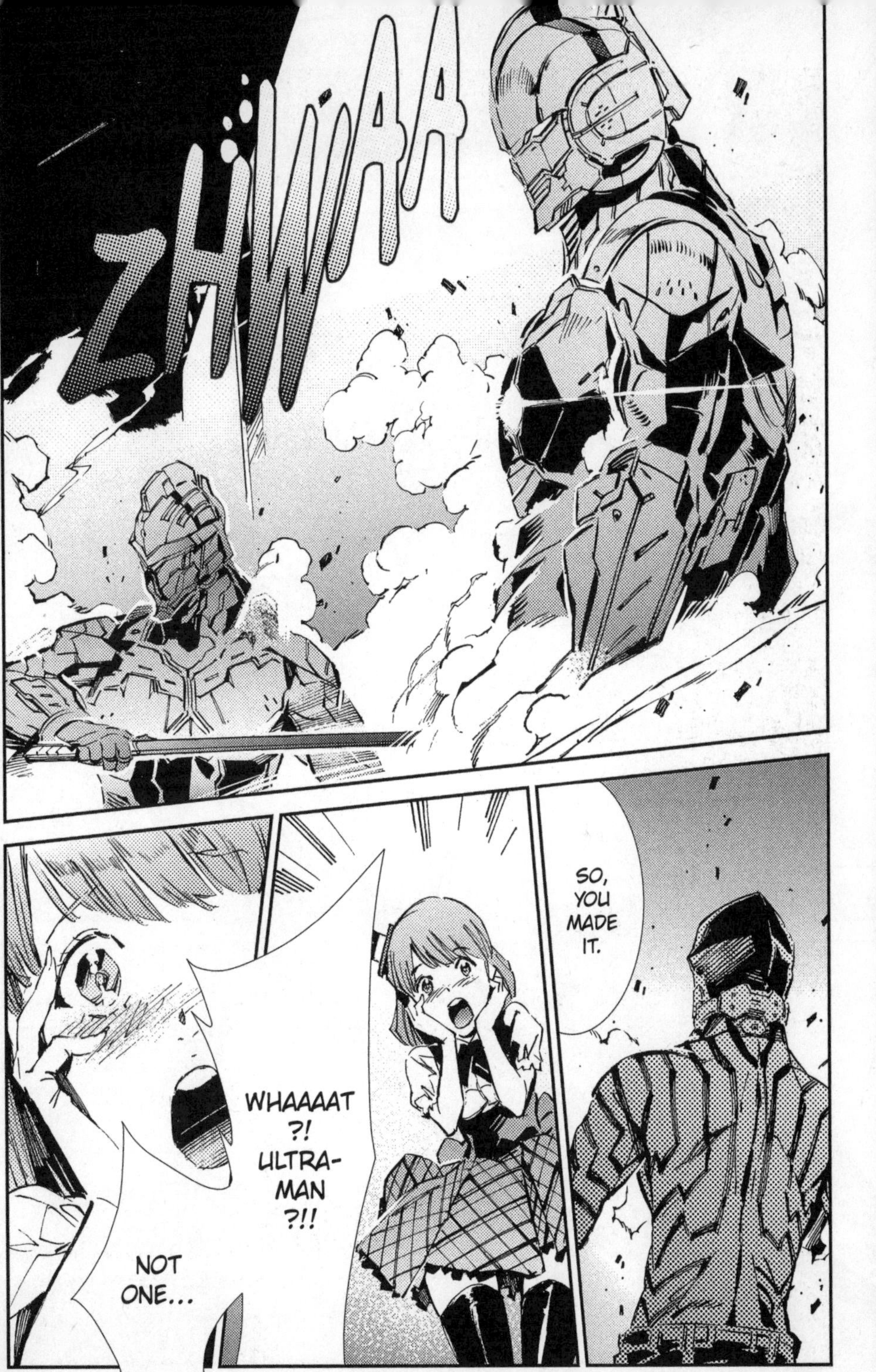
ZHWAA
SO, YOU MADE IT.
WHAAAAT?! ULTRAMAN?!!
NOT ONE...

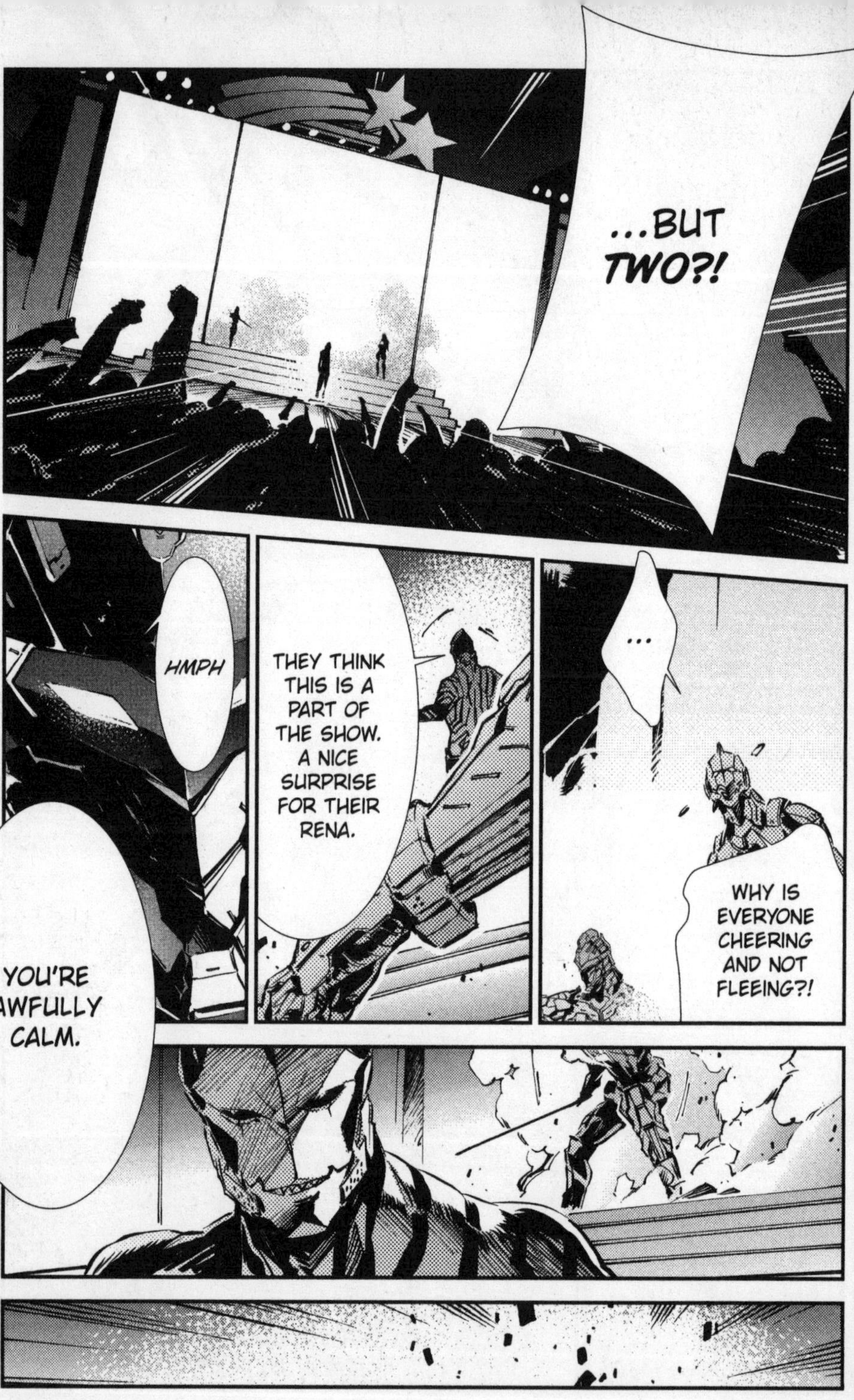
...BUT TWO?!
...
WHY IS EVERYONE CHEERING AND NOT FLEEING?!
THEY THINK THIS IS A PART OF THE SHOW. A NICE SURPRISE FOR THEIR RENA.
HMPH
YOU'RE AWFULLY CALM.

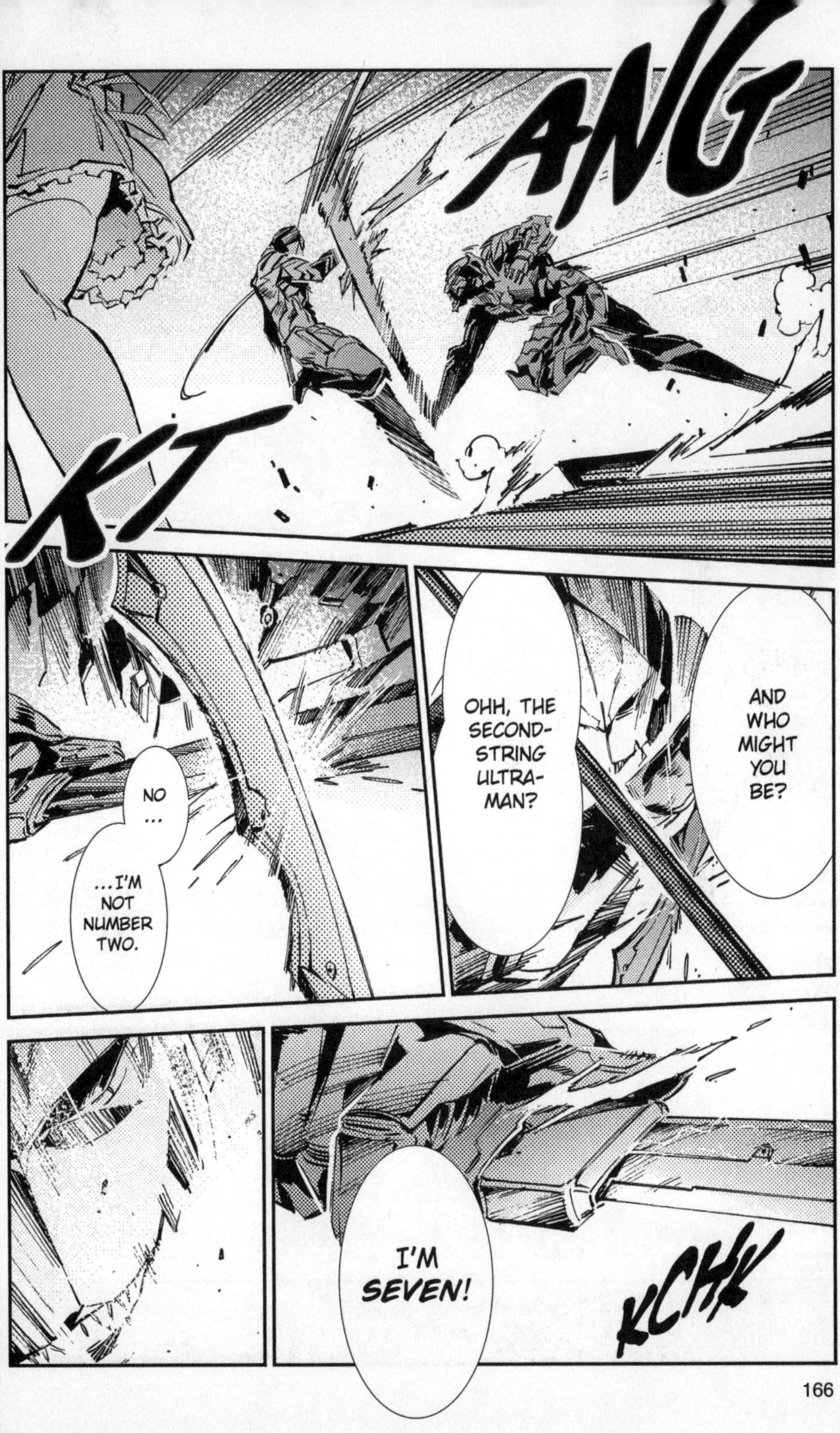
ANG
KT
AND WHO MIGHT YOU BE?
OHH, THE SECOND-STRING ULTRA-MAN?
NO ...
...I'M NOT NUMBER TWO.
KCHK
I'M SEVEN!

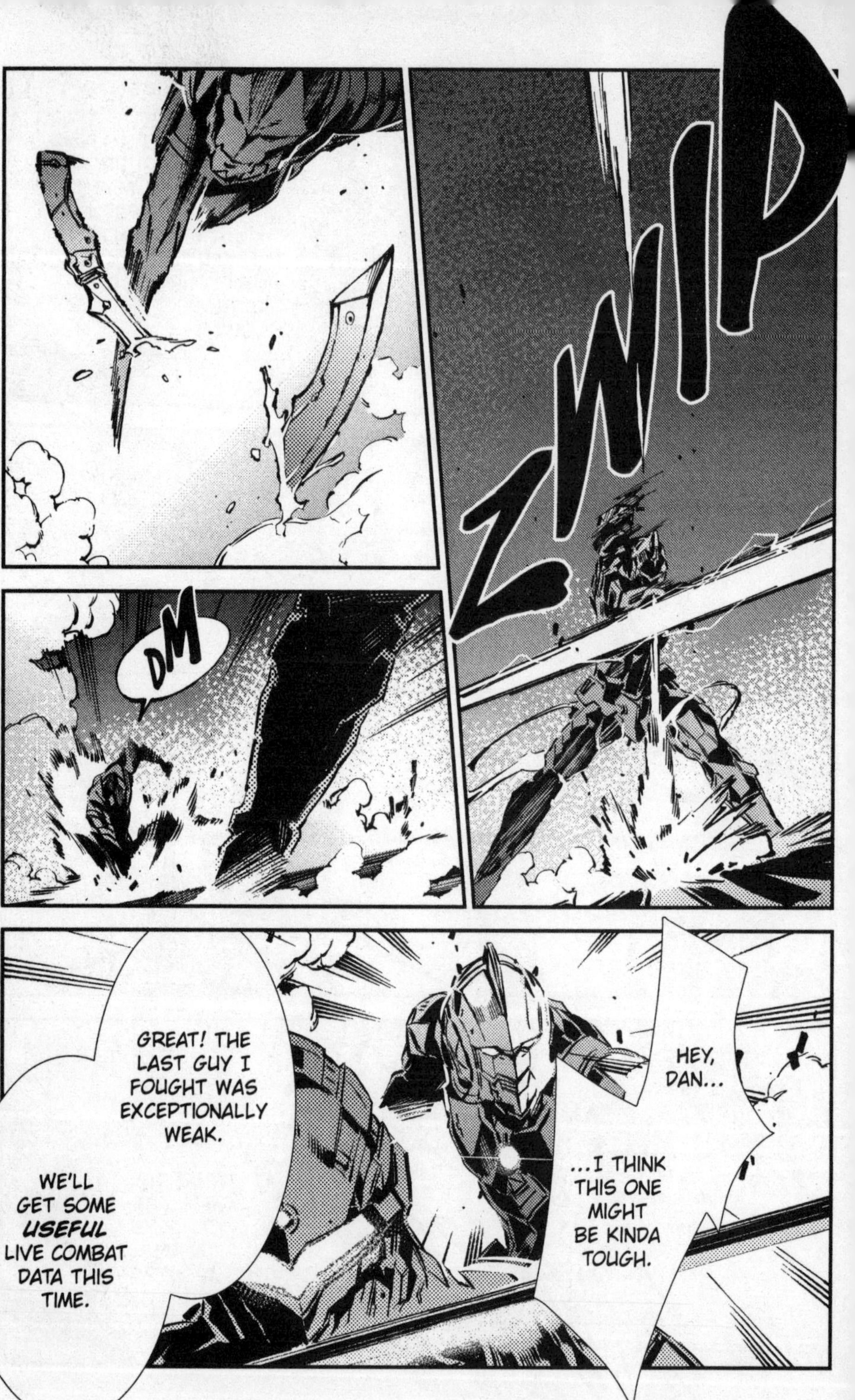
ZWIP
DM
HEY, DAN...
...I THINK THIS ONE MIGHT BE KINDA TOUGH.
GREAT! THE LAST GUY I FOUGHT WAS EXCEPTIONALLY WEAK.
WE'LL GET SOME USEFUL LIVE COMBAT DATA THIS TIME.

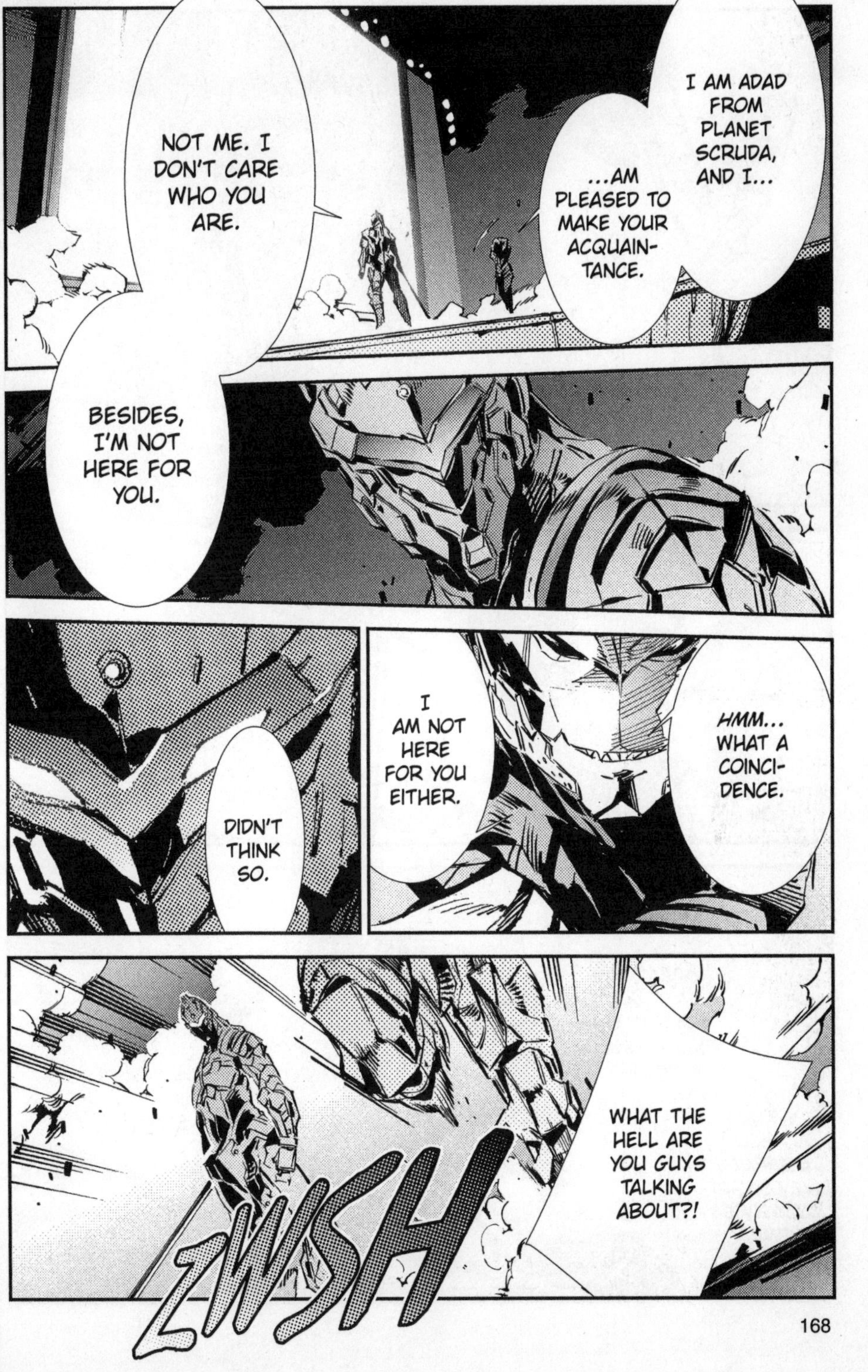
I AM ADAD FROM PLANET SCRUDA, AND I...
...AM PLEASED TO MAKE YOUR ACQUAINTANCE.
NOT ME. I DON'T CARE WHO YOU ARE.
BESIDES, I'M NOT HERE FOR YOU.
HMM... WHAT A COINCIDENCE.
I AM NOT HERE FOR YOU EITHER.
DIDN'T THINK SO.
WHAT THE HELL ARE YOU GUYS TALKING ABOUT?!
ZWISH

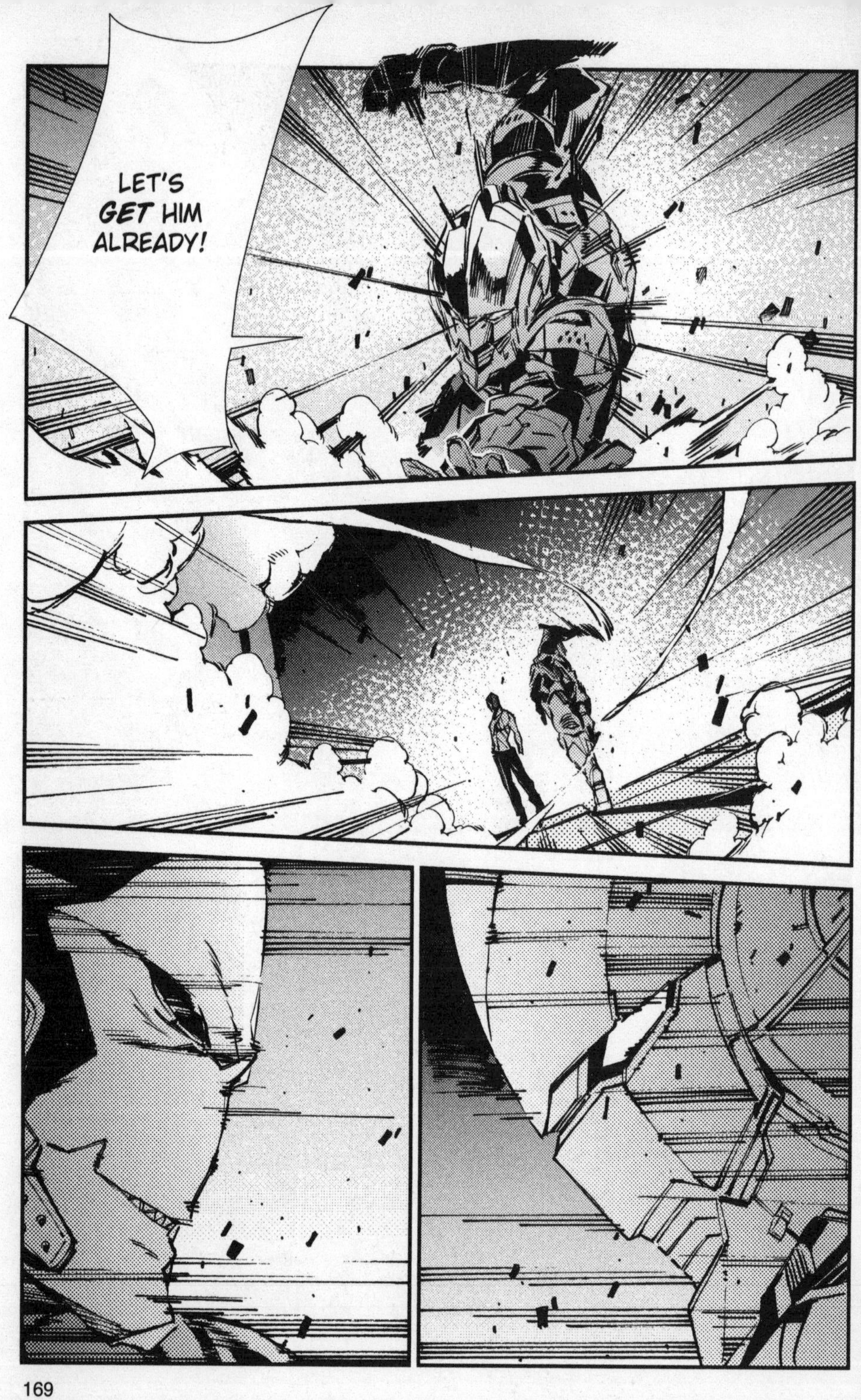
LET'S GET HIM ALREADY!

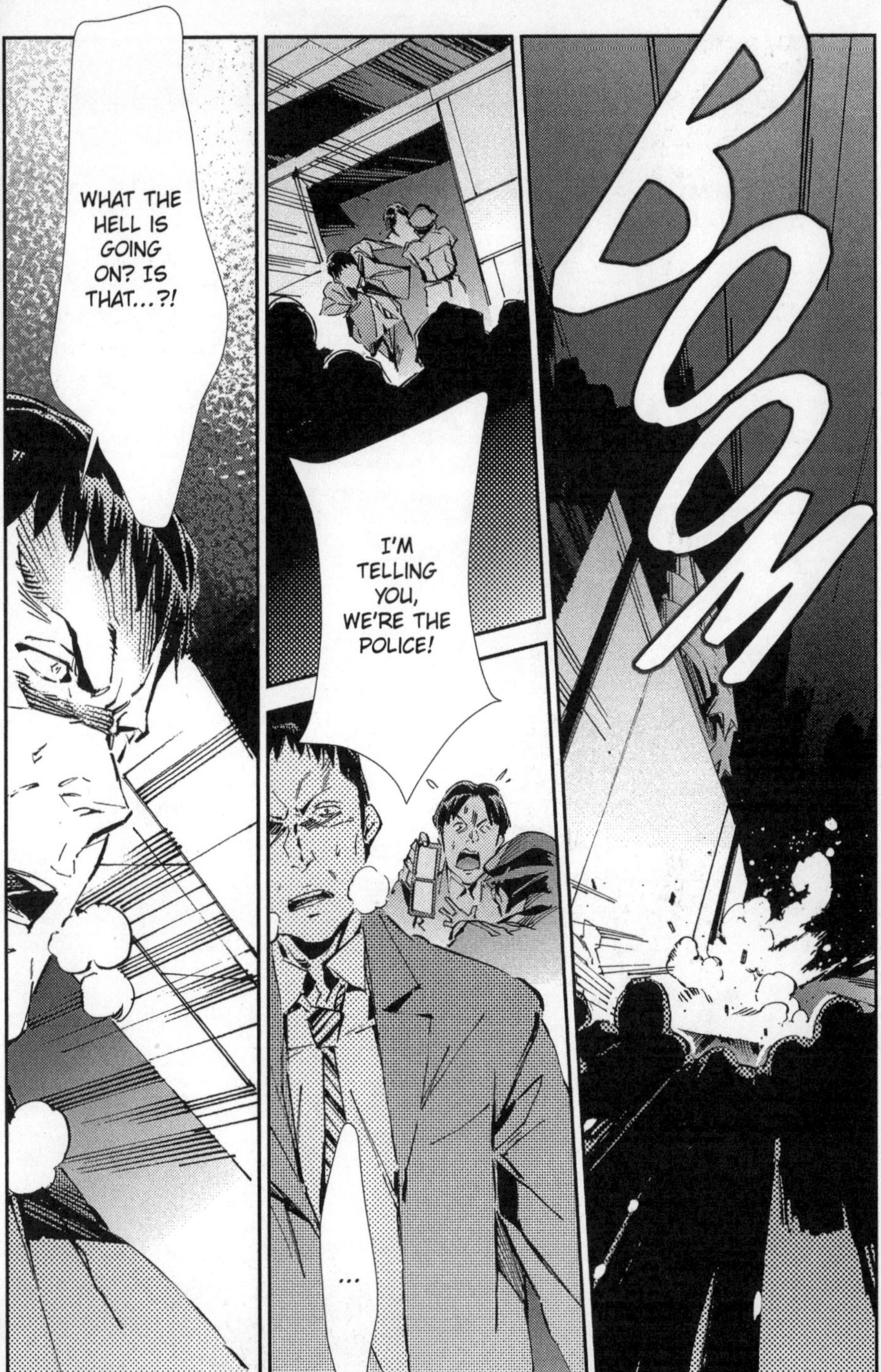
BOOM
I'M TELLING YOU, WE'RE THE POLICE!
...
WHAT THE HELL IS GOING ON? IS THAT...?!

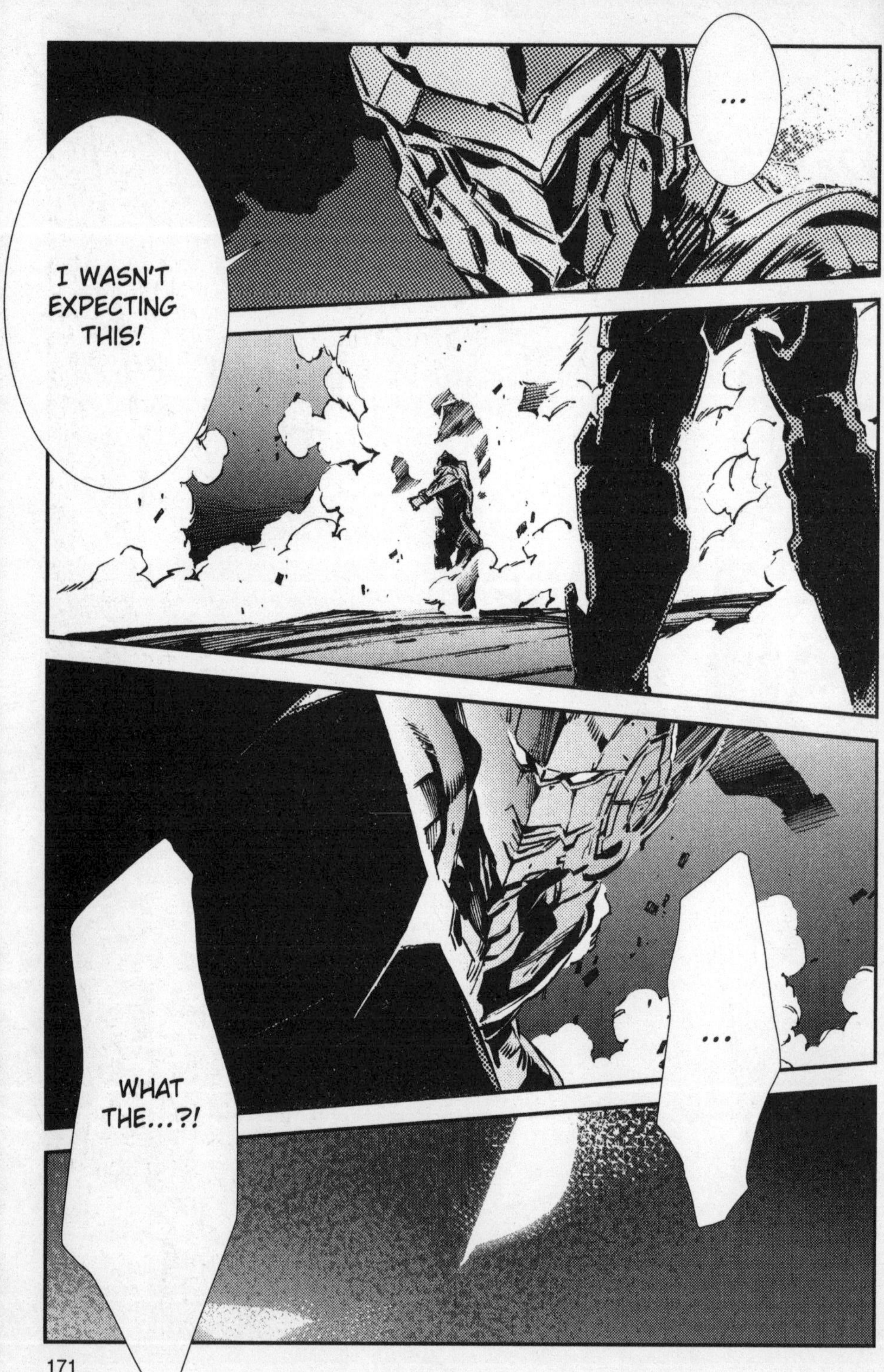
...
I WASN'T EXPECTING THIS!
...
WHAT THE...?!

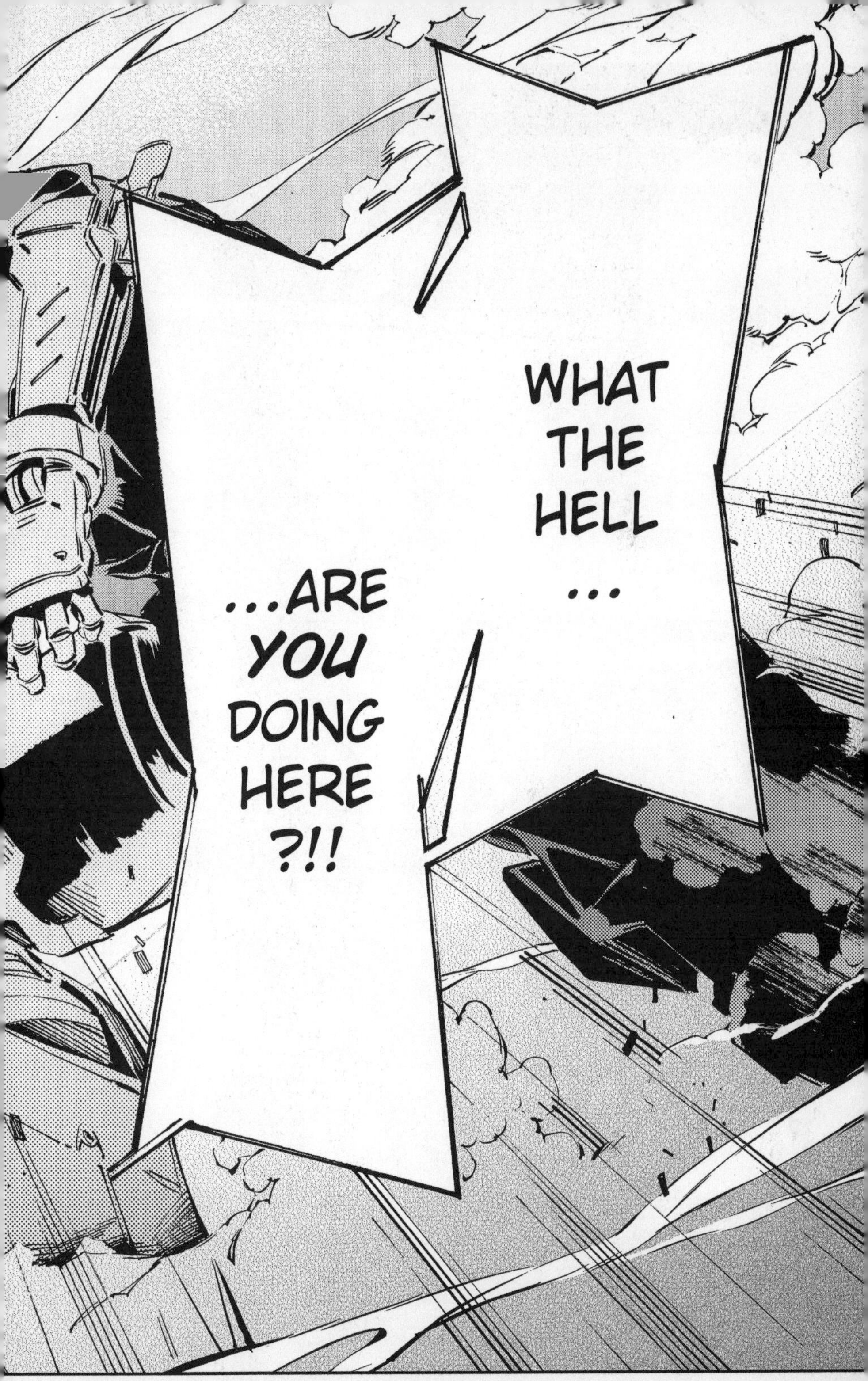
WHAT THE HELL ...
...ARE YOU DOING HERE ?!!

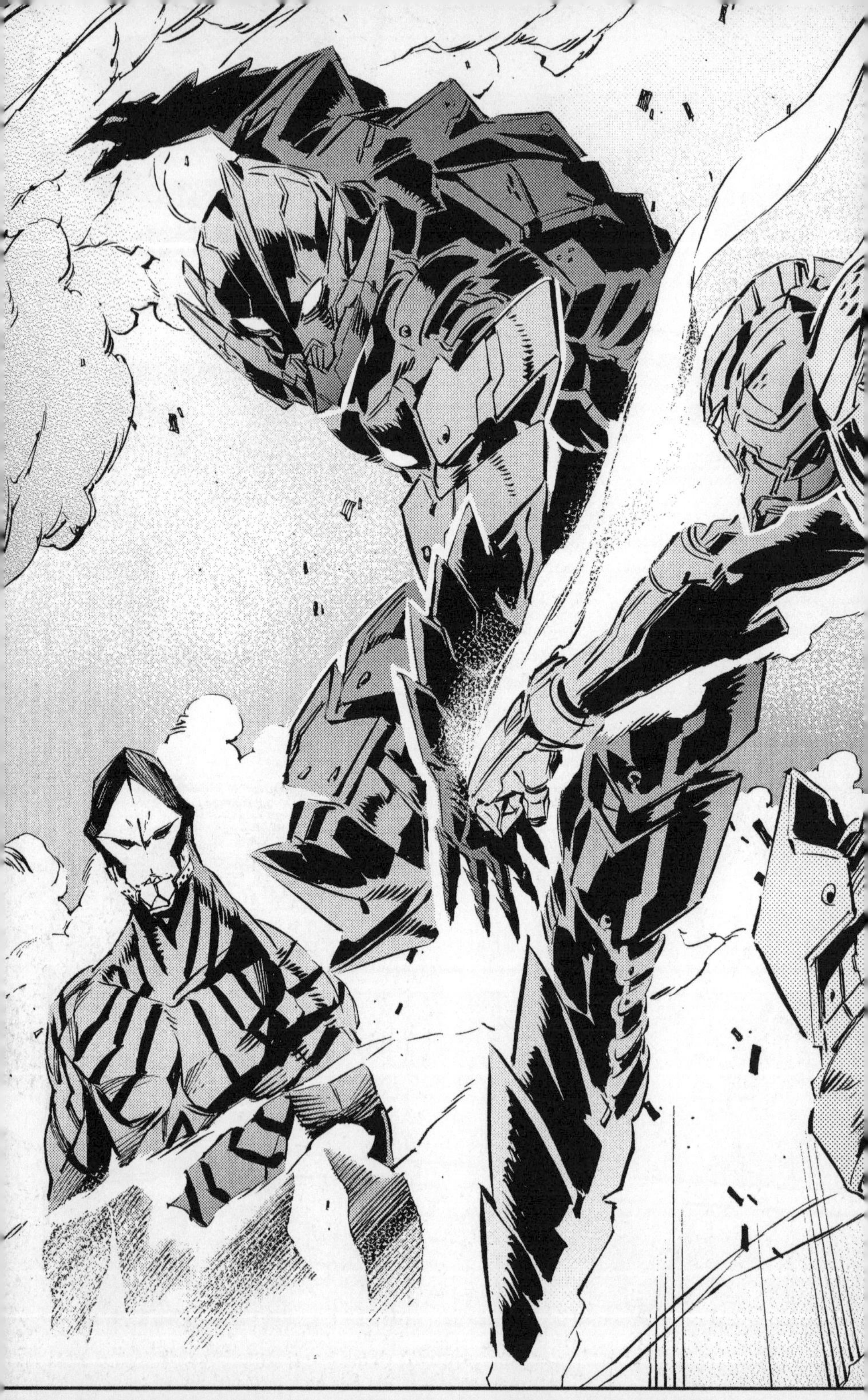

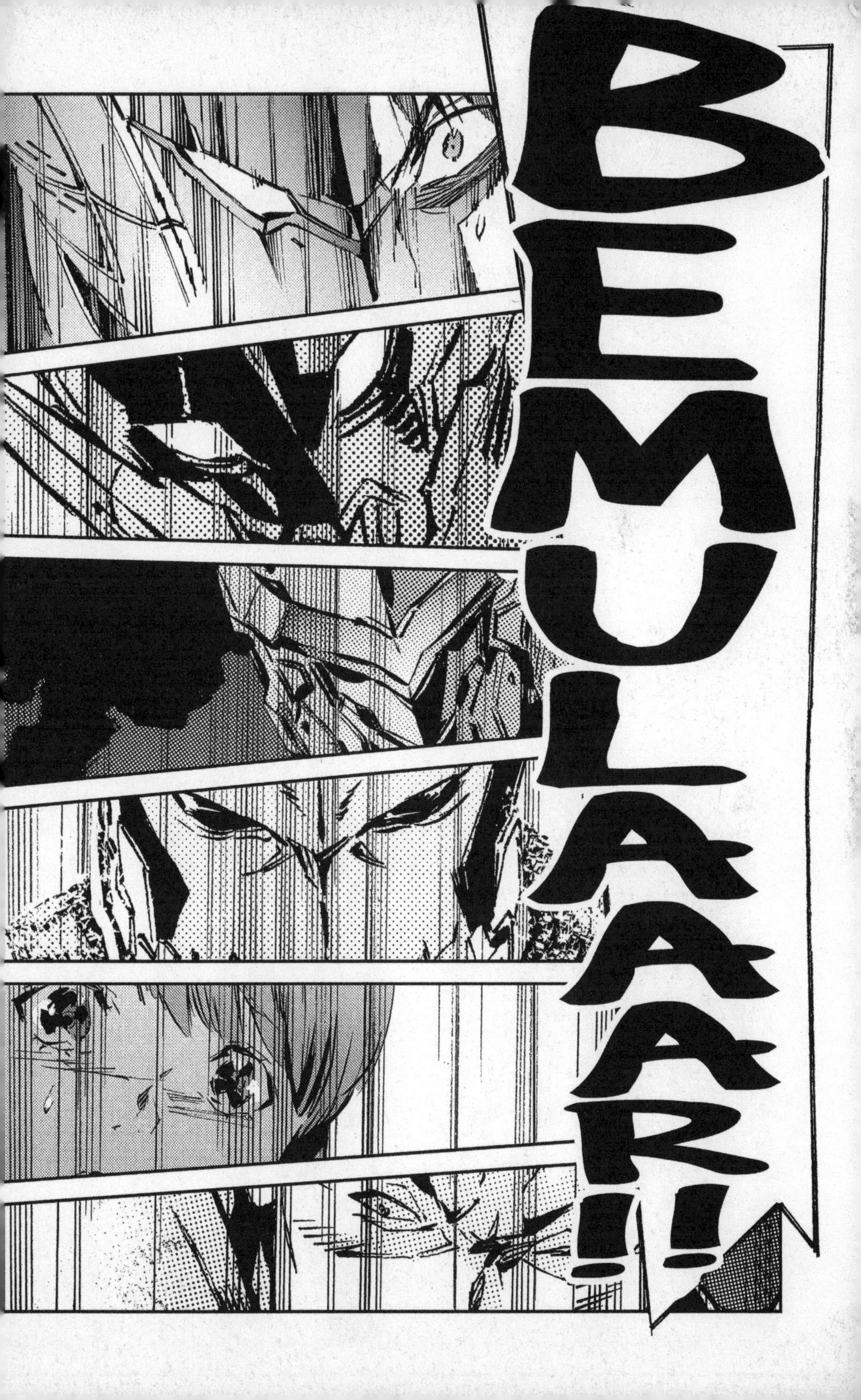
BEMULAAAR!!

THIS IS THE BEGINNING OF A NEW AGE

ULTRAMAN SUIT Ver. 7.1

Ultraman-type exo-armor for Dan Moroboshi. The suit was designed for ordinary humans and thus is equipped with numerous experimental features to cover a wide range of potential situations. However, many issues exist, such as the toll it takes on its wearer. According to Ide, although it's been sent into active service, it is far from finished.

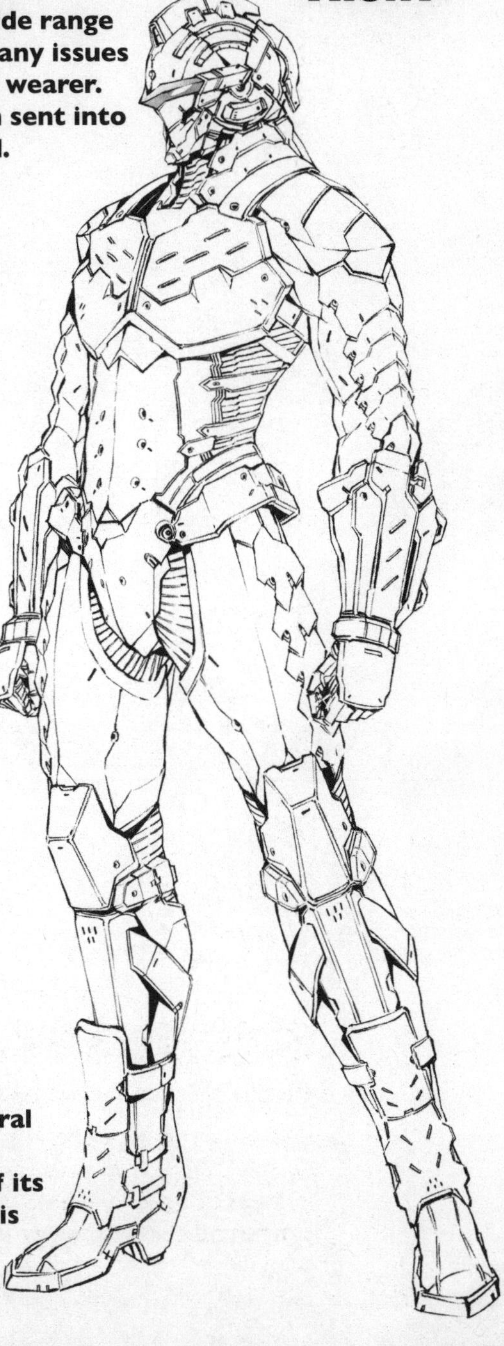
FRONT

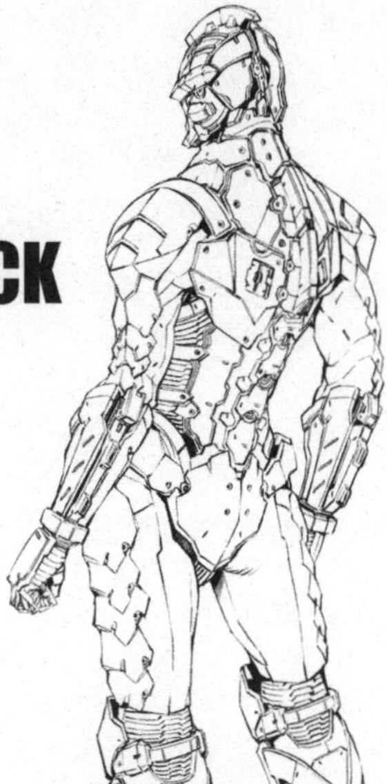
BACK

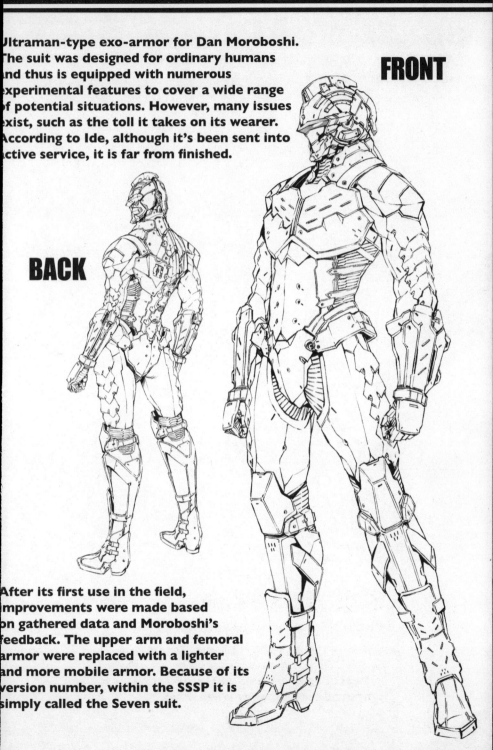

After its first use in the field, improvements were made based on gathered data and Moroboshi's feedback. The upper arm and femoral armor were replaced with a lighter and more mobile armor. Because of its version number, within the SSSP it is simply called the Seven suit.

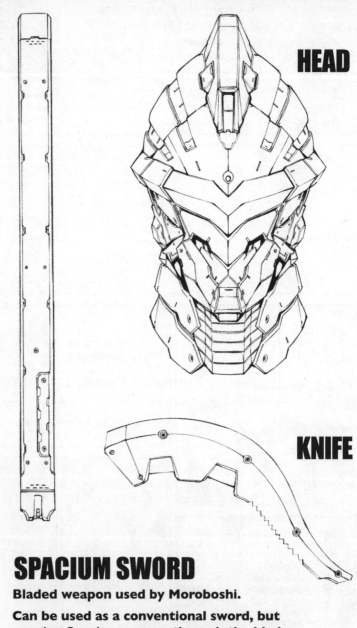

HEAD

KNIFE

SPACIUM SWORD

Bladed weapon used by Moroboshi.

Can be used as a conventional sword, but running Spacium energy through the blade increases its sharpness to the point where it produces a shock wave when used.

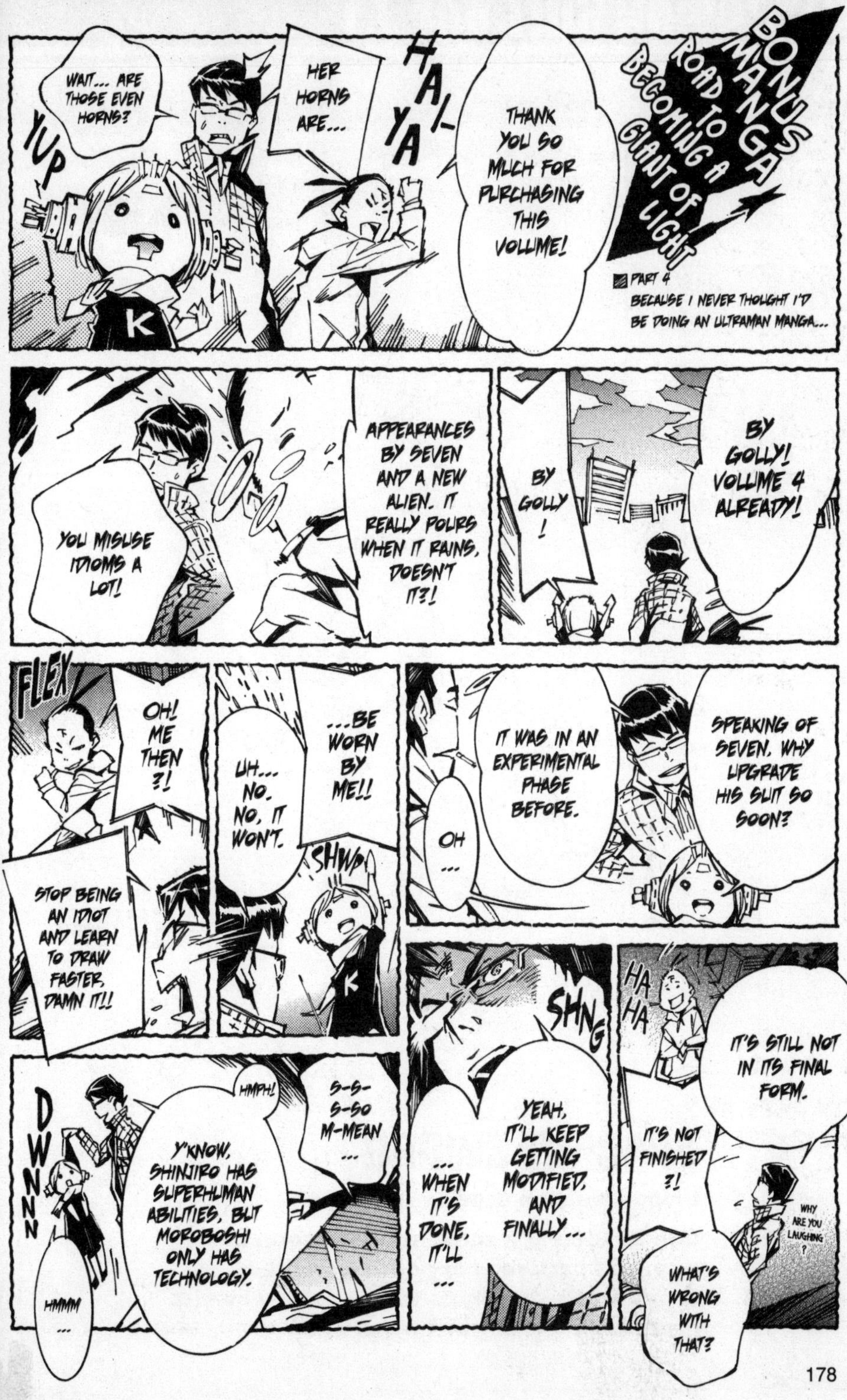
BONUS MANGA
ROAD TO BECOMING A GIANT OF LIGHT
PART 4
BECAUSE I NEVER THOUGHT I'D BE DOING AN ULTRAMAN MANGA...
THANK YOU SO MUCH FOR PURCHASING THIS VOLUME!
HAI-YA
HER HORNS ARE...
WAIT... ARE THOSE EVEN HORNS?
YUP
BY GOLLY! VOLUME 4 ALREADY!
BY GOLLY!
APPEARANCES BY SEVEN AND A NEW ALIEN. IT REALLY POURS WHEN IT RAINS, DOESN'T IT?!
YOU MISUSE IDIOMS A LOT!
SPEAKING OF SEVEN, WHY UPGRADE HIS SUIT SO SOON?
IT WAS IN AN EXPERIMENTAL PHASE BEFORE.
OH...
...BE WORN BY ME!!
UH... NO. NO, IT WON'T.
SHWP
FLEX
OH! ME THEN?!
STOP BEING AN IDIOT AND LEARN TO DRAW FASTER, DAMN IT!!
HA HA
IT'S STILL NOT IN ITS FINAL FORM.
IT'S NOT FINISHED?!
WHY ARE YOU LAUGHING?
WHAT'S WRONG WITH THAT?
SHNG
YEAH, IT'LL KEEP GETTING MODIFIED, AND FINALLY...
...WHEN IT'S DONE, IT'LL...
S-S-S-SO M-MEAN...
HMPH!
Y'KNOW, SHINJIRO HAS SUPERHUMAN ABILITIES, BUT MOROBOSHI ONLY HAS TECHNOLOGY.
DWNNN
HMMM...

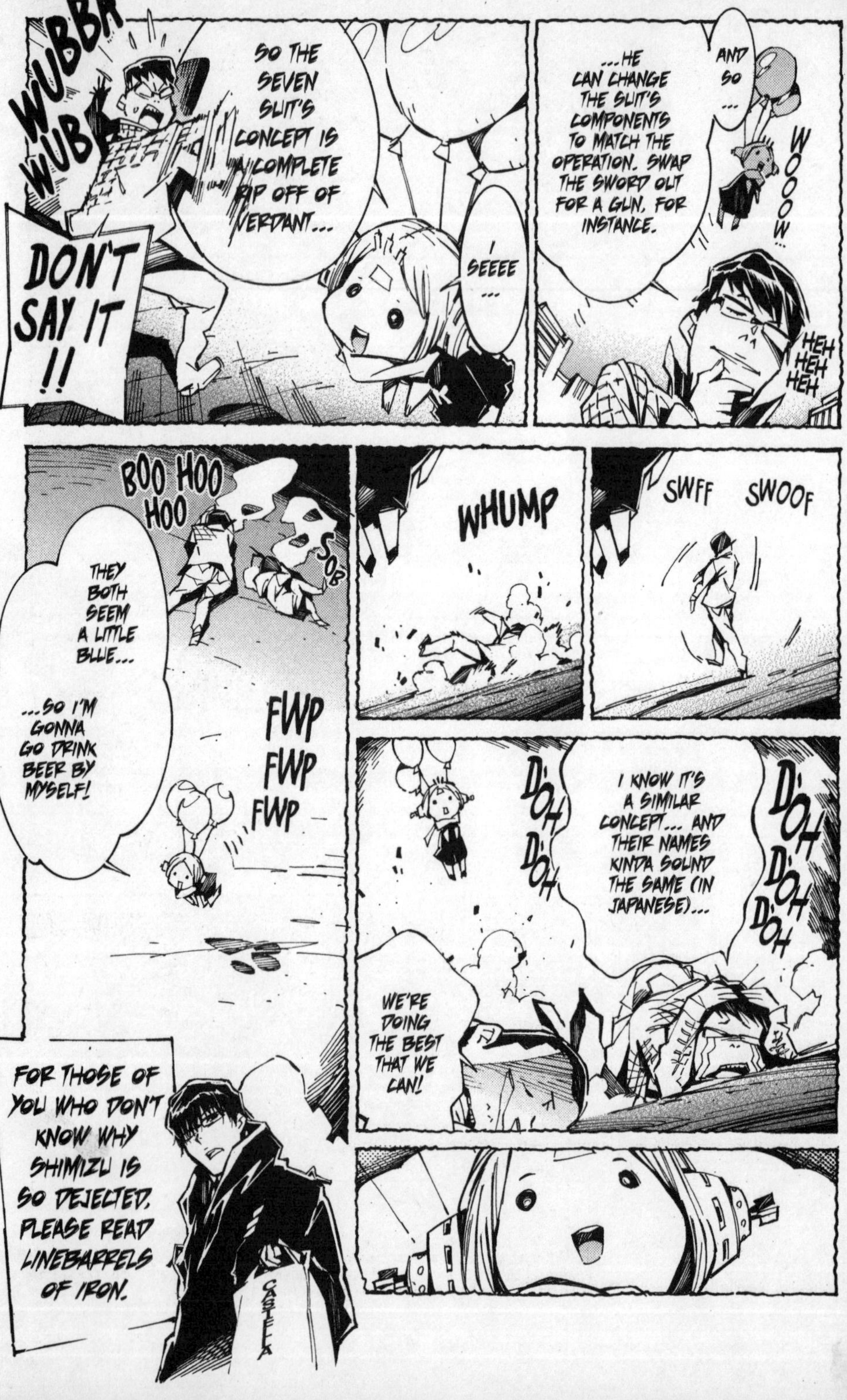

AND SO ...
...HE CAN CHANGE THE SUIT'S COMPONENTS TO MATCH THE OPERATION. SWAP THE SWORD OUT FOR A GUN, FOR INSTANCE.
WOOOOW...
HEH HEH HEH
SO THE SEVEN SUIT'S CONCEPT IS A COMPLETE RIP OFF OF VERDANT...
WUBBA WUBBA WUB
I SEEEE ...
DON'T SAY IT !!
SWFF SWOOF
WHUMP
I KNOW IT'S A SIMILAR CONCEPT... AND THEIR NAMES KINDA SOUND THE SAME (IN JAPANESE)...
D'OH D'OH D'OH
D'OH D'OH D'OH
WE'RE DOING THE BEST THAT WE CAN!
BOO HOO HOO
SOB
THEY BOTH SEEM A LITTLE BLUE...
...SO I'M GONNA GO DRINK BEER BY MYSELF!
FWP FWP FWP
FOR THOSE OF YOU WHO DON'T KNOW WHY SHIMIZU IS SO DEJECTED, PLEASE READ LINEBARRELS OF IRON.
CASTELLA

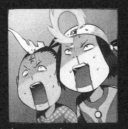

EIICHI SHIMIZU × TOMOHIRO SHIMOGUCHI

Shimoguchi never used to pay much attention to special effects-heavy, *tokusatsu* TV shows, but now he's gotten to the point where he knows quite a bit about *Ultraman*.

But that growth has come with consequences. Regardless of the story's setting or plot, he now foists his ideas on me. Like the other day, he rudely told me to put Antlar in the story.

I decided that one day soon I'm going to smack him...real hard.

ULTRAMAN

VOLUME 4
VIZ SIGNATURE EDITION

STORY/ART BY **EIICHI SHIMIZU** AND **TOMOHIRO SHIMOGUCHI**

©2014 Eiichi Shimizu and Tomohiro Shimoguchi / TSUBURAYA PROD.
Originally published by HERO'S INC.

TRANSLATION **JOE YAMAZAKI**
ENGLISH ADAPTATION **STAN!**
TOUCH-UP ART & LETTERING **EVAN WALDINGER**
DESIGN **FAWN LAU**
EDITOR **MIKE MONTESA**

Printed in the U.S.A.

Published by VIZ Media, LLC
P.O. Box 77010
San Francisco, CA 94107

10 9 8 7 6 5 4 3 2 1
First printing, May 2016

VIZ SIGNATURE

www.viz.com

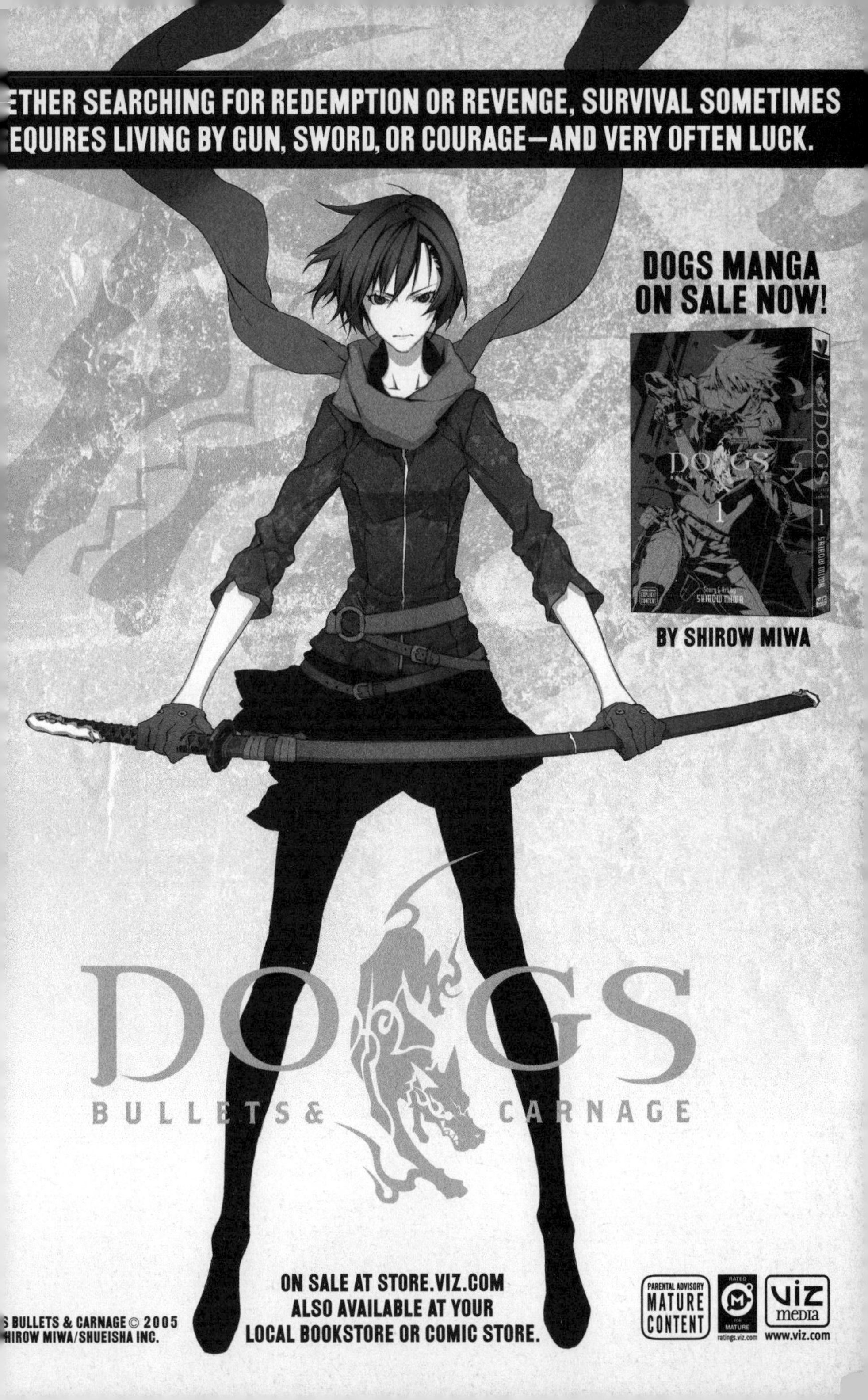
ETHER SEARCHING FOR REDEMPTION OR REVENGE, SURVIVAL SOMETIMES
EQUIRES LIVING BY GUN, SWORD, OR COURAGE—AND VERY OFTEN LUCK.
DOGS MANGA
ON SALE NOW!
DOGS
1
SHIROW MIWA
BY SHIROW MIWA
DOGS
BULLETS & CARNAGE
ON SALE AT STORE.VIZ.COM
ALSO AVAILABLE AT YOUR
LOCAL BOOKSTORE OR COMIC STORE.
S BULLETS & CARNAGE © 2005
HIROW MIWA/SHUEISHA INC.
PARENTAL ADVISORY
MATURE
CONTENT
RATED
M
FOR MATURE
ratings.viz.com
VIZ
media
www.viz.com

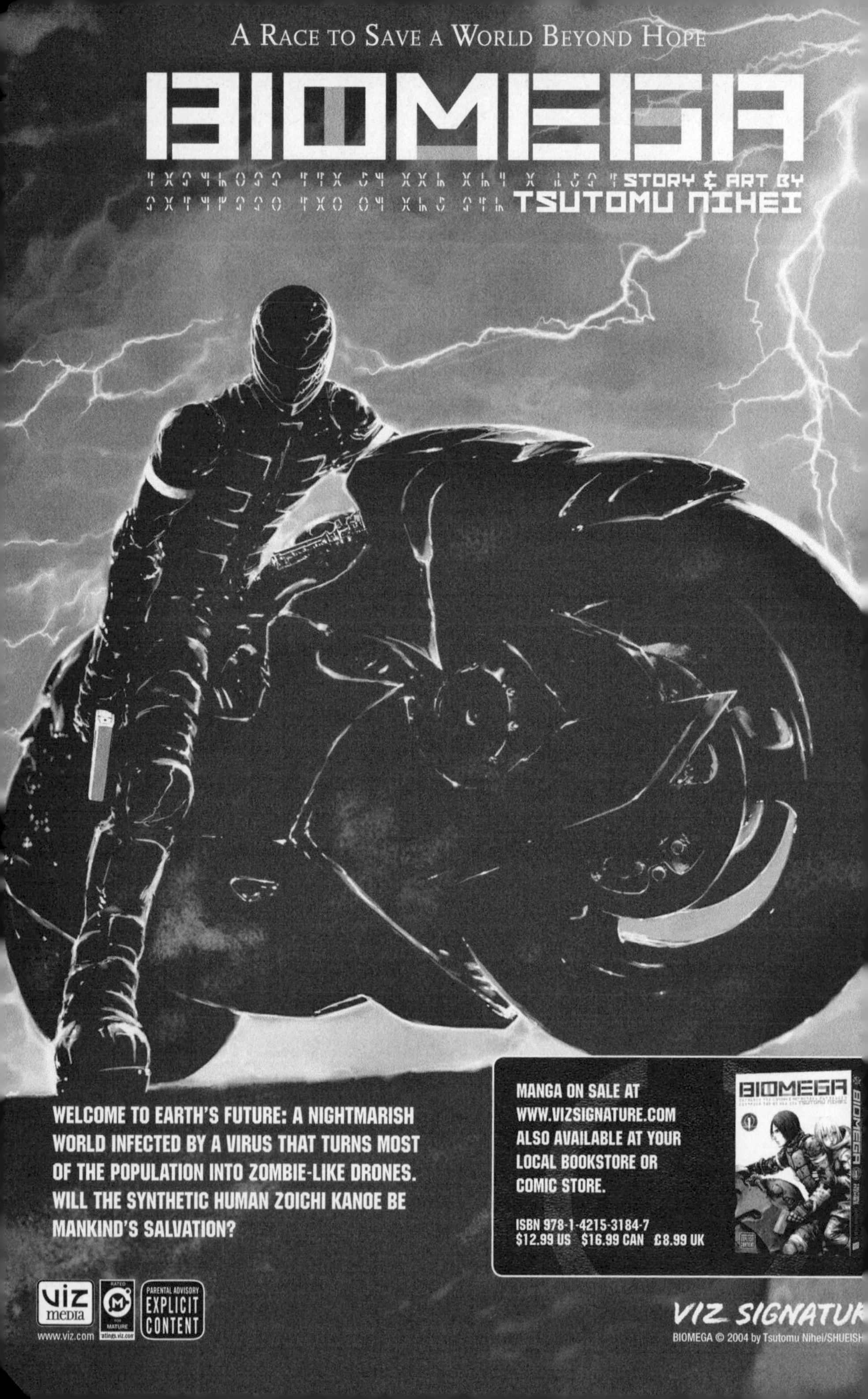
A Race to Save a World Beyond Hope
BIOMEGA
STORY & ART BY
TSUTOMU NIHEI
WELCOME TO EARTH'S FUTURE: A NIGHTMARISH WORLD INFECTED BY A VIRUS THAT TURNS MOST OF THE POPULATION INTO ZOMBIE-LIKE DRONES. WILL THE SYNTHETIC HUMAN ZOICHI KANOE BE MANKIND'S SALVATION?
MANGA ON SALE AT WWW.VIZSIGNATURE.COM
ALSO AVAILABLE AT YOUR LOCAL BOOKSTORE OR COMIC STORE.
ISBN 978-1-4215-3184-7
$12.99 US $16.99 CAN £8.99 UK
BIOMEGA
viz media
www.viz.com
RATED M FOR MATURE
PARENTAL ADVISORY EXPLICIT CONTENT
VIZ SIGNATUR
BIOMEGA © 2004 by Tsutomu Nihei/SHUEISH

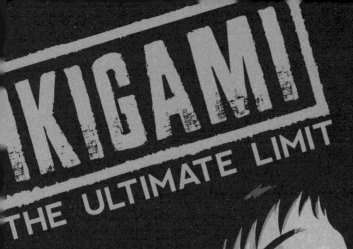
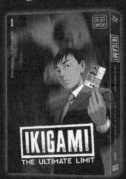

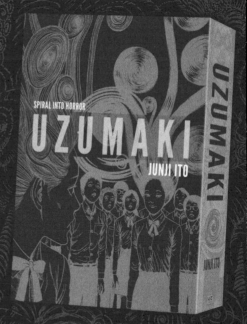

Vagabond

by Takehiko Inoue

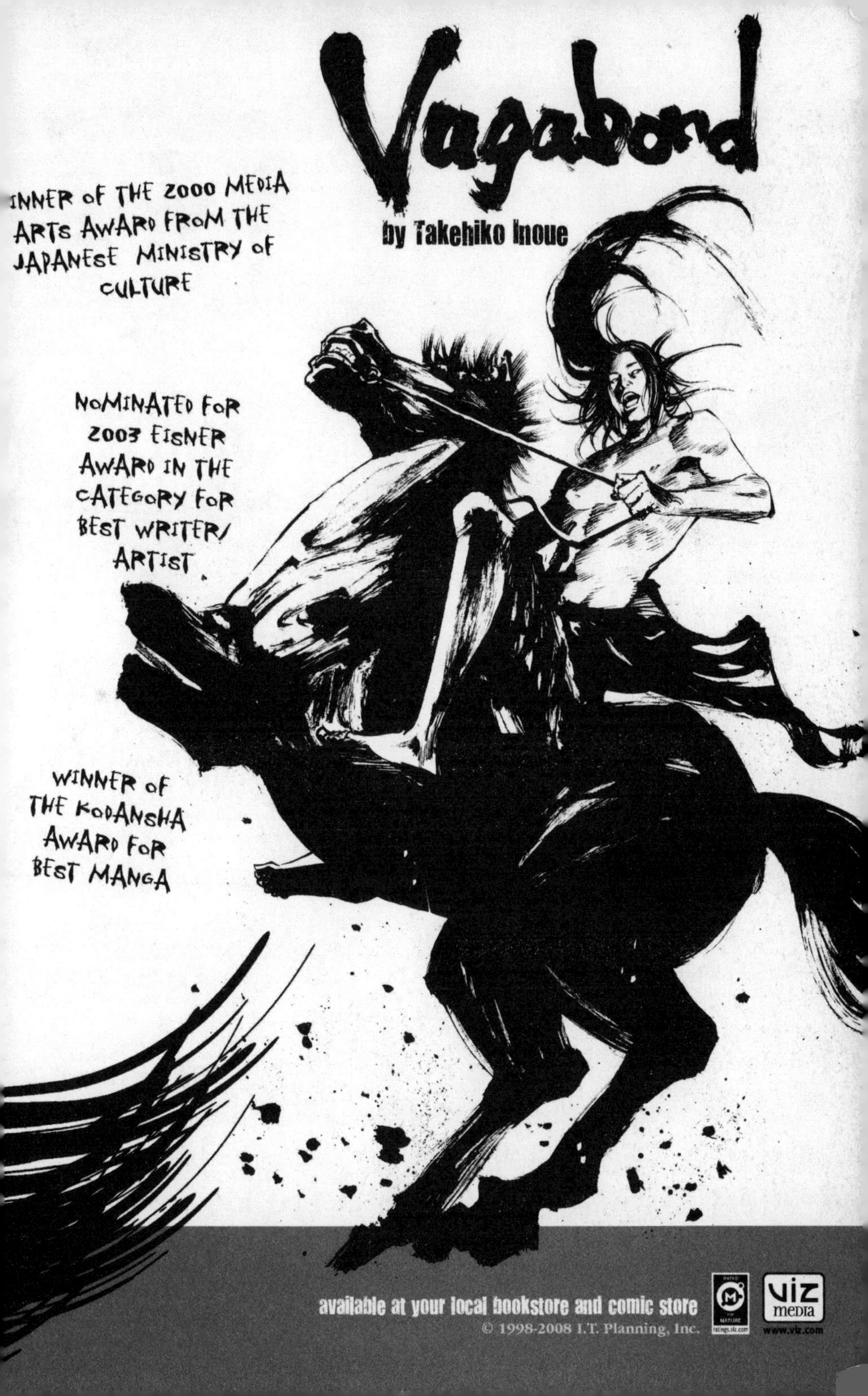
INNER OF THE 2000 MEDIA ARTS AWARD FROM THE JAPANESE MINISTRY OF CULTURE
NOMINATED FOR 2003 EISNER AWARD IN THE CATEGORY FOR BEST WRITER/ ARTIST
WINNER OF THE KODANSHA AWARD FOR BEST MANGA

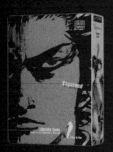
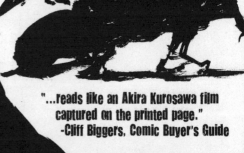
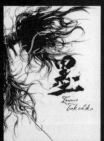
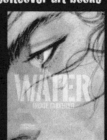

HEY! YOU'RE READING IN THE WRONG DIRECTION!

This is the END of the graphic novel

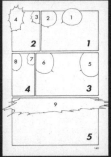

Follow the action this way.

To properly enjoy this VIZ graphic novel, please turn it around and begin reading from RIGHT TO LEFT. Unlike English, Japanese is read right to left, so Japanese comics are read in reverse order from the way English comics are typically read.

This book has been printed in the original Japanese format in order to preserve the orientation of the original artwork.

HAVE FUN WITH IT!